LIFE AND SOCIETY IN THE WEST

Antiquity and the Middle Ages

LIFE AND SOCIETY IN THE WEST

Antiquity and the Middle Ages

CONSTANCE BRITTAIN BOUCHARD
Kenyon College

HARCOURT BRACE JOVANOVICH, PUBLISHERS

San Diego   New York   Chicago   Austin   Washington, D.C.
London   Sydney   Tokyo   Toronto

PREFACE

My grandfather, the oldest living person of my acquaintance, is 104 years old. During his lifetime there has been an upheaval in material culture unprecedented in history. The objects which are now so common that we would have trouble living without them were unknown when he was born. Computers and televisions were of course not invented a century ago, but neither were any of the other machines that require (the then nonexistent) household electricity: ranges, refrigerators, washing machines, radios, and vacuum cleaners, none of which became common until after World War I. In the 1880s, there were no furnaces, no telephones, no flush toilets. The automobile was still in the future, along with everything that depends on the automobile, from interstate highways, to road maps, to McDonald's, to suburban sprawl. Airplanes were considered a physical impossibility, and no one had heard of nuclear war, genetic engineering, antibiotics, or plastic.

But material objects, by themselves, do not determine how people live. They may certainly influence one's life, even determine whether or not one lives at all, but human happiness has always depended ultimately on the relations between individuals. Human institutions, the methods we use to regulate relations between people, have changed far less rapidly than have our material possessions. My grandfather was born as a member of a family, to parents who wanted him to grow up and turn out well. They made sure he was fed and clothed, tried to teach him respect for their own knowledge and experience, and sent him off for formal schooling. He lived in a town where people bought and sold in the shops and gossiped about their neighbors. Both his family and their neighbors were concerned about law and law enforcement, read about political developments, and argued over how they should vote in the elections. The details for a child born now are certainly different, but the underlying concerns have scarcely changed.

Modern material culture, because it makes life today, on the surface, so totally different from life in the past, has erected an artificial wall between us and those who came before us. Sometimes it seems as though we could have nothing in common with people who had never gone to the movies or used a Xerox machine. Even worse, we might find ourselves considering the members of a society that had not invented flash photography or microwave ovens as mentally inferior. And yet individuals in previous centuries were more technically sophisticated than most of us, even though their society as a whole had fewer technically advanced objects. Very few people now understand how their cars or pocket calculators work, whereas the farmer and his wife of earlier generations could make and repair their own equipment, calculate the time to plant and the time to harvest without almanacs or extension agents, and make enough food and clothing to last their family a year, starting with only animals and plants.

The history of Western civilization is the history of people very like us, at least as intelligent as we are, using many of the same institutions that we use to try to solve the same sorts of problems. The bases of what we call civilization have scarcely changed in outline in five thousand years: families living in large, permanent agglomerations, governed by law codes, subsisting from agriculture rather than hunting and gathering or nomadic pastoralism, recording in writing at least some of the events they considered worth remembering. Our word "civilization" comes from the same root as "city." Ancient and medieval cities looked very different from modern cities; for example, they were much smaller and lacked skyscrapers and neon signs. But some western European capitals, like Paris, have the same street layout in the center of town and are dominated by the same church towers as those cities seven hundred years ago, and many of the modern cities of the Near East, like Jerusalem, have been continuously occupied for millennia.

When one realizes the continuity of Western civilization, one realizes that the men and women of the past were not just our physical ancestors, but also our institutional ancestors. Their methods of dealing with basic human problems are the direct predecessors of modern institutions. We are still asking the same questions people have probably been asking since they first developed language: How can I get enough food for myself and my family? How can we keep ourselves safe from our enemies? How can we set up and enforce rules of conduct so that no one takes unfair advantage of anyone else? What should we do about people in our midst who are not like the rest of us, whether they are crippled slow-witted, destitute, or criminal? Why are we all here in the first place and where do we go next?

The theme of this book is how people lived and tried to grapple with these sorts of problems in the ancient Near East and in western Europe, from antiquity, starting roughly 3000 B.C., to the end of the Middle Ages, roughly 1500 A.D. On the one hand, I show the similarities and continuities between the early stages of Western civilization and the modern day. If we today are at all interested in how our institutions function, much less how we might improve them, it is vital to understand how and why they have developed the way they have. Modern institutions did not simply spring into existence in the modern era, and they took the form they have not by accident but because of factors in the way they were formed. On the other hand, I also stress how different in fundamental ways were our ancestors from us. By studying people who made very different basic assumptions than we do, and came up with a different set of answers to the same questions, it may be possible to appreciate that a person can be intelligent, thoughtful, and of an inquiring mind, without having to be just like us. If we today can develop this sort of appreciation for Westerners of previous centuries, people who are after all at the root of all we think of as modern, then there is hope for appreciating modern people of other nations, even if their background and history are radically different.

This book was written to be a supplement to a political history of Western civilization before 1500. It starts with the ancient Near East, covers Greece and Rome, looks closely at the Middle Ages, and concludes with the Italian Renaissance. Because the way people live changes less rapidly than do kings and governments, I have tended to take leaps in time between chapters, so that they form not a continuous narrative from century to century but rather a series of glimpses into society (this is the only way to fit over four thousand years of history into one book). Thus, the chapter on Greece treats especially Greece in the fifth century B.C., that on Rome the first century A.D., and the medieval chapters the sixth century, the ninth, the twelfth, the fourteenth, and the fifteenth. I have not hesitated, however, to lap over these boundaries in order to show either the origins or the later results of a particular practice.

This book is also written in such a way that it could be used on its own in a social history course, if one wanted to make society rather than politics the focus of the development of Western civilization. It is meant to be read sequentially, but the different parts are independent enough that they should also make sense if read separately. If the book is used as a supplement in a course that skips very rapidly through the Middle Ages (a tendency I deplore), then one can read just Chapter 6 through Chapter 8, which cover three aspects of the high Middle Ages of the twelfth and thirteenth centuries, the quintessentially medieval period.

Finally, this book treats social history in the broad sense, as the study of both how people obtained the food they needed to survive and how, once having assured they had enough to eat for the moment, they tried to create a society and a set of beliefs by which to live. My themes, touched on in most chapters, include what food people ate and how they raised it, what sort of clothing they wore, what sort of houses they lived in, the organization of the family, what sorts of laws and government people were subject to, their educational system, how and why they went to war, and the religion they practiced. From pure social history I make forays into economic history, the history of ideas, the history of art, institutional history, and the history of the church.

Constance Brittain Bouchard

CONTENTS

MAPS

INTRODUCTION

HUMAN HISTORY, at its most basic level, is the history of people trying to get enough to eat and trying to find ways to get along with
each other. For the five thousand years of recorded western civilization,
these have been the principal problems, and even now we have not
solved them.

It is often hard for modern Americans to understand the central place
food has had in human history. This is not just because we ourselves are
fairly well fed; few people reading this book will have ever gone more
than twenty-four hours without eating. But we tend to take food for
granted because so few of us are directly involved in its production.
Whereas most people in the world's history spent most of their time,
year around, raising food, only about five percent of the modern American population lives on a farm, and the number is shrinking. To most
of us, food is something that springs into existence, prewrapped in plastic, on the shelves of the grocery store. We may have gardens, but they
are only a supplemental source of food; it will be a shame if the tomato
worms eat all the tomatoes in the garden, but we can always buy some
at the produce counter.

It is therefore hard for us to appreciate that, until very recently in the
West, 80 percent or more of the population was concerned on a daily
basis with raising food, from planting to harvesting, with the cycle starting over again each year. If the harvest failed, one could only hope that
one's neighbors had had better luck. The alternative to raising enough
food was not a trip to the supermarket but slow death by starvation.
Americans are concerned when they read about famine in third-world
countries and are very generous in sending aid, but we tend to think of
famine as something bizarre and unusual, rather than something that has
sat behind the shoulder of all ordinary men and women for thousands
of years.

Food and water are the bases of human existence. In the short run,
water is even more important than food; people can go for several weeks
without food, without any long-term ill effects—but only for a few days

1

without water. Whereas today many people worry about getting less fat and more fiber in their diets, throughout most of the time that *Homo sapiens* has existed the concern has been to get more calories and protein and less spoiled or rotten food. The first humans were hunter-gatherers, as some peoples in remote parts of the world still are. This sort of life entails hunting wild animals and gathering edible plants. Hunter-gatherers must move quite frequently, going to new areas after exhausting the old ones, and this method of obtaining food cannot support a large population. But European explorers, coming to the Americas from countries in which living solely from hunting and gathering had not been feasible for many generations, were able to live on what they gathered and what they shot.

Humans are omnivorous, eating both meat and vegetables—a relatively rare phenomenon among mammals, which usually specialize in one or the other. This has made us very adaptable. Quite early, hunter-gatherers began supplementing their food gathering with agriculture and pastoralism—that is, raising plants and keeping flocks of animals; one could practice either or both. If there is a certain kind of plant that is especially good to eat, it makes sense to gather the seeds and plant a lot in one spot, rather than wandering long distances looking for it. Long before Columbus, the North American Indians were practicing agriculture, at least on a small scale, while functioning also as hunter-gatherers. It is also much easier to domesticate and raise animals in herds and flocks than always to have to hunt for and catch wild animals. Eating animals or their products (such as milk and cheese) is also an effective way for humans to gain nourishment from plants they could not eat themselves, because the animals eat the plants and the people eat the animals. Cattle, sheep, and goats can all eat plants such as grass that are high in cellu-

In this wall carving from ancient Egypt, plowmen drive their teams, above, while harvesters bring in the crop, below.

lose, which humans cannot digest. Some nomadic African tribes today still rely largely on their herds for food.

Civilization began when people began settling permanently in one spot and living from agriculture. This style of living was normally supplemented with animal raising, some hunting or fishing, and some gathering of such things as wild fruit. Only agriculture will support a large group of people in one place, such as a town or city. Hunter-gatherers must always be on the move, if there are more than a very few living together, and pure pastoralists must move their flocks whenever all of the grass is eaten. Only a town or city, with a large number of people living in proximity, provides the opportunity for the exchange of ideas required for politics, law, art, philosophy, and literature. A town or city is not defined purely by size, for many of the cities of the ancient world would seem tiny to us. Rather, it is defined by a certain political and economic complexity. A city has a conscious identity, sometimes made clear by the existence of city walls, and its own local government. It is a crossroads where goods from afar are traded and where at least some people devote themselves entirely to trade or to crafts, buying or bartering for their food, rather than working in agriculture.

The most effective sort of agriculture has always been raising grain. Grain is a fairly high-calorie food that can be stored for long periods without spoiling. Its ability to be stored is very important; although one has to keep it dry and free of rodents, one *can* make the harvest last twelve months, which one could never do with fruit or vegetables. Different sorts of grain predominate in different parts of the world. In China and most of Asia, rice is the major grain. Around the Mediterranean, barley is common. Oats are often grown in northern Europe, and in the Americas before Columbus maize (corn) predominated. In most of Europe wheat has traditionally been the principal grain. (It is interesting to note that in English the word "corn" is applied to whatever is the principal local grain; Americans use "corn" for maize, the English use it to mean wheat, and the Scots use it for oats.)

Grain may be eaten in a number of different ways. Ground into flour, it can be baked into bread or baked on a griddle without leavening (like tortillas), or made into pasta, or porridge. Grain can also be made into beer, which has been drunk throughout history as much for its caloric as its alcoholic content. (Until quite recently beer was very thick, more the consistency of runny oatmeal than modern "lite" beers.) Whereas modern Americans have to be reminded to eat a certain number of servings from the "grain group" every day for a balanced diet, for most of our ancestors—indeed, for most people in the rest of the world today—food *was* bread. Christians still pray, "Give us this day our daily bread," with the understanding that "bread" is here used to mean food in general. But when the prayer was composed in the first century A.D., it was literally a request for bread; all other forms of food were only supplements to this basis of the diet.

Although food is the fundamental human need (as indeed it is the fundamental need for all animals), people need other things as well in order to survive. Above all, they need other people. It is a rare individual who functions well as a hermit. Most tasks, from raising the children to plowing the field to keeping guard, are easier with someone else's help. People are gregarious, needing contact with each other for their emotional and indeed physical well-being. Babies who are kept without human contact will die, even if they are given food and kept warm and dry. Lonely adults, those without family or friends, die at a much higher rate than the general population. But people's need for other people also requires regulations to govern relations between individuals. More than two or three people cannot live in close proximity without some sort of formal rules. The modern family, even at its most casual, always has some rules about coming home or staying out, spending money, and doing chores. As soon as several families live near each other, there must be rules to prevent one from taking advantage of the others, whether by doing violence, stealing food, or shirking work. Such rules may not be formal, codified laws, but they must be understood and taught to the children.

Humans also need objects in order to survive. Because we are hairless mammals without good built-in defenses, we need clothing, shelter, and tools. Clothes keep out the cold and the worst of the sun; shelter, whether a straw hut or palace, helps keep people warm and also provides them a place they can sleep feeling somewhat secure in a world full of dangerous creatures (including other people). A house also is a good place to store things.

The plow (lower center) holds a prominent place in this Mesopotamian stela, demonstrating that agriculture, as the best way to hold people in one place so that a settled culture can flourish, was important to the Assyrians as a prime means of gathering food.

The most primitive cultures have always had "things." The Kalahari bushmen, with no metal or even stone tools, still make tools and weapons of wood. We are not like other animals, who are born with the hunting, fighting, and food-gathering equipment they need permanently attached. Humans are unique in their ability to make and use complex tools, but we cannot get along without these tools either. We need vessels to carry water and to store food, tools to dig in the ground, start fires, skin animals, grind the grain. If a herd of gazelles is startled by a predator, the gazelles can run away and resume grazing wherever they stop. A crowd of humans in the same situation would have to return later and pick up what they had dropped. If a person were put down naked in the wilderness, without car keys or a jackknife or a canteen, he might be able to survive if properly trained; but he would have to begin by making and accumulating tools for the purpose.

Finally, people always need to be *doing* something, whether they are using tools or only their imaginations. As a result of our ability to think and to try new activities, we cannot be happy for long unless we *are* doing something. Most vegetarian mammals spend all day eating, because they need to process enormous amounts of cellulose to gain enough nourishment. Most predators, who obtain a higher amount of nutrition per volume than vegetarians from the meat they eat, spend most of the day sleeping (as do domestic cats and dogs). Humans stay awake as herbivores do, but they are not forced to use all of that time eating. Instead they are always looking around for something to do. Raising food has kept humans occupied for most of history, and if the goal of work is something worthwhile in itself, such as getting the crop in or making an attractive vase, this work will also fulfill the human need to have a goal. If the work is deadeningly dull (such as work on an assembly line), the goal may be to make it until the weekend. Curiously, when we are working hard on something unpleasant, we look forward to relaxing, to doing nothing; but humans can "do nothing" for only a very short time before they are bored and seeking activity again. People who have recently retired die at a much higher rate than those still working, not because retirement came along just in time for someone who was already sickening fast, but because many of those who are suddenly left with nothing to do soon feel no great urge to live.

In this regard, humans always need to use their brains as well as their bodies. As a species we are extremely curious and also eager to express our own particular view or vision to others. Religion and mythology arise from our attempts to deal with the nature of existence beyond our material lives; art and literature, from a need to express a particular viewpoint on life. These then are not just attributes of civilization but the result of a fundamental human requirement—to have and express ideas—for which civilization provides the context for a particular sort of expression.

The history of civilization is a history of different attempts to meet these basic human needs. So far, none of the myriad arrangements humans have tried have been completely successful. Very few people have always had plenty to eat. Modern America, the richest nation on earth, with the highest proportion of people anywhere in history who have never skipped a meal unless they wanted to, still has distressingly large pockets of poverty and hunger. In the world as a whole, probably a third of the population is hungry at any one time. There has never been rewarding, productive work for all the people who wanted it. No society has ever been free from crime (the United States has the highest crime rate of any Western nation), and no individual has spent his whole life completely happy and in harmony with all his neighbors. Part of being human is having the ability to think about society's failure, or humanity's failure, and to try to come to grips with the question of what we are doing here anyway, which has never yet been answered to everyone's satisfaction. Part of being human is being dissatisfied, including being dissatisfied with someone else's answers.

People born into the premodern world could assume that, if they did not catch a fatal disease or have a fatal accident, were not murdered or killed in war, they would have about seventy years to try to find their own answers—the same number of years that a person of the twentieth century can hope to have. This is because the basic human life *span* has not changed since at least the beginning of recorded history. Someone who was seventy would be old and would probably soon die of one of the diseases or complications that hits the old the hardest, although the very rare person might live to ninety or even one hundred. However, although the life *span* has not changed appreciably, the life *expectancy* has changed dramatically in the twentieth century. That is, many more people can now expect to live out their full seventy-year span because their chances of dying of disease or infection before they grow old has been substantially reduced. One now speaks of an "average life expectancy" of about seventy, meaning the average person can expect to live to that age. But if, for example, half of all babies born now died immediately, the average life *expectancy* would be thirty-five, the average of zero (for the half that died immediately) and seventy; those who survived their first year, however, could still expect to live to seventy.

The life *expectancy* in the premodern period was much lower than it is now because a great many people died, long before they had a chance to grow old, of the diseases that modern antibiotics cure. Since children are especially susceptible to infectious diseases, many fewer babies grew to adulthood than is now the case. Yet the overall population was, on the average, much younger than the population of modern America. Whereas today we have a rapidly rising percentage of our total population over sixty-five, the populations of the ancient and medieval world had lost many more of their citizens to famine, disease, and war while they should still have been in the prime of their lives.

Humans are born into a struggle for food and a struggle for love, with the feeling that a lifetime is too short to solve the problems, whether personal or global, and that we are too obsessed with daily requirements to address the underlying issues. But humans are also hopeful, at least some of the time, that better answers could be found, even if not final answers. The study of history, the study of the ways humans have tried to deal with being human, comes out of that hope. The way we live today, both our material and our institutional culture, is certainly not the only way we could live. In order to improve life, for the individual or for broader humanity, we need to understand what solutions have been tried in the past and why they worked or did not work. The people who tried them may have had a very different set of presuppositions about what details or objects are important or worthwhile; but fundamentally they have always been concerned with the same issues as we are, and their attempted solutions are at the roots of the institutions, good or bad, that are in place today.

CHRONOLOGY
ONE

ANCIENT EMPIRES

c. **3500** B.C.	Beginning of Mesopotamian civilization; invention of writing
c. **3300** B.C.	Beginning of Egyptian civilization
c. **3000** B.C.	Approximate beginning of the Bronze Age
c. **2500** B.C.	Building of pyramids and ziggurats; beginning of Stonehenge
c. **1760** B.C.	Hammurabi's law code in Babylon
c. **1500** B.C.	Hebrews settle in Palestine
c. **1250** B.C.	Moses leads the Hebrews out of Egypt
c. **1100** B.C.	Phoenicians established in eastern Mediterranean
c. **1000** B.C.	David and Solomon rule as Hebrew kings
722 B.C.	Hebrew states conquered by Assyrians
c. **700** B.C.	Approximate beginning of the Iron Age
586 B.C.	Temple of Jerusalem destroyed by Babylonians
c. **500** B.C.	Celts settled in western Europe
c. **450** B.C.	Jewish government reestablished in Jerusalem
390 B.C.	Celts sack city of Rome
140 B.C.	Establishment of short-lived kingdom of Judaea
70 A.D.	Final destruction of the Temple in Jerusalem by the Romans

CHAPTER
ONE

ANCIENT EMPIRES

LONG BEFORE AUTOMOBILES and computers, long even before watermills and iron tools, there were empires. An empire is more than a big kingdom; it is a large and diverse territory, including several different peoples, that is all ruled by one man. Starting about 3000 B.C. there were a series of powerful empires around the eastern Mediterranean, with urban capitals, kings, and professional bureaucrats. Out of these ancient empires came the foundations of a writing system, of organized law codes, of religion, all of which influenced later Western societies and eventually modern society.

These empires were able to arise in the eastern Mediterranean (fifteen hundred years or more before empires took shape in India and China) because the region had an excellent climate for growing food. The area between the Tigris and Euphrates rivers, called the "Fertile Crescent," and the banks of the Nile in Egypt received enough water and sunshine that crops could be grown reliably year after year. (The area is much less fertile now, both because the climate has become drier, and because centuries of irrigating the fields have increased their salinity level, as the natural salts in the irrigation water remain when the water itself evaporates; the same process is happening now in California's central valley.) But because the fertile areas were limited to the areas along the rivers, people were pushed together in close proximity and thus had to work out ways to get along in large groups.

Even with the fairly crude stone or bronze tools available, farmers were able to raise good crops, providing not just enough food for themselves, but a surplus to sell to market. Unless there is such an agricultural surplus available, it is impossible to have urban culture or complex administration, for city people and administrators must rely on buying food, since they do not grow it themselves. The growth of cities and of governments then depends on the well-being of farmers and their ability to raise more than is required for their own needs.

Two great technical advances took place not long before 3000 B.C. which made possible the rapid development of civilization. The first was the development of bronze metallurgy. This was based on the discovery that certain metal-bearing rocks may be melted down at high enough temperature to produce liquid metal, which can then be combined, poured into molds and hardened, and then finished to make tools of any shape one wants. The practice of melting gold to shape it into jewelry (gold becomes pliable at relatively low temperatures) had indeed preceded the casting of metal for tools. Metal hoes, axes, knives, and swords, once developed, were much more effective than stone implements.

The first metal to be worked for tools was copper, which has a low melting point (iron has quite a high melting point, and this delayed its introduction). However, it was soon discovered that if one mixed some tin with the copper to make bronze, the result was a much sturdier metal than copper alone. The period from roughly 3000 B.C. to 700 or 500 B.C. is therefore known as the Bronze Age. The other great technical breakthrough of the same period was the invention of writing, which is discussed on pages 10–12. When metal could be fashioned into tools and writing was available for issuing proclamations and for keeping records, the development of empires became possible.

Ancient Mesopotamia

The oldest known villages were probably constructed around 10,000 B.C., at around the same time that agriculture was invented. In subsequent millennia, people in the Near East developed improved architectural methods, invented the wheel and its uses, and perfected the technique of firing pottery. But the first real civilization, with laws, organized government, and writing, was that of Mesopotamia, starting around 3000 or 3500 B.C.

Mesopotamia gets its name from Greek words meaning "between the rivers," because it was located between the Tigris and Euphrates rivers, just northwest of the Persian Gulf, in what is now Iraq. This area was very fertile, good for growing crops, and is therefore known as the Fertile Crescent. It was, however, an area without timber or very much stone; consequently, buildings had to be of mud brick, and both the development of metallurgy and cooperation between people was necessary. Several different ethnic groups flourished in the Mesopotamian region, succeeding each other by conquest or by assimilation. For simplicity's sake, I do not distinguish them here, except for the Babylonians, who created an empire based in the Mesopotamian city of Babylon.

Writing and Mathematics in Mesopotamia

The Mesopotamians invented writing sometime before 3000 B.C. We tend to take reading and writing for granted now, but its original inven-

Group of statues from shrine II of Square Abu Temple, c. 2900–2600 B.C. The beards are typical for Mesopotamian men.

tion was a great breakthrough because it meant that for the first time humans could keep records, either for other people or to jog their own memories, and could communicate with other people without having to speak to them directly. Writing in the Old World seems in fact to have been invented twice, independently: in Mesopotamia and later in China. In both places the original writing was made up of little pictures, but Mesopotamian writing quickly became very stylized. Mesopotamian writing is now called cuneiform, from a Latin word meaning "wedge-shaped," because of the distinctive wedge shapes or triangles the strokes of the letters took. The first writing seems to have been done by pressing pieces of reed into clay tablets and then firing them, to make a permanent record, but cuneiform writing was also very well suited for inscriptions in stone. Great numbers of both clay tablets and inscribed stones have been found with cuneiform characters.

The earliest records are bureaucratic: accounts of royal or temple income, or lists of offerings to the temples. An organized government requires some sort of record-keeping. Soon kings accumulated large collections of clay tablets recording their income and their diplomatic correspondence with other kings. Government tablets were indexed on the ends with distinctive marks to make them easier to classify and to find again and were stored in baskets in royal or temple archives. Among the thousands of remaining Mesopotamian tablets are also many records of sales and purchases. Some of the laws of the city-states specified that before a man could marry a woman he had to obtain the permission of her parents and make them a suitable gift, all of which was recorded in

Mesopotamian pupil's copybook, c. 2500–2000 B.C. The teacher's lesson is on the flat side, and the pupil's copy is on the round side.

a marriage contract; the tablets for some of these contracts still exist. Other tablets are inscribed with historical texts, literary creations, even school books. Mesopotamia produced the first epic literature (or religious literature; there is no clear distinction), which included creation stories and stories of the flooding of the entire world. Such stories were widely spread in the Near East and were later incorporated into the religion of the Hebrews, who are discussed further on pages 28–36.

One of the most significant developments was that of a written law code. The earliest known complete law code is that of Hammurabi, drawn up around 1760 B.C. Hammurabi unified all of Mesopotamia into a single empire under the direction of Babylon, which he made his capital. There had been laws, especially laws regulating trade and commerce, in the different Mesopotamian cities, but Hammurabi was the first to create a uniform law code for the entire empire, covering everything from murder to cheating in trade. As well as forbidding crime, the law code specified rules for such civil matters as marriage and adoption. The law code also provided penalties for all the different offenses. A block of stone with the laws carved on it was set up so that everyone could read it.

Hammurabi's laws divided society into three parts: the aristocrats, who were always a small minority; the vast group of ordinary people in the middle; and the slaves. Slavery has been part of human history since the beginning of civilization. There were different taxes, penalties, and fees depending on which part of society one came from. For example, the law code specified that a surgeon could only charge a slave one-fifth as much for an operation as he could charge an aristocrat. The best slaves were considered to be those captured in the mountains east of Mesopotamia, who were sturdy and hardworking. In cuneiform writing, in fact, the symbol for "slave" was made by combining the symbol for "man" or "woman" with that for "eastern mountains."

The Mesopotamians invented mathematics as well as writing. The ability to count, of course, goes back to the Stone Age, but mathematicians in Babylon were the first to work out the principles of algebra and geometry. They were also excellent astronomers who watched the movement of the stars at night and were able to calculate their courses. Astronomy was used both as a basis for astrology (the two were not separated until about three hundred years ago) and for computing the calendar.

Whereas we have a numerical system based on tens, the numerical system of the Babylonians was based on twelves and sixties. They were the ones who first decided that a day had twenty-four hours, twelve hours of day and twelve of night, and that each hour had sixty minutes. By observing the stars, they were able to calculate that it took 365 days for the earth to move through the year until the stars were again in exactly the same position they were when one started.

Again, in an age of calendars and newspapers with the date printed on the front, it may be hard for us to appreciate how much of an innovation this was. It was only possible because of precise astronomical observations, for the climate shifts enough during the year that one could never reach the exact figure of 365 simply by looking for the first rains or the like. (The Babylonians were also the first to decide that a circle is composed of 360 degrees—and they were probably irritated that the year came so close to 360 days but just missed.)

As well as observing the stars, the Babylonians also watched the moon, with its twenty-eight- or twenty-nine-day cycle. They were the first to speak of months or "moons," divided into four parts for the four phases of the moon, the seven-day week we still use today. Their year had twelve months, but whereas we give all the months but February thirty or thirty-one days, to make the year add up to 365 days, the Babylonians kept the lunar month. This meant, however, that once every year or so they would have to add a "leap-month" by repeating one of the months; which one to repeat was decided by the astronomers. When this happened, proclamations would be sent out to tell people that their taxes were due in a different month than originally announced.

Religion and Government in Mesopotamia

Originally Mesopotamia was a land of scattered city-states, of which Babylon and Ur were the most important. They were quite substantial cities; Babylon, the largest, had a population of perhaps as many as 100,000 people, a size that dwarfs the villages of the millennia before the Bronze Age. Each city controlled the surrounding countryside and had its own laws and government, although the different Mesopotamian cities shared a common language and religion. The people within the cities lived in small houses of mud brick, built next to each other in solid blocks, with no windows and the door in front the only way in or out.

The Mesopotamian economy was primarily agricultural. People had domestic cattle, sheep, and goats and were the first to use wheeled carts to carry their produce. Barley grew well in their irrigated fields and was used to make both beer and barley bread. The residents of each city went out during the day to farm or tend their flocks and came back into the city at night, where they felt safe behind high walls and gates. In the middle of each city were the temples of their religion; by 2500 B.C., or shortly thereafter, the Mesopotamians were building massive brick temples called ziggurats, many of which still survive today.

These temples were in some ways as striking a development as the invention of writing, for they represented a new form of religious life. Archaeological discoveries indicate that men of the Stone Age certainly had forms of religion, which probably included the worship of deities of springs or groves, involved amulets and representations of animals, and burial of the dead as though in expectation of an afterlife. But the temples in Mesopotamia introduced something new—not just religious ritual permeating one's private life, but a series of buildings and people devoted entirely to religious activity. The priests of the temples performed their rituals not for individuals but for society as a whole.

The temple complexes owned much of the land surrounding each city. These huge temples also served as meeting places and as markets. From the rents from their lands, from the offerings that people (especially the kings) made to the gods, and from the sale of pots and textiles they produced in their workshops, the priests were able to generate enough income to feed a large number of people who did not raise food themselves and to garner food for the "god's table." The god was assumed to live in the temple as a person lives in a house, and at mealtimes the priests, using a series of standardized rituals, put out food for the god to eat. The food might be burned or, after having sat a certain amount of time, sent on to the royal palace. There was a slightly uneasy alliance between the king, who was supposed to be the high priest to his city's chief god but who did not live or work in the temple, and the priests, who did.

Whether the individual city-states of Mesopotamia were independent or ruled as part of an empire, they were frequently at war with each other. Warfare was only for the aristocrats, who could afford the weapons and armor; kings were expected to lead their men in battle. (However, as in all succeeding centuries, ordinary workers who never went to war themselves could be financially hurt or even killed in battle.) Wars were short; individual battles were sometimes little more than afternoon excursions of men from two city-states against each other. The battles were often very bloody, however; bronze will take a good edge and thus can be used to make lethal weapons as well as farming implements. Many disagreements were settled at great peaceful banquets.

Much of the fighting was done from war chariots, with aristocrats steering against each other and against the infantry of the other side. The Mesopotamians do not seem to have had horses, instead using more or less domesticated wild asses to pull their chariots. They also did not have proper harnessing techniques; they fastened four asses or so together in a single collar and then arched a pole back from the collar to

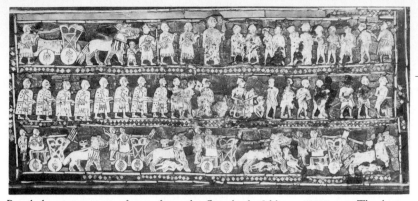

Panel showing scenes of war, from the Standard of Ur, c. 2700 B.C. The lower row shows aristocrats in their war chariots.

the chariot, rather than attaching the harness to the animals' chests and shoulders. Although this method reduced energy efficiency and made the chariot hard to steer, it was perfectly serviceable. The armies also had squads of infantry, men who fought on foot with lances and bows and arrows. They had little armor, other than a helmet, which might be made of bronze but was usually made of leather. They did carry square shields, however, and, when infantry marched shoulder to shoulder, the shields could form an effective wall against incoming arrows and lances.

The city-states were ruled by kings. In most of the cities, most of the time, the kings did not have absolute power but ruled through a council of elders. As long as they governed their people well, they were considered to have the gods with them, much more so than the gods were ever with ordinary men. One of the chief obligations of the king was the protection of his people by maintaining the city ramparts but also by keeping the poor from starving or being unduly oppressed.

It is possible that originally a king could only rule for a year, ending his rule in the spring, at the coming of the new year, the great Mesopotamian holiday. He may even have been ritually put to death at the end of the year. Such a ritual, which is hinted at in the evidence of several early civilizations, seems to have been part of the identification of the king with the year's cycle: As the old year died, so must the king, and as the new season began, renewal must come with a new man. However, the Mesopotamian kings quickly found a way around that, instead establishing the custom of a mock "king-for-the-day" on their New Year's. On this day people could break all the ordinary social taboos, and the mock king wore a grotesque mask, taking part in the revelry. This "king" then may have been put to death; some scholars think that this is the origin of the grave pits at Ur, where a number of people were all buried together. By the time the records are better, however, the "king-for-a-day" was simply deposed, and the old king came back again after one day as the "new" king to greet the new year. At least once, however, the real king died on New Year's, and the mock king became the real king in his place, ruling for over twenty years.

The gods of the Mesopotamians were fairly manlike figures, with concerns similar to theirs; one of the most important of their gods was the farmer-god. According to legend, the leader of the gods, Marduk, only came to be permanent leader when the rest of the gods needed his special talents to drive off the powers of chaos, and they agreed unanimously that he would have such power as a reward. It is significant to note that, although they assumed that all societies, including those of the gods, should be governed by kings, they also took it for granted that kings only governed with the assent of at least the other powerful or wise men. This view of kingship came to the fore again in the early Middle Ages.

Ancient Egypt

Shortly after civilization began to flourish in Mesopotamia, it also developed in Egypt, about eight hundred miles to the west, on the far side of the great Arabian desert. Egypt was the most successful of the ancient empires. It was certainly the longest lasting; Egyptian civilization existed fundamentally unchanged for nearly three thousand years, from before 3000 B.C. until Egypt was conquered by Alexander the Great in 332 B.C., a period of time half again as long as the period from the birth of Christ until now. Although dynasties came and went, the people under the

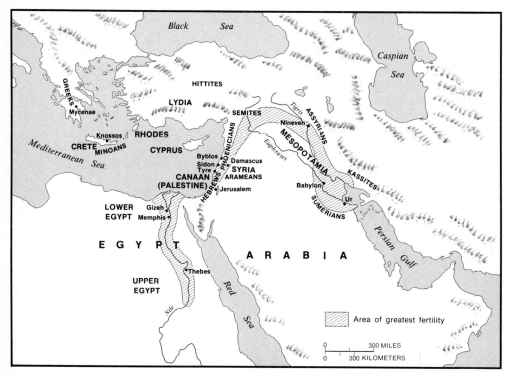

THE ANCIENT MIDDLE EAST, c. 2000–1000 B.C.
Western civilization began in the Middle East. The two major centers were in the most fertile regions, along the Nile in Egypt, and in the "Fertile Crescent" region of Mesopotamia, along the Tigris and Euphrates rivers.

Bronze head of the goddess Mut. She is depicted wearing the double crown of the pharaohs, symbolizing the unification of upper and lower Egypt.

pharaohs, or kings—who themselves varied little in spite of dynastic changes—continued to live under the same political organization and social structure and even to follow the same styles of art. When the Greeks and Romans studied Egypt, they were looking back to a culture whose beginning was already as remote to them as classical Greece is to us. Because of the great influence of Egyptian learning on Greece and Rome, and because it is the best known of the ancient empires, it deserves to be examined in detail.

The ancient Egyptians viewed life as passing through a succession of changes but only as cycles within a greater, repeating pattern that did not really change at all. Egypt used a calendar based on the 365-day year, which they took from the Babylonians. Unlike the Babylonians, they did not try to make the years and the lunar months come out even. Instead, their calendar consisted of twelve thirty-day months plus five extra days. But they did not have leap year. Whereas today we introduce an extra day into the calendar every four years, the Egyptians did not, which meant that their dates gradually became further and further off, by one day every four years. A calendar date that had originally been in the spring gradually worked its way back into the winter, then back into the fall, and so on. Egyptian culture lasted long enough for dates to work their way around the year *twice*.

But the calendar was not a major concern to the Egyptians, whose life was ruled not by dates but by the Nile. This river, longest in the world, starts in the mountains of central Africa and flows northward toward the Mediterranean. Ancient Egypt, built along the Nile, was a country nearly fifteen hundred miles long but in places no more than twelve miles wide. Every spring, when the mountain snow melts, the river rises rapidly. Egypt's long central valley was flooded every year, starting at the beginning of the summer, when the snowmelt reached the lower stretches of the Nile. In this prosperous valley were the two kingdoms of Upper and Lower Egypt ("Upper" was upstream to the south, and "Lower" was downstream to the north around the Delta at the river's mouth). They had been united since the first pharaohs, who always wore a double crown to symbolize control over the double kingdom.

The pharaohs—the kings or emperors of this double kingdom—had much more power than did the various Mesopotamian kings. At least in the early days of Egypt, the pharaohs and the temples seem to have owned all the land; therefore, the population always owed them rent. In order to hold their very long empire together, the pharaohs governed through viziers, men who acted in their name. Normally there were two, one at Memphis, the capital of Lower Egypt (not far from modern Cairo), and the other upriver at Thebes, the capital of Upper Egypt. These men were responsible both for seeing that the pharaohs received their rightful taxes and rents and for maintaining justice and prosperity in the two kingdoms.

The annual flooding of the Nile was the central feature of the year, and the chief officials of the pharaohs were responsible for obtaining word from upstream when the heaviest flooding was coming and for measuring each year's flow with Nilometers. (A Nilometer was a series of marks cut into cliffs along the river, to measure the Nile's height.) The river brought silt with it that constantly renewed the soil, so that it was always very rich, ready to grow large crops. Farmers diked and dammed the water, so that after the flood had receded and the soil began to dry out they could slowly release more water, keeping the soil always damp enough. The sun was hot and shone almost all the time, so that with plenty of sunshine and enough water the crops grew readily and dependably. The flooding of the Nile continued to dominate Egypt until the Aswan dam was completed in 1971: The purpose of this dam was to store all the river's water and to release it slowly over the course of the year in a constant flow, making it possible to grow more than one crop a year, and ending the differences between years of disastrously high floods, disastrously low floods, and normal floods.

Egyptian Hieroglyphs

We know a fair amount about how the Egyptians raised their food, as well as other details of their daily life, both from paintings and artifacts found in Egyptian tombs and from the notes they took themselves. In many of their paintings one can see a process described in a series of pictures drawn next to each other, like a modern comic strip without the

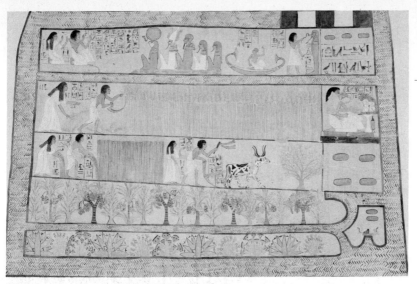

Wall painting depicting the Fields of the Blest, c. 1200 B.C. The middle rows show agricultural scenes. The ripples around the edge are the Nile.

boxes separating the separate events. But even more informative are the hieroglyphs.

Egyptian hieroglyphs, with Mesopotamian cuneiform characters, are the oldest forms of writing in the world. The Egyptians probably got the original idea of writing from the Mesopotamians, but they quickly developed their own unique forms. Hieroglyphs started as little pictures, with the word "eye" for example represented by a picture of an eye. Abstract concepts (such as "home" or "beauty") could be expressed by putting several little pictures together. (Chinese and Japanese characters stand for words and are constructed out of other characters in the same way.) One could also use a character for another word that sounded the same even though it meant something different. An ancient Egyptian writing modern English, for example, would use the same character for "eye" and "I."

Although the complicated little pictures persisted for formal writing carved in stone, for everyday purposes the Egyptians developed a faster hieroglyphic script, in which a complicated picture of an object would be reduced to a few strokes. Scribes, those who could read and write the very large number of Egyptian characters, would have to study for years to become proficient. It naturally takes much longer to learn several thousand characters than it does the twenty-six letters of our modern alphabet (even today, Japanese and Chinese school children must spend years learning characters). In spite of the long training involved, becoming a scribe was a highly regarded profession, because the Egyptian government bureaucracy, the military, the religious temples, and ordinary landlords all used them to keep tally of what was going on. At harvest time, scribes sat under the trees by the fields busily recording the jars of grain and bales of straw. Studying in the scribal schools was an excellent way for someone from a poor background to get ahead in the world.

Most records were kept on papyrus. This material was made from the papyrus reed, which grew wild along the Nile. The reed was cut in thin strips, which were laid out in a double thickness, the two layers at right angles to each other, and hammered with a mallet until the sap in the reeds stuck the whole mass together. The surface, which came out of this process with a texture like a woven material, was then smoothed with a stone. After the papyrus was dried and bleached in the sun it was ready to be written on like paper; our modern word "paper" in fact comes from "papyrus." The scribes used a reed brush dipped in ink or paint.

Papyrus was a versatile reed; as well as using it for paper, the Egyptians also used it for boats and rafts, for baskets and mats, and for sandals—in a pinch they even ate it. The very dry climate in Egypt means that a great number of papyrus documents have survived. Since the nineteenth century, when Egyptian hieroglyphs were interpreted (they had not been in use for over a thousand years; modern Egyptians use Arabic script), it has been possible to learn a great deal about ancient Egyptian life from their own writings.

Egyptian Food and Farming

The principal Egyptian crop was grain (as indeed grain of one sort or another is the principal agricultural crop of all societies), some wheat but mostly barley. Rent to one's landlord (often a large temple complex) and taxes to the royal government were paid in grain; the amounts were fixed, good years and bad. The normal diet consisted primarily of barley bread, which the Egyptians baked in little beehive ovens in their kitchens, supplemented with onions or leeks which they grew in their kitchen gardens, and with barley beer. The kitchen gardens also produced lettuces, radishes, cucumbers, peas, and beans. There were dates and figs in season, and the Egyptians also raised cattle and poultry as well as catching fish and trapping small wild birds; but barley bread and onions were the main food for most Egyptians most days, as indeed they were for all the people who lived around the Mediterranean in antiquity.

No farming could be done during the summer, when all cropland was under water, but beginning around the autumn equinox farming started in earnest. The first step was to determine where everyone's field was; all boundary markers would naturally have been washed away by the flood. Although the Egyptians did not have any complex mathematics, they had worked out basic geometry, so that, using a few fixed points on high ground above the flood line, they could triangulate and reestablish field boundaries.

In the three months known as "the emergence of the soil," while the river receded, the Egyptians planted their grain. Doing the reverse of what we would consider normal, they first spread the seeds across the damp fields, and then plowed. The purpose of plowing for them was to cover the seeds with dirt, to protect the sprouts from the sun and from birds. The Egyptians used a very lightweight plow, essentially a pointed stick with handles. One person steered, while a donkey or a cow or two pulled; the plow was light enough that a man could pull it in the absence of a cow or donkey. (The Egyptians, like the Mesopotamians, did not originally have horses, which were only introduced into the Near East sometime after 1800 B.C.) After plowing, men with hoes went through the fields, making sure that all the seeds were covered and breaking up the biggest clods of dirt.

After planting came the season known as "drought," when the Nile shrank to a trickle and the Egyptians had to let their carefully stored water out from behind its dikes to keep their fields from drying out. At the end of this season came the harvest, when the grain was finally ripe. Egyptians harvested with a sickle made with a wooden handle and a blade of sharpened flint (iron was not in general use until after Egypt's heyday). A lot of grain fell to the ground during this process, and after the harvesting the fields had to be gleaned. This meant that people went through them on their hands and knees, picking up heads of grain that had dropped. Children especially were used for gleaning. A poor family would supplement its diet by gleaning in a rich neighbor's field, and kindhearted harvesters might be deliberately sloppy in gathering in the grain.

The harvesters brought in the whole heads of grain from the field. Further work was needed to separate the actual grain from the hulls and stalks. The harvest was taken to a threshing floor, where it was spread out and threshed by oxen walking around and around on top of it. The oxen's feet broke up the heads of grain, separating the straw and hulls (the chaff) from the grain itself. The threshed grain was then gathered up and winnowed. One could winnow by fanning the threshed grain with a large fan; the lighter chaff blew away while the grain itself remained. The more common method was to throw the threshed grain up into the air, letting the wind carry away the chaff, and catch it again in baskets. People still winnow this way today in parts of the Near East.

The stems of the wheat or barley plants—that is, the straw—were left standing in the field when the grain was harvested. Soon, however, workers went back and cut the straw as well, after the gleaners had had their chance to go through the fields. Straw, along with chaff, was used as oxen fodder, and straw was also used in making the bricks from which most Egyptian buildings were made. By the time the harvest was all in, the river was beginning to rise, and the cycle was repeated the next year.

Egyptian Households

Ancient Egypt was primarily a land of villages, built on outcroppings of rock that were high enough above the river to stay fairly dry during the flooding of the Nile. Over the centuries, these outcroppings rose gradually higher because when an old house was torn down the new house was built directly on the rubble. Even today, many Egyptian villages are built over layers of old houses laid down during millennia of rebuilding. The houses were made of brick, given tensile strength by the addition of straw, as mentioned above. Bricks were either dried in the sun or fired at low temperatures. Although this sort of brick will melt back into mud in a damp climate, it lasted fairly well in Egypt's dry atmosphere, as long as the river did not reach it. Eventually the bricks crumbled and the house had to be rebuilt.

Egyptian houses were very small by our standards and built along narrow, twisting streets no more than five feet wide. Although the number of people in a village might not be large, the need to fit everybody onto a small outcropping made for cramped quarters. Ordinary houses consisted of a few rooms, laid out one behind the other, all on one story, though there was generally a small cellar for storage and a stairway to the roof. The back room was used as the kitchen, and the garden patch was out in back. Houses of the well-to-do were larger, with more rooms, and sometimes even a bathroom. Water was too valuable to be used by the tubful or allowed to drain away, so instead of a bathtub a wealthy Egyptian had a stone slab, on which he stood while someone sluiced him down with a bucket; the slab was cut to carry the water away to jugs for storage and reuse. Instead of a toilet with running water, the Egyptians had wooden seats, with a keyhole-shaped opening cut in them, and a chamberpot underneath.

Most clothing in ancient Egypt was of linen; flax, from which linen was made, was the other principal crop plant besides barley. Linen is very cool in hot weather, and the Egyptian style of dress was very simple and well designed for the heat. Men wore a short kilt or skirt as their basic garment, sometimes with the addition of a shirt or tunic. Women wore a sleeveless, ankle-length dress, cut tight and form-fitting. Fashionable women often left one breast bare, and dresses for fancy occasions were made of cloth so delicate and sheer that nothing was left to the imagination. Neither sex wore underwear, and children went naked. Both men and women wore bracelets, necklaces, earrings, and makeup; women especially wore very heavy eye makeup.

Both men and women went to barbers, who shaved them with bronze razors. Many men preferred to shave off their own hair and wear a wig when they went out. The pharaohs, who always shaved their heads and chins, wore both wigs and false beards. (It is interesting to note that the female pharaohs, of which there were several, also wore false beards!) To keep their skin from drying out, everyone, rich and poor, rubbed themselves regularly with ointment. When the necropolis workers at Thebes went on strike around 1200 B.C., it was because they claimed they weren't receiving their rightful ointment ration.

Clothing and household furnishings could be made or they could be bought. The Egyptians did not have coins, and so all transactions had to be through barter—that is, with one object exchanged for another. Their barter did not mean simply haggling over a price, for objects had set prices, even if that price was not in money. A dress would be valued as being worth a certain weight in silver, or a kitchen pot a certain weight in copper. Egypt was thus on a "metal standard" long before metal was actually used for coins. If one wanted to buy a dress, one had to assemble objects whose total value was the same in silver as that dress (there were methods of converting values in weights of copper, used for more mundane objects, to weights in silver or gold, used for more expensive objects). Housewives seem to have kept worn-out bronze kitchenware, pots that had a known value, on hand as a source of "ready cash" (even if worn out, they were valuable for their metal). The awkwardness of such a system indicates why all of the Near Eastern civilizations adopted the use of coins when they first began to appear around the end of the Bronze Age.

Everyone in Egypt was expected to marry and have children. Although we tend to think of Egypt in terms of brother-sister marriages, in fact this was something reserved only for the royal dynasty, to keep the line of rulers pure. It was only because they *were* royal that such a dispensation could be made at all. Normally Egyptians would have looked at marriages between brothers and sisters with as much revulsion as we would. To have children was a deliberate choice, because the Egyptians, like all civilizations, had various methods of contraception available if they wanted them. A number of papyrus manuscripts have been found that contain formulas for concocting contraceptives; one of the most popular ingredients was crocodile dung.

New children were welcomed, and soon after birth Egyptian parents would have a professional astrologer cast a horoscope for their child, to see what sort of life and career he or she would have. Young children played with toy animals and little carts, of which plenty of examples have been found in children's tombs, and children and adults both played board games. It is interesting to note that children played with wheeled toys long before Egyptian adults used wheeled transport. Most households had pets, dogs, cats, even monkeys. Cats were highly revered, and it is usually thought that the Egyptians were the first to develop the domestic breed of cats we now have. Well-to-do households had servants and foreign slaves.

Death in Ancient Egypt

Egyptian civilization was built around the idea of death. From a modern viewpoint, this preoccupation with death seems strange and morbid, but the Egyptians themselves seem to have been relatively cheerful and optimistic, and the afterlife that they expected, while always described rather vaguely, was going to be very like their ordinary life, involving work in fields that would, even in the afterlife, be flooded annually by the Nile.

The pharaohs, who had much more authority than did the kings of Mesopotamia, expected to be gods after death, and they especially prepared for their deaths. Originally the pharoahs seem to have thought that only they and perhaps members of their households would be revived in the life to come. In earliest times servants may even have been killed to accompany dead pharaohs to the grave, although this practice does not seem to have lasted long. By about 2000 B.C., immortality was believed to be available to anyone, although still only the pharaohs were expected to become gods.

The pharaohs spent much of their lives building massive tombs, suitable homes for gods, of which the pyramids are the most spectacular examples. The pyramids, Egypt's biggest structures, were built specifically as tombs, unlike the Mesopotamian ziggurats, built about the same time or slightly later, which were designed as temples. The pyramids were built quite early in Egyptian history, around 2600–2500 B.C., but

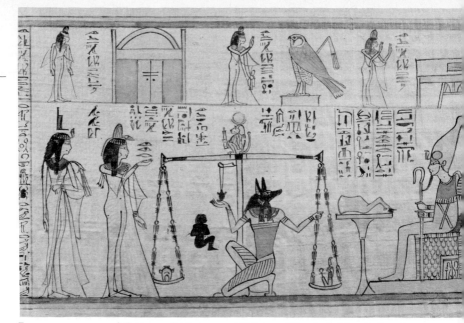

Funerary papyrus of Princess Entiuny, c. 1025 B.C. The jackal-headed god in the center is weighing a human heart in judgment.

later pharaohs also had elaborate tombs, even if not in pyramids. In a society in which all ordinary buildings and even royal palaces were made of mud bricks, only temples and tombs were made of stone.

The pyramids were built near Memphis, the capital of Lower Egypt. They were a remarkable engineering feat, especially as they were built with very primitive tools. The Egyptians had not invented the block and tackle, so the huge stones out of which the pyramids were built, each weighing two and a half tons or more, had to be levered into place from ramps. They did not even use the wheel at the time the pyramids were built, so the stones had to be dragged to the site on sledges. To pull the stones up the ramps, the builders conscripted local people, usually during the season of the floods when they were not able to work in their fields anyway. The flood season was also preferred for building because the stones were usually floated down the river to the building site. The stones themselves were quarried with stone or copper tools, as iron working had not yet been developed, much less steel.

Most of a pyramid was solid stone, but somewhere within it was the burial chamber for the pharaoh. The builders tried to hide the actual location of the tomb, so that it would not be found by grave robbers. A series of labyrinthine passages, false doors, dummy chambers, and carefully walled up real doors were designed to fool anyone who broke in.

Pharaohs were buried with gold, jewelry, and finely made household objects, to be well provided for in the afterworld, but the grave robbers thought that the gold would be even more useful for them in their present lives. In spite of all the precautions, pharaohs' tombs were almost inevitably discovered and broken into. Of all the royal tombs excavated by modern archaeologists, only the tomb of King Tut (built in the fourteenth century B.C. in the Valley of the Kings, 600 miles upstream from the pyramids) had not been thoroughly robbed during antiquity.

Building tombs, whether pyramids or the smaller structures that later pharaohs preferred, was one of the major industries of Egypt. There were whole villages around Thebes, the capital of Upper Egypt, in the so-called Valley of the Kings, where the men did not work their fields at all but rather worked in construction. Thebes itself, on the east bank of the Nile, was the royal capital, but the west bank was given over to the dead. The narrow canyons were full of royal tombs, piles of rubble from the digging of new tombs (rubble from a later tomb covered Tut's tomb, the principal reason it was hidden so long), and the huts of workmen. There were specialists in stoneworking, painters who covered the insides of tombs with scenes from everyday life and scenes of the afterlife, priests for the many temples located there, scribes, the royal embalmers, and guards to try to keep out the robbers.

Although the pharaohs were buried with great amounts of gold, ordinary people were not. Viziers and important officials of the royal administration had rather fancy tombs, but most people were just buried by having their coffins stacked up in a burial chamber with a lot of other coffins. Everyone was mummified, however, and even cats and birds were sometimes made into mummies. The purpose of mummification was to preserve the body from decaying. The Egyptians saw life as composed both of the life of the body and of the life of what we might call the spirit or soul. As long as either the spirit lived or the body remained, a person was not really gone but was ready to live again in the afterworld. Although it was difficult to tell how long a person's spirit might last or how well it could function in the afterlife without the body, the Egyptians felt they had played safe by ensuring that the body would remain as intact as possible.

When someone died, the body was given to the embalmers to preserve it. Depending on how much the relatives had to spend, mummification could be simple or very elaborate. Normally the internal organs, the first to spoil, were removed. For elaborate mummification, even the brain would be removed, carefully pulled out with hooks though the nose. Then the body was dried out with salts and stuffed with spices. The final step was wrapping the body with yards of bandages, held in place by resin or gum. The thoroughly dessicated body would now keep indefinitely. The funeral and burial took place after the body was received back from the seventy-day mummification process. Mummies have lasted extremely well in Egypt's dry climate. The process has not been in use for two thousand years, but the Egyptian sands still yield mummies. They are so plentiful that in the nineteenth century, when the Egyptian railroad system was being built, workers used mummies as supports for the tracks.

Egyptian Religion

In spite of their preoccupation with death, there was a good deal of Egyptian religion that was concerned with life. They worshiped a mixture of gods, including their pharaohs, but especially animals and birds such as the cat and the ibis. The Egyptians believed in a multitude of gods, and although the pharoah Akhnaton briefly tried to establish monotheism in the fourteenth century B.C., based on worship of the sun as the one true god, this had little long-lasting effect.

The Egyptians, looking ahead to life after death, considered that there would be a judgment, in which one would either be blessed or damned. They passed along this idea to the Romans, who in turn gave it to the Christians. There are representatives in Egyptian tombs of a jackal-headed god weighing or judging a man's heart in a scale. The Egyptians had no middle ground between blessing and damnation—nothing comparable to the Purgatory that Christianity developed during the Middle Ages. The Egyptians' hell was an immense region of muddy marshes and lakes of fire, in which the damned were subjected to bloody and terrifying tortures. This hell, like everything else in Egyptian religion, tended to be concrete rather than philosophical: some sarcophagi (stone coffins) even included maps of it.

Although the religion itself seems to have had little structure or dogma, the temple system was fairly well organized. High priests controlled a substantial amount of revenue and were nearly as powerful as the royal viziers. Temples were built roughly along the same plan as houses, only they were much larger and made of stone rather than brick because they were considered to be houses for the gods. The largest temple, Karnak, is in fact the largest temple ever constructed, and it was continually being rebuilt or having additions made to it for two thousand years.

These temples were not places for public worship, in our sense, for ordinary people would never be allowed past the mud-brick walls that surrounded the temple complex. Only the pharaohs, a few high officials, and the priests were allowed into the temple itself, and only the highest priests into the inner temple, where the god himself resided. Worship of the god took the form of a series of rituals following the god's day, which was assumed to be very like an Egyptian's day. (In this way the Egyptian temple ceremonies were like those of the Mesopotamians.) The god started by getting up and getting dressed in the morning, as the high priest changed the decorations on the cult statue. Then he had his breakfast, as the priest laid out food offerings, and so on. Temples owned a lot of land, to provide the food for the priests, the craftsmen, the sculptors, the masons, and all the other people a temple required, but the god also paid taxes on his land to the pharaoh just like anyone else.

The temples, as well as being religious centers, were also educational centers, as most of them had schools attached. These were the schools where boys could go for the scribal training they needed for their careers. Boys usually started at about age six, learning to write the characters by copying old texts, which must have been totally meaningless to them at first. Scribal training involved much more than learning to read and write. It also required learning history and literature, basic mathematics and bookkeeping—even personnel management, because a successful scribe would fill a management role similar to that of an M.B.A. today.

The temples were also medical centers, where anyone could be treated. Medicine for the Egyptians included surgery and herbal medicine but

Egyptian scribes, c. 1350 B.C.

also spells, charms, and exorcism. (The distinction we draw between formal medicine and folk medicine would be incomprehensible to the Egyptians.) Some doctors gained international reputations; other emperors wrote to the court of Ramesses II asking if they could use the skills of a particularly renowned physician. The Greeks, who greatly admired the Egyptians and their learning, later copied a great deal of their herbal cures from them.

The Phoenicians

Although the Mesopotamians and the Egyptians were the first and most successful empires, the Middle East also produced several other empires during the two thousand years before Christ. It seems in fact to have been a standard development for cities to be unified under the control of one city and its emperor. All of these empires were located in the fertile regions of the Near East, where food could be grown fairly easily, and all of them went to war with each other and with Egypt and Mesopotamia. The Hittites, who lived on the northern edge of the eastern Mediterranean in what is now Turkey, and the Assyrians, who lived in what is now Syria, northwest of Mesopotamia, were among the most successful. They eventually fell to the Persians, who were centered in what is now Iran, the last great near eastern empire before the short-lived Greek empire of Alexander the Great (see Chapter 2) and the much longer lasting Roman Empire (see Chapter 3).

But one of the most influential peoples of the ancient world, the Phoenicians, never really formed an empire. They lived along the eastern edge of the Mediterranean and were the best shipbuilders and sailors of the ancient world. Trade routes brought goods overland from India and even farther east to Mesopotamia, and from there to the Mediterranean.

The Phoenicians took over much of this trade by 1100 B.C. or so. They loaded goods both from Mesopotamia and the east onto their ships and sailed west with them to Egypt, northern Africa, even Europe. Phoenician ships sailed the length of the Mediterranean, out through the straits of Gibraltar, and even up to England, where they bought tin. Tin was needed, along with copper, to make bronze, as noted above.

The Phoenician capital at Tyre, in what is now Lebanon, was built half a mile out to sea, inaccessible except by ship. This meant in the first millennium B.C. that it was inaccessible to any but themselves, for their ships were better and faster than anyone else's. From the eastern end of the Mediterranean, the Phoenicians gradually spread their cities around the fringes of the entire sea, always staying very close to the coast, rather than settling inland. One of their largest cities was Carthage, in northern Africa, which Rome considered a major threat to its own growing empire in the third century B.C. Rome eventually conquered Carthage after a hundred years of fighting.

The Phoenicians, as well as being great sailors, also perfected the first true alphabet. Whereas the Mesopotamians and Egyptians had used variations of pictographs, with each symbol standing for a word, the Phoenicians refined certain hieroglyphs into symbols that stood for sounds (the way the letters in a modern alphabet stand for sounds). They developed twenty-two characters that could, among them, spell out all the words in the Phoenician language. These letters became the basis of the Hebrew alphabet, of the Greek alphabet, and, from the Greek, of the Roman alphabet we still use today. If we compare Phoenician and Greek characters, the Greek ones being much closer to our own, it is clear that many of the characters were turned upside down or sideways when the Greeks adopted them; but they still have recognizable similarities. The Phoenician city of Byblos became a specialized center for the manufacture of books and writing materials; our words "bible" (meaning "the book") and "bibliography" both come from the name of this town.

The Ancient Hebrews

The great empires such as Egypt and Babylon were certainly the most politically important cultures of the time. But it was another culture, that of the Hebrews—a small group that passed almost unnoticed on the fringes of the great empires—that had the most long-term impact on Western culture. They never constituted an empire, or even one kingdom; in their most politically unified period they made up two kingdoms, Israel and Judah, not one. But their religion, with one God rather than multiple gods, was the basis of both Christianity and Islam in later centuries, as well as three thousand years of Judaism. Their ideas of law and of morality are still very much part of our culture.

The ancient Hebrews were a group unified by their religion. Modern ideas of the separation of church and state would have been incomprehensible to them, both because the idea of separating their religious beliefs from the rest of their lives would have been impossible, and, even more importantly, because until quite late in their history the Hebrews had neither an organized "state" nor an organized "church."

Although from a modern point of view Judaism is a fairly well-defined religion, governed by the tenets laid down in what the Jews call the Bible and the Christians call the Old Testament, it was never defined by one set of beliefs and practices, and indeed is not now. One need only think of the differences in modern America between the Orthodox, Conservative, and Reformed forms of Judaism to realize how much religious practice can vary within what is officially the same religion. Modern Israel, which is open to immigration by any Jew, had to avoid defining exactly what constitutes a Jew, because there are people who consider themselves Jewish who would not fit any precise definition. The ancient Hebrews were nearly as diverse in their practices. Even the Bible (Old Testament) did not finally take the form it has now until the first century B.C. The essence of Judaism was never a distinct philosophy or specific beliefs so much as a broader belief in being the chosen people of God.

This belief in being a chosen people took the specific form of a covenant, or binding agreement, between God and the Hebrews. This covenant, according to the Bible, was reached between God and the patriarch Abraham, from whom all Jews were considered to be descended. God agreed to watch over Abraham and his descendants and to give them the land of Canaan. As a sign of this covenant, Abraham and all his male descendants would be circumcised (Genesis 17). It should be noted that the biblical account of the Jews being chosen by God and beginning the practice of circumcision was given as a description of an event that took place at a certain time to a certain person, not just a general myth.

This is because Judaism, much more so than other ancient religions, was a *historical* religion. Their religious writings were primarily a historical record of events that happened to the Jews as a people. It was this consciousness of sharing a common history, rather than any centralized temple or precise set of creeds, that tied the Jews together (and still does). Even the hundreds of laws governing the details of daily life and the religious rituals were described in historical terms, as having been laid down at a specific time in reaction to specific events. For example, the ancient Hebrews shared with the Babylonians the idea of a seven-day week, but for the Babylonians it had an astronomical significance, corresponding to the seven planets that they could see and to the four quarters of the moon's twenty-eight-day cycle, whereas the Jews gave the week a historical significance corresponding to the earth's creation in seven days. Similarly, all Near Eastern religions had some sort of special spring religious ceremony, but only the Jews' holiday, the Passover, was tied to a specific historical event, in their case the flight of the Jews under Moses out of Egypt.

The historical aspect of Judaism set it apart from other Near Eastern religions, but perhaps even more unusual for its time was the Hebrews' monotheism: the ancient Hebrews always believed in only one God. Because Judaism gave this idea first to Christianity and then to Islam, it scarcely seems radical in the modern West, but it was certainly unusual in the ancient world. Most religions had a principal or chief god, and occasionally an individual would claim that there was only one god, as did Akhnaton in Egypt, as mentioned above; but for the most part the Hebrews' neighbors were all polytheistic, believing in a multitude of gods and goddesses of various functions and attributes. The Hebrews were the only ancient culture that believed strongly enough in their own god not to feel required to worship their neighbors' gods as well, "just in case."

Hebrew monotheism was not at first quite like modern monotheism. Although the early Hebrews only worshiped and followed one god, Yahweh (whose name is sometimes incorrectly anglicized as Jehovah), he was *their* god specifically, and they were willing to concede that there might be gods for other peoples, even if these gods were not as good and powerful as theirs. The Ten Commandments begin, "Thou shalt have no other gods before me" (Exodus 20:3), which certainly established Yahweh's priority, but allowed for the *existence* at least of other gods. There is throughout the early books of the Bible a strong xenophobia, or fear of strangers. To be sold as a slave to non-Hebrews was something to be greatly feared, and to worship the gods of strangers was something disgusting. This dislike of outsiders was certainly one of the factors that has kept Judaism a coherent religion through three thousand years, during which there has rarely been an organized and centralized Jewish political or church structure.

But early Hebrew monotheism gradually evolved into something rather different, a belief that Yahweh was not just their particular god but the one God, God of all peoples whether they recognized Him or not. This change in attitude was certainly not abrupt, and indeed probably not striking at the time, because ancient Judaism was not a particularly theoretical or philosophizing religion, concerning itself much more with the concrete. But this version of monotheism, which saw in the worship of other gods by other peoples either misguided beliefs in nonexistent deities or else the worship of the real God under the wrong name and in the wrong forms, at least provided the basis for Jews and later Christians and Muslims (occasionally) to talk to each other about religion. (Interestingly, worshiping the "right" God in the "wrong" way has usually been seen as a much more wicked sin than not knowing God at all, which has meant that Jews, Christians, and Muslims, or for that matter different factions within these religions, have generally opposed each other much more bitterly than any have opposed polytheistic pagans, who are assumed not to know any better.)

Hebrew Pastoral Life

Our knowledge of the daily life of the ancient Hebrews comes to a large degree from the Bible. The biblical records have, in the last century or so, been so well corroborated by archaeological findings that it is now generally assumed that these books, written down to describe what were considered historical events, can indeed be taken to have a great deal of what we would consider accurate history in them.

The first Hebrews appeared roughly around 2000–1500 B.C., as tribes of primarily nomadic pastoral people, drifting into what was already a highly civilized and urbanized area. The ancient civilizations of Mesopotamia and Egypt were already in place when the Hebrews appeared with their flocks of sheep and goats, setting up their tents in the open places between developed agricultural areas.

The Hebrews left their tents for the settled city (that is, agricultural) life within a century or two after first coming into Palestine (now Israel). But the nomadic life remained as an ideal. The story of Adam's sons, Cain and Abel, who quarreled because the virtuous Abel kept sheep whereas the fratricide Cain grew crops, reflects the natural antagonism between the two forms of life. (For someone with herds, a person raising grain is selfishly taking all the best potential pasturage for himself, whereas the person engaged in agriculture always fears sheep and goats eating his crops.) It is significant that the bad brother of the story was Cain, whose crops were not as acceptable to God as his brother's flocks.

Even after they were well urbanized, the Hebrews continued to identify the city with sin and corruption and to see redemption and renewal coming from the wilderness. The patriarchs Abraham and Isaac, who are now considered even by secular scholars to have been actual people, though perhaps not necessarily with all the deeds attributed specifically to them, were nomads and pastoralists. Abraham indeed had originally been a city-dweller in Ur, in Mesopotamia, until he left there to become a tent-dweller in the land of Canaan (Palestine) (Genesis 15:7). The cities of Sodom and Gomorrah, which Abraham encountered, were sinful essentially because they *were* cities. Long after the Hebrews were settled city-dwellers with a king, renewal still came in the form of David, a shepherd; and a long-established law was that once a year, for the Feast of the Tabernacles, the Hebrews should live for a week in arbors or tents made from leafy boughs (Leviticus 23:39–42). (Even now, certain Orthodox Jews in New York City observe this festival by setting up tents on the fire escapes.)

The life of the nomadic Hebrews was in many respects similar to the nomadic life still followed by some of the Bedouins in Arabia. The basic unit that lived and traveled together usually consisted of several related nuclear families headed by two or more brothers, or a father and son or sons, with their wives, children, and servants. Polygamy, the practice of a man having more than one wife, was fairly widespread, but far from universal. A man was expected to have no more wives than he could provide for easily. The women were in a secondary position to the men and expected to retreat into the background when strangers came, but within their own tents they enjoyed a good deal of independence and helped make many decisions.

The tents in which they lived, usually made of goat hair, were large and luxurious compared to our modern nylon backpacking tents. With their wooden poles and rugs on the ground they were essentially houses with cloth walls. A family group would have several tents, at least one for every man and wife. They might be set up in a spot for only a short time or for several months, depending on the quality of the pasturage for the flocks. As long as there was enough grass and water for their herds, they ate well, a diet rich in protein, lamb, beef, butter, and milk. Because they were living among agricultural people, they could barter or buy grain to make bread, both wheat and barley, as well as fruit, olive oil, and wine. In times when the harvest was bad in Palestine, they could travel the relatively short distance southwest to Egypt, where the waters of the Nile meant consistently good crops. Abraham is recorded as making a trip to Egypt with his family and flocks, and the settling of Joseph and his brothers in Egypt is one of the most significant events of early Jewish history.

The Hebrews in the Cities

The age of the patriarchs, the nomadic period in Jewish history, was succeeded after about 1300 B.C. by the settling of Hebrews into cities and city life. In the Bible, the beginning of this period is recorded as the flight out of Egypt under Moses, the wandering of the Hebrew tribes in the wilderness for forty years, during which wilderness experience they received the definitive codification of their religious laws, and their settlement, with a fair amount of antagonism, into urban life next to new urban neighbors.

Moses, like Abraham, is considered a historical figure, an inspired religious leader, who came from Egypt with a certain number of Hebrews. He was able to persuade the people in Palestine who had the same traditions as the Jews from Egypt, traditions of being a chosen people and of being the heirs of Abraham, that they *were* all one people, that the Yahweh from whom Moses had received a new codification of law was the same God the Palestinian Jews had worshiped. Moses was so effective in persuading them that they shared in the laws given on the way from Egypt that Hebrew history subsequently had *all* the Jews share in the experience of "bondage" in Egypt and dangerous flight and return to the "promised land." The Exodus became the one historical event in which all Jews were later considered to have taken part.

The Hebrews of the subsequent centuries lived a life in which most everyday events were regulated by the Torah, the over six hundred laws of Moses. These laws included every aspect of life, from how to wear one's hair, to circumcision of infant boys, to dietary regulations, to the cleansing of ritual impurity. The dietary regulations have perhaps received the most attention. Among other regulations, the Jews were ordered to eat meat only from animals that had a divided hoof *and* chewed their cud—that is, cattle, sheep and goats, both wild and domestic, and wild deer. Horses were not specifically mentioned but would certainly have been excluded because they neither have a divided hoof nor chew their cud. Pigs *were* explicitly excluded, as they do not chew their cud even though they have a divided hoof (Deuteronomy 14:4–8). Therefore Jews, then as now, were not supposed to eat pork. The Muslims, who adopted the Mosaic laws, also do not eat pork, although the Christians abandoned quite early most of the Jewish regulations for daily life, including the dietary restrictions. (Although modern Jews who do not eat pork may be teased about this, they are at least rarely told how delicious camel meat is—another food specifically forbidden because the camel does not have a divided hoof even though it chews its cud—much less the "unclean" birds of prey, including owls and vultures.)

The Hebrews' neighbors had their own religious rituals, and some, like the Semitic worshipers of the god Baal, were ethnically very close to the Hebrews. They too worshiped one god, though a different one (Baal). There was a fair amount of influence back and forth between the Hebrews and their neighbors, especially as the Hebrews, who were not yet tied to a central priesthood or sanctuary, were more concerned with the ethics of family and neighborhood. The Hebrews, like their neighbors in the small cities of Palestine, lived in houses built close together. Because the people were outdoors most of the day, their houses could be very small and were actually used for little besides food preparation and sleeping. Indeed, in warm weather people often slept on the roof.

The family groups of urbanized Hebrews tended to be smaller than the rather extended groups of relatives who had herded flocks together. Now increasingly men had only one wife. Women enjoyed a reasonable amount of autonomy and could even own property in their own right. Although husbands had the right to divorce their wives, this was rarely done. It was always felt that a man *ought* to be married and have children. Yet there was a constant shortage of women, because the men who could afford it still practiced polygamy. Without enough women to go around, and unmarried men considered sort of nonpersons—ancient Hebrew had no word for an unmarried adult male—the men had a strong incentive to stay with their wives. Although some urban households had slaves and servants, they were not very common. Someone who had become destitute might sell himself into bondage in order to survive, but the laws of Moses specified that a Hebrew bondsman had to be freed within six years, so servitude was not a permanent condition.

Once they became agriculturalists more than pastoralists, the Hebrews ate less meat and more grain and vegetables, though they still kept herds for ritual sacrifices. They raised both wheat and barley; wheat was considered preferable, as it made much better bread, but barley grew better in the hot, dry climate. The Hebrews harvested the grain rather inefficiently, as did the Egyptians, by seizing the tops of the grain stalks with one hand and using a sickle to cut them loose. There was always a fair amount of grain left lying on the ground among the cut stalks after the harvest. This could be gathered up or gleaned as the Egyptians did. With the growth in population and the settlement in cities, there began to be urban poor—people with no land and little to eat—and many landowners considered it a kind act to leave the gleanings for those who needed the grain the worst. (This practice is described in the biblical book of Ruth.)

Besides grain, the Hebrews grew fruit in their orchards, especially dates and figs. They also grew olives for eating and for making olive oil, and grapes for wine. Their fruit was shipped over much of the Mediterranean area, just as Israeli fruit is found today in supermarkets throughout Europe. Their flocks provided milk. In the ancient world, Canaan really was the "land of milk and honey" as it is described in the Bible (especially if "honey" is rendered, perhaps more accurately, as "fruit juice"). Their bread-and-fruit diet was supplemented with some fish, both salted and fresh, mostly from the inland Sea of Galilee.

The Hebrews themselves had very little use for the Mediterranean, but there were "sea people" on the coast, the Philistines, who *were* great traders, and they took much of what the Hebrews had to sell. (The word "Palestine" comes from the Philistines.) The Philistines seem to have been closely related to, though not identical with, the Phoenicians, whose cities were somewhat farther north. Although the Philistines were a Semitic people, like the Hebrews, their cultural system was quite different, and the Hebrews considered them more threatening than the other dwellers in Canaan. It was partly in reaction to these sea people that the Hebrews first began to establish a monarchical system in self-defense, in which they were ruled by kings who could organize them for battle.

The rise of the Hebrew kings is marked in the biblical record by the story of Saul, the first king, who fought the Philistines, and of David, who slew their giant, Goliath, and went on to succeed Saul sometime about 1000 B.C. But it was David's successor, Solomon, who changed much of the face of Hebrew society by establishing Jerusalem as a central holy city, with a permanent centralized priesthood at a central temple. Jerusalem, unlike virtually all other major cities in the world, was not built on a sea or river and was not even on an important land route; hence its growth was due solely to its being a religious center, not an economic capital.

There were in fact not one but two Hebrew states: Israel and Judah. But the "nation" was never really identified with either state; the "nation" was the Hebrew people, not the royal government. Unlike Egypt, where the kings were considered gods, the Hebrew kings were quite definitely *under* both God and the law, ruling only with the good will of the Hebrew nation. The priesthood, which became increasingly important once the temple was built in Jerusalem, also provided a strong counterweight to the power of the kings.

It was at this point that much of the detailed ritual law that had been part of the Jewish religion since Moses, including a complicated legal system for assessing sins and crimes, took its fully developed form. It should again be noted that, as the nation was defined as God's chosen people, there were none of the distinctions we would draw between civil and religious law, or for that matter between social reform and religious renewal. Prophets and preachers who tried to make improvements in the condition of the urban poor or who deplored uneven distribution of wealth always did so in terms of warnings that God might withdraw his favor from a sinful people, leaving only a remnant of the "seed of Abraham," keeping the covenant with this chosen remnant but turning against the rest.

Keeping free of sin and obeying the law were always treated as a collective responsibility of the chosen people. We tend to think of responsibility in individual terms today, but for the Hebrews, who had a collective covenant, each individual was supposed to observe that covenant in order to help maintain the well-being of the group. Ancient Judaism did not have the emphasis, which Christianity later developed, on obeying God's command for the purposes of individual salvation; the group's historical survival was much more important than the life or death of one person. Judaism originally gave very little thought to personal rebirth or life after death, stressing instead the continuity of the chosen people—a continuity possible only if people did not become "stiff-necked" and turn away from the commandments of the God who had chosen them.

Judaism in the Diaspora

The distinction between the nation or people on the one hand and the actual state on the other, as well as the collective responsibility to uphold a highly detailed law, served the Hebrew people well in the Diaspora. Diaspora means the scattering of the Jews among people whom they considered strangers and outsiders. Their religion and culture made it possible for them to resist assimilation into the customs of these "outsiders." Since the Jews have lived among non-Jews for most of the three thousand or more years of Jewish history, the continued cohesion of the people and their religion can only be considered remarkable.

Already in the eighth century B.C. many Jews had been captured and carried as slaves to Assyria, and in subsequent centuries many more were taken to Babylon. The temple at Jerusalem was destroyed by the Babylonians in 586 B.C., when as much as one-third of the population of Judah were killed or deported. Although a large Jewish population remained in Palestine, many were scattered through other areas of the Near East. In the fifth century B.C. a group of priestly Jews from Babylon reestablished Jewish government at Jerusalem, but not long afterward the whole Near East came under the domination first of Alexander the Great and then of the Roman Empire. The kingdom of Judaea, independent of the Romans, was established in 140 B.C., but this was quickly crushed. The kings of Palestine were clients of the Romans for the next two hundred years, until a final abortive revolt, and the second destruction of the Temple, this time by the Romans, in 70 A.D. ended any further hopes for an independent Jewish state until the twentieth century.

But these centuries of dispersal and exile did not by any means lessen the Jewish faith in God. From the sixth to the second century B.C., each new disaster was met in part by rewriting and reworking their religious history. The disasters were seen as God's punishment of a people he was trying to correct and discipline, not the destruction of their God by other stronger gods. Because Yahweh was increasingly seen by the Hebrews as the universal God, He was God in Babylon as much as in Jerusalem, and His people were still His people no matter what state they lived in. The complex ritual that governed the Hebrews' lives kept them distinct from their non-Jewish neighbors. Looking back at their past gave the Jews a hope for the future.

By the second century B.C., there began to be hopes for a Messiah. He was sometimes seen as a leader of military victories, but more frequently the anticipated Messiah was seen as someone who would correct the people's sins and bring them again into harmony with God. This hoped-for event, it was clear, would be a *historical* event, occurring at a specific place and time (though neither were known yet), and happening to all the chosen people, not just to individuals within their individual consciousness.

The Diaspora naturally changed many features of Hebrew life, even while leaving their central religious beliefs intact. The Jews taken to

Babylon, for example, while they did not remain in a subservient or servile position for long, could also not be farmers as they had been in Palestine. This was for the good reason that in Babylon they owned no land. Many of them instead became merchants, bankers, and artisans, positions many urban Jews continued to hold for the next two thousand years. Although they continued as much as possible to observe their religious rituals, some, such as the majority of the sacrifices, were really not feasible, and so a greater emphasis was placed on prayer rather than sacrifice as a way of establishing and maintaining a relationship with God.

Although the Jews resisted assimilation for the most part, they did pick up many of the customs and especially the languages of the people among whom they lived. Greek, in the *koiné* or trader version, became as important a language for the Jews as the Aramaic version of Hebrew spoken in Palestine. By the third century B.C., it was necessary to translate the Hebrew Bible into Greek, the so-called Septuagint; it was this Greek version which the (Greek-speaking) Christians later took as their Old Testament. The influence of the Greeks on Judaism was intensified because a number of Greeks and educated (and therefore Greek-speaking) Romans also made conversions to Judaism, and initiation into the religion also meant entry into the nation or people. The morality and laws, which provided a structure for one's life, as well as the elements of the supernatural, were very appealing to many members of Greek and Roman society, just as Christianity proved very attractive a few centuries later. The Greeks had developed a much more sophisticated philosophy and abstract logic than had the Hebrews, but their religion had never made demands on all a person's thoughts and actions in the same way.

Northern Europe in the Age of Near Eastern Empires

Bronze Age Culture

Not nearly as much is known about northern Europe as about the empires of the eastern Mediterranean, because there are no written records from the north; we therefore have to rely on archaeological evidence and on the few occasions when the people of the Mediterranean happened to mention northern people. It is clear, however, that at about the same time as the Egyptians were building the pyramids and the Babylonians were building the ziggurats, roughly 2500 B.C., there were also enormous stone structures going up in northern Europe. The most famous of these is Stonehenge, in what is now England. It is made up of concentric circles of gigantic standing stones, lined up in such a way that, on the summer solstice, the sun comes straight down the middle of the array. Stonehenge was actually built and rebuilt over a period of a thousand years, with the biggest central stones, which were brought all the way from Wales, the last to be erected.

Very little is known about the culture that erected Stonehenge. It is called the "megalithic" culture, the word "megalith" meaning "large stones," because modern scholars find it necessary to call them *something*. Whoever the people were who built it, they had quite sophisticated astronomical

The enormous standing stones of Stonehenge are still an impressive sight, over four thousand years after its construction.

knowledge to be able to line their stones up so accurately with the sun and stars; some people have even suggested that Stonehenge can be seen as an early observatory. It is also obvious from their monuments that they were capable of a high degree of social organization. Building Stonehenge was a remarkable engineering accomplishment: to be able to bring stones that size from nearly two hundred miles away and then to be able to set them up on end. Each phase of construction would also have required the mobilization of large numbers of people over extended periods of time.

The megalithic culture also erected many other monuments across Europe, although Stonehenge is the most striking. There are still circles of stones and individual standing stones on many European hilltops. Near Stonehenge, Avebury combines a large ring of stones, none of them as big as those of Stonehenge, but impressively large nonetheless, and enclosing an area of close to thirty acres (many times the area of Stonehenge), with a double aisle of standing stones over a mile long leading up to the ring. Similar aisles are found in Brittany. Brittany also has megalithic tombs in which a number of people were buried together in structures made by laying enormous flat stones across other stones. Some of these tombs, a good thousand or two thousand years older than the pyramids, are the oldest man-made structures in the world.

The people who populated northern Europe during the Bronze Age did not spend all their time erecting stone monuments; that was only an occasional part of their lives. Archaeology suggests that they lived mostly in small agricultural villages, a community of perhaps a hundred people, often on a hilltop, surrounded by fields of barley and millet. They lived in wooden houses that seem to have served both as dwellings for the family and barns for the cattle, sheep, and horses. The human population was scattered thinly enough that there was still an abundance of wild game, and they supplemented their barley bread and domestic meat with deer, boar, and hares. These Bronze Age Europeans also seem to have been the first to cultivate pear and apple trees.

The villages were too small to have anything like the city-state organization of the Near East, and they seem to have been independent of each other. There were trade networks, but these were primarily in such luxury goods as amber, hides, and glass beads, which are found in graves across northern Europe. The only real necessities that villages could not produce on their own were salt and bronze. It is significant of the importance of salt that the first northern European town of any size was Hallstatt, a salt-mining town that first grew at the end of the Bronze Age. Bronze was used for tools, weapons, and jewelry, and occasionally for vessels for food, although most cooking and storage was done in kiln-fired pottery. Broken weapons and worn-out tools were saved and recycled; all but the smallest villages probably had a craftsman who could melt and cast bronze.

The Celts

At the end of the megalithic period, a new group of people entered western and northern Europe: the Celts. They came out of eastern Europe and ultimately out of Central Asia, where most of the peoples of the West seem to have originated. The Celts may have been closely related to the megalith builders, but it is difficult to say exactly. All that is clear is that by roughly 500 B.C., at the time of the emergence of the Greek and Roman civilizations (discussed in Chapters 2 and 3), the Celts were settled in most of what is now Germany, Switzerland, France, the Low Countries, and the British Isles. Though certainly not unified politically, the Celts seem to have shared a similar language and material culture, which makes it possible to consider them one people. The areas in which they settled were already populated, though quite sparsely. They merged with the local populations fairly readily, though some of the earlier peoples, such as the Basques, retained their own identity through the Celtic age—as indeed they have through twenty-five hundred years of subsequent history until now.

The Celts first appear as a distinct people around 700 or 500 B.C., at the beginning of what is now known as the Iron Age. There is even some thought that the Celts may have been the first to work iron. They mined iron ore in what is now Germany, smelted it, and traded it to the people along the Mediterranean. They were primarily a farming people, living in scattered settlements as had the people who preceded them in Europe, working the light soils of the uplands rather than the richer but also much heavier river-bottom soil. The Celts were also a very warlike people, specializing in making heavy swords and war chariots with their iron. On the highest hills they built forts by digging ditches and piling up high earthwork walls; these hill forts can still be seen in many places, especially in England. (In fact, many of these hill forts, with their circle of earthworks, were used as the sites of castles in the high Middle Ages.) With the advent of iron in northern Europe, archaeologists have also found the bones of the first people there they can identify as slaves; improved technology and slavery (perhaps due to the enslavement of one people by those with better weapons) came in together.

The Celts were described with both admiration and horror by the Romans. They sacked the city of Rome itself in 390 B.C., before the Roman Empire began to spread, and although they quickly left again, the Romans never forgot this humiliation. They described even the Celtic women as great warriors, standing as tall as their husbands, their red hair swirling around their heads as they landed kicks and blows. According to some Roman writers, these warlike people burned captured enemies alive in wicker cages. The Romans called them the *Galli*, or Gauls, and called their principal territory Gaul (this is the area we now call France). When the Romans began to develop an empire, as discussed in Chapter 3, they made sure to conquer the Gauls and integrate them into the empire. Julius Caesar's achievement of subjugating all of Gaul solidified his position as the foremost man in Rome and made it possible for him to become the first emperor.

The religion of the Celts is somewhat difficult to describe because they had mostly been Christianized by the time they started writing anything down themselves, and the Romans tended to call the Celtic gods by the names of Roman gods, which makes things even more confusing. But it is clear that their religion was governed by high priests, called druids, who also functioned as lawgivers and as educators. Druids committed traditional wisdom to memory, made sure it was taught to the young, judged disputes and criminal cases, healed wounds, and interceded with the gods. (Contrary to popular belief, the druids did not have anything to do with Stonehenge, built two thousand years before the druids emerge in history.) The Celts worshiped a variety of gods and goddesses, including Epona, the horse-goddess, one of the few that the Romans did not try to turn into one of *their* gods or goddesses.

Their religion, befitting a warlike people, seems to have had a quite bloody side, and even human sacrifices took place occasionally. We do not know of priestesses, only of male druids, but women did play an important role in the society. For example, inheritance seems normally to have passed not from father to son, but from a man to his sister's son. Although the Celts were eventually pushed back to the fringes of Europe first by the Romans and then by Germanic peoples (as described in Chapter 4), who were the next wave of people coming out of central Asia a few centuries behind the Celts, the ethnic group and the Celtic language still persist in Brittany and in parts of the British Isles, in Scotland, in Wales, in Cornwall, and especially in Ireland.

The Celts were scattered fairly thinly over northern Europe, which made it relatively easy for the Romans to absorb them into their culture, and for the Germanic peoples to settle among them. This meant that by the Middle Ages the area that had been populated by the Celts in antiquity was populated by a people who had absorbed many of the ideas of civilization that had started with the Egyptians, Babylonians, and Hebrews. But this is jumping ahead of the story. The development of western European culture—the culture that eventually crossed the Atlantic to become America's culture—was a long process. The ideas that began on the banks of the eastern Mediterranean were modified and augmented by the Greeks and the Romans (discussed in the next two chapters), before coming via the conquering Roman legions to western and northern Europe.

CHRONOLOGY

TWO

—

ANCIENT GREECE

c. **1400** B.C.	Destruction of Minoan civilization on Crete
c. **1300** B.C.	Fall of Troy
c. **800** B.C.	Homer composes the Iliad and the Odyssey
776 B.C.	Traditional date of the first Olympian games
c. **500** B.C.	Beginning of Greek democracy
490 B.C.	Greeks defeat Persians at battle of Marathon
431 B.C.	Beginning of Peloponnesian War between Athens and Sparta
404 B.C.	Athens surrenders to Sparta
399 B.C.	Execution of Socrates
338 B.C.	Conquest of Greece by Philip of Macedon
336 B.C.	The coming of Alexander the Great; beginning of Hellenistic Age
323 B.C.	Death of Alexander the Great

CHAPTER
TWO

ANCIENT GREECE

THE CIVILIZATION THAT we now consider "Western," which we identify with the United States and western Europe, took much of its original form in the eastern Mediterranean. The Hebrews, discussed in Chapter 1, gave the West much of the religion and morality we still follow, and the Greeks, discussed in this chapter, developed ideas of politics and political obligations which are still very important. The flourishing of ancient Greek civilization, like that of the ancient Hebrews, took place in the first millennium B.C. Both civilizations were based in small cities, scattered through rocky lands of which much was never good for agriculture. The individual cities might not be thought of as urban in our sense, for a great many inhabitants were directly engaged in farming, going out in the morning to work their plots and coming back to the city at night. But these agglomerations of houses, although their usual size was perhaps two thousand people, and even the largest cities rarely had more than ten thousand inhabitants, should be considered cities rather than villages, for they had their own governments and their own walls to define them. The cities were both the basic economic units and the basic political units of Greek society.

Indeed, although the area of Greek culture was quite small—modern Greece, like modern Israel, is still a small country—there was no national government that took precedence over the self-governing cities. Even though there was a fair degree of cultural similarity, the Greeks did not want to translate this into union in one state. The Greeks at their most unified formed two leagues of cities, one headed by Sparta and one by Athens. The Greeks, like the Hebrews, then, developed their unique contributions to Western culture in settings that revolved around the family and the city, not any wider political allegiance.

There were many similarities between Greek and Hebrew attitudes and ways of life. They worked out their religion and philosophy in very similar physical settings and stressed duty and obedience, even though that obedience was to quite different institutions. As the Jewish religion was the basis for the religion and morality both of Christianity and of Islam, so Greek philosophy and politics are now considered the basis of their counterparts in the modern West. Although the greatest flourishing of Greek culture lasted less than a century (the fifth century B.C.), it has had an enormous influence on later civilization. The democracy of Athens has even been considered, although not entirely accurately, the origin of Western democracy. (The impact of the Greek ideal may be seen in the United States in the late eighteenth and nineteenth centuries, when large farmhouses and townhouses were built in the Greek revival style, with Greek-inspired columns, to show the owners' democratic beliefs.)

Ancient Greece was a country greatly influenced by its geography. Greece is a mountainous country where there is a strong contrast between the rocky coast, the plains along the coast where crops may be grown, and the wild upland. The mountains divide the country into separate valleys between which communication is possible but never easy. These mountains continue south into the Aegean Sea, their peaks forming the multitude of Greek islands. The different valleys and different islands were almost all separate political states.

The sea was always a feature of Greek life, as communication between different parts of the mainland was usually easier by boat than overland, although the Greeks were not adventurous mariners. In the often treacherous waters of the Aegean and Mediterranean, they preferred to keep their small boats always in sight of land. During the winter, when vicious storms could come up without warning, they preferred not to sail at all. In spite of the proximity to salt water, Greece has little fresh water and a low annual rainfall. This scarcity of water meant, as it did in Palestine, that the grape vines, figs, and olives had to be carefully irrigated. This scarcity also meant that every well or spring was considered holy, usually with a resident minor deity.

Bronze Age Greece

The origins of Greek culture, like the origins of the Hebrew people, go back to the second millennium B.C. Between about 2000 and 1500 B.C., the ancestors of the later classical Greeks came wandering into the Aegean basin, probably from Asia. Although extremely little is known about them, the small amount of archaeological evidence suggests a pastoral people who used bronze tools and ox carts, and had a strong warrior ethos. They first introduced horses (originally no bigger than ponies) into the eastern Mediterranean. Until they arrived in Greece, they seem never to have seen a large body of water. They had no word for the sea or for boats and seem to have been ignorant of the cultivation of wine grapes and olives. But they quickly learned these from their new neighbors.

Like the nomadic Hebrews, the first Greeks appeared in a world that was already highly civilized. The most important center in the Aegean basin was the island of Crete. On Crete an extremely elaborate civilization flourished, the Minoan civilization. The Minoans were literate, and

Statue of bare-breasted goddess from Crete.

a fair number of inscriptions have been unearthed that were written in what is called Linear A, a language no one now can read. The Minoan capital on Crete was centered on the royal palace, which consisted of a great number of rooms and dwellings built haphazardly around an opulent center.

The culture of the Minoans seems to have been devoted to pleasure rather than war, for the palace was unwalled and all the frescoes seem to show happy enjoyment. One of the most intriguing features of the frescoes are the "bull dancers," apparently a form of athletic contest or show, possibly with religious associations, in which young men and women did what amounted to gymnastic exercises on the backs and horns of bulls. (In contrast to the modern bullfight, there was no attempt to kill the bull.) The great palace appears in the Greek legend of the Minotaur, a monster half bull and half man, in the center of the labyrinth.

There seems to have been a great deal of influence back and forth between the Minoans and the early Greeks, for, starting in the fifteenth century B.C., Linear A was replaced in Crete by Linear B for royal accounts and records of dedications at shrines. This style of writing borrowed its letter forms from Linear A, but they were adapted to write an archaic form of the Greek language. The capital of Minoan culture on Crete was destroyed around 1400 by a major earthquake. The attendant tidal waves, flooding, and general destruction are now thought by some scholars to have been the origins of the story of the destruction of Atlantis, a story first written down by Plato a thousand years later.

Greek history is obscure for at least five hundred years after the destruction of Minoan culture on Crete. Archaeology suggests that a related although more warlike culture, the Myceneans, flourished for a century or so on the Greek mainland after the great earthquake, and another Greek people, the Dorians, seem to have come out of Asia and joined those already in Greece. But around the eighth century B.C., while the Hebrew kingdoms in Palestine were flourishing, real Greek written records begin; this is also the point at which the Greeks started using iron rather than bronze. This is the beginning of the period now known as that of classical Greek culture, which reached its peak in the fifth century B.C.

The classical Greeks, like the Hebrews and Phoenicians, wrote a script composed of a relatively small number of letters, each standing for a specific sound, as we still do today, rather than writing a separate letter (or pictogram) for each word, as the Egyptians had and the Chinese still do. (Linear B, the earliest form of Greek writing five hundred years earlier, had been a combination of syllabic letters and pictograms for such things as man, woman, horse, barley, and so on.) Whereas the Hebrews wrote from right to left, and later Greeks wrote (as we do today) from left to right (there is no necessary reason why one method should be more "correct" than the other), the first Greek writing went *both* left to right and right to left, on alternate lines. The letters on the lines to be read from right to left were written "reversed," mirror images of the letters on the lines written left to right, so there was no confusion over which direction one was supposed to read. Thus, when one reached the end of the line one would simply drop down and continue reading from there, rather than having to jump all the way back the width of the page to the left margin, as we do. The words were normally written without punctuation and without even spaces between them. Although this may seem odd to us, it would be no harder, once one was used to it, than separating words while listening to conversation; most people while talking put no more of a pause between words than they do between syllables of the same word.

Whereas the first known written works of the Hebrews were the early books of the Bible—that is, Hebrew history and law—the first known

Fresco from the Minoan capital on Crete, showing male and female bull dancers.

Greek works were epic poems. Although only written down in the Iron Age, they referred to events of centuries earlier, during the Bronze Age. The Iliad and the Odyssey, traditionally said to have been written by a poet named Homer, were first written down around the eighth century B.C. But they seem to have been the product of a long, oral tradition, going back to events of the Mycenean culture five centuries earlier. The Iliad tells of the Trojan Wars, which culminated in the Myceneans' destruction of the city of Troy. Troy was located in what is now Turkey, although in ancient times its position on the eastern coast of the Aegean sea made it part of broader Greek culture. The Odyssey tells of the adventurous wanderings of the hero Odysseus around the eastern Mediterranean for twenty years after the fall of Troy.

Although for a long time the events of the Iliad were considered fanciful, in the late nineteenth century the archaeologist Heinrich Schliemann discovered the actual site of Troy using the Iliad as his guide. The archaeological record does indeed show a major destruction of the city at about the right time (although it was intermittently repopulated in later centuries). Thus the writing down of the Homeric poems was only a late stage in a tradition that maintained the glorified but still quite real history of a much earlier Greek people. Once written down, the Iliad became a cultural center for all Greek speakers, taking the place that the Bible took for the Hebrews as a statement of their common heritage and a guide to all religious, ethical, and practical problems.

Once writing became common, Greek history is reasonably well known. One cannot date all events with the precision one might like, but one can take the year 776 B.C. as the beginning of "classical" Greece. This was the year the Greeks themselves used, because it was supposed to have been the year of the first Olympian games (so called because they were held at the town of Olympia). They naturally called this year 1, rather than 776 B.C. The games became a symbol of common Greek culture, and were held every four years for over a thousand years; the four-year cycle of the games was used to date many other events. Wars would stop for the games, such was their importance. (The modern Olympic games were founded in imitation of the Greek Olympian games, but fifteen hundred years after the Olympian games ended.) It tells us a lot about the Greeks that they should have chosen an epic story of war and a regular cycle of competitive games as their unifying symbols.

The Governance of the Greek *Polis*

In classical times, Greek language and culture unified a fairly broad area—not just what is now mainland Greece and the islands, but also the eastern Aegean coast, where Troy had been. Yet ancient Greece never formed one united country; rather, it was divided up among a very large number of city-states. The city-state, or *polis* (the root of our word "politics"), was the basic unit of society and the primary focus of a man's loyalty.

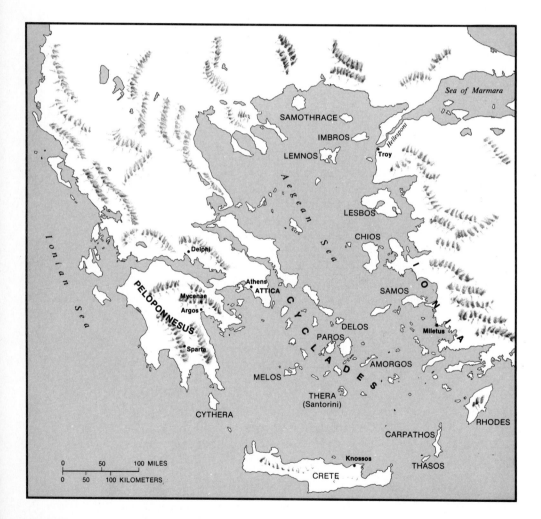

THE ANCIENT GREEK WORLD, c. 1500–300 B.C.
Ancient Greece was a mountainous land, where the sea was never more than a short distance away. The entire Aegean basin, including the islands and Ionia on the eastern shore, were as much a part of Greek culture as the mainland. There was, however, no political unity among the different city-states.

The *poleis* (the plural of *polis*) were more than just cities. Each included a fair amount of the surrounding territory as well as the central cluster of buildings. As in Palestine, people generally lived in the city but went out into the countryside to work their fields during the day. People who lived full-time in the country were always considered second class compared to those who lived in the city itself. *Poleis* were religious as well as political units, each one having its own special god or goddess—for example, Athens was dedicated to the goddess Athena—although there were always temples to other gods as well in every city. Today one can draw maps with reasonably distinct boundaries between the territories of the different *poleis*, but for the ancient Greeks a *polis* was not a certain geographical unit so much as a certain group of people.

The Greeks defined themselves by the *polis* to which they belonged, but not everyone who lived in a certain city-state was a citizen. Citizenship was restricted to men only, those who were free and who had been born there to a citizen father. (Other men could become citizens under certain circumstances, but this was unusual.) Even men who had lived in a *polis* most of their lives would be considered foreigners. The citizens were always in a minority in the adult male population, and certainly a minority in the total population when one counts the women, the slaves, and the "foreigners." Only citizens could take part in government, and in most of the *poleis* they were the only ones who could own land. Not all of them were wealthy by any means, but it was rare to have a wealthy person who was *not* a citizen.

The *poleis* originally were all ruled by hereditary kings. A king was the chief intermediary between a people and their god, as well as their political head. Kings were not absolute, by any means; they ruled with the assistance of a council—men (usually aged and learned) who accompanied and counseled the kings—and of an assembly, which was made up of all the citizens of the *polis*. The rule by king, council, and assembly was potentially unstable, due to the constant possibility of factionalism and infighting between different powerful families, especially within the council. Just as American politics has been dominated almost from the beginning by political parties, even though they are not mentioned in the Constitution, so Greek politics were often dominated by such parties.

By the sixth century B.C., men called tyrants, essentially party bosses with no constitutional claim to rule, had come to dominate many of the *poleis*. It was partly in reaction to the rise of the tyrants that many city-states started searching for new ways to define and distribute political power. At Sparta, some of the problems were avoided by having two separate hereditary kings, who were expected to counterbalance each other. At Athens, much more power was given to the assembly, leading to the rise of Athenian democracy.

Although Athenian democracy has often been invoked as the pattern for American democracy, it was actually of quite a different sort. To begin with, as already noted, citizenship was only open to free males born in the *polis*, thus excluding many people who would now have the right to vote. Perhaps an even more significant difference is that Athenian democracy was direct rather than representative. In the United States, the major decisions, the budget, declarations of war, foreign aid, welfare benefits, and for that matter most of the minor decisions, are voted on by Congress. Congress is made up of representatives voted into office by the citizens, but once they are in office the public has no direct control over how they make decisions—only the threat not to reelect them. In Athens, in contrast, all these major decisions were voted on directly by the citizens as a group.

Direct democracy is still found in a few places in the world today, as in some Swiss cantons and in the town meetings often held in New England towns; but for the most part it is too unwieldy, which is why representative democracy is preferred today. Even in Athens, with its thousands of citizens, it was often extremely difficult getting enough people together to vote on many issues. No one wanted to arrive too early, preferring to stand around the agora (the main marketplace) with their friends until they thought something might actually start happening. The Athenian police often had to go through the city with pieces of rope dipped in red paint stretched between them, quite literally herding the citizens. No one wanted the shame of a red stripe across his clothes, so this process usually rounded up enough citizens for crucial votes.

The Athenians had no separation of powers within their government, as is the case in the United States, so judicial and legislative functions were not distinguished. Accusations were heard and judgments given by enormous juries of about five hundred citizens, chosen by random lot from the assembly (that is, all citizens). The Greeks had no professional lawyers, so both the accuser and those trying to defend the accused were ordinary citizens. Naturally, with a five-hundred-man jury it was impossible to have a unanimous decision, the way one hopes for with a twelve-man American jury. Rather, for someone to be convicted, he had to have a majority of the jury vote against him. In order to discourage people from bringing suits too readily ("nuisance suits," as they are called today), an accuser who was not able to persuade at least 20 percent of the jury to vote to convict had to pay a heavy fine.

The usual penalties for those convicted were banishment, seizure of property, or death. The Greeks had no prisons and no regular system of fines. A slave might be whipped for a serious offense, but citizens were not whipped. The Greeks drew a distinction (as we still do) between crimes depending on intent. For example, a premeditated murder was much worse than accidental homicide. In Athens there was literally a prescribed route, a designated series of streets and roads out of town, which someone could follow if he had accidentally killed another citizen, and as long as he stuck to the route he would be safe from revenge. However, he had to stay out of town until the dead man's relatives had forgiven him. For most serious crimes, a citizen was executed by having to drink poison hemlock, which killed him quickly and without great suffering. The penalty was much worse for captured pirates; sometimes they were pegged to a board and left out in the sun to die of shock and exposure. The Greek *poleis* had no uniform penal code, which meant that the juries could be swayed, both in determining guilt and innocence and in determining the appropriate penalty.

The real novelty of Greek democracy was that a single individual could not impose his will on the majority. This was what the tyrants had tried to do; by making all the important decisions require a majority vote, the Athenians were able to ensure that no one could force the citizens as a group into doing something of which they disapproved. It also kept the richer citizens from being able to influence the poorer citizens too much, as they all had only one vote apiece. This direct democracy, however, did little to safeguard the rights of those who held the minority opinion.

Because direct democracy, even with the police rounding up the citizens, was too cumbersome for many civil functions, Athens, like other *poleis*, continued to have both a king and a council. The king at Athens was in effect not one man but nine, the nine "archons," who were elected by the assembly and who rotated the office of king among them. To be an archon, one had to be a citizen with a certain minimum of land and income. (The idea was that a poor person who was elected archon might use his political position to make his personal fortune in an improper way, whereas a relatively wealthy person would not need to do so.)

The council was originally made up of former archons. But around the year 500 B.C., in an attempt to break up the power of some of the powerful families that usually produced the archons and threatened to produce tyrants, it was decided to divide all Athenian citizens among ten artificially created clans or tribes. Each of these tribes elected fifty men for short-term office; between them they constituted the Council of Five Hundred. This was a form of representative democracy, but the purpose in establishing it was not really a democratic one. Rather, the purpose was to restore and maintain the basic unity of the *polis*. The chief threat to this unity was the presence of warring families, and the creation of the artificial tribes, which divided some families while throwing other previously antagonistic families together, maintained at least a reasonable measure of internal peace in Athens.

Athens used one other method to try to keep dangerous men from seizing power, and this was ostracism. Once a year, all citizens were asked to vote on the question of whether there was someone in the city who ought to be banned, who might not have committed any crime but was definitely tending toward becoming a tyrant. All the citizens who wanted to could write the name of such a person on a piece of broken pottery (an *ostrakon*, hence our word "ostracism") and deposit it in the ballot box. There would have to be at least six thousand votes cast for the balloting to count at all. If there were this many, then the person whose name was mentioned most often on the potsherds would be required to leave town for ten years, taking his possessions with him. Both ostracism and threat of ostracism were intended to keep someone from swaying the opinion of a small but powerful group enough to become a tyrant, and to keep anyone from expressing too freely views that were contrary to the interests of the state.

The Pursuit of Politics

It should be noted that Athenian democracy did not involve many things that modern Americans often assume are a natural part of democ-

Ostraka, or pieces of broken pottery on which, once a year, Athenian citizens scratched the name of a person who they believed ought to be banned from the city. These are from about 470 B.C.

racy, such as freedom of religion or freedom of speech. Although Athenians typically spent hours of every day arguing politics, no one could be allowed to say anything that was considered actually dangerous to the state or insulting to the gods. Socrates, the mild-mannered philosopher, was executed in 399 B.C. because he was believed to be corrupting Athenian youth with novel and impious ideas.

The state and the other citizens kept a very close eye on one's behavior, including what we would consider personal moral issues. But the Greeks do not seem to have considered this restrictive, for it was enforced obedience to impersonal and generally applied laws, not degrading subjection to an individual. Where arguing politics could become unpatriotic was a thin line, but this does not seem to have stopped the Athenian men from doing such arguing most of the day. The agora, the central marketplace, was where they met their friends and their political opponents to discuss the issues of the time. Indeed, in a period when there was no distinction drawn between the state and society, politics was considered a man's natural occupation. Someone who did not interest himself in politics was both scorned and pitied; since women and slaves were not citizens and could not vote, they could not be considered fully human. Most Athenian men were much more interested in their political life than their personal life.

In modern America, where people act as citizens primarily through voting once every two to four years (if at all), government is often considered a rather sordid business, carried on by professional politicians some distance away. The chief purpose of government is now often seen to be providing the security to allow private citizens to carry out their own lives in domestic privacy. But in classical Greece there *were* no professional politicians, because every citizen was supposed to vote on every policy decision, and each one might be elected, for a shorter or longer term, to the council, or even to be an archon. There were no career bureaucrats and not even a professional army because the citizens of a *polis* were also its army. Modern politics is often considered dreary because so much of it is concerned with administrative details, but the politics that excited the Greeks was primarily composed of policy decisions. Athenian citizens seem to have been much more ambitious for glory and power—to become an archon or a great leader in war—than they were to acquire personal wealth or social status within private society.

Greek Warfare

There was no distinction made between the army and the citizenry, for all citizens were supposed to be part of the army. The first sign of a professional body of soldiers was the use of some mercenaries in the wars of the fourth century B.C. The sons of citizens were all trained in warfare. (Slaves could not be soldiers, although some might accompany the army.) The identification of citizen and soldier was a new development that some scholars have linked to the rise of the assembly as a political body. Certainly, in the great Near Eastern empires, both governing and warfare had been restricted to the aristocracy, whereas in cities such as Athens, both were the responsibility of all citizens (still a restricted portion of the population).

In most of the Greek cities, young men spent almost all their time in military activities between the ages of eighteen and thirty. All the young men of the same age trained together. They were divided into "age-classes" and were given more responsibility each year. At around thirty they would usually marry, taking a wife only about half their age, and start living in their own houses. Nevertheless, they might still be called on for participation in war until they were in their sixties. At Sparta, the most militarized of the city-states, training for warfare began when boys were about seven, when they were taken away from their families to be raised and trained in age-classes. Even after Spartan men finished active duty and married, they still normally took their meals with the men of their age-class rather than with their wives and children.

The armies of Greece in the classical period were "hoplite" armies— that is, composed primarily of citizen infantrymen called hoplites. Much earlier, fighting in the Greek peninsula had been done by men in chariots, but it was possible to have appreciably larger armies by relying on foot soldiers, as horses and chariots were expensive, and an army of well-trained infantry was just as effective. The citizens were all expected to provide their own armor and weapons. They carried round shields, called hoplons (hence the term hoplites), and marched in close formation so that each man's shield helped protect the man next to him. Besides his shield, a Greek hoplite wore a breastplate, a helmet, and often greaves— that is, armor strapped to the fronts of his legs. He wore no shoes, going barefoot into battle. The helmet, made of bronze, covered the top of his head and much of his face, with slits left for eyes. Often there was a plume on top of the helmet. The main weapons were a sword and a short spear, used mostly for thrusting at close quarters. Sometimes soldiers carried throwing javelins as well.

Greek cities were well fortified, and normally armies did not bother to attack them. Battles consisted primarily of clashes between phalanxes of well-drilled foot soldiers, although a Greek army would also have a small cavalry made up of wealthy men, who could afford a warhorse and the time to practice riding it. The cavalry played only a small part in war both because the Greeks had not invented saddles and stirrups, the lack of which made riding in battle difficult at best, and because only the wealthy could afford to ride at all. These men also served as military commanders; increased wealth and power in the city meant increased responsibility on the field of battle. Armies were also often accompanied by a small, specialized band of archers. In spite of the proximity of the ocean, naval battles were relatively rare, except in the wars against the Persians. For a period, however, Athens was able to dominate the peninsula because of her fleet of "triremes," light, very maneuverable warships rowed with three banks of oars, which were used primarily to ram other ships.

Warfare was tremendously exciting to the Greeks. There was no pacifism in ancient Greece; participation in war, along with participation in politics, was considered a man's natural occupation. Even now, one of the most exciting things a person can do is to go off to face dangers bravely, for a cause that one considers worthwhile, with one's best friends in the whole world at one's side. (It is this excitement that makes war movies consistently popular.) Because the hoplite armies were made up of men who had been raised together since their youth and were all citizens of the same city-state, the sense of camaraderie in the army was tremendous. There was little room for considering the disadvantages of war in such an atmosphere. Fighting and winning with their friends was a psychological high that nothing in peacetime could duplicate; it is thus not surprising that there was scarcely ever peace over the whole Greek peninsula except during the Olympian games. Sparta was completely devoted to war; although Athens is now thought of as a home of democracy and philosophy, it was scarcely less warlike. All Greek citizens engaged in physical exercise for the purpose of keeping themselves fit for battle, though only the Spartans wore magenta tunics and scarlet cloaks "so the blood won't show."

There was a great deal of violence in classical society, including piracy

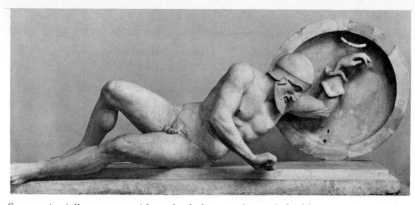

Statue of a fallen warrior. Note the helmet and round shield.

and banditry, which were admired unless they affected one personally.
But war was considered to be more than one of many forms of violence.
It was a confrontation between two willing political communities, carried
out according to the "rules of war." As is still the case, it was expected
that there be a formal declaration of war. Such a declaration would be
made only after the deliberation of the king and council, or, in Athens,
of the assembly. The government, like modern governments, would present
a formal "cause" of war, whether it was self-defense or the gross impiety
or immorality of the enemy. This was more than just a pretext, for no
one wanted to start a war unless "right" was on his side. The decision to
declare war was always accompanied by sacrifices and the consulting of
oracles and portents. It was useless to start a war with the gods against
one's side, which was why it was so necessary to be sure that one was
right. (Although modern military commanders no longer consult oracles,
they too want to be sure they are acting for what they consider a just
cause.) Of course, *both* sides generally went to war convinced that the
gods and the cause of justice were with them; in the Iliad, Homer makes
a nice ironic point from the fact that some of the gods were fighting for
one side, some for the other.

Most wars did not last long; those that did, such as the Peloponnesian
wars between Athens and Sparta, were actually composed of a series of
relatively short campaigns. If the results of the war were inconclusive (as
they generally were), the two sides would sign a peace treaty, and one
or both would erect monuments to their victory. Such monuments were
hung with the weapons and armor of the dead and captured. Prisoners
were ransomed at the end of a war, a man's relatives raising the money
to pay for his freedom. Being captured, however, was fairly shameful;
hence the saying that was attributed to the Spartans, "Come home with
your shield or on it," meaning come home victorious or dead, not as a
ransomed prisoner whose shield was added to the victor's monument.

If one side clearly prevailed in war, the other would be forced to
surrender. Surrender was both humiliating and devastating, so that even
a city that was clearly defeated might try desperately to keep on fighting
rather than surrender. After a city had surrendered, all its citizens' possessions and property were in the hands of the victors. Women and

children were made into slaves, and anything of value was carried off, including the statues of the gods. But cities going down to defeat were often able to negotiate a surrender that was not total, for the victor too would not want to keep on fighting until both sides were utterly exhausted.

Greek Slavery

The citizens of classical Greece were able to spend most of the day involved in some aspect of the public life of their *polis*, whether involved in military exercises, discussing politics in the agora, sitting on juries, or voting in the assembly, because ancient Greece was a slave society, and the citizens often did not have to work themselves. A middle-class family typically had a dozen slaves. As well as cooking, cleaning, grinding the grain, fetching the water, and doing other useful tasks around the house, the slaves also did much of the heavy labor, such as construction or work in the mines. They might even be schoolteachers or policemen (the police were slaves who were owned by the state rather than by individual citizens). A good deal of agricultural labor was also carried out by slaves. Poorer members of a *polis* usually had no choice but to work their own fields, and in Athens there was an ideal of a "gentleman farmer" who did at least some of his own farming, but in Sparta the citizens shunned agriculture altogether, leaving it entirely to their slaves. In Athens, even those who farmed avoided such manual crafts as weaving and pottery-making since they considered them below their dignity. Even trade and commerce were often left to "foreigners" rather than being carried out by the citizens.

Slaves were men and women who could be bought and sold like animals, for they were not considered to have the rights of freemen. Slaves were considered a man's personal property, but he was not supposed to mistreat them. The real distinction between slave and free is not in the amount of work that one does, because a freeman can (and often does) work as hard as a slave. Nor is the difference one of taking orders, for almost everyone has a boss. Rather, the distinction lies in whether one has to accept arbitrary orders and whether one has any options except to obey. Greek slaves had no choice but to obey their masters. A modern American is subject to his boss's orders, but only so long as those orders are considered reasonable. If they are not, an American worker can refuse to obey them, protest to the boss's boss, organize a strike, or simply quit. None of these options are open to a slave.

In spite of their subjection to arbitrary orders, there was in Athens a good deal of variation in slave status, and a rather large and murky gray area between slave and free. Many slave owners found it profitable to set their slaves to a trade—for example, making and selling pottery. Such a slave would lead an essentially independent life, living away from his master, deciding for himself what tasks to do each day, in fact able to behave essentially like a freeman as long as he paid his master his share of the profits on a regular basis. The schoolmaster slaves and police slaves were empowered to give orders to citizens under the appropriate circumstances. Slaves could be freed for service to their master or after the payment of a fee and then become indistinguishable from the large mass of foreign freemen who lived in every Greek city but who were not citizens.

Because a great many slaves were culturally Greek themselves, having perhaps been brought home as captives after a war with another *polis*, or perhaps even being former citizens who had become slaves in payment for serious debts, they fitted in well with the society of their masters. (The Athenians ended the practice of enslaving a man for debt, but they were the only *polis* to do so.) It is always easier to mistreat someone and try to draw arbitrary boundaries if he or she is culturally different. Household slaves were always better treated than field slaves and indeed were welcomed into a house by being showered with nuts and dried fruit, the same ceremony used to welcome a bride into the family. Most household slaves even participated in the family religious rituals along with their masters. The citizens of any particular *polis* always looked down at the noncitizens, including the "foreigners," who might be citizens of another *polis* and who often did much of the commerce; but because it was often hard to tell real slaves from free "foreigners," the slaves were not often badly mistreated. (They still deeply resented their subjection.)

The above discussion has focused on slaves in Athens and most of the other city-states. The situation was somewhat different in Sparta, where the slaves, called "helots," were a special class of people subject to the state as a whole. The helots did all the agricultural labor for the Spartans; whereas the Athenians always did at least some of their own farming, the Spartans considered such activity demeaning. Every Spartan man was allotted a certain amount of land and the helots to work it, but they were not the *personal* possessions of their master and could not be sold. Some scholars have thought, with good reason, that the helots were the original inhabitants of the region whom the Spartans had enslaved as a group when they first arrived.

Every year, the Spartan government officially declared war on their helots, not to engage them in actual battle, but rather to justify their treatment of them. Because the Spartans were always officially at war with their slaves, a Spartan could kill one without trial (which could not be done in any other *polis*). If he did kill one, he was not subject to the ritual defilement that normally attended manslaughter. It is indicative both of the harshness of the treatment the helots received and the unity they found with each other from this mistreatment that the Spartan slaves were the only slaves in Greece ever to have an organized revolt.

Women and Family Life in Ancient Greece

Although to the eyes of modern women's liberation, the position of Greek women, who were never allowed to be citizens, might seem little different from slavery, the Greek women themselves knew there was an enormous gap between them and the slaves. In terms of the outer or public world, a Greek wife was subject to her husband, not even being allowed to own property in her own right, but within the household she reigned supreme. She organized the household affairs, commanded the slaves, and raised the children. Although a man's superior position was supposed to be maintained even within the house, men were frequently not there, and the comedies and satires of the time show plenty of husbands being summarily ordered about by their wives. Socrates's domineering wife brought him much good-natured teasing without reducing the respect he was given by other men.

Lower-class women had to work in the fields or in retail shops, but the middle-class ideal was for the wife to stay home. She was not even supposed to go out to do the marketing; her husband or a slave did that. She was certainly not idle, however, for a middle-class woman had the responsibility of making clothes for the entire household. Spinning and weaving were considered to be a woman's natural occupations, just as a man's natural occupations were considered to be politics and farming. The Greeks did not have spinning wheels, so the wool had to be spun into thread using a distaff (a staff that held the wool) and a spindle (the spool that held the newly spun thread). The identification of spinning with women is so strong that even today the term "distaff" is often used as a synonym for female. Once the thread was spun, it had to be woven into cloth. The Greeks used vertical looms, in which the lengthwise threads were hung from a horizontal bar, each one weighted with a clay weight to make it hang straight. The crosswise threads were woven in and out between the lengthwise threads by hand—a slow, laborious process that was not speeded up until the invention of the horizontal loom in the Middle Ages (see Chapter 7). Between weaving the cloth for the family, cooking, or at least overseeing the food production, and raising the children, Greek women certainly had plenty to keep them occupied. By controlling the home, they played an essential role in Greek civilization.

But a woman's authority at home could not make up for her exclusion from the political and intellectual life of the city. When men had parties for their friends, these friends all came without their wives. The banquets, or *symposia*, at which men ate, drank, watched various entertainments, discussed serious issues of the day, and told bawdy stories, were typically all-male affairs. The only women involved were either dancing girls or the women serving the food. At *symposia*, men reclined on couches, two or three to a couch, at low tables, so that both private and open conversations were always going on along with the eating.

Marriages were normally arranged, in agreement between the man and the girl's father. Girls typically married in their teens, but men only married when they were thirty or so and had finished their active military service, as noted on page 51. Although there is some indication that the men of Sparta were married younger, at about age eighteen, they continued to live in the barracks until they were thirty, seeing their wives only occasionally until then. Girls were supposed to bring a dowry to the marriage, a lump sum in cash or some real estate, which the father gave the bridegroom. The dowry was intended to support the bride if she was widowed, freeing the husband from some of the financial burden taking a wife would otherwise entail. The dowry was also a symbol of a girl's worthiness as a wife, and no self-respecting man would marry a girl without one. Once a girl's father and the husband-to-be had agreed on

A young Greek woman at home, assisted by a slave.

the marriage and the father had given him a dowry, the actual ceremony took place. January, which was the goddess Hera's month, was especially popular for weddings (just as June is very popular now).

The ceremony did not involve anything directly comparable to our wedding ceremony because the promises that are at the heart of a modern ceremony had already been made between the men. The modern wedding ceremony also has nothing comparable to the special sacrifices that would be made on the Greek wedding morning. (Flesh from the sacrifices was used later in the day for the feasting.) The similarity between Greek and modern weddings began at the point of what we would call the wedding reception. There was a great feast at the bride's house, to which all friends and relatives were invited, followed by a torchlit procession through the streets to her new husband's home. Here the couple was tucked into bed together, and the wedding guests sang special wedding hymns outside the door, to assure the fertility of their union (which was, after all, a man's chief reason for getting married). The next day, the bridegroom would give a banquet, but this was a man's banquet, and no women (including the bride) were present.

With respectable women excluded both from politics and from social gatherings, it is scarcely surprising that homosexuality was an accepted part of Greek life. Ordinarily women were just not considered very interesting people. A small number of women, generally intelligent and accomplished women whose families could not provide them with dowries, became high-priced courtesans, "hetaerae." Hetaerae were free to attend the men's *symposia* and engage in learned debates, but they were the exception.

A man might have a wife to run his household and produce sons, have sexual relations either with his own slave girls or with the state-owned slaves of the municipal brothel, and have a concubine as well—many concubines were freeborn women whose families, like those of the hetaerae, had not had enough money to marry them off suitably—yet still have a homosexual interest in a younger man. In a liaison of this sort, the ideal was for the older, more experienced man to be a guide and tutor for his young lover. Such a tie was generally described as involving love and affection—much more affection, in fact, than might be admitted between husband and wife—even when it did not include physical consummation. Indeed, Plato advocated that male lovers refrain from physical union to purify their love (hence the term "platonic love"), although this was not the general practice. (It should be noted that Greek wives were allowed none of the sexual license that was expected of their husbands.)

Although men were usually not particularly interested in the details of household management or running a family, they *were* eager to have sons to succeed them. A man without sons was a man to be pitied. Children were born at home and, after a week or ten days, were formally admitted to the family with a special religious ritual. At this point they were named; the oldest boy was usually named for his paternal grandfather. One of the principal tasks of a son was to ensure that his parents received a proper funeral and burial. Unlike modern America, where birth and death take place in hospitals and funeral parlors take over funeral arrangements, all these fundamental events took place in Greece at home (as indeed they have in most premodern cultures).

Funerals and weddings were the two occasions for which the Greeks really believed in ostentatious display. A body in Greece was laid out in good clothes in an open casket. Close relatives and slaves put on mourning, which involved cutting off one's hair as well as wearing black. It was expected that the women especially should wail and cry; if one did not have enough mourners in one's own household, one could hire professionals. After being on view for a day, the body was carried to the cemetery outside of town and buried. Sometimes a body was cremated instead. As now, a family typically owned a plot, where family members and their slaves were all buried. It was common for gravestones to have a bas-relief sculpture of the person. These funerary monuments (*stellae*), many of which still survive, were a common sight to anyone approaching a Greek city. Like the Hebrews, the Greeks followed a funeral with a ritual purification of both the house and the family members.

A funeral could not be so elaborate if someone died in battle; even so, the Greeks had enough respect for the dead that they commonly called truces in their wars so that both sides could bury the fallen. A great many Greeks *did* die in battle, for it was extremely rare to have peace in the entire Greek peninsula at any one time. Those who fell hoped that they and their deeds would be commemorated in glorious stories and songs told in future generations.

Daily Life in the *Polis*

Even with slaves who greatly outnumbered them, the Greek citizens would not have had the leisure for politics, war, and banquets had not the material requirements for life in classical Greece been relatively simple. Because the climate was good, the crops usually grew well, and people needed only very simple houses and clothing. Furniture too was very simple, consisting of little beyond tables, chairs, beds made of mats spread on a rope webbing, and the chests and pots used for storage. The Greeks did not have the books, papers, extra clothes, or extra kitchen appliances that fill up modern houses. They had neither rugs nor framed pictures, although walls might be decorated with paintings. They did not even have much bedding; they had pillows and blankets but no sheets.

Greek houses, like those in Palestine, were very small. The better-quality ones had a room upstairs and a room downstairs; the poorer ones consisted of only one room. By our standards they would seem dark and squalid. These houses were the province of the women while their husbands spent their days in spacious and elegant public buildings. Houses were made of brick or stone, without particularly good mortar, and built very close together. To rob a house at the time, rather than trying to break down the door, it was considered easier to come in through the wall, preferably from the house next door. Houses generally had no heat; even cooking was done outside. They also had no plumbing. Water had to be carried from the public fountains for cooking and washing. However, people usually bathed at the public baths, where, for a few pennies, one could steam comfortably and gossip with friends. (Respectable women were the exception; they preferred to bathe in hip baths at home.) Lacking toilets, the Greeks used chamber pots, and dung collectors (slaves of the state) went around every morning to collect the refuse and carry it out of town.

The Greek diet consisted primarily of bread, usually made from barley flour and baked on a griddle (like pancakes or English muffins), although they also had some wheat bread. By classical times, Greece was not growing enough grain for the population and subsequently had to import it, primarily from Egypt. Barley bread could be baked at home from flour ground at home in hand mills, or it could be bought from a baker. It is significant of the importance of bread in the Greek diet that they had a word, *opson*, to mean everything in the meal that was *not* bread, that was rather the "accompaniment."

Breakfast was usually eaten before dawn. People were generally at work or going about their affairs at first light, which indeed was always the pattern in society before the spread of electricity (most of us are still asleep several hours after sunrise, at least in the summer, which would have seemed inexplicable to our ancestors, especially since we make up for it by staying up long after dark). It also made sense in a hot climate to get as much done as possible before the day warmed up. Breakfast was small, usually consisting of a little barley bread soaked in wine. (They had no tea, coffee, or orange juice, much less coffee cake or corn flakes.) Lunch was similar, perhaps with the addition of a few olives or some cheese.

The main meal was dinner, which was served at the end of the day. The major component was, again, barley bread. The Greeks ate very little meat, except at feast times or holy days when a pig or ox was sacrificed. (Unlike the Jews, they had no objection to eating pork.) They did eat fish, but most meals were vegetarian. Along with their bread they often had lentils or dried beans, cooked into a puree. Onions and garlic were the other principal vegetables, and olives and goat's milk cheese rounded out their cuisine. For dessert they might have figs, raisins, nuts, or maybe a honey cake. (Chocolate is New World and hence was unknown.) Wine was the chief beverage, usually drunk diluted with water. Since bottles for storing wine under airtight conditions would not be invented for another two thousand years, wine became vinegary quite quickly, and diluting helped kill the bitterness. Another popular beverage was a thin barley-meal porridge, about the consistency of undercooked oatmeal, essentially unfermented beer. This was called *kykeôn* and was flavored with mint, thyme, or other herbs.

As was natural in a hot climate, the Greeks wore very little clothing, and what they wore was very revealing (as underwear was still unknown). In most of the United States, outside of southern California, the Greeks would be considered positively indecent. The basic garments were simple rectangles of cloth, made of linen, wool, or occasionally goat's hair— they had no cotton or silk. These rectangles were draped around the body, rather than cut and sewn to take its shape the way modern clothes are. The cloth was held in place by a belt and a few pins or knots, only occasionally by stitches. Most people wore two garments, both made of these simple rectangles, the tunic underneath and the cloak, or himation, over it.

The tunic was the principal garment for both men and women. For men, a fairly small rectangle of cloth was wrapped around the body, under the left arm, and knotted or pinned at the right shoulder. This left the right side open, but a belt around the middle kept the cloth more or less in place. This knee-length (or shorter) tunic still showed a man's right thigh nearly up to his waist at every step. At night, a man took off his belt and slept in his tunic.

Young Spartan women, who engaged in vigorous physical exercise along with the boys, wore a very similar tunic, but in general a woman's tunic was made from a much larger piece of cloth. It was ankle-length, rather than knee-length, and indeed often longer; if longer, a deep double fold would have to be made along the top before it was wrapped around the body. The cloth was wide enough that there was usually plenty of slack, after the corners were pinned at the right shoulder, to draw up some fabric and pin it or sew it at the left shoulder as well. Sometimes the open right side was stitched together part of the way down, but normally it was left unstitched. There was enough cloth at the side of a woman's tunic to be made into a cascade of folds, of the sort that look very attractive in vase paintings. These folds provided enough overlap that, with their belts holding the folds in place, women did not have to worry about indecency at every step.

Over the tunic, Greeks often wore a cloak, called a himation, a very large ankle-length garment that was again made of a single folded and draped rectangle. (Some men, as is clear from the statues, only wore the himation, without a tunic under it.) To put on a himation, one started by draping it across one's back, with the two ends both coming over one's shoulders to the front. One then took the two ends together, passed them to the right and under the arm, across the back, and to the front again over the left shoulder. A knot or pin might be used to keep the himation from slipping. As the himation could be quite unwieldy, soldiers preferred a much shorter cape, a waist-length square draped over the shoulders with the top corners pinned together at the left shoulder.

The Greeks normally went barefoot inside, but outdoors they wore sandals, which cobblers made to the measurement of their feet. For journeys they wore boots. Although men were normally bare-headed in town, if they were outside for an extended period of time or were traveling they wore flat, broad-brimmed hats, such as one still sees on representations of Mercury the Winged Messenger. Greek women wore a lot of jewelry—bracelets, earrings, necklaces, and ankle bracelets—but men rarely wore any jewelry beyond a signet ring. Men wore beards but had fairly short hair, which was kept clipped by professional barbers. Greek women shaved their legs and wore makeup.

Greek children played with toys that were not very different from many of the toys children still have. They played with dolls, with toy animals, with hoops, with tops, and with marbles. Miniature chariots filled the niche now filled by toy trucks. Many people had pet dogs, and larger households usually had a cat, although a cat was considered less a pet than a means of keeping down the mice.

A Greek city had a great deal of art on display, primarily stone and bronze sculpture. There were a number of religious statues representing the gods. Although there were rarely statues of private individuals, the statues representing the gods used real people as their models. Although the Greeks enjoyed art, decorating the vases that held their grain and wine with scenes of everyday life, monumental art was not private but municipal. It was also highly idealized; the gods were uniformly handsome, except for traditionally homely gods such as Hecate or Pan.

The Parthenon, the great temple to Athena that still stands on the Acropolis (the hill in the center of Athens), was built in the fifth century

B.C. with money Athens had acquired by the conquest of other cities. Originally it held a statue of Athena that stood forty-five feet high and incorporated an enormous amount of gold, over a ton by some estimates. (The gold plates were cleverly made in such a way that, in case of emergency, they could be removed from the statue's wooden core and melted down to provide money for the treasury.) Most statues however were stone. The Greeks developed stone sculpture to a high degree, and many of their statues were later copied by the Romans. The statues in the temples were not the pure white marble we now associate with Greek sculpture but were painted realistically and dressed elaborately.

Exercise and Sport

The Greeks had no equivalent to sweatsuits or jogging shorts because exercise was almost always done while naked. Every city had a gymnasium where men would come to work out (our word "gymnasium" is directly from the Greek, from a root meaning "naked"). Before exercising, they rubbed their bodies with oil and sprinkled them with fine sand. The exercise was usually done to flute music. The sand and oil with the accumulated sweat was all scraped off afterwards, followed by a hot bath.

Exercise was not just for fun or for the purpose of making the individual healthier. Rather, its aim was to develop each man so that he could better take part in the moral and military life of the *polis*. The exercise at the gymnasium often took the form of competitive individual sports, especially wrestling, which was extremely popular. Other sports were carried out at the stadium; every Greek city had a stadium, one *stade* long (about 200 yards). These sports included foot races, long jumps and high jumps, boxing, and javelin and discus throwing. Boys liked to go to the gymnasium or stadium with their friends, as did mature men. All these sports were the basis of competitions at the Olympian games as well as friendly competitions within a city.

The Olympian games, as mentioned above, were treated as a symbol of Greek unity. Every four years, wars would stop and participants would gather at Olympia. The games were part of the religious festival in honor of Zeus and went on for a week. There were events for men and for boys, but none for women. Events included footraces of various lengths, including races run in full armor; the long jump; wrestling and boxing; javelin throwing or discus throwing—all events (except for the race in full armor) that would be at home in a modern sports competition. But they also included such things as poetry contests or chariot races. It should be pointed out that the Greeks had nothing comparable to the modern marathon. This race is a recent invention, even though it does commemorate an event in ancient Greek history. After the Greeks had defeated the Persian armies at Marathon, a city twenty-six miles from Athens, one of the soldiers, already exhausted from fighting all day, ran the distance to Athens to give the good news. He then fell down dead, and though he was remembered with great honor, no one thought of trying to run that distance as a competitive event until extremely recently.

Training for the ancient Olympian games, as for the modern Olympics, was a full-time occupation. One's *polis* usually paid for one's training because victory in the games reflected glory on the city as well as the individual. There was then, as now, a great deal of controversy and different opinions over what foods an athlete should or should not eat; for example, some fish were allowed but others were not, depending on what kind of seaweed they had been eating. For the last month before the games began, the athletes were all required to be at Olympia, training under the gimlet eyes of the judges. If they broke training, tried to foul their opponents, or passed bribes, they were fined or, for very serious offenses, expelled from the games or even whipped—the only time that a Greek citizen could be whipped. The fines athletes paid were used to erect special statues to Zeus. The final month of training served as a sort of mini-games, in which those who clearly had no chance of win-

Black-figured Panathenaic amphora depicting a footrace. Note that the men competed naked.

ning were weeded out, rather than having to face the humiliation of
losing in the actual competition.

Winning was what mattered at these games; there were no consolation
prizes, no equivalent to the silver or bronze medal. The Greeks did not
keep "Olympic records," as we do today, only lists of the winners. The
crowd, who sat on the hillside above the track, cheered wildly for their
hometown heroes. The most popular events were the bloodiest—boxing,
which was carried out without any break into rounds, the opponents
fighting with their fists wrapped in leather thongs rather than cushioned
by boxing gloves, and the *pancratium*, an all-out combination of wrestling
and boxing which continued until one of the opponents was knocked
out, gave up, or died.

The Greeks participated naked in all these events. They declared that
their willingness to strip in public, displaying bodies of which they were
very proud, separated them from the over-modest (and perhaps not as
shapely) barbarians. There was a legend that in the first Olympian games
the men had participated wearing shorts, but after one participant's
waistband broke, dropping his shorts (either allowing him to run much
faster unencumbered, or else causing him to fall and crack his skull,
depending on which version of the legend one believed), everyone had
appeared naked.

Participants took part for glory, for themselves and their *poleis*. The
winners of the different events were given a crown made of olive leaves
as a prize. Although the olive wreath was the only reward that winners
received at Olympia, they did nonetheless get substantial financial rewards once they returned home. Olympian victors would also be paid
handsome sums for their appearance at other sporting competitions. There
was no sense of an "amateur status" that they had to preserve, and those
who had been voted a lifetime pension by their *poleis* for their victory at
the games were back again four years later to compete again. Therefore,
the lack of monetary prizes at the Olympian games themselves should
not be seen as precursor to the late nineteenth-century leisured class's
"amateur ideal," which the modern Olympics are trying desperately to
keep alive.

Greek Education and Philosophy

While Greek boys and men were supposed to train their bodies for
the service of the *polis*, they were also supposed to train their minds for
the same end. An educated man was considered to be a wise man—not
just someone who had mastered a certain set of skills, but one whose
wisdom made him capable of vision and leadership.

Except in Sparta, where, as noted on page 51, boys were taken away
from their families at age seven to start their military training, early education took place in schools where students went during the day, returning home afterwards. Public education was for boys only; girls received
a rudimentary education in reading and writing at home. Although *poleis*
hoped for general literacy, there was no requirement that boys go to
school, and the schoolmasters were paid by the parents, not by taxes.

Schools taught reading and writing, music, and the classical poets, especially Homer. The well-to-do had tutor slaves, who accompanied the boys to school each day, carrying their stylus and wax tablet, their books, and their flute and lyre, and in the afternoon made sure they got their lessons done. There were no regular days off from school; whereas the Hebrews had the Sabbath, one day off in every seven, the Greeks had no comparable break in their schedules. However, there were various religious holidays (about one a week on the average) scattered throughout the year when all work, including schoolwork, would stop.

When students first began writing, they practiced on wax tablets, which were made by putting a thick layer of wax on a board. They wrote with a pointed stylus, using the blunt end as an eraser. Paper was not yet invented, and papyrus, which was made from reeds that were soaked, matted, and beaten together into sheets (see Chapter 1), was too valuable for beginners to use. Upper-level students, however, were taught to use reed pens and ink on papyrus sheets. All Greek books were of papyrus, having been copied out by hand, for the printing press was still two thousand years in the future. The Greek they wrote was based on a twenty-four-character alphabet (our word "alphabet" comes from *alpha* and *beta*, the first two letters of the Greek alphabet). They also used these same twenty-four letters, plus three other characters, for numbers. The twenty-seven "numbers" included nine for the numbers we write as 1 to 9, nine for the "ten's place" of 10 to 90, and nine for the "hundreds," 100 to 900 (Greek numbers, like Roman numbers later, had no zero).

After the boys had finished learning reading, writing, and music, the Greeks had no organized system of higher education. Because boys started military training to become hoplites as soon as they were through school, there would not really have been a place for it. However, beginning in the late fifth century B.C., wandering teachers first appeared. They would come to town and set up under a tree for a period of time, discussing philosophical topics with whomever was interested, in return for a small fee. These men were called "Sophists," from the Greek *sophia*, meaning "wisdom," because they were interested in trying to gain wisdom on the basic philosophical questions, the nature and purpose of the universe and man's place in it.

Today we try to answer such questions by formulating experiments and inventing complex measurement devices. The Greeks instead used observation and logic. The use of logic was new and considered very exciting; the Sophists had no trouble attracting the citizens of the cities where they came. Their system of postulates, statements, and conclusions is the same one we use in logic today. ("Socrates is a man. All men are mortal. Therefore, Socrates is mortal.") The Sophists also taught such "useful" skills as medicine. Greek medicine, which is now considered the basis of modern medicine, was also built on reason and observation.

The real founders of philosophy were three men of Athens who lived in the fifth and fourth centuries B.C.: Socrates, his pupil Plato, and Plato's pupil Aristotle. They distinguished themselves from the Sophists because they wanted to instill moral virtue in their students, not just intellectual achievement. Like the Sophists, they taught very informally.

A popular meeting place outside of town was a sacred grove of trees, called Academe; this grove is recalled in our word "academic." Socrates especially taught in even less formal settings, at dinner parties, the *symposia* at which a group of friends would recline at their tables, eating, drinking, and talking all evening. It is indicative of how seriously the Greeks took philosophical debate that Socrates was executed, as noted above, when it was feared his teachings were becoming impious.

Socrates wrote down nothing himself, although many writers of the time left us a record of his habit of "buttonholing" people on the street, questioning them about their views of such issues as justice or citizenship, continuing to probe and question until they had to define their views on a topic they might before have scarcely considered; this sort of questioning is still called the "Socratic method." Plato described the *symposia* to which Socrates was often invited as "dialogues," in which Socrates's deep insights into the nature of the world were interspersed with the ribald jokes and the confused questions of the other people present. We also have very little of what Aristotle wrote himself, although it seems fairly clear that he intended, like Plato, to write down his ideas. Instead, we have what are essentially lecture notes that some of his students took. (This means that Aristotle 'is much more difficult reading than Plato.)

Plato (and Socrates's ideas as interpreted by Plato) and Aristotle were quickly taken as the two foundations of philosophy. They took very different approaches, Plato extrapolating from what we can see to what we do not see, and Aristotle more concerned with categorizing and describing what we do see. Both the Romans and the Christian philosophers of the Middle Ages read Plato and Aristotle, discussed their ideas, and made them the basis of their own philosophical treatises.

Closely related to Greek philosophy was Greek science (Aristotle lectured extensively on both). This science was studied, memorized, and copied throughout antiquity and the Middle Ages. The Greek thinkers Pythagoras, in the sixth century B.C., and Euclid, in the third century B.C., are considered the fathers of modern mathematics. They and their followers worked out the arithmetic and geometric principles that are still taught in school, but they were not simply interested in mathematics for itself; the followers of Pythagoras, for example, considered that the best way to understand the universe was to determine how to translate matter into numbers, for numbers for them were the real basis of material existence.

Both astronomy and music were considered by the ancient Greeks as mathematical expressions. In astronomy, the Greeks tried to calculate such things as the diameter of the earth, which they knew was a sphere, and its distance from the sun. (It is a mistake to think that people of the ancient world thought the world was flat, as it was quite easy to determine that it is spherical, from such things as watching the earth's shadow during an eclipse of the moon, or even watching ships sail out of sight, where their hulls sink beyond the curve of the earth before their sails disappear into the distance. Their error, perpetuated over the next two thousand years, was in thinking that the sun went around the earth rather than vice versa.) They adopted and expanded on Babylonian astronomy and astrology. They thought of the stars as divine, which is not so odd when one considers that phases of the moon directly affect the tides, or that the passage of different constellations is directly related to changes in weather and season. The astronomer Ptolemy, who lived in the second century A.D., under the Roman Empire, worked out a catalogue of the stars and planets and their movements which served as the basis for the great Arabic astronomers of succeeding centuries.

The Greeks are also now considered the founders of modern medicine. Hippocrates, a semi-legendary figure of the fifth century B.C., is attributed with the first medical texts, which initially revolved purely around diet, with different diets being recommended to cure different ills. Other material was quickly added, including an emphasis on hygiene and exercise, and the use of amulets and potions to ward off disease. Many remedies and purges were taken over from the Egyptians. The biggest emphasis in the Greek medical schools was put on observation—on learning to recognize diseases by observing the symptoms. There were also treatises describing human organs in great detail, which doctors were expected to commit to memory; some of these books, especially those of Aristotle, became essentially sacred texts, with his description of a pig's liver being treated as a description of a human liver (which is actually quite different) for the next two thousand years.

Greek Religion

Both Plato and Aristotle spoke of an absolute God, a god above the plethora of Greek gods, approaching monotheism from a philosophical viewpoint. (In the Middle Ages, some people who read Plato were quite surprised by this and decided that Plato must have known Moses and gotten his ideas from him.) But the Greeks as a whole were not a monotheistic people. Their culture was permeated with religion—religious ceremonies and rites punctuated daily activities—but theirs was a religion of multiple deities.

The whole Greek peninsula subscribed to essentially the same religion, but it was one without any sort of central organization, scriptures, or dogma. The landscape was scattered with shrines and temples, each of which was independent of the others. Twelve main gods and goddesses were assumed to live on Mount Olympus, headed by Zeus and Hera, but there were also a great many minor gods and demigods, nymphs attached to springs, and the like. The twelve Olympian gods tended to absorb other "heavenly" gods (though the more "earthy" gods resisted assimilation). Thus, different cities seem originally to have worshiped their own gods and goddesses, but because they tended to have similar attributes, all moon-goddesses became a variation of Diana, and so on.

The cult of the gods was carried out through a combination of sacrifice, purification rituals, and prayer. Sacrifices, usually blood-offerings, were made to obtain a personal favor. To make an offering, one killed an animal and burned some of its fat, bones, and flesh on the altar to the god. (The rest of the flesh was eaten; sacrificial offerings were one of the major sources of meat in the Greek diet, although for an especially important favor one might burn the entire animal.) As with the Hebrews, a sacrifice for the Greeks was an indication of the fervency of one's desire, but the Greeks also thought (unlike the Hebrews) that the gods ate the food that was burnt to them. In the same way, before one started drinking, it was thought good to spill out a little wine for the gods and also to sprinkle a little flour for the gods when one was baking.

The Greeks, unlike the Hebrews, did not think in terms of sins or sinfulness, but rather in terms of defilement. A great many things could defile. Certainly the committing of a cowardly act defiled, as did murder and other crimes, but other things that we would not group with these also produced defilement, such as a birth or death in the house. When one was defiled, one would have to be cleansed, usually through sacrifices, to make oneself ritually pure again and ready to rejoin society.

Drama

We tend to think of Greek drama as the ancestor of modern drama, and thus a secular activity, but for the Greeks it was part of their religious ritual. Plays were always put on during one of the festivals of Dionysius (there were several during the year). Dionysian festivals were an opportunity for people to let off steam, to engage in activities that would normally not be proper, and to go to the theatre. Just as every Greek city had a gymnasium and stadium, so every one had a theatre. Normally part of the festival was a play contest, in which all the playwrights would produce their new plays, and the writer judged to have written the best new plays received a crown of laurel.

The plays were put on four or five a day, for four days. The whole city came to the plays, both men and women, to watch a combination of tragedies and comedies. The tragedies addressed deep issues of man's relations with other men and the gods and how one can try to deal with conflicting responsibilities; the comedies on the other hand were often vulgar or obscene. Usually the plots were based on Greek legends that everyone knew, so that how the story was going to come out was not much of a surprise, but the audience wanted to see how well the author handled the material and how successful he was at giving it fresh ideas. The audience did not hesitate to stamp or cheer if it liked a play, trying to influence the judges' decision.

The actors were men only (the parts of women were also played by men), dressed in boots with very thick soles, to make them tall, and wearing oversized masks, so that even people at the back of the theatre could see them easily. The action was accompanied by a chorus, a group of actors peripheral to the action who commented on what was happening. (In the sixteenth century, when the Italians were trying to revive Greek drama, they misunderstood the purpose of the chorus and thought that instead of chanting their lines they *sang* them. Consequently, rather than reviving Greek drama, they invented opera.)

Although most Greek religion was public, there was also private religion, concerned with the salvation of the individual rather than the well-being of the state. This took the form of mystery-cults, of which the most important for Athens were the Eleusian mysteries, held at Eleusis, fifteen miles from Athens. They were "mystery" cults in the sense that those initiated into them would receive hidden knowledge, unknown to the general public, which would assure one of a happy life beyond the grave. For the most part, the Greeks viewed the afterlife as rather a grim, dark place, which is why they hoped to be able to live on in the glorious memory of this world. The mystery-cults provided a chink in that grimness; their popularity continued into the Roman period.

Divination

A major part of Greek religion was divination, trying to determine the will of the gods. The casting of lots was often used for processes that we would vote on instead, such as the election of the members of the Council of Five Hundred, discussed above. This was because it was assumed that the gods would have a hand in picking the "right" names out in a random drawing. Any special sign, such as an unusual flock of birds, was taken as an omen and had to be analyzed.

A vase painting: consulting the Oracle at Delphi.

Before undertaking anything important, such as a war, the government always consulted oracles. There were full-time oracles, the most famous of which was at Delphi. Oracles were people who went into hypnotic trances and supposedly spoke the words of the god. The Delphic oracle was supposed to speak in the voice of Apollo. The problem with this oracle was that its utterances tended to be very obscure, or at best couched in riddling terms, so that one would think the utterance meant one thing and find out later that it meant just the opposite. (The advantage of ambiguous answers, of course, is that they can always be interpreted later to have been right.) The actual oracle at Delphi was always an uneducated young woman of the region, whom the priests who served the temple seem to have made pass into her trances by the use of drugs. This should not be taken to mean that either priests or even educated observers considered the oracles a fraud; the drugs were supposed to draw the woman's mind away from ordinary things ("expand her consciousness" as we might say today), and her lack of education was supposed to assure that she did not cleverly guess what the questioners were hoping to hear. Although there was always a good deal of questioning of individual oracles, and people were on the alert to make sure that attendant priests did not suggest the answers to the oracle in a trance, no one doubted that the gods could and did, if they wanted, make their will known to men through such means.

Hellenism

Greek culture, as mentioned previously, only really flourished for a century or so: the fifth century B.C. Then wars of the Athenians with their allies, against the Spartans with theirs, ended up badly weakening both, and in the fourth century Greece fell under the control first of Philip of Macedon and then of Alexander the Great.

Philip was king of Macedon, the region immediately north of what we now consider Greece, although it was heavily influenced by Greek culture. He turned the Greek peninsula into a Greek protectorate in 338 B.C., when the *poleis* were unable to unite against him. Two years later, Philip died, apparently assassinated at the orders of his twenty-year-old son Alexander, who set out to conquer for himself the largest empire anyone could imagine. During the next thirteen years, until his death, he was constantly on the move, conquering the entire Near East, including Persia and Egypt, then moving through Mesopotamia as far as what is now India. (Even now Alexander the Great appears in stories in India, threatening bad children who do not go to bed when they are supposed to.)

Alexander, whose tutor had been the Greek philosopher Aristotle (discussed on page 66), apparently intended to use Greek culture to unify his enormous empire. He founded cities, including Alexandria in Egypt, and settled Greeks in them, encouraging them to marry local women but to bring their children up speaking Greek. Although he died long before he had completed his planned conquest and unification, and his enormous empire was partitioned among his generals, one part of his plan survived, and that was the spread of Greek language and culture. For the next three hundred years, Greek was the language of government and education throughout the Middle East.

This is the period known as the Hellenistic Era, from the term "Hellenes," which is what the Greeks called themselves. Although Alexander's empire had never reached as far west as Rome, which was just beginning to expand, the Romans very quickly absorbed Greek culture when they brought their own empire as far as the Near East. Greek philosophy, education, and religion, all much more sophisticated than anything the Romans had had, were adopted and spread in turn throughout the western Mediterranean and even into northern and western Europe. Thus the empire of Alexander, although it only lasted thirteen years, managed to perpetuate and disseminate much of Greek culture and lead to its general adoption in what we now think of as the West.

CHRONOLOGY
THREE

THE ROMANS

c. **500** B.C.	Foundation of Roman Republic
312 B.C.	Construction of Appian Way; beginning of Roman road system
146 B.C.	Rome destroys Carthage; Roman hegemony over Mediterranean assured
55 B.C.	Caesar reaches Britain
44 B.C.	Caesar declared dictator for life; assassinated
27 B.C.	Rule of emperors begins with Augustus
33 A.D.	Crucifixion of Jesus
c. **50** A.D.	Christian church organized under Paul and Peter; Pauline letters written
66 A.D.	Great Fire of Rome under Nero
70 A.D.	Final defeat of the Jews by the Romans; destruction of the Temple at Jerusalem
c. **75** A.D.	The Gospels begin to be written
c. **100** A.D.	Last books of New Testament written
312 A.D.	Constantine begins toleration of Christianity

CHAPTER
THREE

THE ROMANS

THE HISTORY OF ROME is the history of a highly practical, highly militarized, highly expansive society that established an empire which at its broadest covered all the countries around the Mediterranean, including Spain and north Africa, most of the Near East, and the areas that are now England, France, and the Low Countries. Although there had been many empires earlier, Rome's was much larger. It absorbed most of the territory that had been part of earlier Near Eastern empires, including Egypt. Much of the culture of the civilizations that Rome absorbed, especially that of the Greeks, was integrated into Roman culture and spread, with Roman rule, far beyond its earlier boundaries. The term "empire" is somewhat misleading, because the city of Rome, which had thrown off its kings and become a republic around 500 B.C., about the same time as Greek democracy was beginning, actually ruled a very large territory while it was still governed by the Senate and the Assembly. Therefore, even before Julius Caesar and Augustus became the first emperors in the first century B.C., Rome controlled something that could be called an empire. Usually the term "Roman Empire" is reserved, however, for the period of the emperors, from the first century B.C. until the last emperors in Rome in the fifth century A.D.

The Roman empire was built on military conquest, and Rome was at war nearly constantly. This empire lasted as long as it did (five or six centuries) in large part because of the Romans' organizational abilities. They tied together their vast territory with an administrative system centered on Rome, and built excellent roads to make (fairly) rapid communication possible between different regions, nearly two thousand years before automobiles and telephones. Their language and religion spread through an empire that was also unified by a common set of laws. A crucial organizational difference from the Greek *poleis* was that citizenship came to be open to men from all parts of the empire and of every racial or ethnic origin, and the same laws and rights were applied to all Roman citizens, wherever they might live.

Rome was an urban culture. Even though 90 percent of the population of the empire was always rural, all government and culture was based in the cities. Rome had begun as a small city-state, comparable to those of Greece, but it grew much larger than any city of Greece had been. The city of Rome, both during the time of the Republic and then under the emperors, was a real city, recognizable as such even to people of the twentieth century. The government, religion, and culture that were developed in Rome and passed along to later centuries were all products of an urban society. At its height, Rome had a million people, more than San Francisco has even now. It was burdened by all the readily recognizable urban problems, such as enormous gaps between the fabulously wealthy and the hopelessly poor, street crime, overcrowded housing, unemployment, and rioting, as well as the excitement of being at the center of everything (the same excitement that keeps many New Yorkers today from wanting to live anywhere else).

Roman Citizenship and the Toga

The right to be a citizen of Rome was originally a very narrow and very important right, extended only to free men born within the city and the immediately surrounding countryside. But, already in the days of the Republic, citizenship was extended to people living elsewhere. Roman citizenship was first granted to residents of Rome's Italian allies in the second century B.C. At this point, the chief value of citizenship was the right to vote in the Assembly, although one had to be present to cast one's vote (there were no absentee ballots), and the Assembly was always overshadowed by the Senate. Over the next centuries, the number of people considered Roman citizens continued to expand. Finally, in the third century A.D., citizenship was extended to all free adult males living within the borders of the Empire. By this time the Assembly was gone, but citizens still kept one important right: that of being tried in Rome if they wanted to be (and could afford to be).

Although Roman citizenship conveyed a (theoretic) judicial equality, in practice and indeed in law there were enormous economic and political differences between the patricians, the small group of wealthy and powerful families who ran Rome as an oligarchy during the days of the Republic, and the plebeians. This latter group ranged from fairly well-off urban dwellers, to small landowners or agricultural laborers, to the desperately poor "proletariat," that group which was not expected to bring any sort of weapon or armor with them when conscripted for military service, because they had neither property nor money.

The patricians' wealth was based on ownership of most of the land around Rome. They provided all or almost all the magistrates, made up virtually all the members of the Senate (the equivalent of the Greek council), which had to pass on the validity of any decrees passed in the

Bronze funerary statue of an orator. He is wearing a toga over a short-sleeved tunic.

Assembly, and dominated that body as well through their clients. The priesthood, which was responsible for the temples that the Romans identified with patriotism as well as with religion, was made up of members of patrician families. Roman history was marked by repeated struggles between the patricians and the plebeians, with the plebeians gaining rights to their own "tribunes" to represent their interests, their own temples, and their own magistrates, and with organized food subsidies for the poorest citizens. But the many laws and concessions never ended the fundamental gap between the few with wealth and power and the great mass struggling to get along.

There was a distinctive garment for all citizens, patricians and plebeians, rich and poor: the toga. The toga was more than a piece of clothing; it was a symbol of citizenship. Only male citizens could wear one, although, by the late Empire, it had become complex and voluminous enough that many citizens preferred not to wear one except on special occasions. In fact, the many complicated folds in which fashion dictated that a toga be worn led to the first use of safety pins to hold together one's clothing. (Archaeologists have found vast numbers of Roman safety pins, plain and not decorated because they were not supposed to show.)

Like the Greek himation (discussed in Chapter 2), the Roman toga was essentially a large piece of cloth (perhaps four yards long), worn draped and folded around the body. It was woven out of lightweight white wool. The Romans wore it over a short-sleeved tunic, which would be all someone would wear if he was not entitled to wear a toga or did not want to bother. The toga was oval, having been woven that way, and the outer edge of the oval normally had a purple (actually dark garnet) border woven on. One folded the toga lengthwise before wrapping, so that the straight, folded edge was closest to one's neck and the curved, outer edge, with its purple border, was on the outside.

To wear a toga, one starts by extending the left arm and draping one end of the toga over it, with the fold at the neck and the purple border at the wrist. At this point, the cloth should reach almost to the ground in front, while most of the toga is in back. The next step is to wrap the long end of the toga, across the back, under the right arm, across the chest in front, and then over the left shoulder to the back, where, if the toga is the right length, it should almost reach the ground. It is much easier to wrap a toga with help, and all domestic slaves had to become adept at helping their masters here. Once the toga is wrapped, to keep it from sliding off, it is normally necessary to walk around with the left arm bent, the hand in front of the chest or stomach, so that this arm can support the weight of the draping. Because the outer, oval edge of the toga is longer than the straight, folded edge which encircles the body, and because there is a double thickness of cloth to work with, it is possible for the helper to pleat the extra material into all sorts of attractive designs. The use of safety pins came in here, to hold the pleats in place (it would have been embarrassing to need the safety pins to hold the toga on at all). Fashions in togas came and went, based on whether the cloth was wider or narrower, longer or shorter, and especially on exactly how all the pleats were arranged. It is possible even now to date a portrait sculpture or painting by the style of toga, and no Roman would have wanted to be seen in an outmoded style.

The Roman Army

One of the responsibilities of citizenship in Rome, as in Greece, was service in the army. However, whereas Greece's hoplite armies were made up of the same men who normally stood in the agora arguing politics, Rome's army was a *professional* army. It was made up of career men who served twenty or twenty-five years in the legions, and therefore army service never involved more than a small percentage of Roman citizens, even when citizenship was restricted to Rome itself. Whereas for the Greeks war had been the proper and glorious avocation of all citizens, for the Romans the army was responsible for keeping the peace so that the majority of citizens could go about their other business unmolested.

Many men volunteered for military service; others, especially young men from farming families of the country near Rome, were conscripted. Under the Republic, Rome was intensely proud of its young men who had grown up in the Roman countryside. Here, they felt, was the virtue and sturdy hard work that made Rome great. It was certainly an army made up of such people that made possible the conquest and establishment of the Roman Empire. The correlation between military service and citizenship continued long after the army ceased to be made up of these yeoman citizens, but in reverse. Even in later centuries, when barbarian recruits made up a majority of the legionnaires, soldiers were normally granted full citizenship upon retiring.

The only people in the army who were not professional soldiers were the generals. These were upper-class citizens, often from old and wealthy patrician families, who could have lived out lives of idle pleasure but who considered leadership of the army either their duty to the state or a means of getting ahead politically. A good many of the leaders left home to lead troops hundreds of miles into unknown territory, without knowing if they would be back again. These men were often Stoics, adherents of a philosophy that put little value on the individual but rather said that one had to bear what came with fortitude, doing one's duty, being reincarnated again and again until one finally did it right. At this point one finally died for the last time. Putting no real value on their own lives, believing that fulfilling one's duty was all that was important, these generals also put little value on the lives of their men.

Throughout the history of Rome, both when its soldiers were young men from the Tiber valley and when they were Germanic soldiers, the army was a highly organized and disciplined body. The Roman genius was for organization, and it showed to its best in the army. New recruits were trained in disciplined marching and in warfare, and the army itself continuously practiced, holding military exercises when they were not actually engaged in a war. The Field of Mars outside of Rome was in constant use for such exercises. New soldiers, who had to be at least five feet ten inches tall originally (the height requirement was lowered in the later Empire), would start by fighting against stakes planted in the ground until they became accustomed to the armor and weapons.

Roman soldiers were primarily foot soldiers, although each legion had a cavalry contingent as well. Each soldier wore armor consisting of a breast plate and back plate, worn over a wool tunic, and a bronze helmet. The helmet was fitted with decorative plumes on special occasions. All soldiers carried a rectangular, convex shield, long enough to protect their legs, so that they did not need to wear greaves. On their feet Roman soldiers wore heavy sandals, with soles several inches thick. The straps of these sandals extended up the leg almost to the knee.

The basic weapons were throwing javelins and a short sword. The javelins, fitted with iron heads, were made in such a way that the head snapped off the shaft on contact, so that someone could not pick up a soldier's javelin and hurl it back at him. The sword was two feet long but only a few inches wide, used for stabbing rather than cutting. It was carried in a scabbard on the right side of the body, where it would not interfere with the shield (medieval warriors in later centuries carried their much heavier swords on the left side). A knife, worn on the left of the Roman soldier's broad belt, completed his weapons.

In addition to their basic armor, most Roman soldiers wore necklaces, decorative collars, bracelets, and pendants. Such decorations were often distributed to the soldiers at the end of a successful campaign. Shields too were garishly painted with emblems identifying the unit or commemorating a great victory. Officers were especially highly decorated, and only they could wear bright red cloaks. (Khaki had not yet been invented.) The legions on parade, wearing all their decorations and with elaborate plumes on their helmets, must have been an impressive sight.

The Roman legions were highly organized, just as is the modern army. The basic military unit was the "century," which one might assume from its name had originally been a hundred men, but which usually had eighty by the time that we have detailed information. The century was commanded by a centurion, a career officer, comparable in this respect to a sergeant in a modern army. The century was made up of ten mess units of eight men each. Each mess unit shared an eight-man tent and did its own cooking while on campaign. There were six centuries in a cohort and ten cohorts in a legion, which thus was composed of a little under five thousand infantrymen, plus its officers and auxiliaries, which group might be nearly as large as the legion itself. Roman legions existed over long spans of time, though individual soldiers came and went, and most legions had their own traditions, history, and symbols. The eagle standard that led each legion was the focus of religious ritual; soldiers gave their oaths by their standard, and its loss in battle was a devastating blow that might require the disbanding of the entire legion.

A legion on the march, moving in columns of ten, normally expected to cover about fifteen miles a day, although it could do twenty-five if necessary. (The Roman mile was considered to be a thousand paces long, each pace consisting of the right foot's and left foot's step, and was slightly shorter than our mile; the word itself comes from the Latin *mille*, meaning "one thousand.") A day's march was always halted with two or three hours of daylight left, so that the army could build a fortified camp. The legions did not want to take a chance on a surprise attack at night. To make a camp, a rectangular area of perhaps forty acres was leveled and cleared. A ditch was dug all around the perimeter, and the dirt made into a wall inside the ditch. Stakes were then driven into the wall to form a palisade. Because every soldier knew exactly what he was supposed to do, such a camp could be constructed very efficiently.

Everything required for the march and for building a camp was carried by the legionnaires at all times. Each soldier carried a certain number of stakes with him on the march, to build the palisade, as well as such tools as shovels, saws for clearing timber, and buckets for carrying dirt. These tools, along with a soldier's armor and weapons, his bronze mess kit and kettle, the tent with its poles, and food for at least several days, made a pack which must have weighed a good sixty pounds per man. (Nylon tents, aluminum pots, and freeze-dried food were still two thousand years away.) However, pack mules and pack slaves helped the legionnaires carry their burdens.

The Roman legions ate porridge as their principal food, since it could be quickly cooked in the evening, unlike bread, which would need time to rise and to bake. This porridge was made of wheat as well as barley; wheat was considered a superior grain, and only the best was good enough for the army. In addition, the soldiers made and carried hard biscuits with them on campaign to eat in the field. This diet was supplemented with whatever vegetables and meat (usually pork) they could buy or take on their trip. Their normal beverage was vinegar mixed with water.

Temporary camps were broken down in the early morning as the legion prepared to move on (Roman soldiers ate no breakfast). But a camp might also be more or less permanent if a legion were stationed in a particular location for a while. In this case it kept the same rectangular layout, with officers' headquarters at the center, but some permanent structures were added. The most important was a covered hall or basilica, with a shrine to the gods. Other buildings included barracks, to replace the tents, lavatories and baths, kitchens, granaries, a hospital, and workshops where weapons and tools could be made and repaired.

Roman troops were an important part of the life of the Empire, being much more than a force which conquered territory. Since at the end of twenty or twenty-five years soldiers were pensioned off and could settle down, and often settled in the provinces where they had been stationed, they helped spread Roman culture to far parts of the Empire. They married local women for the most part, and their sons were a major source for new recruits into the legions, especially by the second century A.D., when most soldiers were recruited locally rather than being sent out from Rome. Many Roman generals, including Caesar, were able to take power because they had the troops to allow them to march triumphant into Rome. The imperial guard in Rome made many decisions itself about who should succeed as emperor during the more tumultuous days of the Empire. The Roman army, then, like the army in many modern countries, could be an important political force at home as well as a tool of foreign policy.

The Roman Roads

To make it easier for the legions to move quickly from one part of the Empire to another, the Romans built an elaborate system of roads, many of which still exist (often underneath modern asphalt, which continues to follow the same route two thousand years later). These roads made trade and communication between different parts of the Empire much easier than they would otherwise have been, as well as allowing rapid troop movement. The roads linked the entire Empire, including Europe, Asia, and north Africa. They stretched from northern England to Jerusalem, and one could travel between these two places in a space of six weeks, a time not matched again until the advent of railroads in the nineteenth century.

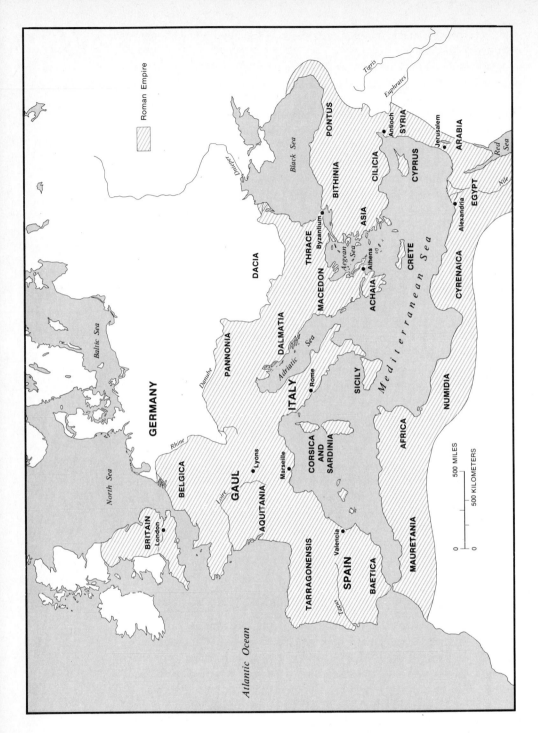

THE ROMAN EMPIRE AT ITS HEIGHT, SECOND CENTURY A.D.
The Roman Empire had, by the second century, gained control of the entire Mediterranean basin and much of what is now western Europe. The earlier kingdoms of Egypt, Palestine, and Assyria, much of Alexander the Great's Greek and Macedonian empire, the trading centers of the Phoenicians in Africa, and much of the territory of the Celts had all been absorbed.

The road system became necessary once Rome had conquered a large empire which extended far beyond the Mediterranean basin and thus was not easily accessible by water. Land transportation is much less energy efficient than transportation by water, and it is indicative of how important it was for the Romans to hold onto their vast territory that they were willing to go to the tremendous labor and expense of building the roads to keep the empire tied together. Just as the American interstate highway system, in spite of its value for commercial and personal travel, was only built in the first place because it could be used to move missiles from place to place, so the great Roman roads would never have been built had they not been so useful for troop movements.

The road system began in the fourth century B.C., when Appius Claudius persuaded the Senate to build a road south of Rome to Capua, some 130 miles away. This "Via Appia" (named for him) was the longest paved road ever built in the world until then. More roads quickly followed, and a more or less complete network was in place by the first century A.D. Some of the Roman roads followed the same routes along Europe's ridges that had been used since the late Stone Age. Since geography rather than politics determines what is a good location for a road, many of these Neolithic tracks are still preserved today in modern divided highways across Europe. In other cases Roman engineers laid out perfectly straight roads on maps, linking one place to another, and the road builders had to grade the hills and fill in bogs to keep the road so straight.

The roads were built by the Roman armies in between campaigns, assisted by locally conscripted labor. Though some secondary roads were just graded earth, all the important ones were paved. They were built as wide as thirty feet, to allow wheeled traffic to pass freely in both directions, and were built up above the surrounding countryside, to avoid flooding. First a subsurface of loose stone and gravel was laid down, to allow drainage, and then carefully fitted blocks of stone were laid on top. These blocks were put together without mortar, because mortar would have required periodic maintenance, whereas it was hoped that properly laid stones would never shift. The Romans also built bridges; their bridge across the Thames in London continued to be used until the twelfth century.

In building their roads, as in making their buildings and aqueducts, the Romans were willing to put a great deal of time and effort into the original construction, hoping they would last indefinitely with minimal attention. It is a tribute to how well they were constructed that, after even the minimal maintenance they had received came to a halt in the fifth century, the Roman road system continued to be used as Europe's main roads for another thousand years.

The great roads of the Empire were all charted on a giant map that the emperor Vespasian erected in the forum in the first century A.D. There were small maps and guidebooks one could buy for planning a journey. Both the major and minor roads were marked by mile stones, telling how far to the next city. Inns catering to merchants and travelers were dotted along the roads. Every ten miles or so there were posting stations, with horses and veterinarians, for the benefit of those carrying urgent official messages. Such messengers (not available for ordinary personal mail) could travel as far as 100 or 150 miles a day.

Commercial traffic on the Roman roads was primarily by pack mule. Although carts were used to transport bulky goods short distances, these carts were all ox-drawn—the Romans had not worked out an effective harnessing system for attaching horses to heavy loads—and as a result very slow. For longer trips, merchants usually strapped their wares to mules. Although mules are stubborner than horses, they are also much less high-strung and thus less likely to spook and run away, and both their hide and their hooves are tougher. This means that their skin was less likely to be chafed by the packs, and their hooves did not wear down as quickly (the Romans did not have horseshoes). Horses were used, however, for the light chariots in which imperial messengers rode. As long as Roman administration was in place, the Roman road system was always thick with commercial travelers, messengers, and the marching legions.

Slavery

Rome was a slave society; almost all citizens, except the poorest plebeians, owned at least a few slaves, and the wealthiest people owned hundreds. A slave in the classical world, as noted in Chapter 2, might be a member of any ethnic group, including that of his master. The first Roman slaves were indeed mostly inhabitants of Rome who had been sold into slavery or enslaved because they could not pay off their debts, or else captured people from other city-states of the Italian peninsula. A slave, whatever his ethnic origins, was someone who had no control over his own life, who was subject to the arbitrary will of his master. Roman slaves could be bought and sold, punished, even tortured to death, with no more official rebuke than one would receive today from maltreating a pet. It has been estimated that a good third of the population of the Empire were slaves. The easy availability of slaves freed the upper classes from having to work and gave them the leisure necessary for politics and culture. It is therefore necessary to realize that the grandeur of Rome was based on the exploitation of a large part of the population.

Although all ancient civilizations had slaves, slavery only became the major basis of Roman society with the gradual spread of Roman rule through Italy and then the Mediterranean basin, in the fourth and third centuries B.C. Soon the wealthy were competing among themselves over who had the most slaves. Enormous numbers of captives were taken in the wars and were brought back to Rome and set to work in the fields. Because so many of the young men of the countryside around Rome were conscripted into the army, the big landowners faced a labor shortage, which they solved by relying more and more heavily on slaves. Most slaves, especially in the countryside, were worked mercilessly to produce as large harvests as possible. Better-educated captives might be made household slaves. Some slaves were treated no better than machines— for example, those put to work in the mines—to labor away until they died. A few, however, enjoyed a good deal of power and prestige, such as the chief domestic slaves in a wealthy household, who would have scorned to think that they were in the same social class as the chain gangs of slaves raising grain for Rome. Slaves could be set to work by their masters in a great variety of occupations, depending on their background, from manual laborer to hairdresser to even doctor or teacher. The gladiators, discussed later, were slaves.

After a great campaign, a successful general came back to Rome with sometimes thousands of captives, whom he then sold to a slave dealer. The slave dealers also bought slaves from outside the Empire. Typically slaves were put up on an auction block, naked so that would-be buyers could be sure they had no hidden defects. Foreign slaves who did not speak Latin had their feet marked with white chalk. Sometimes slaves with special attributes or abilities would hold placards advertising their features while the buyers strolled among them, examining them, making sure a healthy complexion was not really just rouge. The slave market was big enough that certain dealers could specialize, for example, in sturdy slaves good for work in the mines, or in attractive young boys for those with perverted appetites.

The steady importation of slaves always threatened to overwhelm Rome, and Roman law early drew very sharp distinctions between slave and free. This was unlike Greece, where there had been a large gray area between full slavery and full citizenship, including slaves who essentially ordered their own activities and free men who were still not citizens. The Romans also treated their slaves much more harshly than had the Greeks. In part this was because a great many Greek slaves were Greeks themselves, whereas, once Rome's empire spread beyond Italy, there was a sharp distinction between the native Romans and the "barbarians" from other areas whom they brought in as their slaves. It is always easier to treat someone as an inferior being if he or she is different from you. The Romans soon had more slaves than any other ancient civilization had had and began feeling rather uneasy about their numbers. When someone proposed in the Senate that slaves be required to wear a distinctive type of clothing, the proposal was quickly voted down, "For then they would see how few we are."

To control the huge numbers of their slaves, the Romans kept them under sharp surveillance, so that any sign of rebellion could be crushed before it was too late. The slave uprising led by Spartacus in the first century B.C. was the only one to last any length of time before being brutally put down. The slaves who worked the big plantations were kept chained in individual cells at night so that they could not run away. Many slaves had iron collars welded on with the names and addresses of their owners (like modern dog collars), to make it easier to identify and return runaways. Professional slave catchers did a good business in finding any slaves who tried to escape. Although household slaves were much better treated than those working in agriculture, and some even developed close personal relationships with their masters, the treatises written at the time on the topic of good treatment of one's slaves always make it clear that the real value of good treatment, such as proper food and promises of a day off from work, was that it made the slave work harder.

Initially slaves had very little family life. When they were captured they were separated from whatever family they had, and the work in the fields and in the mines did not lend itself to the slaves' developing new personal ties. However, once Roman expansion slowed down, so that hordes of slaves were no longer brought into the city with every new conquest, it became necessary to begin breeding them to produce the next generation. The Romans also realized that a slave with a family was less likely to run away. Thus, those slaves put in a position of authority, such as the overseers on the plantations, were usually encouraged to marry as a reward for their faithful service and as a tool to make sure that faithfulness continued. But for the most part, until the end of the Roman Empire (discussed in the next chapter), agricultural slaves had no families, although the Romans soon found it advantageous to raise their domestic slaves at home. For work in the fields, they continued to import slaves, if not men captured by the Roman legions, then slaves brought in by slave traders from beyond the borders of the Empire.

Domestic slaves (though usually not the slaves who worked in the fields or the mines) could be and often were freed, as a reward for long service, or sometimes as a pious act at the end of the master's life. A slave who worked in an occupation that made him money might even be able to save enough over the years to buy his freedom, but this was rare. One aspect of the very sharp line that Roman law drew between free citizens and slaves, with no gray area between, was that as soon as a slave was freed he became a citizen. This did not mean that he had any real power, and indeed many former slaves continued to serve their former master as his clients, but it meant that they could now marry other citizens. The result was that, by the first or second century A.D., essentially everyone in Rome was related to a former slave. This is why Roman citizens, originally a fair-skinned people, are represented in portraits from the late Empire as dark-haired and dark-skinned, the "Mediterranean" type one still associates with southern Europe. Generations of marriage with people from north Africa or the Near East left the fair-skinned type very unusual.

The City of Rome under the Emperors

The Romans were indefatigable builders, as the enormous number of their surviving structures makes clear. They built temples, monumental arches, stadiums, aqueducts, palaces, and apartment buildings. After much of the city burned in the first century A.D., the Romans rebuilt most of the central city's housing. The emperor Nero, in spite of his well-deserved unsavory reputation, had enough foresight to impose orderly ideas of town planning on the rebuilding process, including minimum street widths and an improved water supply.

The center of the city, the forum, served as a marketplace, meeting place, and religious center. The forum (or actually forums, as several emperors built elaborate extensions or additions to the original Roman forum) was centered on a large basilica, a rectangular hall with rows of colonnades down the sides. This could serve as a market, a meeting

Trajan's Column, erected in the Roman forum by the emperor Trajan to commemorate his wars.

place, and a law court. Next to the basilica the emperor Trajan constructed a huge column in the second century A.D., decorated with carved and painted scenes of his wars. Commemorative arches were also scattered around the area. Monuments had inscriptions chiseled on them in the same "Roman capital letters" that we use today. The forum also included a produce market and many shops, as well as temples linked by colonnaded promenades. It was in the forum that Romans met their friends and argued politics.

Whereas Rome always had the same sort of small, one- or two-story houses that were the rule in the ancient Near East and in Greece, it also had the world's first tenement blocks. Many of the structures built after the great fire were four stories high or more, large buildings that included shops on the ground floor, craftsmen's studios and workshops, and apartments on the upper stories. Balconies looked out over the streets.

The Romans were able to build such structures relatively economically because they were the inventors of concrete. Their concrete was both durable and inexpensive, made from a mixture of lime and a dark red volcanic sand, combined with pebbles and pieces of broken stone and brick. The Romans did not leave their concrete exposed (as modern architects often do) but used it only for the structural core of their buildings. They then faced their concrete with the thin, flat Roman bricks that can still be found by just a little digging in many parts of Europe. The Romans fired their bricks at high temperatures, to ensure that they would last indefinitely (unlike Mesopotamian or Egyptian bricks). The brick was then normally covered with plaster or stucco.

The Romans were excellent architects, using their concrete, brick, and stone to make buildings that have survived, in many cases, for two thousand years. They were the first to make extensive use of the arch and

Roman relief of a clothing merchant's shop. Note the tiled roof.

the vault, which had been used very little by the Greeks. An arch, in which the stones are supported by a central keystone, makes a very firm top to a window or tall door, and made it possible for the Romans to build much taller buildings than had been in use earlier.

The four-story apartment buildings, made of concrete, became the home for the majority of Rome's population. They were extremely primitive apartments by modern standards since they had no kitchen or bathroom facilities, no heat or electricity, and were very small; but to the Romans these sunny and airy rooms, with their perfectly straight walls, provided comfortable and civilized living. The only constant complaint was that the rents were too high.

The rooms were sparsely furnished by our standards, the principal furniture being stools for sitting and chests for storing one's possessions. In this respect, the apartment dwellers were not much different from those in the large houses, for the wealthy also believed in only a few pieces of furniture, although they often had chairs made of expensive wood, such as cypress or cedar, as well as stools. Lighting was provided by flat earthenware lamps that burned olive oil; this lighting was poor enough that no one tried to do much after dark. People living in the apartments used the public lavatories and public baths, as discussed further on page 88. They brought their drinking water from public fountains in jugs. For food, they either bought what could be eaten cold at home or ate at one of the thousands of stalls throughout the city that prepared and sold hot dishes. They could also grind flour for bread at home and take it to a public bakeshop.

Although some of the wealthy also lived in tenement blocks (though perhaps with a whole floor to themselves), those who could afford it usually preferred a free-standing house, even in the city. In the country, the villa or country-house was the normal dwelling for the well-to-do. A city house was built around an atrium, a large room with an opening to the sky in its ceiling. The front door opened from the street onto the atrium, and the family altar and ancestral statues were placed here. The ancestral statues were carved very realistically, even with separate pupils of darker stone set into marble eyes. The private family rooms, the bedrooms, kitchen, and dining rooms, were at the rear. These had windows opening sometimes into the atrium and sometimes onto the enclosed garden that many houses had at the very back. An elegant house would contain different dining rooms and sitting rooms for winter and summer, where the sun would enter more or less directly depending on the season, and where the views were different, to provide a change of scene. The houses were heated with charcoal-burning braziers in the winter but had no way to keep out the heat in the summer, other than the small size of the windows. There was in fact some criticism of the new layout of Rome after the great fire, because the old narrow, crooked streets had been quite shady, whereas the wide, open streets of the rebuilt areas offered no protection from the summer sun. Those who lived in fancy houses were always afraid of thieves, just as modern city dwellers are. Because there was no police force, the houses were always heavily barred and guarded with dogs and slaves.

Many of the features of the city house reappeared in the villa, or country estate. The wealthy built villas in the countryside around Rome and escaped to them during the summer. In the provinces, where the cities were much smaller, the well-to-do often lived year-round in their villas. A villa in some ways was its own miniature city, including from a few dozen to a few hundred people. The main building, where the master lived, was normally rectangular and built of bricks, with the same sort of atrium plan found in town. Because there was more room to expand, however, and because urban amenities such as baths were not readily available, a country villa tended to be larger, sometimes having large private baths of its own, which a town house would never have. Barns and houses for the tenants were attached to the main house. In the major agricultural areas, the large, comfortable villas of the landowners dotted the landscape.

Urban Life in Rome

Even more than by its buildings, Rome was defined by the feeling that civilization and politics were inconceivable except in an urban context. As Rome's empire spread, it spread the idea of the city into western and northern Europe, and the Empire was soon dotted with towns that reproduced, on a smaller scale, many of the monuments of Rome. The basic administrative unit of the Empire was the *pagus*, consisting of a city and the surrounding countryside, which was assumed to be dependent upon it. The Romans took over the local settlements when they conquered; after all, the geographic features that had made a certain place a good place for a Celtic town also made it a good place for a Roman provincial capital, or for that matter a modern European city. Roman provincial capitals were not large, sometimes only a few thousand people, but they were political, religious, and cultural centers, the features that even to-day define a "real" city, regardless of size.

Roman provincial cities were originally built on an open plan, without walls, although by the third or fourth century A.D. walls began to be added. The center was the basilica, the center of government, with an adjoining temple. In imitation of Rome, all cities had a forum at the central crossroads, usually adjoining the temple and basilica. This was an open-air paved area, meant for public congregation, as was Rome's, and rimmed with covered porticos for protection in rainy weather. Many local notables built baths or other public monuments as a personal display of wealth. Normally these cities had an amphitheatre, or a separate theatre and amphitheatre, for plays and spectacles. Amphitheatres are still the most visible remnants of Roman civilization in many cities in France.

An elegant city house, with its blank white walls and tile roof hiding the life within from the street, was unusual among houses in Rome in its stress on self-contained privacy. Generally one might sleep at home, but most of the rest of one's life was carried out in public. The streets, from which wheeled vehicles were banned during the daylight hours, were essentially extensions of one's home. Those who lived in the apartments did not consider them too small because everything from bathing to entertainment took place outside the home.

The Roman baths are the best example of something we consider private being carried out in public, for bathing was normally done at the public baths. Not only Rome but most other cities of the Empire had central baths, where all local residents could bathe for a nominal fee. (The city of Bath, in England, is named for its Roman baths.) There would be hot and cold baths and usually a large plunge-bath, or swimming pool. Men and women were usually segregated. The baths were much more than a place to get clean. They were also a place to lift weights, to receive a massage, or be depilated. Sausage and pastry vendors sold their wares to the patrons. Some of the fancier bath houses had large, comfortable sitting rooms as well as the disrobing rooms (the locker rooms, we would call them), and even libraries and art exhibits. Successive emperors were proud of building new baths. The city of Rome alone had several hundred different bath houses.

Roman cities also had public lavatories, where flushing was provided by a continuous flow of water under the seats. Men went to barbers for their daily shave, or, during the periods when a beard was in fashion, to have their beards trimmed. Thus most of the things that we do in a bathroom at home the Romans did in public facilities.

All of this was possible because the Romans were excellent waterworks engineers. A few baths were built over thermal springs (as was Bath in England), but in most places the water had to be piped in. Rome was served by eleven principal aqueducts and many smaller ones, all of which brought water to the city from as far as fifty miles away. The aqueducts, normally made of concrete, were built directly through hills and on high

Pont du Gard (Nîmes, France). The Romans built this three-tiered aqueduct over the Gard River to carry water to the city of Nîmes.

arches across valleys, bringing the water on a carefully calculated, gravity-fed, slow descent into Rome.

Theoretically, the water would have reached Rome even without such a steady descent because siphoning will keep water in an enclosed pipe moving as long as the lower end is below the upper end. But the Romans did not want to put undue stress on their concrete. They felt it was worth the extra difficulty and expense to engineer a smoothly descending aqueduct rather than risk having their concrete split by constant water pressure in a few generations. Although they could have laid enclosed pipe more cheaply than building aqueducts, such pipe would be very hard to clean if it started to silt up, and, if the pipe broke, the siphoning and the water flow would be difficult to start up again. When the Romans built, they built for the future, making their structures as maintenance-free as possible. "Planned obsolescence" would have made no sense to them.

Aqueducts still stride across the Italian landscape, and at Segovia, in Spain, the Roman aqueduct is still in use today. The city of Rome was also equipped with a complex series of drains, the oldest and biggest of which, the "Cloaca maxima," had been in place since the earliest days of the city.

Roman Family Life

A Roman family was governed by the father; the *pater familias*, as he was known in Roman law, had absolute authority in legal matters over his wife and children. During the early Republic, he even had the right to sell his children into slavery. A father's authority over his sons lasted until he died, at which time they could own property and enter into legal transactions in their own right for the first time; this might not happen until the sons were grown men with children of their own. Daughters always had to have a male "tutor," their fathers until they married and sometimes even afterward, and then their husbands.

Under the Republic, married women had no legal rights independent of their husbands, although a widow might have rights in a few areas, such as approving the new tutor who was appointed when her husband died. Under the Empire, the only way for a woman to free herself from male guardianship was to bear at least three children; the emperors put in this law as an inducement for women to have large families. However, in Rome, as in all societies that are officially governed by men, there are plenty of hints that, at home, husbands often had to agree with their wives' opinions.

Marriage was a civil rather than religious arrangement. Roman law governed who could and could not marry; for example, a patrician could not marry a freed slave, whereas people of lower status could and did. State law forbade marriages between first cousins, but cousins related more distantly could marry (this was changed during the Middle Ages, when more distant cousins were also forbidden to marry). Some of the emperors, wishing for various dynastic purposes to marry their own nieces, forced exceptions to this general rule through the Senate.

Most parents tried to marry their daughters off between the ages of twelve and fifteen. Normally marriages were celebrated publicly, with witnesses, but there was nothing comparable to our marriage licenses and registration. One of the important decisions for the families to make was whether the father's authority over the bride would pass to her new husband or whether the father should keep it, in which case she would continue to worship her ancestral gods rather than her husband's. The requirements for a valid marriage were that both parties be free (slaves could not marry unless freed) and have the consent of the *pater familias* or the woman's tutor, unless the husband-to-be had been freed by his father's death or the bride by having already born three legitimate children, in which case their own consent was required. The actual moment of marriage was considered to be the time that the bride arrived at her new husband's house; as in Greece, families often had a torchlit procession accompany her through the streets. Any children born more than six months after the bride's arrival there were considered legitimate.

A woman was supposed to bring a dowry to the marriage, her share of her family property, which then became her husband's. However, if he divorced her he was supposed to give the dowry back to her kin, unless he divorced her for adultery, in which case he was entitled to keep half. Divorce was fairly easy for the man, consisting of little more than sending a wife home because she was found disagreeable, but it was much more difficult for a wife to divorce a husband.

There was a somewhat murky line between being a wife and being a concubine. A Roman man could legally have a concubine, but only one at a time and not at the same time as he was married. A concubine was someone with whom he lived and to whom he could not be validly married (for example, if he were a senator and she a freed slave) or someone with whom he had not established "marital affection," an extremely vague phrase. Even though women were not required to bring a dowry for a valid marriage, the presence of such a dowry made a strong presupposition of "marital affection"; a father marrying his daughter to someone more wealthy would always want to give her a dowry to make sure no one thought he was giving her as a concubine rather than a wife. A concubine's children were not legitimate and had no rights to their father's inheritance.

Normally men married women, but Roman law also allowed marriages between two men, formalizing the sort of relationship that had been informal in Greece. The emperor Nero himself twice married another man. Those who did not like Nero—that is, most of the city—joked that it was too bad that the emperor's father had not married the same sort of "wife" as he had because then Nero would never have been born.

Families wanted to have children, especially sons, but there were always attempts to limit family size, both in poor families that could not afford large numbers of children and in rich families that did not want to have to divide up a sizable inheritance. Various herbal contraceptives were used (with greater or lesser effectiveness), but one of the most common ways to limit family size was to "expose" unwanted children. This exposure did not mean leaving them out to die, but rather leaving them out for someone else to take.

There were streets in which children—girls more frequently than boys and illegitimate children much more frequently than legitimate—were regularly set out, and anyone who wanted a child came by to look over the selection. Those who ran houses of prostitution came by frequently to collect baby girls, and someone who wanted a household slave could pick out a baby and take it home to raise, but so did the attendants of Roman matrons who had not been able to become pregnant. Even some fashionable women who could have become pregnant seemed to prefer taking in an exposed baby to losing their figures and facing morning sickness. There were always jokes about someone finally having his long-awaited heir after the slaves had been seen sneaking into the house carrying something concealed in a basin.

Children were not considered full members of the household until they were eight or nine years old. It was only at this point that they were given a formal name, to replace the nicknames they would have been called as infants. A Roman name had three parts. The rhetorician we normally call Cicero was actually named Marcus Tullius Cicero. The first of one's names (Marcus in this case) was the name of one's official tribe, which might be quite large. The second (Tullius) was one's personal name, what would be a first name or a Christian name in modern usage. The third name (Cicero), called the *cognomen*, was one's family name, the same *cognomen* as one's father (like the modern last name). Many fathers named their sons for themselves, all three names, and in fact they might name several different sons all exactly the same thing. (It was a good thing that they still had their childhood nicknames to identify them.) Girls were given feminine versions of male names, such as Claudia from Claudius; there were not yet distinctive women's names unrelated to men's names. When children were named, they received a special amulet that they then wore until they were married, for girls, or reached their majority in their mid-teens, for boys.

The Romans, like modern Americans, disposed of their property after their death by testament. When they first encountered the Germanic people, they were rather surprised to find that these people did not make wills but rather had their children inherit everything. Roman law commanded that one leave one's children (or nephews in the absence of children, or paternal relatives in the absence of nephews) a certain minimum of one's property, but after that one could dispose of it as one liked. It was fairly common for a wealthy Roman without children to adopt someone (possibly an adult, not necessarily a child) and then leave that person everything.

Roman Education

The purpose of Roman education was not intellectual attainment, nor the promise of better job skills. Rather, for the Romans, education was a process that molded character and conduct. Originally all education took place at home, the wealthy buying educated Greek slaves to serve as tutors; all cultured Romans prided themselves on their mastery of Greek. Later Romans considered that their society was becoming decadent when fathers no longer personally oversaw their sons' training. Starting in the late Republic, there were schools to which one could send one's son (girls received their education at home). After school, the boys went home to a lunch of bread and cheese, with probably some olives as well and perhaps figs for dessert. In the afternoon, schoolboys might go to the public baths to meet their friends, accompanied by the slaves who carried their towels.

The schoolmasters, then as now, were underpaid and had to deal with overcritical parents and rambunctious boys, but the masters could whip boys who had not learned their lessons. The boys went off in the morning with their personal slaves running beside them, carrying the wax

A Roman school scene. The schoolmaster, who has a beard, was doubtless a Great slave.

tablet and stylus on which they learned to write (the ancient equivalent of the slate). Like the Greeks, Roman schoolboys were only allowed to use papyrus, the reed-based paper on which permanent records were kept, after they had proved their proficiency with the stylus on wax. (The cheap newsprint that elementary-school children now learn to write on was not invented until many centuries later.)

The basis of Roman education was the "seven liberal arts" ("liberal" meant "related to books," *liber* in Latin). These liberal arts continued to form the base of all education throughout the Middle Ages. The first three learned, the "trivium," were grammar, rhetoric, and logic. Grammar was basic reading and writing, rhetoric was the art of speaking well, which was very important in Roman politics and law, and logic was the ability to reason and argue effectively. A person properly trained in the trivium was ready to take his place in a society where public speaking was highly prized. Because one learned grammar, rhetoric, and logic before anything else, the trivium, which originally just meant "three things," gave rise to the word "trivial," which we still use in modern English to mean something minor and elementary.

After the trivium came the "quadrivium," the other four liberal arts. These were arithmetic, geometry, astronomy, and music. The study of music, with its emphasis on the relationships between notes, was studied almost as a form of mathematics, rather than as a performing art. Astronomy involved both learning to observe the movements of the stars and using them as signs and portents; astronomy and astrology were treated as one discipline.

If one compares this basic Roman education to a modern education, one will be struck by the absence of natural or physical science. Scientific inquiry in our sense—the formulation of hypotheses and experiments to test them—was unknown to the Romans. An educational system whose purpose was moral development and the ability to speak well in public had no room for science. The closest they came was in the study of medicine, to which a student could advance after a basic education. Their form of medicine would scarcely seem scientific to us, as it was composed primarily of the close study and memorization of Greek texts on anatomy. Besides medicine, the other major forms of higher education were the study of architecture and of law. Of these three professions, only lawyers were considered to be following an honorable trade. (Unlike the Greeks, who had no professional lawyers, the Romans, with their emphasis on written law codes, always had such professionals.)

A good deal of education involved close reading of the Greeks, their philosophy, their drama, their poetry. Intellectually, the Romans always felt slightly inferior to the Greeks, although they tried to make up for this by producing their own versions of philosophy, drama, and poetry in Latin (modeled directly, however, on the Greek). The best example of this is the long poem, the Aeneid, written by the poet Virgil. It was intended to be an epic poem of the foundation of Rome which would serve the same place in Roman culture that the Iliad had in Greek culture. The Aeneid was the story of the wanderings and adventures of Aeneas, who had supposedly been a Trojan who had escaped from the destruction of Troy (Homer had mentioned Aeneas as someone who escaped, although Virgil made the rest of the story up himself) and eventually came to Italy. In spite of its somewhat derivative character, the Aeneid was very successful and became part of the basic education of Roman schoolboys, and it was also studied closely throughout the Middle Ages.

Public Entertainment

Rome was provided with a theatre, for plays, and a great amphitheatre for spectacles, something also found necessary in every provincial capital of the Empire. In the provinces, the theatre and amphitheatre were often combined into one structure, but in Rome they were distinct, and also distinct from the "Circus Maximus" outside of town, where chariot races were held. The theatre and amphitheatre were made solidly of concrete and stone, designed to last forever, although the Circus was a wooden structure. The Colosseum, the Roman amphitheatre, which would seat 50,000 or more spectators on its benches (the same number as in a modern football stadium), and whose floor could even be flooded for mock naval battles, was truly a colossal structure. Even today it creates an impassable barrier to smooth traffic in the center of Rome. (Unfortunately, carbon monoxide and the vibrations of traffic are now weathering the Colosseum faster than it has aged in any comparable period since it was built.)

Public entertainment was a central feature of Roman life, and many emperors relied on free entertainment to keep the masses happy. Spectacles were scattered at regular intervals throughout the year, and any free man could come to them, as could privileged slaves. Free tickets were given out based on social status; the wealthier were given good seats on the lower tiers, and the plebeians jostled for seats in the bleachers. The stone benches became very hard by the end of the day, but one could bring or rent cushions.

Rome's chief entertainments (next to which the clowns and trapeze artists of a modern circus would doubtless pale) were at the Colosseum. They can only be described as bloodthirsty and brutal, even to a generation raised on thousands of television murders. Fighting was the chief form of entertainment, fights between men or between men and beasts. The animals were mostly from Africa, such as lions, brought north to Rome via a thriving trade from south of the Sahara. The spectators wanted to see a good battle—not just someone meekly killed, but fights to the death. This meant that Christians made very poor viewing and were only rarely sent into the Colosseum.

Important prisoners of war or people accused of major crimes against the state were often put to death in the Colosseum, but the crowd grew restless if they did not put up at least some resistance. The spectators preferred the fights between professionals, the gladiators. The first gladiator fights seem to have had some religious significance, perhaps a blood-offering to appease the dead, but they quickly degenerated into violence for its own sake. Many emperors boasted of the numbers of men they had sent to their deaths in the Colosseum. Gladiatorial contests, which are first mentioned in the third century B.C., continued until the fifth century A.D., long after the empire was officially Christian.

Gladiators were the stars of the Colosseum. They were slave-warriors, specially trained at imperial schools for the fighting. These schools taught them how to fight with a variety of weapons and how to die with dignity. The schools also employed doctors who patched up the wounded and nursed them back to health so that they could fight again. The gladiatorial schools were such effective teachers of fighting methods that the professional army adopted some of the schools' techniques. Theoretically a gladiator who survived for three years would be given his freedom, but it was rare that one lasted that long. Normally they only had a life span of a few months, if anywhere near that, once they finished their training and began appearing in the fights.

But for a brief period, during which they might fight as often as once a week, gladiators were heroes. Lovesick girls scribbled their names on walls and carried their images with them. Gladiators, in their short and intense professional lives, had great pride and even *esprit de corps*, which was reflected in the traditional greeting they gave the emperor as the fights began, "We who are about to die salute you." Being a gladiator was so exciting (and, if one survived, offered so many opportunities for wealth) that even some free men enrolled at the gladiatorial schools. The emperor Nero, wanting to prove his manliness, himself fought in the Colosseum, even declaring that he wanted to engage in real battles with gladiators rather than simply being allowed to win, although he seems to have been terrified that he would lose.

Gladiatorial contests involved fights between men arrayed in very different sorts of armor and weaponry. Sometimes a gladiator would have a small shield, a helmet that encased his entire head, and a sword with a very sharp bend in the center, like a sickle. Another gladiator would have no armor but a straight sword and a very large shield that covered his entire body. Still another gladiator would be outfitted with a long trident and a heavy net that he could slap over his opponent. The fights were not just contests between men but contests between different forms of weaponry, and there was intense betting between adherents of the small-shield versus the large-shield styles.

Unless both men were poor fighters, sooner or later one would incapacitate the other. At this point the fighting would stop, while the crowd yelled for the defeated man's death or, if he had fought exceptionally well, for him to be spared. After a few moments, the emperor would signal his verdict from his special box: thumbs up to save him, thumbs down for his execution. If the verdict was thumbs up, the defeated man was carried off and patched up, to fight again in a few weeks. If the verdict was thumbs down, then the defeated man was expected to sit perfectly still while the victor slit his throat. The body was then dragged off, and the next pair of gladiators came out as soon as slaves had sprinkled fresh sand over the blood.

At the end of the day, it was common to distribute free gifts to the crowd. The emperors arranged a system of machines that, during the closing ceremonies, would spew hundreds of tallies into the seats. These tallies were marked with what one could win, usually a few loaves of bread or a chicken, but sometimes a ship or a country house. Even the bread and chickens were valuable prizes to many residents of Rome, and there were violent fights in the stands as people scrambled for as many tallies as possible. The well-to-do often left early to avoid the fights, while sometimes the poor came for the distribution of prizes more than for the gladiatorial contests themselves.

Slightly less violent were the chariot races at the Circus. The stands, which would hold close to a quarter of a million people, were always packed on race days. The lightweight chariots were driven by professional charioteers. Usually these were low-born men or slaves, although a few hot-blooded young aristocrats always wanted to drive their own horses, and Nero once drove a team. The charioteers thought of themselves as better than gladiators, for at least the purpose of the races was not to have them killed.

The races were very long by modern standards, fifteen times around the stadium, with the horses exhausted and foaming at the end, while the charioteers whipped them ruthlessly, and the bettors and supporters of different factions screamed and cheered. In many ways these races were closer to the Indianapolis 500 auto race than to modern horse races. There were twelve or more races a day (as many as twenty-four under Nero), usually a race of four chariots against each other. Very close track was kept of the statistics of all the drivers, just as modern baseball keeps statistics on all players. After a charioteer retired or was killed, he or his family would erect a monument at the Circus Maximus, recording his statistics proudly, in such categories as "led from wire to wire" or "came from behind to win."

A team consisted normally of four horses, although there were also races with larger or smaller teams. (The four bronze horses on San Marco in Venice, which the Venetians brought back from Byzantium in the thirteenth century, originally were part of a sculpture of a chariot.) Each of the chariots was sponsored by one of the principal aristocratic factions, which were identified by their colors, white, blue, red, and green. In the late Empire, when the capital moved from Rome to Byzantium, these racing factions, especially the blues and greens, became the basis of political parties.

Especially in the final laps, a great deal of maneuvering went on to try to drive one's opponent out of control. With any luck, the opponent's frail chariot would overturn and the horses, hopelessly tangled in the harness, would crash to the sand and break their legs. Because the charioteers raced with the reins tied around their waists—no one could have controlled the horses just with his arms for fifteen laps—they had about a second and a half, once they realized that the chariot was going over, to slash their way out of the reins before they too were mangled in the crash. Charioteers drove with a special slashing knife between their teeth, ready for action. They wore light crash helmets of leather, but these provided little protection. There was nothing the crowd liked better than several good crashes during a day at the races.

As soon as a charioteer went over, people of his faction raced out to drag him and the wreckage out of the way before the rest of the horses came around again. A charioteer who was just badly shaken up—a surprising number of them had long careers—was given a supposedly restorative drink made largely of wild boar dung. Originally the charioteers were supposed to compete in a footrace at the end of the horse race, but, scarcely surprisingly, this custom soon died out. As soon as the winner was announced and the charioteers received their prizes, and the bets in the stands were paid off (betting was informal, not organized as at modern race tracks), the crowd began calling restlessly for the next race to begin.

Although the Romans were principally interested in spectator sports (much more so than the Greeks had been), they also continued to honor the athletes of the Olympian games. Even after Greece was made part of the Roman Empire, the games continued to be held at Olympia every four years until late in the fourth century A.D., and fashionable Romans made a point of attending. The games had naturally changed from the days when they were the symbol of Greek unity and culture. Successful athletes received much more substantial rewards than leafy crowns. With larger rewards at stake, the athletes complained about the referees and judges much more loudly and forcibly than they had before. There were sometimes special races for women as well as men, although these seem to have been less sporting events than chances for the men in the audience to enjoy watching female legs in action. The women wore tunics, whereas the men continued to participate naked. But the same mixture of racing, jumping, wrestling, and discus- and javelin-throwing continued to dominate the events as had been the case centuries earlier.

Roman Bread

Many emperors relied on keeping the masses happy by providing "bread and circuses." Bread was provided for the people at artificially low prices; such subsidies were in fact necessary to keep much of the population from starvation. Rome had a great many displaced people living in the city, many of whom had been farmers on small farms but had gravitated to the city after they were outcompeted and bought out by the large slave-worked plantations. Such people hoped for, but did not find, a better life in Rome. (The same sort of immigration from the countryside to the city took place in the United States in the twentieth century.) By the second century B.C., Rome already had a large mass of urban poor, the plebeians, many of whom were citizens of the republic but had no real rights or property. The Gracchi brothers, acting as "tribunes" for the plebeians, first introduced subsidized grain prices at this time, a move so popular that no one dared rescind it. Caesar in fact later made grain free for certain citizens.

Rome, like all cities of the ancient world, was originally supported by the grain grown in the immediate vicinity, much of it in fields worked by people living in the city. But when Rome began to grow rapidly, it increasingly had to import its grain from some distance away. Egypt

Fresco of a Roman grain barge being loaded by slaves.

became Rome's breadbasket. Here, on large plantations known as *latifundia*, grain was grown by gangs of slaves. Egypt was not yet as dry as it is now, and the steady supply of water from the Nile made it possible to grow reliable crops every year. Barley was the principal grain, but wheat was also grown. Great grain barges, loaded with food for Rome, crossed the Mediterranean to Ostia, at the mouth of the Tiber River, from which the grain was brought upstream to the city. The grain barges were sailed— they were too heavy to be rowed—but because they had to tack against the wind coming north, a very difficult and slow maneuver with the square-rigged ships of the time, it took weeks to make the crossing from Egypt to Ostia. If there was bad weather or other delays, it might only be possible to get one flotillon of barges across before the autumn storms. The Romans were always nervous that someone could cut off their food supply by intercepting the barges, so grain shipments were always heavily guarded.

Once the grain reached Rome, it was sold to individual households, and then ground into flour in handmills. Handmills are quite inefficient; it took at least one person per household essentially all day, doing nothing else, to grind enough flour for that family's bread for the day. To avoid constant grinding, many people ate porridge instead of bread at their principal meal, in the middle of the day, because for porridge the wheat and barley could be cooked whole. It may be surprising, considering the high level of Roman technology, that they did not have windmills or watermills. (In fact, the Romans *did* have mills, but they were used primarily as toys.) The reason behind this acceptance of energy inefficiency among people as practical as the Romans was that they felt it important for there be something for the plebeians and the slaves to do.

Roman Religion

A large part of the public life of any Roman city, Rome itself or one of the provincial capitals, focused on religion and concern for the dead. Rome worshiped the same basic twelve Olympian gods and goddesses as the Greeks, but under different names: Zeus and Hera were Jupiter and Juno, Ares had become Mars, and so on. (The name "Jupiter" comes from *Zeus pater*, "Zeus the father.") The Roman gods were originally different from the Greek gods, but assimilation was a strong force in Roman religion. Eventually all sky gods in the Empire were determined to be Jupiter in one form or another, all war gods Mars, and so on. These gods were more distant, less accessible than their Greek counterparts, and religious ceremony did not revolve around their personalities as it did for the Greeks. The public worship of the great gods was identified with patriotism, but for personal worship the Romans paid more attention to household gods, to mystery religions, and to their ancestors.

The Romans put a great deal of emphasis on formal reverence for the dead. Whereas the Greeks primarily wanted to be remembered in song and story, the Romans wanted to be commemorated by monuments. Normally when someone died, including someone very poor, his relatives would erect a stone monument to him, called a *stella*. The Greeks had also had *stellae*, as mentioned in Chapter 2, but those of the Romans were much more elaborate. They normally included a realistic carved portrait of the deceased, sometimes holding tools of his trade or represented with his family around him. Someone with an illustrious career might have a very large *stella* erected, decorated with highlights of his various achievements. Because the Romans did not want the dead in the city with them, they buried both bodies and cremated ashes along the roads outside of town. The Via Appia, stretching south from Rome, was lined with *stellae* for a hundred miles, many of which were unusual or striking enough to become tourist attractions. Besides these commemorations of individuals, all Roman households had a shrine to the *Lars familiaris*, or ancestral spirit of the family.

More important on a daily basis than the great gods were the many minor deities who influenced every aspect of daily life. In the house, the two most important were Janus, the god of doors, and Vesta, the goddess of the hearth. Vesta was worshiped in an official temple in Rome, where women sworn to perpetual chastity, the Vestal Virgins, kept her fire alight. These Vestal Virgins, the only six women in Rome not to have a "tutor" before Augustus allowed women freedom from guardianship for bearing three children (noted on page 90), were supposed to be extremely pure in order to maintain the city's religious purity; a Virgin who lost her virginity was entombed alive. Such a drastic punishment is an indication of how closely the Romans identified womanly virtue and the well-being of the state. But Vesta was also invoked every morning when a woman lit a fire to cook her family's food; daughters were carefully instructed both in cooking and in reverence to Vesta.

All of the important turning points in life, such as marriage or childbirth, had gods and goddesses invoked for every step or aspect. There were separate gods for plowing, for sowing the seed, even for manuring the field. Besides gods and goddesses for every activity, there were deities for every stream, mountaintop, and many trees. The Roman countryside was always thickly dotted with shrines and holy monuments.

The Romans also paid reverence to the goddess of Chance and the goddess of Fate. These concepts are actually different, although in modern parlance they are sometimes treated the same. Chance is the "luck of the draw," things happening by accident, while Fate or Fortune is the goddess who has predetermined what will happen. Religion sometimes took on a philosophical aspect, such as among the Stoics, who, believing that all has been predetermined, thought the only rational response was to bear it as well as possible, or the Epicureans, who believed that the purpose of life was pleasure, which they felt lay in avoidance of activity or fame. There was also plenty of witchcraft in Rome, potions brewed from odd parts of animals and enemies confounded if one could use a few of their hairs or nail clippings to curse them. For determining the future, the Romans used signs and portents; this was not just a matter of simple superstition but of official religion, for the legions would not march until sacrifices had been made and inspection of an animal's entrails showed positive portents.

This great mixture of religion could become rather dry, at least in its official aspects. This was especially true when official religion began to turn on the worship of the emperor, who was supposed to undergo apotheosis and become a god when he died, and whose guiding spirit was divine even while he was alive. One aspect of Roman religion, however, was not at all dry, and that was the mystery religions. Mystery religions were mysterious in the sense of unrevealed secrets, known only to the few, not in the sense of a detective "whodunnit." As mentioned in Chapter 2, mystery religions had been found in ancient Greece, and they became increasingly common during the Empire, in spite of intermittent attempts to suppress some of them—although in other cases emperors themselves joined them.

The mystery religions met a deep need, for they did not turn on official cults or adherence to certain rituals but rather on an emotional response to the divine. The worship of the Olympian and the household gods was identified with patriotism and the peaceful continuity of hearth and home, but only the mystery religions promised personal salvation. In origin, the mystery religions seem to have been eastern, drawing on material from Persia or Egypt in many cases, having affinities with the regular letting down of barriers that characterized the Greek Dionysian revels (discussed in Chapter 2). Citizens and slaves alike became adherents to the mystery religions. We cannot be sure today of the details of any of these religions, because they were supposed to be kept secret, but enough people at the time revealed details that we can get a general impression. Although they worshiped a variety of gods, the different mystery religions all shared a ritual purification of the initiates. The rites might include eating a special sacrificial meal or fasting, flagellation or orgies. In all mystery religions, the worshiper hoped to be in some way united with the hero or the goddess, to share in their death and rebirth and eventually immortality. Many followers of the mystery religions joined as many as possible, for example following the rites of Mithras on Monday and of Isis on Tuesday.

Typically a mystery religion involved the story of a hero-figure, half human and half divine, who died and was reborn again. The hero might also be a woman, and many scholars have seen in some of these religions the continuation of the worship of the "Great Mother," which seems to have been the prevalent form of religion in the late Stone Age and early Bronze Age. For example, one of the most highly revered mystery cults was that of Demeter, the goddess of grain and fertility, at Eleusis in Greece. This cult had been established long before Athens came to prominence, and it continued under the Roman Empire. So many people wanted to become initiates of this cult that the priestesses put firm restrictions on who might join, not even letting in the emperor Nero.

One of the most important of the mystery religions was the cult of Mithras. This was very much a male religion; women could not participate in its rites, although most of the other mystery cults were open to them. Its greatest popularity was among the soldiers on the frontiers of the Empire. Mithras was a hero who, in the simplest form of the legend, overcame a bull, dragged it to a cave, and then killed it, watering the earth with its blood so that life could grow. The cult of Mithras was therefore followed in underground cave-temples, and the ceremonies included the spilling of blood.

Mithraism was a dualist religion whose followers believed in a perpetual struggle between the forces of good and evil, with neither ever able to win. Mithras, who himself took part in death and rebirth with the bull, acted as a mediator between sky and earth, between man and the gods. Mithras was also a sun-god. When the emperor Aurelian decided to find a religion that would unify the Empire, replacing the huge hodge-podge of practices with a single imperial cult in the late third century A.D., he decided on Apollo, who quickly became identified for the soldiers with Mithras. The feast of Apollo, which was naturally the winter solstice—the day that the sun "returned" and the days first began growing longer, December 25 in the Roman calendar—became for the followers of Mithras their god's birthday. (Aurelian's plans never had much effect on unifying Roman religious practice.)

Jesus and His Message

When Christianity first began to spread in the Roman Empire, it was initially treated by those in authority as another mystery cult. In fact, many of the early adherents of Christianity viewed it as such themselves and were surprised when told that if they were followers of Christ they could not also worship Isis. And indeed many aspects of early Christianity had strong parallels to the mystery religions: the cult of the half-divine hero, who is reborn, and in whose rebirth the initiate can share through revealed learning and a sacred meal (the bread and the wine). However, these similarities, which certainly touched a chord in people looking for answers in religion, are overshadowed by the differences. Christianity could not help but absorb some influences of the climate around it, as discussed further below, but in origin it was not a mystery religion but a form of Judaism, with a very different understanding of the relationship between man and God.

This can be seen most clearly in a comparison between the figures of

Mithras and Jesus. Jesus was a historical figure, who certainly lived and said and did many of the things that were said about him by his followers, whereas Mithras was always divorced from time. Jesus's background was Jewish, and he had all of Judaism's sense of a historical relationship with God and its hope for redemption of an entire people. Mithraism, with its emphasis on individual salvation, only slowly allowed the initiate to gain the hidden knowledge, but the whole purpose of Jesus's mission, as he saw it, was to make his understanding of men's relations both with each other and with God as clear as possible.

Aramaic, the dialect that was spoken in Palestine in the first century A.D., was not a subtle or complex language; it was better suited for the transactions of the marketplace than for philosophy. This is doubtless why much of Jesus's teaching took the form of parables, using the terms available to him to explain the Kingdom of God, and also using objects and events that would be familiar to his listeners. Jesus's message had, in common with Judaism, a very strong element of morality and responsibility, which was not found in Mithraism. The most radical part of his message had no parallels in Mithraism, or even really in Judaism: that if God is the loving father of His people, not just their king (an idea that many Jewish thinkers of the time were also expressing), then all men are brothers. Jesus specifically included the poor, the sinners, and the outcast in his ministry, as expressed in the table fellowship in which he ate and drank with them. This is probably part of the reason why Christianity, which began to spread slightly earlier than Mithraism, came to enjoy an enormous popularity that the cult of Mithras never did. (In close to two thousand years of people trying to follow Jesus's teachings, the acceptance of brotherhood with and love for the ungodly has always been the most difficult part for the determinedly godly.)

Jesus's message spread rapidly among women and slaves, those whom Christianity welcomed though others rejected, but also among the powerful and well educated. His story of the Good Samaritan, although it is now read primarily as an admonition for people to help each other, would have shocked Jesus's original listeners with the suggestion that even a Samaritan, a member of a people treated with hostility by the Jews of the time, could be "good." Because Jesus was preaching specifically to the Jews, he did not worry overly much about whether the absolute brotherhood he preached extended to non-Jews as well, but that was certainly the direction of his teaching. This is especially so as it was broadly considered among first-century Jews that Yahweh, their God, was also God of the rest of the world.

The second part of Jesus's message, along with the brotherhood of man, was the preaching of the Kingdom of God. Precisely what he meant by this has been argued both within the church and by modern scholars. There is still no general agreement after close to two thousand years, although most scholars now would argue that, for Jesus, the Kingdom of God was an inner awareness of God in one's own life, a source of power already at hand for those who recognized it. However, this philosophical concept was difficult to express in Aramaic, and even while Jesus was alive many people seem to have assumed he meant an apocalyptic event, the sudden appearance of God and the end of the world as we know it. When it became clear, however, that this apocalypse was not going to happen soon, it was sometimes moved into the indefinite future and sometimes redefined in personal terms as the Judgment that would happen to each individual. (Even today some people use everything from disastrous wars to strange arrays of stars and planets as signs that the long-awaited apocalypse is finally arriving.)

Another possible interpretation of the Kingdom of God was a more practical one: the violent overthrow of the Romans, who ruled Palestine through client kings in the first century A.D., and their replacement by kings who would be like David and Solomon. There were certainly plenty of Jews in Palestine waiting for a leader to begin such a revolt, which did break out eventually in 66 A.D., more than thirty years after Jesus's death. Although the Jews managed to hold off the Roman legions for four years, they were much too seriously outnumbered to resist indefinitely, and in 70 A.D. the Jewish Wars ended with the destruction of the Temple and the dispersal of the Jewish population of Palestine. This dispersal, called the Diaspora, continued until the foundation of the modern state of Israel after World War II. Although this kind of violent revolt was not Jesus's intention at all, the Roman authorities of his time decided not to take any chances when they heard a charismatic leader was speaking of the imminence of the Kingdom of God. They arrested him as a revolutionary, had him convicted on trumped-up charges, and had him crucified. Crucifixion was an especially painful form of execution in which the victim usually took several days to die of shock and loss of blood; the leaders of the Spartacus slave revolt a century earlier had all been crucified.

Although the Romans expected the execution of Jesus to disperse his followers, in fact the number of adherents to his teachings continued to grow rapidly. To his followers, not just Jesus's message but Jesus himself continued to live. And very quickly that message began to spread beyond the Jews to other people of the Empire. The Christians, as they quickly began to call themselves (from the Greek *Christos*, meaning "the annointed one," the description of the expected Messiah in Jewish apocalyptic writings), began to receive converts who had *not* started as Jews. Much of the spread of Christianity to non-Jews, or Gentiles, was due to the influence of Paul.

Paul was a well educated Jew who was very familiar with Greek philosophy and was a citizen of the Roman Empire. Although he had not known Jesus personally, he greatly influenced the early development of Christianity. Paul was able to express Christian concepts in Greek, in complex philosophical terms, which made the religion intellectually acceptable to educated Greeks and Hellenized Romans. He early joined forces with Peter, who had been the leader of Jesus's apostles, and with James, Jesus's brother. Paul and Peter persuaded James (very amicably, according to the description in Acts of the Apostles, written forty years or so later) that one need not become a Jew first in order to become a Christian, that converts did not have to adopt Jewish dietary restrictions and, for the men, undergo adult circumcision (which would certainly have held down the number of converts). Although the early Christians certainly recognized their debt to the Jewish tradition, they also believed that with Jesus there was a new covenant, a new relationship between God and man, that made some of the regulations of the old covenant unnecessary.

The Christianity that Paul advocated (his letters are the oldest part of the New Testament) had a different emphasis than the message Jesus had preached. He took Jesus's teachings on the brotherhood of man and the nearness of God as givens, but he himself was very little concerned with the details of Jesus's ministry. Rather, for Paul, the Crucifixion and Resurrection (which, since they had come at the end of Jesus's life, were of course not part of *his* teachings) were the heart of Christianity. Paul added to Jesus's basic message an emphasis on redemption from sin and the salvation of the individual, specifically in a triumph over death. Paul's version of Christianity was accepted without question by Peter and James, the men who had known Jesus best, so in spite of his different emphases it must have been close to what Jesus had been saying.

The Spread of Christianity

With Christianity open to conversions by Gentiles, the religion began to spread very rapidly. When the Jews were dispersed at the end of the Jewish Wars, in 70 A.D., the Christians among them were also dispersed throughout the Mediterranean basin. It was at this time, immediately after the destruction of the Temple, that the Gospels first began to be written, accounts in Greek of the life and teachings of Jesus. These accounts were based on oral tradition and also on written records of some of Jesus's sayings, of which a few scraps still survive; but the Gospels were the first effort to integrate Jesus's sayings into an account of his life and activities. It is indicative of the variety within early Christianity that, within a thirty- or forty-year period, four different men (whom we now call Matthew, Mark, Luke, and John) each found it necessary to write down his own version of the "real" meaning of Jesus's life.

There were converts to Christianity from all social classes. The religion spread rapidly, but probably most converts had only the slightest idea of Jesus's message. Christianity and Judaism were the only religions in the ancient world with actual doctrine; and adherents to the various forms of Roman religion, who were accustomed to worshiping one god or goddess or another because he or she seemed powerful, were "converted" to Christianity in the same way. They simply decided that the Christian God seemed powerful and therefore worthy of worship, without having it occur to them that this religion might have a complex philosophical base or require sincere dedication of all one's heart and mind. Those doing the converting did not worry much more about such details; early church historians spoke proudly of how, after one particularly marvelous miracle or another, dozens or even hundreds of people "converted on the spot."

Where Christianity differed from other religions—and this *was* a point brought home to new converts—was that, unlike the Roman gods, who

Jesus as the Good Shepherd, a third-century wall painting from the Catacomb of Domitilla.

were tolerant of one worshiping as many other gods as one liked, the Christian God was actually antagonistic to other gods, who the Christians argued were in fact only false or weak divinities anyway. Intermittently the Roman rulers denounced Christianity and blamed the Christians for all the decline they saw from the morals and habits of the "good old days" of the Republic (interestingly, during the Republic, several rhetoricians had denounced *their* age as having lost the morality and religion of their ancestors in the good old days). Even after the emperor Constantine announced the toleration of Christianity in the early fourth century and was baptized himself while dying, those members of the imperial government who became Christians were usually new men—men who had risen from lower ranks in the service of the emperor, while the men from families which had long governed Rome still venerated the gods of the old state religion.

Christians were persecuted because they seemed to be undercutting the state when they refused to take part in the state religious rituals, especially when they refused to acknowledge the emperor as a god. The emperor Nero, fearing that this was sedition, made it a crime to be a Christian and tried to blame the great fire of 66 A.D. (which some people were blaming on him) on the Christians. The secret meetings of the Christians looked very ominous to outsiders, and the Christian communion, partaking in "the body and blood of Christ" by drinking the wine and eating the wafer, was sometimes feared to be real cannibalism. As a result, Christians in the first two centuries faced intermittent persecution. In some ways, however, this actually helped spread the religion, for pagans who saw the Christians gladly going to martyrdom began to wonder if there might be something in a religion that offered rewards so powerful as to be stronger than death.

The Structure of the Early Church

During the first two centuries of Christianity, the religion was especially concerned with surviving in a frequently hostile climate, but it was also adopting the organizational structure that the church would keep in subsequent centuries. Jesus does not seem to have foreseen a formal church structure for his religion, but those adhering to Christian beliefs quickly found such a structure necessary. Local churches, originally semi-independent, were headed by priests (our word comes from the Latin *presbyter*, which in turn comes from the Greek term for "elder"; all the vocabulary of the early church was Greek). These men were commonly married. Though Paul had said it was best to remain chaste, as he did himself, he also made it clear that marriage was preferable to burning with unsatisfied lust, and priests of the early church rarely sought the "best" course of celibacy. The churches were organized by city, as was natural in a city-dominated civilization, with each city having its bishop, who was responsible for all the Christians in the city and its surrounding *pagus*. (Our word "bishop" comes from the Latin *episcopus*, from a Greek word meaning "overseer.") The bishop was normally selected by the Christians of his community.

Because early Christianity spread by word of mouth, without any organized central authority, it inevitably developed a number of variant forms almost immediately (even among the educated people who *did* try to think about the message of the gospels). By the second century A.D., a major concern for Christians was trying to sort out what the essential features of the Christian religion actually were. The early church was run by its bishops, leaders of the Christians in each city of the Empire that had Christians; and the bishops of the different cities, though they had no particular institutional ties with each other, still tried to coordinate their efforts in defining and living Christianity. For example, it was due to a compromise that the New Testament we have now has four Gospels in it, four similar but still essentially different accounts of Jesus's life. Rather than choosing among different versions, the bishops who were assembling Christian holy writings included them all.

The church's organizational structure was refined in the second century, and by the third century, even before Christianity was officially tolerated, there was at least a general consensus of what Christianity entailed. Where there was no such consensus, there was at least an organizational structure that could attempt to find out. The goal of the bishops was, having once converted people to Christianity, to try to instruct them in Christian doctrine. The bishops of the different cities essentially ran organized Christianity among them. Any question, any heresy, would be met by organizing a council of bishops of the region to argue it out and reach a decision. A heresy is maintaining that one's version of Christianity is correct even if ecclesiastical authorities call it erroneous, but first the bishops had to decide if something *was* erroneous. The bishops of the first centuries had no real overarching authority higher than themselves, which made the council system necessary, both to reach decisions and to spread them. (Interestingly, seventeen hundred years later, with the pope and cardinals holding an authority undreamed of in the early church, the Catholic hierarchy still cannot make major decisions or change the church's direction without holding a council—for example, the Second Vatican Council of 1962, which first allowed Catholics to hear the Mass in their own language rather than Latin.)

It is important to note that much of Christian doctrine was only worked out in reaction to a challenge; that is, the bishops had never really considered a number of issues until someone came up with his own interpretation, which seemed wrong but could not be rejected until the bishops had formulated a statement of what was *right*. For example, the decision to make the Jewish Bible part of the Christian Bible as the Old Testament was only finally reached after someone began preaching that the God of the Jews was actually not the same as the God of the Christians, but the devil in disguise. Similarly, Christianity made a break with the whole concept of secret knowledge, revealed to initiates, when they denounced the Gnostics, a sect who considered themselves Christian but emphasized secret knowledge in the same way as had the mystery religions. (The Gnostics also had a reputation for libertine practices, which the rest of the Christians would not tolerate.)

The Acceptance of Christianity

Early Christianity was a proselytizing religion, one that tried to gain converts. One of the methods Christians used was to make the transition as easy as possible for the new recruit. They drew a thin line between practices that were certainly not Christian and must be rejected, and the observance of holidays and the habit of going to certain places of worship which could be made Christian with a little effort. Thus a great many pagan temples were rededicated as Christian churches, and December 25, the "official" birthday of the sun-god, was taken over and used as Jesus's birthday. (The exact date of Jesus's birth was unrecorded and not observed on any particular day in the first centuries—in fact, from the Biblical account of the shepherds, it might have been in the spring.) In the same way, the Christians took over the Roman idea of hell, where people burned in agonies in order to punish them for sins they had committed during their lives, and made it into the Christian hell (the Bible is very vague on hell). The Christians were willing to accept some things that still had pagan aspects as long as they had been made *officially* Christian; hence, some scholars have seen in the early devotion to Mary the old religion of the Great Mother coming to the surface again in a new form.

Eventually, once Christianity was officially tolerated, the bishops of the five major Christian cities of the Empire became the "first among equals," the patriarchs. These five were the bishops of Rome, Constantinople, Jerusalem, Antioch, and Alexandria. The bishop of Rome, the man now known as the pope, claimed preeminence over the other patriarchs, both because Rome was the capital of the Empire and because Peter, the first of the apostles, was supposed to have been the first bishop

---

CONSTANTINE

The emperor Constantine ruled Rome from 307 to 337 A.D. He began official toleration of Christianity within the Empire and also moved the empire's capital to the Greek-speaking region of Byzantium. His new capital was named Constantinople for him (this city is the modern Istanbul, in Turkey).

Constantine's toleration of Christianity began in the year 312, when, just before an important battle, he had a vision of a cross in the sky, with the words, "In this sign you will conquer." When indeed he did conquer (defeating another claimant to the imperial title), he decided that this was a powerful religion and ended all persecution of Christians. He also took it upon himself to oversee church councils and, at the end of his life, was baptized as a Christian himself.

His move to Constantinople exacerbated a tendency already underway to split the empire into two halves: the eastern, or Greek-speaking, and the western, or Latin-speaking. In succeeding generations there were often co-emperors, one at Rome and one at Constantinople. The ones at Constantinople continued to hold the title of Roman emperor continuously until the fifteenth century, but there ceased to be emperors at Rome in the late fifth century.

---

of Rome. Paul, the other leading apostle, had also certainly taught at Rome. The other four patriarchs were not so sure about this preeminence; Antioch as well as Rome claimed Peter, and it was not until the fifth century that the bishop of Rome gained exclusive use of the title *papa*, meaning "father," from which we get "pope." In practice, although the bishop of Rome enjoyed a vague moral authority, coming from his position as heir to the principal apostles, it was not until the eleventh century that the pope began to exercise real power as the head of Catholicism.

In the fourth century, the price that Christianity paid for being officially tolerated was to have the emperors begin to take an active role in its governance. For example, several of the early church councils that defined Christian doctrine were assembled by, and presided over by, the emperor Constantine. As the pagan emperors had been virtual gods themselves and certainly the chief priests of the Roman state religion, so the Christian emperors considered it reasonable that they take charge of sorting out any questions or disputes within Christianity. The concept of the separation of church and state was still fourteen hundred years in the future. Christianity might not have survived without official toleration, but it also could not remain unchanged.

In spite of the emperors' best efforts, however, Christianity never fell under actual control of one man. Like Judaism, Christianity was a religion in which all rulers, even the most powerful, were under God and under God's law. Although Christianity recognized the social distinctions of the world, the huge gulf between an emperor and a slave, and was not even particularly concerned with trying to bridge that gulf in the here-and-now, it also made it perfectly clear that, ultimately, all men were equal before God. Not only was the emperor not a god to the Christians, he would be judged for his sins in exactly the same way that a slave was judged.

Although the Roman Empire collapsed between the fourth and sixth centuries, due to a combination of internal and external pressures, it left a legacy to the Middle Ages that followed in Europe. Latin, the language of Rome, became the basis of French, Italian, and Spanish. Western Europe had been Christianized when the emperors became Christian, and this religion, with its center at Rome, long outlasted the Empire. Even after the men who called themselves Roman emperors were exclusively emperors in Constantinople, with no more interest in Rome itself, the West kept alive the ideal of an emperor, who would keep the peace and protect the church. The amphitheatres, aqueducts, baths, and roads that the Romans had built continued to stand long after the institutions that had shaped them were gone.

Rome had absorbed many of the ideas of the ancient world, from the astronomical observations that had started with the Babylonians to the Judeo-Christian ethic. The Near East, where civilization had begun, became part of the Roman Empire, as did both Greece itself and the wider area that had absorbed Greek culture during the Hellenistic period. All of this ancient learning, distilled and accompanied by the Roman sense of organization and central government, was spread into western Europe. Although the disintegration of the Empire, discussed in Chapter 4, meant that Roman learning survived only in small pockets, the memory of Rome was a living presence and incentive for the next thousand years.

CHRONOLOGY

FOUR

THE END OF THE ROMAN EMPIRE AND THE
BEGINNING OF THE MIDDLE AGES

FOUR

THE END OF
THE ROMAN EMPIRE
AND THE BEGINNING
OF THE
MIDDLE AGES

The Question of the "Fall" of Rome

IT IS AGREED by all modern scholars that the Roman Empire fell; the only question on which scholars disagree (and they do disagree quite strongly) is on the reason for this fall. However, no one at the time noticed anything of the sort. There ceased to be emperors in Rome in the late fifth century, and the year 500 is therefore usually taken as an arbitrary turning point between the end of the Roman Empire in the west—that is, the end of classical antiquity—and the beginning of the Middle Ages. The term Middle Ages, or medieval period, was later chosen because the Middle Ages came in the "middle" between classical antiquity and the modern period. People of what we call the Middle Ages called their own time "now," as indeed everyone always has with his own period.

The people who lived in what had been the Roman Empire noticed nothing new in the year 500. Although there were no emperors living in Rome after the 470s, this had often happened before, and there were still emperors at Constantinople who called themselves Roman emperors and were recognized as such in the west; in fact, their line continued until the fifteenth century. In the first part of the fourth century, as

112

FOUR
*The End of the
Roman Empire and
the Beginning of the
Middle Ages*

mentioned in Chapter 3, the emperor Constantine had decided he did not like living in Rome and would instead make his home in the region of Byzantium, in what was then a Greek-speaking region and is now part of Turkey, and renamed the city there Constantinople, after himself. In the sixth century the whole Mediterranean basin was still unified, politically and culturally.

Perhaps more significant than the end of emperors in Rome in the fifth century was the disappearance of the meetings of the Roman Senate in the late sixth century, although there continued to be men who called themselves senators. Even though Rome was no longer directing the gov-

THE BARBARIAN INVASIONS

The "barbarian invasions" of the late Roman Empire were not so much sudden invasions as the gradual settlement of Germanic peoples in the Empire, some coming as conquerors but many settling on land that Roman administrators gave to them. For a long time, the Rhine river was supposed to be the boundary, and the Roman legions tried to keep Germanic peoples east of the river.

In the third century the Germans were held at the Rhine, but in the fourth century they began to come across in waves. The Germanic people included several different tribes, very large groupings of people who spoke a similar dialect, some of which were organized under their own kings. The push that seems to have propelled them into the Empire came from the Huns, a non-Germanic people coming behind them. The Goths, one of the Germanic tribes, were the first to be allowed into the Empire, in the second half of the fourth century. After Alaric, king of the Visigoths (one of the branches of the Goths), sacked Rome in the year 410, many more Germanic tribes moved into and through the Empire. The Visigoths eventually settled in Spain; the Franks (discussed on page 117) settled first on the Rhine and then in what is now France; the Lombards settled in northern Italy; the Ostrogoths (another branch of the Goths) also settled in Italy; the Burgundians settled in eastern Gaul; the Vandals went through Spain and across the Straits of Gibraltar to northern Africa; and the Angles and Saxons crossed the North Sea to land in Great Britain.

The Huns also made a brief foray into the Empire, especially Italy and Byzantium, in the middle of the fifth century. Attila and his Huns reached the gates of Rome but did not actually attack the city, persuaded not to do so by the pope; the legend was that Saints Peter and Paul appeared to Attila and terrified him. When Attila died the next year (453) on his wedding night, having just taken a new bride, the threat to the Empire from the Huns collapsed. The disorganized remains of Attila's armies retreated and settled in what is now Hungary.

ernment of the Empire, the administrative machinery in the provinces was, for the most part, still functioning in the year 500. But while politically the Roman Empire was still intact in the sixth century, economically and socially it had already been in decline for a good two hundred years.

The integrity of the Empire was threatened for several centuries by the invasions of Germanic peoples, but this was a very long and slow process, not a sudden turning point. The Romans called the Germanic tribes "barbarians," borrowing the word from the Greeks, meaning anyone who could not speak Latin and instead spoke a language that they said sounded like "bar bar baa." German-speaking families and tribes had been entering the Empire since the fourth century, sometimes resisted by the Romans, sometimes officially admitted. By the fifth century, the pressures had built to a maximum, and the city of Rome itself was sacked in 410, although there continued to be emperors there. The Germanic tribes came not just as conquerors but as settlers, taking up residence with their flocks and families.

The settlement of the various Germanic tribes within the Empire was facilitated by the long-standing Roman practice of recruiting local men into their legions. Already in the fourth century, many of the civil wars within the Empire, between different men who each claimed to be the "real" emperor, were fought not by the traditional legions but by barbarians, who in fact fought in their leather breeches and heavy cloaks, rather than in the uniforms of the imperial army. New kingdoms (referred to as "barbarian" kingdoms by modern scholars) were established in the fifth and sixth centuries in what had once been the Empire, including the kingdoms of the Franks, the Burgundians, the Visigoths, and so on, but even this should not be seen as a radical change, for the barbarian kings all considered themselves to be living within the Empire and were intensely proud of any official recognition from the emperor in Byzantium (which many in fact received).

It is therefore difficult to speak of "causes" for the fall of Rome, as though one were describing causes for an *event*; what actually occurred was a series of gradual changes, each of which passed essentially unnoticed. Classical historians would say that the Roman era came to an end by the late fifth century, but many medievalists would argue that the real end of the Roman empire came only in the seventh century, when the cultural unity of the Mediterranean basin was broken by the rise of Islam. Scholars today rarely agree on what aspects of late Roman history actually were signs of decline, and one gets a very different picture if one is discussing Rome or discussing the provinces. And of course it is hard to characterize as a "fall" a process that seems to have taken five hundred years.

But whether or not one uses the term "fall," it is clear that the period from roughly 400 to 700, the period to be covered in this chapter, was very different from preceding centuries. This is the beginning of the early Middle Ages, a period which is called Merovingian in what is now France, because the Merovingian dynasty of Frankish kings ruled then. In some places during these centuries, in Anglo-Saxon England and in north Africa once it was conquered by the Arabs, Roman culture was nearly effaced and replaced by a new culture. In other areas, where waves of Germanic peoples settled within the Empire, they tried to meld their own culture with Roman culture.

In most areas, men living within the old boundaries of the Roman Empire still thought of themselves as Roman, but they seem to have forgotten much of what the Romans had known. This can be seen, for example, in the rapid changes in written Latin: spelling became erratic, classical case endings changed and disappeared, verb tenses and sentence structure became simplified. Spoken Latin had always tended in this direction; some of the graffiti scrawled on the walls of Pompeii in the first century A.D. are written in the same simplified way. But formal, written Latin had continued to be a complex, highly sophisticated language until the fifth century or so. At this point, however, it began to change rapidly. The educational system was no longer adequate for classical Latin training. The local spoken languages were evolving, turning from Latin into French or Italian or Spanish, and those writing what they thought was Latin were in fact writing something closer to the spoken language of their particular region.

Even more striking is the change in art and architecture. In the flourishing days of the Empire, as noted in the previous chapter, roads out of Roman cities were often lined with funeral *stellae*, highly realistic representations of the dead carved in stone. There continued to be funeral *stellae* in Gaul under the Merovingian kings, but these became progressively cruder; rather than being molded, three-dimensional representations, they became little more than stick figures, roughly sketched on a flat piece of stone. Similarly, the Merovingian kings issued coins with their images on them, as had the emperors, but these images were now reduced to very awkward representations, almost cartoon-like faces with bulbous noses, and the laurel wreaths that had crowned the emperors had become indistinct squiggles.

Complex artistic representation, as is stone sculpture, can only be learned through a lengthy apprenticeship. One cannot look admiringly at a statue, pick up a chisel and a piece of marble, and set out to duplicate it. The skill can only be learned with one-on-one training and coaching from an expert; this is still true today. From the time of the Greeks, the art of realistic stone sculpture had been taught to each new generation. But it only took one break—one generation that did not learn the techniques because, in a time of turmoil and disaster, no one ever taught them—for the techniques to be lost. They were only reinvented and repolished in the eleventh and twelfth centuries, and not until the thirteenth century can one again see the sort of realistic stone sculpture that had been common in Rome before the fifth century.

The Collapse of Roman Cities

Many of the changes between the fifth and seventh centuries resulted from the disruption of urban culture, due both to the barbarian invasions and to the shrinking of the population. Because the barbarians concentrated primarily on cities when they looted and sacked, these were often deserted in their wake. The cities might have been repopulated, except that it was also becoming much harder to produce enough food to feed a city's population. The trade routes that had once brought food to market were seriously disrupted by the frequent turmoil, and there was also less food available. The climate became wetter and cooler in the sixth century, entering what is now known as a mini ice age. This meant that early frosts and disastrous hailstorms became more frequent, and farmers could not count on being able to raise as much food as they once had. Raising less, they had less surplus to sell to market.

The worsening of the climate in the early Middle Ages was especially a problem in northern Europe, where the richest soils were also the heaviest and the wettest. The lightweight Roman plows had only been able to cultivate these soils in dry years, and now with the wetter climate many of these soils could not be cultivated at all. Grain crops thus were often disastrously small. With grain, a constant dilemma arose from the fact that the food and the seed for the next year's crop are actually the same. This gives one the unenviable choice in a really poor year of starving now and saving the seed, or eating the grain now, having nothing to plant, and starving next year. Rarely was there enough surplus to stockpile against a bad year. In the sixth century, as the cities where the poor might have been able to get subsidized grain under the Roman Empire shrank to tiny enclaves, peasants whose crops had failed formed desperate bands roving the countryside.

Also in the sixth century, the Black Death, or bubonic plague, swept through western Europe, decimating many cities, where the close proximity of city-dwellers allowed infection to spread rapidly. This plague was not seen in the West again for eight hundred years, but it effectively ended the already weakened urban civilization of the old Roman provinces. Those whom the plague spared often left the cities for good, taking up farming because that seemed the only way to assure themselves enough food. As noted in Chapter 1, one cannot have large cities unless the countryside is producing substantial surplus food over what the farmers and their families need, which they can sell to market. And in the early Middle Ages the farmers were unable to produce much more than the minimum they needed themselves.

Those left in the cities retreated toward the centers. The baths, circus, theatre, and mint which had been in every Roman provincial capital were either abandoned or were turned into semi-fortified dwelling places. A Gallo-Roman city that might once have held several thousand people usually shrank to several hundred. The abandoned houses and monuments of the outer rings of the city were used to build city walls as protection for the small city centers; during the flourishing days of the Empire, most of the provincial cities had not been walled. Western Europe had become predominantly rural by the end of the sixth century, and it would so continue for over five hundred years.

Because of the disasters of the fifth through eighth centuries, the period is sometimes referred to as the Dark Ages. The real darkness of the

116

FOUR
*The End of the
Roman Empire and
the Beginning of the
Middle Ages*

period is one of information; the disintegration of the educational system, mentioned previously, meant that many fewer people could write, and those who could kept few records. The wars and invasions of the succeeding centuries destroyed many of the records they *did* keep. Because the expression "Dark Ages" has a tone of moral judgment, it is probably better not to use it, instead referring to "the beginning of the Middle Ages," or, in France, the "Merovingian period." (It is highly incorrect to use "Dark Ages" as a synonym for the entire Middle Ages.)

The Integration of Germanic and Gallo-Roman Peoples

If one concentrates on the Roman Empire, the Germanic people look like invaders, but if one looks on the other hand toward the history of subsequent centuries, then it is clear that they as well as the Romans had something to pass on to the Middle Ages. The Germanic tribes did not replace the Romans so much as these two separate cultures fused together. The process can be seen most clearly in France, where the Gallo-Romans, that is the native people of Gaul who had become thoroughly Romanized in language and culture in the late imperial period, were joined by the Franks. The Franks were a Germanic people who came from the area around the mouth of the Rhine but were settled in Gaul under their own kings by the end of the fifth century (France is named for the Franks). Although the Franks came as conquerors, they did not supplant the Gallo-Romans but rather joined them. They adopted their language, many of their habits, and the bases of Roman provincial administration while intermarrying with them.

The Merovingian kings of the Franks ruled through counts, nobles who were their trusted friends and advisers, and they used the same administrative boundaries the Empire had used before them. (The word "count" comes from the Latin *comes*, meaning originally a companion, and thus has nothing to do with counting from one to ten or the like. A county is the area ruled by a count.) The basic imperial administrative unit was the *pagus*, a city in the center of a fairly large territory. The territory was named for the city; thus, the city of Poitiers was the capital of Poitou, and the city of Le Mans the capital of Maine (the French region after which the American state was later named). Generally, each Roman *pagus* became a Frankish county.

The intermarriage of the Gallo-Roman senatorial families and the Frankish noble families meant that the ruling segments of both societies quickly fused. Both Gallo-Roman and Germanic names were often found in the same noble family by the sixth or seventh century. There were never enough Germanic people to have completely ousted the Gallo-Romans as secular rulers. The Germanic people who settled near the Gallo-Romans tended to imitate them, living like them in large villas, while the Gallo-Romans also imitated the Germanic Franks. One of the signs of the influence of Frankish customs on even the most Romanized

The crown of Agilulf of the Lombards, from the early seventh century, illustrates conquered cities making offerings to the king. The Kingdom of the Lombards was one of the Germanic kingdoms formed within the old Roman Empire.

peoples was the change from giving children three names to giving them only one. As noted in Chapter 3, Roman children had all had three names, their tribal name, their personal name, and their family *cognomen*. The Germanic peoples, however, only gave their children one name, the personal name, and this became the rule even in families that claimed to be descended from Roman senators. Only in the late eleventh or twelfth century did nobles once again start to have a second or "last" name (usually the name of their castle), and common people did not normally have last names until the fourteenth century. Until then, throughout the early Middle Ages and the high Middle Ages, people had only one name, that given to them at baptism.

While the Franks were building Roman-style villas, the Gallo-Romans were copying Germanic weapons. One cannot tell by excavating a tomb from the seventh century or later whether a pure Frank or someone who claimed descent from a Roman senator is buried there: in either case, one will find heavy gold jewelry, gaudy by Roman standards but made with energy and flair and often decorated with people and animals, in addition to well-made and highly decorated swords. Under the barbarian kings, warfare became again what it had been for the Greeks, a glorious occupation for those who could follow it, not the professional service it had been for the Romans, who kept battle far from most citizens. Among the Franks, the nobles especially went to war, but ordinary freemen did so as well. Wearing chain-mail shirts, or leather shirts sewn with metal rings, carrying round shields and swords, and throwing their battle axes, they made a formidable army. Many of their names are warlike, such as Hrotgar, "glorious spear" (from which we get Roger); Garhard, "strong spear" (our modern Girard or Gerald); Charibercht, "bright army" (Herbert); or even women's names, such as Gartrudis, "spear might" (Gertrude). War continued to be considered a glorious occupation until the final centuries of the Middle Ages.

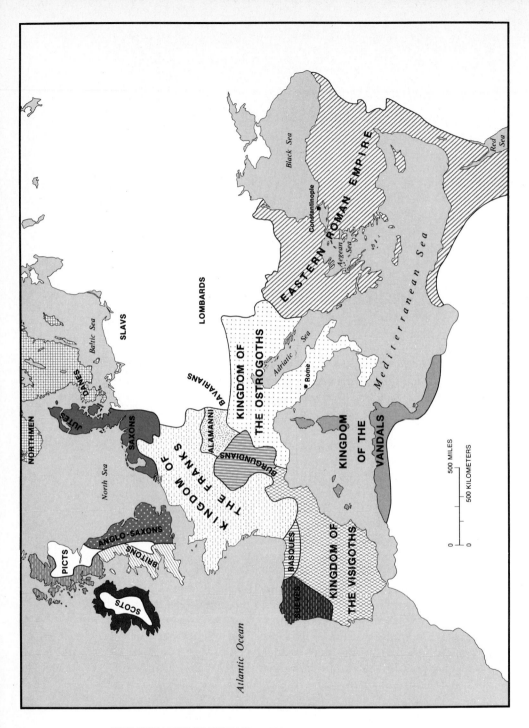

THE GERMANIC KINGDOMS, c. 500
During much of the fifth century, there were two Roman emperors, one in the West, with his capital at Rome, and one in the East, with his capital at Constantinople. By the late fifth century, however, there were no more emperors in the West. The old imperial territory there was divided into a series of kingdoms, most ruled by Germanic peoples who had migrated into the Empire over the previous two hundred years.

Family Life among the Franks

Many details concerning Frankish family life can be perceived through their law codes. Their legal system, which had originally been oral but was written down in the sixth century in imitation of Roman law codes, was based on giving everyone a monetary value. This value, called a person's "wergeld," was the amount that someone who killed or seriously injured a person would have to pay the relatives in recompense. The establishment of the wergeld system seems to have come out of a desire to end the blood-feuds that the Frankish men would otherwise have started to get revenge for every insult or injury.

Frankish families were dominated by their men, who made all the major decisions, but they were also very careful that their daughters received suitable dowries, and the laws backed them up in protecting their wives and daughters from any other men. Frankish law codes gave women of child-bearing age a wergeld triple that of a man, because of the loss to her husband of their potential children. A Frankish woman was under the legal domination of her father until she was married and of her husband afterwards, but when widowed she might control her own property without having to go through a male guardian. This Frankish family structure fused without difficulty with the Gallo-Roman structure, in which the *pater familias*, the father of the family, had also always been the dominant voice.

Because marriages deeply influenced inheritance and the composition of that group of people for whom one might be recompensed by the payment of wergeld, marriage was considered too important to be left to the young people. Fathers or uncles normally arranged marriages, which, among the most powerful segments of society, might mean marrying someone one had never met. Children who tried to object to their parents' choice of marriage partners were simply overridden. There was as yet no "marriage ceremony" in the later, Christian sense; rather, the new couple was tucked into bed by the relatives, and at most a priest blessed the bed. There were strict penalties for adulterous wives, but nothing comparable for adulterous husbands, and Frankish men seem frequently to have had concubines. It was easy for a husband to divorce his wife, but not for her to divorce him.

During the Merovingian period Christianity first began to influence family life and to create a sexual code of conduct. The church emphasized the importance of monogamous and permanent marriages. Although early Christianity emphasized that the best possible state was to be a virgin, it always recognized sex within marriage. This meant, however, that for the church those who were not married were not supposed to engage in sex, and there was to be no adultery, by either man or woman. (Fornication, sex by the unmarried, was however always less serious than adultery.) Even within marriage, sex was supposed to be for procreation alone, not for pure pleasure (this is still Catholicism's official position). Certain types of sex positions were acceptable, and others were not.

Priests naturally had trouble trying to impose these new ideas, even

FOUR
*The End of the
Roman Empire and
the Beginning of the
Middle Ages*

Merovingian pendant from the seventh century, depicting horse and rider, is of bronze with silver overlay.

though, from the sixth century on, they had "penitentials," guides to inappropriate behavior, which gave them suggestions on how to question the behavior of the people committed to them and what sorts of penance to make the sinful undertake. But the Christian sexual ethos did have at least some influence on laymen, in that it gave a rationale for the asceticism that swept through the late Empire and an impetus to the monastic movement, discussed on pages 125–32.

Christianity in the Early Middle Ages

The cities of the Merovingian period were more than relics of imperial rule. They were also the centers of Christianity. Christianity was one of the principal legacies of the Roman Empire in the West, and it was not accidental that it was centered in the old Roman cities. Missionaries had started from Rome to what is now France as early as the second century, though initially many of them were murdered by the local pagans. Nevertheless, the faith they brought ultimately prevailed over the hodge-podge of pagan beliefs in most cities. Between the third and the fifth centuries, essentially all the French, English, and Spanish cities got their own bishops (Italy had had its own bishops slightly earlier, and Germany was not yet Christianized).

Each bishop was assigned to a *pagus*, the basic unit of Roman provincial administration. That is, just as the Roman civil government had an administrator for each *pagus*, often a man from a senatorial family settled in the region, the church had a bishop. The city was the bishop's cathedral city, and the surrounding territory his diocese. Originally the bishops had to share this territory with the civil administrators. The administrators held court at the center of town, which usually meant on a hilltop, whereas the bishops were usually relegated to a church at the edge of town, perhaps one built on the spot where an early Christian missionary had been murdered. But once Roman provincial administration collapsed, and the civil administrators lost their connection to Rome, the bishops moved into the center of town, taking over the administrative palaces, building their cathedrals on the highest points in their cities.

Within their cities, bishops of Merovingian times often had conflicts with the counts, who also considered these *their* cities. Although the civil administrators disappeared, they were replaced with counts, as discussed above, and the boundaries of the counties and the boundaries of the bishops' dioceses were the same. At first glance, it might appear that the bishops represented the old Gallo-Roman families of imperial times and the counts the Germanic peoples who had invaded the Empire, because often the bishop had a Gallo-Roman name and the count a Germanic name. However, one cannot make too much of this distinction. In many cases the bishop and the count who both claimed control of the same city were cousins or even brothers. It just seemed appropriate to families sending a son into the church, a Roman institution, to give him a Roman name.

Although the local churches took over the Roman provincial administrative structure, it should be noted that their orientation toward Rome was not the same as the dependency of Catholic churches on the pope in the twentieth century. The bishop of Rome, the man who later became known as the pope, was certainly more important than most bishops, but he was first among equals, not an absolute master. Indeed, as noted in Chapter 3, the bishop of Rome was originally only one of five patriarchs, the five bishops of the five most important Christian cities, Jerusalem, Antioch, Alexandria, Constantinople, and Rome. Heresies and different religious interpretation often divided these five. Even after the first three cities were taken over by the Muslims in the seventh century, the pope in Rome and the patriarch in Constantinople had major differences of opinion. In western Europe, in the area supposedly under the spiritual guidance of the bishop of Rome, wars and heresies threatened constantly. With communication poor, and most popes more concerned about survival than with what the provinces were doing, the bishops of the west essentially ran the church. New bishops were elected locally, not appointed by Rome (the pope in fact only started appointing bishops in the thirteenth century), and made decisions on spiritual matters jointly, meeting in regional councils, rather than by writing to Rome.

FOUR
The End of the
Roman Empire and
the Beginning of the
Middle Ages

Originally the Christianity of the western bishops was Greek. The liturgy and the Bible itself were only available in Greek, since Christianity had come out of the eastern Mediterranean, where the language of literature and culture *was* Greek. This had not posed a problem in the early days of the Roman church, because all educated Romans knew Greek as well as Latin. But it increasingly became a problem in the later days of the Empire, when the Greek east, centered at Constantinople, drew away from the Latin-speaking west. When Saint Jerome translated the Bible from Greek into Latin, a massive task he was still finishing at his death in the early fifth century, the Latin-speaking west quickly abandoned the Greek liturgy. Latin became the language of western Christianity and remained so for Roman Catholicism until the middle of the twentieth century.

One of the major responsibilities of the bishops was to convert the people of their dioceses to Christianity. While the Empire was still flourishing, in the early fourth century, most of the educated urban population adopted Christianity (at least officially), following the imperial lead. It was indeed a wise career move to profess Christianity when the emperor had done so. Pagan practices, however, continued to flourish in the countryside for several centuries. (Indeed, the very word "pagan" is drawn from the Latin word *pagus*, meaning "countryside," as mentioned previously.) Although there are very few written records of the pagan religion practiced by the Celts of Gaul, and most of those were written by Christians, it does seem clear that it was a religion centered not on temples so much as on holy trees or fountains. There were some gods and goddesses worshiped in many places, such as Epona, the horse-goddess, but for the most part deities were local, attached to a particular stream or tree. People brought offerings, such as small statues, to the shrines. The spring that is the source of the river Seine, for example, has yielded a great many wooden statues, as well as carvings representing various body parts. Apparently people who were suffering an injury in some part of the body, for example the leg, would throw a representation of the leg into the stream as an offering while asking for help from the goddess.

As well as trying to obliterate the pagan religion of the native Celtic people, the bishops also had to try to obliterate the Roman pagan religion. This initially proved extremely difficult, because, as noted in Chapter 3, adherence to the Roman political system and adherence to the Roman state religion were the same thing. Many early bishops in the west were in fact martyred by the local governors. However, once the emperor Constantine officially tolerated Christianity within the Empire in the early fourth century, the bishops' task became much easier. They tore down the pagan statues in the Roman temples and rededicated the temples to Christian saints.

As a practical aspect of their work of conversion, the bishops found it easiest, rather than just forbidding religion at the old sites, to co-opt them for Christianity. The Romans before them had done something quite similar, in erecting temples to the Roman gods over the springs

This Frankish casket, c. 700, combines both pagan (Weland the Smith, Egil the Archer, Romulus and Remus, and the death of Sigurd) and Christian (the Three Magi, Jerusalem) themes. Small in size and made of whalebone ivory, it was used as a reliquary.

which had been holy to Celtic gods and goddesses. Thus the bishops cut down holy trees and knocked down Roman statues, but also tried to persuade people that they had actually been worshiping God and His saints all along, but had just not known it, and were doing it in the wrong way. Springs of various goddesses were rededicated to Mary; even today, a number of churches to Notre-Dame in France still have holy springs in the basement where Celtic goddesses were once worshiped.

In addition to converting the Gallo-Romans, once the Germanic tribes began settling in the Empire, the Christian bishops had to try to convert *them.* In some ways these were even harder men to convert than the Romans, for although the Romans had identified their gods with patriotism, they often did not have a close emotional tie to these rather distant gods. The Germans on the other hand were intensely religious, moving in a world that they saw as populated thickly with gods and demons. The Merovingian kings themselves, long after they became Christian, were proud of being the descendants of a sea god or sea monster.

The bishops of the fourth through seventh centuries were thus faced with the necessity of trying to convert several different sets of pagans. They usually tried to convert the leaders first, in the hope that their followers would convert as well. For example, when Clovis, first Merovingian king of what is now France, decided to become a Christian at the end of the fifth century (according to legend, after the miraculous appearance of a cross under circumstances that have suspicious parallels with Constantine's conversion), the rest of the Frankish warriors were all baptized *en masse.* They cannot have understood much of the religion

FOUR
*The End of the
Roman Empire and
the Beginning of the
Middle Ages*

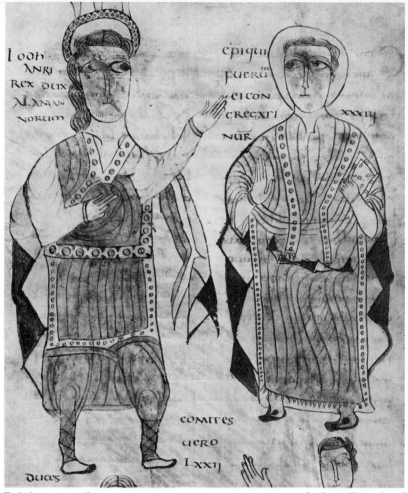

Eighth-century illustrations accompanying the manuscript of Alaric II's code of law show aristocratic Frankish clothing. Alaric is depicted in the figure at upper right, a clergyman at upper left.

they now adopted, but the bishops thought it better to try to teach Christianity to people who were formally converts, and at least were no longer opposed to the very idea of Christianity. From the point of view of the kings, being Christian meant that they could work much more effectively with the bishops, the main link with Gallo-Roman institutions.

One of the most effective tools for conversion that the early medieval bishops had, the same argument that often proved decisive in the late Empire, was that Christian saints and Christian relics could heal the sick. In the unhealthy early medieval period, the power to heal was an important one indeed. Sixth-century bishops kept careful records of the people who came to Christian shrines, the diseases they had, and how they were healed. One of the principal curative agents was considered to be the dust from a saint's tomb, which a sick person would either imbibe or have sprinkled on him. If a saint was popular, dust would be swept off his tomb as soon as it collected, and if there was not enough more could be generated by scraping at the stone sarcophagus in which most people in Merovingian times were buried. At the most highly regarded shrines, the sarcophagi developed holes from the constant dust gathering and scraping. The saints also had power to sicken as well as heal, to strike with boils, for example, someone who was making bread on Sunday rather than praying. With the help of powerful saints like these, the bishops gradually pushed at least some version of Christianity onto the men and women of their dioceses.

The Foundations of Monasticism

Although the bishops thought of themselves as the spiritual leaders of their dioceses, they often encountered opposition from the monasteries. Monasticism, like episcopal administration, came out of the Roman empire, but it was always a form of the religious life somewhat independent of the bishops. It had begun in Egypt in the third century and quickly spread throughout the Empire.

The growing toleration that Christianity was accorded in the third century, even before its official recognition in the fourth century, meant that in many areas it became relatively easy to be a Christian. In Egypt, for example, Christians could follow their religious practices quite openly, without fear of persecution, and could essentially live as ordinary Roman citizens, even if they did receive communion on Sundays. As mentioned in Chapter 3, because a great many early converts were only converted in the sense of agreeing that the Christian God seemed more powerful than His rivals, such conversion did not really change their ordinary lives at all. Of course, even without persecution, early Christianity was not an "easy" religion, at least not to those who tried to understand and think about its message. Once one was baptized, which wiped away one's previous sins, one was supposed not to sin again, because one could not be rebaptized. The only way in the early church to rid oneself of the stain of later sins was to undergo "major penance," in which one confessed all one's sins in public and then spent the rest of one's life in absolute celibacy and humble living.

The danger, however, was that those who did not actually commit any serious sins could become complacent, calling themselves Christians but living essentially the same sort of life as their pagan neighbors. But Christianity is not well designed to be only a religion on Sundays. For two thousand years, it has repeatedly been threatened with becoming little more in many communities than a set of rote ceremonies, but it has always undergone some sort of upheaval that has prevented anything of the kind from becoming permanent or general. The words of Jesus in the New Testament are too direct and radical a challenge to allow long-term complacency. In the third century, the threat of complacency was met by the rise of monasticism.

Monasticism is a general term for the institutionalized way of life followed by monks. In the early Christian world, these were originally men, but in short order women also sought to live a holy life by withdrawing both from the pleasures and from the cares of the ordinary world, to devote themselves to prayer and contemplation. The word "monk" is from the Latin *monachus*, meaning "someone who lives alone" (the Latin is from the Greek, as are all words describing institutions and functions of the early church).

Monks always adopted some sort of austere and difficult life. There had been ascetic religious movements among the ancient Hebrews, of which the best-known group is the Essenes, who were actually contemporaries of Jesus, living in caves along the Dead Sea. Their copies of certain books of the Old Testament, the Dead Sea Scrolls, were rediscovered after World War II and are the oldest copies of these books which we have. (Jesus, who ate and drank with his friends and went to banquets, was certainly not an Essene, but John the Baptist, described in the New Testament as wearing animal skins for clothes and living on grasshoppers, might have been.) But the development of Christian monasticism owed nothing institutionally to earlier ascetic movements, even if the impulse to find holiness in retreat from the world was similar.

Christian monasticism had its beginning in the third century with a man named Antony (251–356; he lived to be 105). When he was twenty, this son of well-to-do Egyptian parents heard a priest reading a passage from the Bible in which Jesus says to a rich young man, "If thou wilt be perfect, go and sell that thou hast, and give to the poor . . . and come and follow me" (Matthew 19:21). Without further ado, Antony set off to do precisely that. He became a hermit, a man living alone in the desert away from the Nile, spending his days in prayer, eating and drinking a bare minimum. His solitude was soon broken, however, because other people began to flock to his cave, to seek his wisdom. Before long he became the head of a small community of hermits.

This mode of holy life soon spread with the formation of other such communities, and monks and hermits became an important feature of Christianity. The fourth and early fifth centuries were a golden age for monks in the Egyptian desert. Centuries later, monks read the accounts of the Egyptian life and hoped to try to recreate it wherever they were. The cities of Egypt, which was then a part of the Roman Empire, provided plenty of potential converts, and the short distance between the civilized Nile valley and the dry reaches on either side made it easy for the would-be hermit to reach uninhabited territory. The warm climate made it possible to live year-round in caves or rough shelters. The desert quickly took on almost the aspect of suburban sprawl, with hundreds and thousands of monks settling in Egypt, and enterprising innkeepers setting up nearby to serve the fashionable tourists, who soon considered a stop to see the hermits a must on any tour.

There were two major forms of monasticism in Egypt, and these two forms continued in later centuries. One form was that of the hermits, who lived essentially alone, and the other was a community life, consisting of men who lived like brothers. The latter are usually known now as monks, to distinguish them from the hermits. The distinctions were not absolute. Many hermits, although living in individual cells, still met on a regular basis for services. In the communities, the brothers lived essentially like a family, and their leader, the abbot, was their spiritual father (the word "abbot" comes from the Aramaic word *abba*, meaning "father"). Whatever their form of community, their principal daily activities were praying and reading the Bible. Both hermits and monks ate bread supplemented with vegetables from garden patches behind their cells. When not praying, they were occupied with simple crafts like weaving mats and baskets or spinning linen. They sold these to tourists and used the money to buy such things as fish and cheese, but they felt it would be too much of a luxury to eat red meat. Some of the communities were large and well-organized enough to be able to sell their crafts on a regular basis to Alexandria.

Monasticism spread out of Egypt during the fourth century. It was enthusiastically adopted in Palestine and Syria, where many of the monks adopted lives of severe harshness to drive sin from their bodies. They tried to outdo each other with the severity of their self-imposed punishments. Simeon the Stylite, for example, lived for thirty years, during the first half of the fifth century, on top of a pillar without coming down.

With the spread of monasticism, it became clear that it would be necessary to have rules for the monastic life. A community that was well run under a revered abbot would want to perpetuate their way of life in written institutes, which both later generations and other monastic communities would be able to copy. For the first several centuries of monasticism, monastic rules proliferated, as many abbots throughout the Empire wrote down their particular versions. Different ones tended to be more popular in different areas, but the church hierarchy made no attempt to favor any particular ones.

Monasticism in Western Europe

By the late classical period, then, monasticism had developed its principal features, but it continued to change and develop during the Merovingian period. Monasticism reached Gaul at the end of the fourth century with Saint Martin, originally a soldier in the imperial army. According to legend, he decided to devote his life to Christianity after he divided his cloak on a frosty night with a freezing beggar, who turned out to be Christ in disguise. (Martin's cloak became a powerful relic for later French kings.) In the fifth through early eighth centuries, a great many monasteries were founded in the west. Many were very small communities, founded in the churches which had been built on the graves of early Christian martyrs. These were just outside the city walls, in what had once been Gallo-Roman graveyards.

The churches were usually dedicated to local saints—for example,

FOUR
*The End of the
Roman Empire and
the Beginning of the
Middle Ages*

The church of St. Pierre-aux-Nonnains, in Metz, considered the oldest church in France, was a Merovingian monastery, founded in the seventh century. It was built on the site of a fourth-century Roman basilica.

Symphorien, Valerian, Ferreolus, and the like. They were small, rectangular structures, very simple and built of unfinished stone; the cathedrals of the time were scarcely bigger. But the simplicity of architecture did not mean a sterile church, for the interiors were highly decorated with silk hangings in bright colors and frescoes on the walls, representing lives of the saints or scenes from the Bible. Such frescoes were supposed to convey Christian stories to those who could not read. The building itself was only in effect the scaffolding on which elegant decorations were hung—decorations which, in their magnificence, were supposed to draw the mind toward paradise.

It is interesting to note that the monks built their churches on top of old graves, for this indicates one of the important changes that Christianity brought about in attitudes toward the dead. The Romans had feared dead bodies, as sources of ghosts and malevolence, which is why their cemeteries were always outside of town. To Christians, however, the dead were not malicious ghosts but friends, even saints, who had God's ear and had real power on earth to help those who paid them reverence. Saints who healed the sick were certainly not in the same category as Roman ghosts. Christians therefore built their churches in the graveyards where those whom the Romans and Gallo-Romans had martyred were buried, and they put the bones of these martyrs in jeweled reliquary boxes and into the altars. Whereas the Romans had prayed *to* dead ancestors (once they were safely cremated so they could not come back as ghosts), the Christians prayed *for* their dead relatives. They could be friends to the dead, just as the dead were friends to them.

The bishops, who had taken over the centers of town by this point, usually named their cathedrals for Roman rather than local saints, such as Saints Peter or Paul. Saint Stephen, described in the New Testament as the first Christian martyr, was very popular in France. The bishop thus identified his church and his rule not just with local Christian events, as did the monasteries, but with the organized structure of the church. The monasteries therefore had an immediacy to their saints, whose bodies were buried in their churches, which the bishops lacked, even though most bishops tried to obtain some relics from Rome. The bishops, on the other hand, always claimed that *their* saints were more powerful.

The squabbling over who had the most effective saints was a symptom of a conflict of spiritual authority between bishops and monasteries which was not satisfactorily resolved during the Middle Ages. The bishops felt that, as the chief Christian officers of their diocese, they were directly responsible for overseeing the morals and orthodoxy of the monks. The monks, on the other hand, who had adopted the life they had because they believed it was holy, felt that the bishops, who did *not* lead such a life, should have no right to judge them. It was quite common, for example, for bishops to have wives as late as the sixth century, a practice generally accepted by most Christians but not by the monks, who themselves followed lives of strict celibacy. The bishops claimed that their authority was the institutional continuation of the authority Jesus had given the apostles; the monks on the contrary claimed that they, and only they, were following the life of the apostles and thus had much more real spiritual authority than the bishops.

The forms monasticism took in the Merovingian period were many and various. There were three or four main rules in circulation, and every monastery adopted one or parts of several, or even created its own. Whatever rules they followed, most of the monasteries were similar in expressing a strong streak of asceticism and self-denial. This asceticism also was found among many well-to-do people of the early medieval centuries.

There were hermits in the early Middle Ages, greatly admired, who gave up every physical comfort. One hermit of the sixth century, for example, set out to imitate Simeon the Stylite (mentioned previously) by living year-round on a pillar, something much harder to do in wintry Gaul than in the warm climate of Syria. A contemporary description says that his toenails froze and dropped off "not once but several times." (The local bishop, deciding that this was showing off rather than the expression of humility, lured the hermit off his pillar and had it chopped down, to the hermit's bitter disappointment.) Numerous stories were told of young noble women who decided to devote themselves to Christ and therefore fled from home when their families tried to marry them off. The motif of concealing themselves in a cave or tree, often relying on

130

FOUR
*The End of the
Roman Empire and
the Beginning of the
Middle Ages*

the guidance and counsel of an old and holy hermit, was a common one. Such women often used their considerable wealth to establish nunneries, where unmarried women would find an alternative to marrying whomever their parents picked out. The nunneries also became charitable institutions, giving away food on a daily basis to the beggars at their gates. Many of the nunneries of the early Middle Ages were actually parts of double monasteries, where men in one cloister and women in a separate but adjoining cloister, usually both halves under the rule of a single abbess, sought holiness by leading lives of deliberate harshness.

Although the strict asceticism of the period might be interpreted as a hatred of the body, it is better to see it as an attempt to gain control of the body. When one's family treated one as a pawn in the marriage market, it was hard to have any say over one's physical being. Running away from home, swearing to live and die a virgin, reestablished that control. One might say then that many people of the Merovingian period, both hermits and the girls who defied their families, were not turning against their bodies so much as trying to reintegrate their physical and moral selves. Christianity taught that body and soul would be saved and resurrected together, and by subjecting their bodies to the same discipline to which they subjected their minds, the late Roman and Merovingian ascetics hoped to prepare themselves for salvation. It was at this time that the ideal of an unmarried clergy became firmly established in the West.

Eighth-century drawing of St. Benedict giving his Rule to monks. He is sitting within a depiction of an abbey church.

While in the fifth and sixth centuries there was an enormous number of monastic rules in circulation, in the West, by the late seventh century, the prevailing form had become Benedictine monasticism. (In the Greek East, there continued to be a great variety of forms.) Benedict, abbot of Montecassino in Italy, originally composed a rule for his monks in the first half of the sixth century, the Benedictine Rule. This rule was intended only for Montecassino, but it soon began to be copied and adopted at many other monasteries. The real surge in its popularity came around the year 600, when Pope Gregory I wrote a highly laudatory "Life" of Saint Benedict. Benedict's rule was unique among monastic rules of its time in its practicality and flexibility, and in its combination of spiritual rigor with physical moderation. It described the ideal of a small group of monks living in harmony, like a family, under the fatherly direction of the abbot, rather than having the brothers engaged in a rivalry for individual mortification and holiness.

The Benedictine Rule, which set up standards for a self-contained monastery, was also especially suited for the rapid ruralization of society. The monks of a typical sixth- or seventh-century house were self-sufficient, producing their food in their own grain fields, orchards, and vegetable patches. Most of the work in the fields was done by tenant farmers, and some by the monks themselves. Necessary crafts, such as weaving, shoemaking, and toolmaking, were also carried out within the monastery. The monks did not need to sell or to buy anything. As many western cities had shrunk to a thousand people at most, even "urban" monasteries did not have an urban civilization on which to draw. Monasteries became charity centers; the poor flocked to them as in the twentieth century they have flocked to the cities. Most monasteries set aside a certain amount of food and often clothing and firewood for the poor they knew they would find on their doorstep every day.

Monasteries soon assumed a vital role in the preservation and transmission of Western civilization. Although monasticism in its early days had been a retreat from the political and social hum of civilization, during much of the early Middle Ages the monasteries were isolated islands where the learning and culture of Roman civilization were kept alive in memory, copied in the books the monks produced, while all around them that civilization disappeared. Monasteries remained oases of stability while kingdoms were formed and broken up, Gallo-Roman and Frankish landowners came and went, and the glories of Rome seemed more and more distant.

The monastery of the sixth and early seventh centuries, idealized in Benedict's rule, was able to survive and even flourish, but it also changed in subsequent centuries. Some houses continued to be small, but others grew rapidly and became important economic forces. While the nucleus remained the same, a family of monks living under an abbot as a self-sufficient economic community, by the late seventh century many monasteries had become larger, wealthier, and more powerful than anything that Benedict would have imagined.

In the late seventh or eighth century a monastery might be a large complex, with dozens of monks, and a collection of buildings that made it almost a miniature civic center: dormitories, an eating hall (refectory), workshops, guest houses, a hospital, offices for the administration of the estates, schools for the boys who would grow up to be monks, even courts for hearing civil and criminal lawsuits among the abbey's tenants. The monastery generally had a large church, which served the tenants as well as the monks themselves, and was often visited by pilgrims. It became a storehouse of relics and works of art, paid for by gifts from powerful laymen. The monks of such a monastery spent an increasing part of their day in the performance of the liturgy, praying not just for themselves but for society as a whole, especially for their noble donors. Such monks performed very little manual labor on their estates themselves, leaving that to their tenants. Their "work" consisted primarily of labor in the scriptorium (a special room for writing), where they copied books and occasionally did a little original writing.

The Development of Manorialism

The monks with their tenant farmers constituted an economic unit, with the monks acting as landlords. This sort of landlord–tenant relationship became very common during the Middle Ages. The system is now known as manorialism, with the basic unit, the manor, consisting of land owned by the landlord and rented or let out to tenants or serfs. A manor typically also included some land that the lord did not rent out but kept for himself, called the "demesne." The demesne land was worked in part by the lord's tenants, during the time they were not working their own land, and in the early Middle Ages also by his household slaves.

Manorialism was far from universal; probably the majority of peasants worked their small plots of land either on their own or in villages made up only of other peasants, with no landlord over them. But manors, from their size and their ability to concentrate resources, tended to take the lead, both economically and in the spread of new farming techniques. Although it is important not to see manorialism as a fixed system—every manor was different, and the structure changed markedly over the course of the Middle Ages—it is a system uniquely medieval, different from anything seen in classical antiquity.

Rome had been a slave society, and although there had always been plenty of free peasants working their own lands, the big estates were worked by slaves. These estates, where grain had been grown for the urban markets, were worked by gangs of slaves whose social position and lives were rather similar to those of the slaves who worked on the plantations in the American South before the Civil War. These estates were known as "latifundia." But the latifundia disappeared by the end of the sixth century. The manors which replaced them were different in several ways. Perhaps most importantly, a manor grew food primarily for the people who lived on it, not for the urban markets, which no longer existed. The landlord was in many cases much closer to his land and to the work on his land than the wealthy city man who had owned vast latifundia had ever been. And, perhaps most strikingly, the slaves who had worked the latifundia were gradually replaced during the early Middle Ages by serfs.

The difference between a slave and a serf is not an enormous one. The same Latin word, *servus*, was used for both, indicating that the people who lived at the time when serfs first appeared did not initially distinguish them from slaves. But there is a real and important difference between them, for while a slave is ultimately a piece of property, something which can be bought and sold, a serf cannot be sold, even if he cannot get out of the obligations he is born into. A serf is a person with servile obligations, but he is a person nonetheless, not an animal or object. In the same way, a serf may have very heavy burdens weighing on him, dues he has to pay, services he has to perform, but he is not subject to his lord's *arbitrary* will. That is, a slave has to do whatever he is commanded, whereas a serf knows there are some limits on what may be commanded. His obligations are set, and cannot be increased by the lord.

The most visible difference between the serfs of the early medieval manors and the slaves who worked the latifundia is that serfs had their own houses, their own families, and, for the most part, determined for themselves how they would spend their days. The transition from slavery to serfdom on the great estates must have been a gradual process, and since it happened during the fifth through seventh centuries, a period in which there are very few existing documents, the precise process cannot be known, but it is fairly clear that one of the chief causes was economic.

As long as slaves were cheap and easily available, it had made sense to work them until they dropped, producing large crops for market. But once the markets dried up, and the worsening of the climate made it harder to get any large crops in at all, there was less gain to be made in driving the slaves. Since slaves have to be fed, they would indeed become proportionately more expensive to keep, once their labor was no longer producing large cash crops. They also became more valuable and harder to replace once the Roman legions were no longer making conquest after conquest, bringing back the conquered peoples as slaves.

At this point it seems to have made sense to many landlords to divide up what had been enormous fields among the different slaves, giving each his land in return for rents and dues, and encouraging him to marry and raise a family. Slaves who are worked in gangs and kept for the night chained in cells will, naturally, not tend to have families, but slaves given their own houses will, thus producing the next generation of slaves without the lord having to go out and buy them. Slaves working their own fields and raising their own food feed themselves, thus relieving the lord of the necessity of buying them food, or for that matter of hiring overseers to watch them and keep them working. Men will always work much harder for themselves than they will for a slavemaster. Economic considerations then made it practical for the great landlords to turn the latifundia, which had been worked by slaves, into manors worked by serfs.

FOUR
*The End of the
Roman Empire and
the Beginning of the
Middle Ages*

Several other factors besides economics also encouraged the dying out of slavery. One was a concern, which many landlords felt, that their slaves would revolt if they did not make them concessions. There had always been scattered slave revolts during the Roman Empire, but the imperial machinery had crushed them so quickly and so thoroughly that they never had a chance to spread. But without the Roman armies ready to march in and take charge, landlords feared that there was no way they could stop a revolt if it started. Another contributing factor was the spread of Christianity. Although Christianity did not actually forbid slavery, it did make it clear that it was a sin to enslave someone who was a Christian and was not already a slave; the spread of Christianity made many potential slaves unsuitable, therefore, if a landlord was trying to replace his. Christianity also preached that it was virtuous to free one's slaves; once freed, they could not be reenslaved, although they could be charged steep rents. Also, during the plagues and upheavals of the sixth century, many slaves just ran away. Some areas became underpopulated, and landlords, desperate for anyone to work their fields, were willing to take on runaway slaves without putting any of the more severe burdens of slavery upon them.

By the middle of the seventh century, then, most work in the fields was being done by serfs, rather than slaves. These serfs were described as being bound by servitude, which meant that they were born with obligations. They were servile "in their bodies," and they would pass their servile status and obligations to their children. The lord who owned the land they worked was not just their landlord but their "lord of the body." In return for their land, the serfs owed their lord rent, usually paid as a combination of money and food (a certain number of bushels of wheat, for example). This rent was fixed and was not a percentage of the crop. This meant that in good years a serf would find it very easy to pay his rent, but in bad years he might have to stint his own family. In addition, on most manors the serfs owed a certain number of "work days." These were the number of days a week that the serf was obligated to work on the lord's demesne land, the land where the lord grew the food for his own use. Typically a serf would have to work one or two days a week on the demesne; the lord spread out the obligations of his different serfs so that there was always someone there. The lord then lived both from the rents he received and from the produce of his demesne lands.

In addition to rents and labor dues, there were several specifically "servile dues" which serfs of the Middle Ages were forced to pay. These were not particularly important economically but were very important psychologically because they symbolized the serf's personal dependence. The most important of these was the head tax, in which the peasant had to come before the lord on his knees, sometimes even with a rope around his neck, and with a penny on his head. This indicated the absolute subservience of the serf and was considered degrading. Many lords placed restrictions on inheritance and choice of marriage partner by their serfs. (In our time romantic novels would lead one to believe that a lord had the right to the virginity of all his female serfs, but this is untrue, being something created by an overexcited mind in the nineteenth century.)

Another key distinction between slavery and serfdom is that, under serfdom, both lord and peasant had obligations to each other. While a serf owed his lord a lot, the lord also owed a lot to his serf. The personal nature of the relationship made it clear that the responsibilities were reciprocal. Above all, a lord owed his serf protection from the wars and invasions sweeping across Europe. Serfs could also demand protection from starvation. If the crops failed, they could throw themselves on their lords' mercy. Of course, since whatever caused peasants' crops to fail often caused the crops to fail on the lord's demesne land at the same time, this might have no practical result—crop failures and famines were a constant feature of the sixth and seventh centuries.

The prevalence of serfs should not hide the fact that there continued to be both real slaves and free peasant workers in the early Middle Ages. By the seventh or eighth century, most of the slaves were household slaves, living with their masters, doing household chores for them. Many lords had their household slaves do much of the work on the demesne, coming back to the house at night. Even serfs could own slaves. Within the household, one of the chief duties for a slave had been, in the time of the Empire, the daily grinding of grain into flour. Women slaves had typically spent much of the day grinding the grain in hand mills. Although the water mill seems to have been discovered by the first century B.C., the Romans did not use it very much, preferring to use human labor instead. But with the decrease in the population in the sixth century, men had to find more energy-efficient ways to do many chores, and the water mill spread rapidly between the sixth and eighth centuries. Its spread made it possible for someone to take a sack of grain down to the mill and come back with a sack of flour, enough to last his family for a long time. Thus keeping and feeding slaves just to work the handmills was no longer necessary. By the ninth century, household slaves had become much less common than they had been earlier.

In the meantime, there were also free peasants. Some of them lived on their own, or in small villages with other peasants, far away from the great lords, but many of them also lived on or at the edges of the manors. There was no obvious way to distinguish, at first glance, a serf from his neighbor who might be free, although the free man was always intensely proud of his freedom. These free men often rented at least some of their land from the lord. Like the serfs, they owed a combination of rents and labor dues, but their rents were almost always lighter, and the lord was only their landlord (in the same sense that anyone today who rents has a landlord), not a personal lord or lord of the body.

Some free men had always been free; others were serfs who had been freed by their masters. Free men could become serfs; someone who was hungry and desperate might "commend" himself to a lord, agreeing to become his serf, in return for a house and land on which to raise food. Someone who was a serf might also rent additional land from a landlord other than his personal lord, paying the same sorts of rent for it a free man would pay. These variations in status and position were all the more confusing because they were preserved almost entirely in memory, rather than written form; the serfs and peasants could not read or write, and, unless the landlord of a manor was a monastery, the lord could not write either. Memory, however, was a powerful tool; lords were not likely to forget what was owed to them, and a serf's neighbors, who did not want him unfairly trying to get out of what they themselves owed, helped keep him honest.

The diet of peasants, whether serf or free, was based on grain, as had been the case for the Romans. The Germanic invaders of the Empire had practiced more pastoralism than had the Romans; the milk, cheese, and butter from their cows were the main supplement to the basic diet of bread or porridge. Whereas the Germanic people had drunk beer as their principal beverage, the lords started drinking wine as soon as they came in contact with the Romans. This meant that every manor had to have vineyards, as well as its grain fields. In some areas in the north, the climate was really not suitable for wine grapes, but the fashionableness of this drink, along with the church's requirement of wine for the liturgy, meant that viticulture spread from the Mediterranean across much of the west.

England in the Period of the Historical Arthur

The above discussion has especially focused on the areas where Roman and Germanic society were fairly smoothly integrated, in Italy, Gaul, and Spain. But in Britain, Roman society was essentially eradicated. Julius Caesar had first landed in Britain in 55 B.C., and, all during the first four centuries A.D., Britain had shared in the general culture of the Continent. The names of British towns were found frequently on Roman maps and in their roadbooks; Roman coins found their way into Britain in large numbers; and the Romanized population built baths and villas on Roman models. Many old Iron Age hill forts were rebuilt as Roman fortified camps. This was the era of Hadrian's Wall, when the Roman legions built and were able to defend a wall across the entire width of northern England, to keep the non-Romanized population back. Remains of this wall, which was built of stone and was fifteen feet high and eight or ten feet thick, still survive today. But Rome's part in England's culture ceased with the Germanic invasions.

The Romans had never been as well established in Britain as they had been on the Continent, and the native Celtic population was overwhelmed in the fifth century by the invasions of the Angles and Saxons. These Germanic tribes, who came across the North Sea to settle in England under the direction of their semilegendary leaders, Hengest and Horsa, drove the Romanized Celts out of central Britain. The Celts fled to the mountain regions on the fringes where the population is still largely Celtic even today: Wales, Scotland, and Ireland. The remnants of Christianity in the British Isles held on only among some of these Celtic people. In the center and eastern parts of Britain, or England as it was soon called (for the Angles), the Germanic invaders soon obliterated both Christianity and Latin.

This is the period of the "historical" Arthur, the man who became one of the major legends of the Middle Ages. The stories told about him later contained an enormous number of elements (like the "chivalry of the round table") that were not originally part of the story, or that were originally separate stories (like the story of Lancelot and Guinevere), only grafted onto Arthur in the twelfth century. But the basic story, of a king fighting desperately to protect his civilization against the onrushing hordes of barbarians, seems based on a British (that is, Celtic) general. He had been thoroughly Romanized and strove with great courage, though only temporary success, to withstand the Angles and Saxons. This "real" Arthur has been debated at great length by modern scholars, and probably always will be, but it seems fairly clear that Arthur fought a great battle at Mount Badon, in the southwest of England, at the end of the fifth century and was buried when he died at Glastonbury, in Somerset. Somerset is one of the warmer parts of England, and Glastonbury is on a solid piece of ground rising out of marshy countryside, and these details seem to have become in later legend the story of Arthur's burial in the "island" of Avallon, "where it is always summer."

When Britain fell almost entirely under the rule of the Anglo-Saxons, the memory of Arthur, the last man to withstand them, lingered on in Celtic memory. In the twelfth century, these stories from Wales emerged again, in very different form but with all their magic and power intact and indeed enhanced. The monks of Glastonbury dug up a skeleton they identified as Arthur's in 1191 (it may indeed have been his), and they had good reason to anticipate that this discovery would make their rather out-of-the-way monastery a pilgrimage site, as no discovery of a saint's bones would have done. Arthur's bones were on display from the end of the twelfth century until the English Reformation of the sixteenth century, when, together with the relics of Catholic saints the English were rejecting, they were broken up and scattered.

Although in the decades after Arthur the Anglo-Saxons were able to take complete control of most of what is now England, replacing Roman Christianity with their pagan religions, England was Christianized again starting just before the year 600. Missionaries came to England both from Rome and from the Celtic parts of Britain which had never fallen under the Anglo-Saxons. The fringes of the British Isles had been the last to be Christianized, originally by men going out from Romanized Britain, like Saint Patrick, who converted many of the kings of Ireland in the fifth century. In the sixth century Saint Columba came from Ireland to Scotland to reintroduce Christianity into Britain. Columba appears to have been a man of strong character, impressing even the ferocious, and he is also the first man recorded to have met the Loch Ness monster. According to an account written at the time, Columba reached the loch, wanted to cross, but had no boat. His servant saw a boat pulled up on the opposite bank and offered to swim across and get it. But as he was swimming "the monster who lives there," according to the account, "tried to attack him." The saint waded into the fray (the sixth-century monster seems to have been much less shy than the monster modern scientists are trying to photograph) and, by making the sign of the cross and commanding the monster to release his victim in Christ's name, was able to drive away the monster and save the faithful servant.

In the early seventh century, missionaries sent by the pope from Rome and missionaries sent out by Saint Patrick's and Saint Columba's successors met in England. The Celtic church had not been in contact with Rome for a good century and a half, since the coming of the Anglo-Saxons, and they had developed many practices different from the Roman church. For example, many monasteries in Ireland consisted of a king as abbot, with his family and court serving as "monks." The Celts celebrated Easter at a different time than did the Romans. The Celts yielded, however, when faced with the unanswerable argument that Saint Peter, who by now was considered to have been the first pope, was said in the Bible to hold the keys of heaven, whereas Saint Patrick did not have the keys to anything. By the end of the seventh century, the British Isles had reentered the Christian mainstream, after the lacuna caused by the Anglo-Saxon invasions. New monasteries were founded where Roman education was revived and the Latin classics were closely studied. It was from these Anglo-Saxon monasteries that classical learning was reintroduced to the Continent a century later, as discussed in the next chapter.

The Rise of Islam

Although the coming of the Germanic Anglo-Saxons made a sharp line of demarcation in Britain, the Germanic invasions were not nearly as clear a turning point in the rest of Europe. As noted above, the Germanic tribes, who crossed the borders into the Empire only gradually, did not replace the native Romanized population so much as become integrated with it. Many of the leaders of the Germanic tribes on the Continent had been men who had already served in the imperial army, and many settled down with some degree of imperial approval or recognition. In some ways the real break between the ancient and medieval worlds came not with the Germanic invasions but with the rise of Islam.

Islam, or the Muslim religion, was begun in the seventh century by an Arab named Mohammed. Like Jesus, he is a historical figure. We actually know his own ideas on religion more directly than we do those of Jesus because Mohammed wrote (or dictated) a great deal during his life. (Jesus's teachings were only recorded, from oral tradition, a generation or two after his death.) Mohammed's teachings, which were believed to have been dictated to him by the Angel Gabriel, were edited and organized by his pupils. These constitute the Koran, the Muslim holy book. Like Jesus, Mohammed took a good deal of inspiration from the Jewish Bible (the Christian Old Testament); Islam, Judaism, and Christianity constitute the three "religions of the Book." Mohammed emphasized obedience to the will of God (Allah) and stressed ethics and family and community responsibility. Charity to the poor was one of the five "pillars" upon which the religion was based; the others were the declaration that there is no god but Allah; daily prayer; annual fasting; and, if possible, a pilgrimage to Mecca once in one's life. Mohammed believed that Jesus had a great many insights into the nature of God, but he treated him as a prophet, not as the Son of God as did the Christians. Mohammed himself refused to accept any suggestions that *he* was divine, being only the last of the prophets (or, as he was later known to his followers, "The Prophet").

At the time of Mohammed, Arabia was (as it still is now) an arid country, a wedge between the fertile areas of Egypt and Mesopotamia. It had never, except for its very northern parts around the Sinai Peninsula, fallen under the domination of Rome. The people of Arabia were primarily bedouins, moving with their flocks from one oasis to the next. Although they had very few towns, they still had some of the attributes of civilization. They admired education and honored their poets. They had a complex knowledge of astronomy, perhaps not surprisingly, since stars can be observed very well in the clear desert air, away from the cities. Many of the names for stars that we still use are their Arabic names. The Arabs had their own alphabet and literature, as well as having an acquaintance with some of the culture of the Hellenistic world. The nomadic life tended to make the Arabs very tough fighters, for only the strong could survive the harsh life of the desert, and the weak and sickly were generally killed. Before Mohammed, the Arabs were polytheistic, worshiping animistic nature-gods, the gods of the Greeks and Romans, and the Judeo-Christian God, without much discrimination between them. All the gods were worshiped at the city of Mecca, at the Kaaba or holy temple. Worshiping together at Mecca was a unifying force for the very independent tribes, and one Mohammed used.

Mohammed initially received a good deal of opposition when he argued that worship of the one true God, or Allah, required turning away from other gods and destruction of their idols. In fact, he had to flee from his native Mecca in 622, the year his followers later took as the beginning of the Muslim era. However, he quickly gained many supporters and converts in his new city of Medina and was able to return to Mecca within ten years. At this point, he destroyed all the idols of the Kaaba, making it the principal temple for the worship of Allah, as it has been ever since. The one element he left of the old polytheism was the "black stone" (perhaps a meteorite), which had been considered a sacred object since very ancient times, and which, according to Mohammed, had been placed in the Kaaba by Abraham as a symbol of God's power.

When Mohammed died in 632, much of Arabia had acknowledged him as their spiritual leader and accepted his teachings (in many cases, without more than a cursory idea of their content). Within a few years the Arabs, newly united, were beginning the conquest of their neighbors. This was called a *jihad*, or holy war, forcing the conquered people

FOUR
*The End of the
Roman Empire and
the Beginning of the
Middle Ages*

to accept both political and religious control from the Muslim Arabs. Egypt, Palestine, Syria, and Persia fell very quickly, for the weakened Roman emperors at Constantinople were not able to resist the armies of desert-hardened fighters. Their own sphere of control shrank to regions relatively close to their capital and never really expanded again.

An Arab empire, centered first at Mecca and then at Damascus, quickly took form, governed by caliphs who were both political and religious leaders, and with its own administrative system. By the middle of the eighth century, when the *jihad* had spread Islam throughout the Middle East, North Africa, and Spain, this Arab empire controlled a territory even greater than that once controlled by Rome. The Arabs incorporated much of the learning and culture of the areas they conquered into their own educational system. The science, philosophy, and literature of the Greeks, Persians, and Jews, and even philosophy from India, was translated into Arabic. When the West began to rediscover Greek learning in the twelfth and thirteenth centuries, as discussed in Chapter 8, it was primarily through translations from the Arabic.

This is because, by the twelfth century, the West was no longer directly in contact with the Greek culture that was still alive at Constantinople. By ending the old unity of the Mediterranean, as it had once existed under the Roman Empire, the spread of Islam marked a turning point for much of the old Roman civilization. Western Europe had already undergone many changes between the fifth and the seventh centuries, as noted previously, so the spread of Islam after 622 cannot really be considered a *cause* of the end of Roman culture. That the *jihad* was able to spread so far and so fast is indicative of how thoroughly the old Roman military and administrative system was gone. Constantine's successors in Byzantium might still call themselves Roman emperors, but the ease with which the Muslims conquered North Africa and parts of southern Europe indicates that the emperors had long lost the ability to maintain control of the Mediterranean, once the Empire's heart. As Constantinople saw the Muslims creeping closer to its gates virtually yearly, it had less and less attention to spare for the West. After the seventh century, northern and western Europe increasingly turned its focus to the north, away from the Mediterranean.

Christianity, which had once surrounded the Mediterranean, was now restricted to Europe and Byzantium. By converting or killing many of the Christians of the Near East or northern Africa, the rise of Islam actually simplified many of the disputes within Christianity by eliminating many of the disputants. The heresies of Donatism in north Africa, Manichaeism in the Near East, and Arianism in Spain disappeared when Christianity disappeared from those areas. There were no more major heresies within Roman Christianity until the late twelfth century. The absorption of the cities of Jerusalem, Antioch, and Alexandria under Muslim rule left only two of the original five patriarchs of Christianity, those of Rome and Constantinople. Christianity was thus further polarized into two camps, Latin Catholicism and Greek Orthodoxy, with neither willing to accept the other's version of religion. The differences between Latin and Greek Christianity were already sharp in the seventh and eighth centuries, and the final breach between them in 1054, not healed until the 1970s, only marked the end of a long period of disagreement.

In northern Europe, the Merovingian kings of the fifth and sixth century had presided over the slow disintegration of Roman culture. By the middle of the eighth century, the time that the Carolingians came to power, as discussed in the next chapter, the rise of Islam meant that the remains of Roman unity were gone, not just forgotten but destroyed. Rome itself remained, but only as a city and a symbol that both popes and emperors used in subsequent centuries. The Empire was no more, and in its place medieval Europe was being formed.

FIVE

THE CAROLINGIAN ERA

CHAPTER
FIVE

THE CAROLINGIAN ERA

THERE IS MUCH MORE known about the ninth and tenth centuries than there is about previous centuries. Although the documents from this period are also very scanty, it is at least possible to discover what the most powerful members of society were doing, and sometimes even ordinary people, whereas historians of the fifth through eighth centuries often have to put their information together from indirect clues.

The ninth century was also a time when central government and an organized educational system reappeared after a long absence. The period is usually referred to as the Carolingian period, named for the Carolingian kings and emperors who established kingdoms in what is now France and western Germany. (Charles the Great, or Charlemagne, was called *Carolus* in Latin, hence the word "Carolingian" for members of his family.) The improvement in education and material culture have even led some historians to use the term "Carolingian Renaissance" for this period, with "Renaissance" being used in the sense of a "rebirth" of learning.

It is important, however, not to push the idea of rebirth too far. The entire Carolingian era was a period of constant warfare between the Christian kingdoms of the west and the Germanic peoples who were still pagans, and also among the Christian kingdoms themselves. Civil war and invasions in the later ninth and tenth centuries led to a breakdown of the central government and the educational and religious systems that had so recently been revived. But the Carolingian era is a vital one for Western history. Throughout both the advances and the disasters of the time, it is clear that western Europe was no longer trying to creak along on dim memories of the Roman Empire; its own instrinsic civilization and culture were now being formed.

CHARLEMAGNE

Charlemagne, king of the Franks from 768 until his death in 814, conquered and ruled an area that covered much of western Europe. He was the second man in his family to be king. His father, Pippin, originally "mayor of the palace" for the Merovingian king (that is, he was his chief household official and did much of the running of the kingdom), deposed the last Merovingian, with the approval of the pope, and had himself made king instead in 751. Charlemagne, who succeeded him, was a tremendously active king who went to war nearly every year, creating a kingdom that included most of modern France, the western part of Germany, northern Italy, and northern Spain. In the year 800 the pope crowned him Roman emperor, the first emperor in the West for several centuries. Although there continued to be emperors in Constantinople who called *themselves* Roman emperors as well, Charlemagne's descendants and successors, with a few gaps, kept the title of emperor until World War I. Although Charlemagne's huge empire was divided up and fought over by his grandsons and great-grandsons, his age was looked back to by later kings as a glorious golden age.

Silver denarius of Charlemagne, showing him as a Roman emperor.

Economic Improvements of the Carolingian Period

The basis of all the advances (such as they were) of the Carolingian era was an improved agricultural economy. The evidence is scarce but real. The climate had once again begun warming up after the mini ice age of the sixth century. In some areas, organized efforts were made to drain and cultivate rich, marshy soil. Some areas produced enough agricultural surplus that trade in foodstuffs became relatively common, as it had not been when peasants felt lucky to grow enough to feed their own families and their immediate lords. This trade in food made it possible for there to be groups of people who did *not* grow their own food, but rather bought their food from others—that is, towns, royal courts, and monasteries. Carolingian towns were tiny even by the standards of two centuries later, but they were still bigger than any towns in the West had been for several centuries.

Long-distance trade, in such lightweight but highly valuable items as spices, silk, and saints' bones, began again after nearly disappearing. Much of this trade was with the Greek East, specifically Constantinople. Constantinople had three-quarters of a million people in Carolingian times, close to what ancient Rome had had, and was a different world than the predominantly rural West. People from France and Italy who had occasion to visit it came back stunned. It had never lost its urban civilization, as had the West, and its workshops churned out an enormous number of luxury goods, from the purple-dyed silks, which by law could not be exported, to jewelry and extremely ornate liturgical vessels. In the ninth century, men of the West began to trade again with Constantinople, as they had not for several centuries, but the West had little to offer except for raw materials. Iron and timber from Germany were exported, as were slaves, most of them Slavs from along the eastern frontier of Charlemagne's empire who were captured in battle (the modern word "slave" comes from "Slav"). By the high Middle Ages, however, as seen in Chapter 7, the most important Western export to Constantinople was wool.

In the ninth century, the West also established trading contacts with the Islamic caliphs of Baghdad. These trade routes were separate from the ones that traversed the Mediterranean to Constantinople; rather, those who traded with the Muslims took a more northern route, starting at the point that a web of commercial routes bound the Continent to Anglo-Saxon England and to Scandinavia. As well as crossing the North Sea and the Baltic Sea, trade routes, with heavy investments by the Carolingian kings, went from the lower Rhine up the rivers and overland, across what is now the countries of eastern Europe, to the Black Sea and hence to Baghdad. Some of the centers of this northern trade, such as Dorestad, located in Frisia (what is now the Netherlands), were the biggest agglomerations of people then in western Europe—although with 10,000 people at the most, it was still completely dwarfed by Constantinople.

These ninth-century trading centers sent the same sorts of raw material to the Muslims as the more southerly trading centers were sending to Constantinople. In return they brought back gold and silver to swell

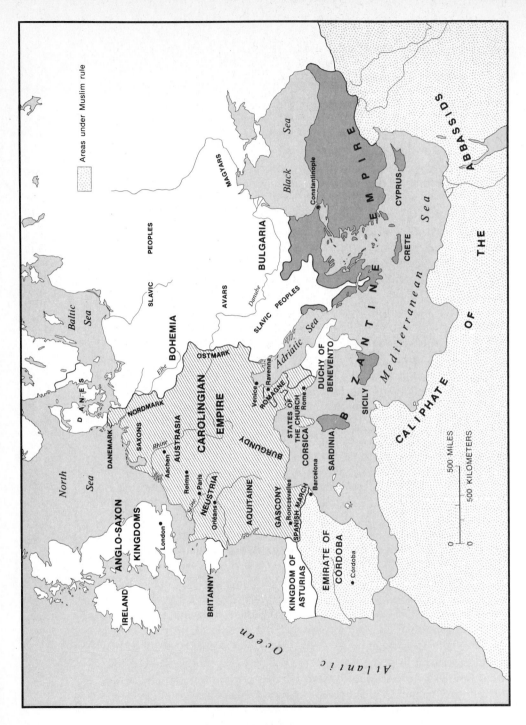

Areas under Muslim rule

ANGLO-SAXON KINGDOMS

IRELAND

BRITANNY

AQUITAINE

GASCONY

KINGDOM OF ASTURIAS

EMIRATE OF CÓRDOBA

• Córdoba

• Barcelona

SPANISH MARCH

Roncesvalles

NEUSTRIA

Orléans • • Paris

Reims •

• Aachen

AUSTRASIA

Rhine

SAXONS

DANEMARK

D A N E S

NORDMARK

North Sea

Baltic Sea

SLAVIC PEOPLES

BOHEMIA

OSTMARK

Elbe

CAROLINGIAN EMPIRE

BURGUNDY

Venice •

ROMAGNE

Ravenna •

STATES OF THE CHURCH

Rome •

CORSICA

SARDINIA

SICILY

DUCHY OF BENEVENTO

Adriatic Sea

AVARS

Danube

SLAVIC PEOPLES

BULGARIA

MAGYARS

Black Sea

Constantinople •

B Y Z A N T I N E   E M P I R E

Mediterranean Sea

CRETE

CYPRUS

CALIPHATE   OF   THE   ABBASIDS

Atlantic Ocean

500 MILES

500 KILOMETERS

THE EMPIRE OF CHARLEMAGNE IN 814
By the time of Charlemagne's death in 814, he had conquered and politically
unified much of the territory that had once been separate Germanic kingdoms.
He pushed the eastern border of his realm far past the old Roman border of the
Rhine and turned the West's attention away from the Mediterranean, where much
of what had once been part of the Roman Empire was now controlled either by
the Muslims or the Byzantine emperors.

Europe's supplies of these rare metals. Some scholars have even thought that the artistic and religious Carolingian Renaissance was financed by Muslim coinage. Although we would call trading centers such as Dorestad towns, they existed only for commercial purposes, being neither governmental nor religious centers, unlike both the earlier Roman cities and later medieval cities. Unlike many of the cities of the high Middle Ages, they were built in areas that had never been subject to the Romans and thus naturally had never been Roman provincial capitals; they thus represent a way-station before the real reurbanization of Europe in the eleventh and twelfth centuries, which *was* for the most part based on old Roman cities.

One can get a better glimpse into ordinary peasant life in the Carolingian era than one can for the previous centuries because for the first time manorial surveys were being done. These surveys or inventories of property and rights were called polyptyques. They were carried out at the orders of several of the greatest landlords, including Charlemagne himself. Although Charlemagne's polyptyques for his own estates no longer exist, some of those commissioned by the great monasteries still do. Polyptyques were not censuses in the modern sense; they did not survey all the people who lived in a certain area, only those who owed certain dues, and even then the surveyors were more interested in the services owed than in the people themselves. Because the polyptyques were generally revised over the years, with new information written in between the lines or scribbled in the margins, it is now impossible for modern historians to say precisely what were the rights and duties of the peasants on even one manor at one given time. But the polyptyques still provide a good deal of information that is lacking for the Merovingian era. In the Carolingian era, starvation was still a constant concern, and the polyptyques were especially concerned with the growing and distribution of food.

The world of the ninth and tenth centuries was still very much a rural world. Peasants lived in small villages in clearings in the forest, with the next village many miles away. People would normally only see from day to day people they had known all their lives—unlike our modern urban civilization, where by far the majority of people one passes are strangers. The houses of the village were usually made of wood; nearby were what archaeologists have called "sunken huts," structures for storage or for those animals who did not share the house with the family, made very simply by digging a hole and putting a roof over it. The tiny village of the ninth century had no castle looming over it, for there would be no castles in Europe for another century, and usually no church, for almost all the churches in the West were either in or just outside the old Gallo-Roman cities.

The forest was the enemy, home of wild animals, of brigands, of fearsome monsters. There were still wolves in Europe then, but the most terrible animals were the wild boars, who weighed four times as much as a man or more, and (unlike the wolves) were not at all shy. Even a man on horseback was not safe from an angered boar's tusks. But because of its wildness the forest was also an exciting frontier. It was the home of marginal people, some criminals, others men possessed by religious fervor, who found in its wildness and solitude an atmosphere conducive to prayer and contemplation.

The weapons of the peasants against the forest were the axe and the plow, to cut down the trees and cultivate the land so the trees would not at once return. It was not until the eleventh and twelfth centuries, when three centuries of attack on the forests had reduced them in much of western Europe from limitless and fearsome expanses to little more than large woodlots, that people began to see forests as a limited resource, needing protection and tending, rather than as the enemy. (The same thing happened a thousand years later in the United States, where conservation only became an issue after the enormous forests the first settlers had found had been reduced to a fraction of their original size by these settlers and by western Europe's appetite for timber of a quality that was no longer found in Europe.)

There were certainly some valuable aspects of the forest to the Carolingian peasant; the trees provided the lumber for building, oak trees provided the acorns upon which domestic pigs were fattened, the honey of wild bees provided the only sugar in the diet, and wild mushrooms in the spring and summer and nuts and wild berries in the late summer and fall provided welcome supplements to the peasant diet. (In Europe, the majority of wild mushrooms are safe to eat, unlike the United States, where half of all species are unpalatable or poisonous.) But the main food, for peasants and aristocrats alike, was bread, and wheat fields required an attack on the forest.

Food and Clothing in the Carolingian Period

The Carolingian Diet

Bread was normally made from winter wheat, which was planted in the fall, not long before the first snowfall, grew rapidly in the spring as soon as the frost was out of the ground, and was harvested in midsummer. If there was not enough wheat, bread could also be made from rye, barley, or oats, but these were considered to produce inferior bread. The advantage was that these grains were planted in the spring and not harvested until the fall, so they could be used to supplement a disastrous winter wheat crop. Without these spring-planted grains, a peasant might be faced at the end of the summer with a choice of having to save all the miserable yield of a bad wheat crop for seed for next year, and thus starving, or else eating the entire crop, saving nothing for next year's seed, and thus starving the next year.

Peasant bread was definitely high-fiber, made from whole wheat, with bits of chaff and straw often still mixed in. By the Carolingian era, however, the aristocracy had developed an appetite for white bread. Americans raised on "sandwich loaves" would not recognize the Carolingian aristocracy's white bread as white, but it was certainly whiter than the peasants' bread. It was made of pure wheat flour, without any rye, oats, or barley added; and although the flour was unbleached and was still mixed with a fair amount of wheat germ, all the hulls and chaff were sifted out.

Both peasants and aristocrats ate a number of other cultivated foods besides bread, though bread was for both (and especially the peasants) the major source of nourishment on a daily basis. Peasants normally had small garden plots next to their houses, where they grew lettuce, peas, beans, onions, leeks, and turnips. Potatoes, corn, and tomatoes, being New World vegetables, were of course unknown.

Dairy products were much more common in medieval diets than they had been in the ancient world. Whereas the Greeks and Romans had cooked with oil, especially olive oil, the Germanic peoples who had settled within the boundaries of the old Roman Empire had brought dairy herds with them, cows, goats, and sheep. Coming from a part of the world without olive trees, they naturally did not use olive oil, instead using butter (which the Romans found disgusting) for cooking as well as for spreading on their bread. (The invention of margarine was fifteen hundred years ahead.) Fondness for dairy products continued in western and northern Europe and even infiltrated the Mediterranean to some degree during the Middle Ages.

Because medieval cows (unlike modern dairy cows) only produced milk part of the year, when they had just given birth to their calves, milk was not available all the time. Even when the cows were producing, lack of refrigeration meant that fresh milk would spoil quickly. As a result, it was necessary to find ways to preserve milk for later use, generally by making it into cheese. Cheese had certainly been known in the ancient world, but it only became a staple of the diet in the Middle Ages. Already in the Carolingian era different regions produced their own very distinctive sorts of cheese, just as France today makes several hundred different varieties. Some of the cheeses were hard, some soft, some (like modern Camembert) were meant to be eaten rind and all. Although most cheeses were eaten where they were produced, a few varieties were shipped long distances. After Charlemagne found a kind of cheese he especially liked while visiting one area of his realm, he arranged to have large shipments sent to him every year.

Eggs and poultry provided another source of protein. Chickens were to be found in every village street or manor courtyard, wandering around in search of insects and seeds to eat. Modern chickens are fed on grain, but medieval peasants preferred to eat the grain themselves and let the chickens eat whatever they could find. The eggs these free-roaming fowl produced were very small, nothing like the "large" or "extra-large" eggs we now take for granted; they were more like what are now called "pullet" eggs. Because the hens tried to hide their nests, it was always a challenge to find the eggs before they had started to grow chicks inside (medieval eggs, unlike modern eggs, were generally fertilized). The chickens themselves were not a regular source of meat, because they were only eaten after they had grown too old to lay eggs. However, wild birds were netted and eaten, including tiny songbirds that would scarcely seem to modern well-fed eyes worth trying to find the meat on.

Fish were an additional supplement to the diet. They were caught in rivers and streams, and most monasteries and manors had fish ponds, kept constantly stocked, so that fish could be kept alive until it was time to cook them. In areas without access to fresh fish, smoked or salted fish could be bought by the well-to-do; eels especially were considered a great delicacy.

The basic diet then for the peasant and aristocrat alike was bread, supplemented with vegetables, cheese, eggs, and fish. This was all that peasants could afford most of the time, and all that monks were supposed to eat. Their diet did not include much red meat, which today in the United States is our major source of calories. Red meat was considered highly desirable; it was just too expensive and difficult to obtain for the peasants, and too luxurious for the monks. Although they raised cattle both for dairy cows and for the oxen that pulled their plows, they ate very little beef, for both cows and oxen would be worked until they died, at which point their tough carcasses were not particularly desirable. Sheep were not eaten for mutton very often, because they were too valuable as a source for wool. Pork was the major domestic red meat, but the word "domestic" is not completely appropriate. Pigs were generally set loose in the forest to forage for acorns on their own, only rounded up in November, after the harvest, when they were at their plumpest. Rounding up pigs that had been running wild was not especially easier than rounding up wild boars, although the domestic pigs were somewhat smaller. The November pig-slaughter was a high point of the year, with everyone eating as much fresh pork as they could hold, the rest being smoked and salted to last the winter (modern hams would be considered extremely insipid compared to medieval hams, which had to keep for months or a year without refrigeration).

The aristocrats loved red meat, just as they loved white bread (the very things that nutritionists now warn us against), and they supplemented their pork and stringy stewed beef with wild game. Hunting was very popular among the aristocracy, providing them with a chance to combine lively sport, real danger, and the search for supper. Game was generally roasted over the fire; Charlemagne became extremely irritated with his doctors when they told him to cut back on the roasts he loved in favor of stews. Stags were the principal game animals; in the ninth century certain areas were already being set aside as game preserves, where only the lords could hunt, and the practice grew in succeeding centuries.

Because meat was often either rather tasteless or else "off" (by modern standards), cooks used a lot of herbs and spices to improve the flavor. Every important household prided itself on the quantity of costly herbs and spices used in its kitchens, and the spice cupboard was as tightly locked as the jewel box. Herbs, like thyme, chives, or sage, could be grown in kitchen gardens, but spices, like pepper, cinnamon, and cloves, made from the bark and bulbs of plants that were foreign to Europe, had to be imported. They were brought thousands of miles overland, from southeast Asia, and were as a result extremely expensive. This naturally increased the prestige of serving one's guests heavily spiced foods, even when the meat was fresh and did not need a masking flavor. Throughout the Middle Ages, spices were a major part of the annual budget for an aristocratic household.

Guarding both spices and jewels as the responsibility of the woman of the house, who therefore went around with a heavy ring of keys on her belt and permitted no one else to open the cupboards. Holding the keys was identified so closely with a well-to-do woman that, when one was being laid out for burial, it was thought necessary to represent the keys among the grave-goods. One could naturally not bury the keys themselves (as they were the only copies), but many Anglo-Saxon graves of women included stylized representations of the keys that would have been hung from the dead woman's belt.

The normal drink in the Carolingian period was beer, brewed on a weekly basis in most manors and villages. Taverns were already becoming common, both as places for travelers to stay and as gathering places for the local people. However, wine was considered highly desirable, even though a lot of wine had already turned to vinegar by the time it was drunk, and great effort was expended in unsuitably cold areas to produce wine grapes. Good wine was highly prized and could bring a high price at the market, although it was too bulky to be transported any distance (markets downstream from wine-producing regions did the best, as the wine casks could simply be loaded onto barges and floated down to market). Monasteries treasured their cellars; monks fleeing from the Vikings often tried, unsuccessfully, to take their wine barrels with them.

Clothing in the Carolingian Age

The clothing of western Europe in the Carolingian period was very different from that of the classical period. It was based more on Frankish than Roman styles and was much more suited to a cold climate than the draped rectangles of Greece and Rome. Charlemagne was described by his biographer as wearing "the national dress of the Franks," and his clothes, except for being made of finer material, were very close to those of the ordinary people of his time. The basic garment was a long woolen tunic reaching to the knees; Charlemagne's was trimmed with silk. Underneath, the king wore a linen undershirt and linen drawers, and probably other Franks did as well. On their legs they wore stockings (woven, not knitted, as knitting was not invented until much later), wrapped with bands of cloth or leather below the knee. On their feet the Franks wore soft leather shoes. Over everything went a long cloak, typically dyed blue.

In the early ninth century, this traditional cloak was starting to seem old-fashioned to some people at court, who instead began adopting a much shorter, striped cloak, woven in Frisia and thus called a "Frisian" cloak. But this innovation was not universally popular, and one opponent was Charlemagne himself. It might be fashionable, the king complained, but it was not nearly as serviceable as his good old cloak. The new cloak, Charlemagne said, would not keep him dry when riding in the rain, was too small to be used as a blanket, and, worst of all, would not cover his bottom when he pulled down his pants.

Clothes for women were essentially the same as for men in the Carolingian era, except that the basic wool tunic was always ankle length. Women with any fashion sense had their tunics cut very close to the body and made with wide sleeves. Aristocratic women belted their tunics with heavy, elaborately decorated belts, often plated with gold and set with jewels. On special occasions they also wore heavy necklaces, bracelets, and rings, as much gold as they could carry. Very little Carolingian jewelry survives, unfortunately, because most of it was melted down in subsequent centuries and recast, sometimes as church ornaments, when a woman gave her jewels to the church, or as more "modern" jewelry. But from the jewelry that survives, as well as pictures and descriptions of the time, it clear that Carolingian women liked to show off whatever wealth they had; they were not believers in subtle or modest display.

Most people, even the fairly well-to-do, had only two complete sets of clothes, one to wash and one to wear. Because they slept nude, they needed no special nightclothes. Although by the ninth century there was some commercial production of cloth, such as the Frisian cloaks mentioned above, most clothing was made at home. Ninth-century descriptions of a "good woman and wife" always mention her with a distaff and spindle at hand, ready to spin thread in every available moment. Even when each family member only owned two outfits, the woman of the house was constantly occupied in making new ones in preparation for when the old ones wore out, which they naturally did quite quickly from being worn all the time. She had to start with the raw material, whether flax stalks or fleece, make the thread, weave the thread into cloth, dye it, and then cut and sew the garments, all very slow processes before the invention of modern textile machines.

Linen and wool were the two basic fabrics from which most clothes were made. Cotton was not yet known in western Europe (much less rayon, polyester, or other twentieth-century fibers). Silk production was unknown in the West, so silk, like spices, had to be imported thousands of miles overland from Asia and was as a result extremely expensive. Wool sheared from the sheep and flax, however, were always at hand. Before being spun into thread, wool had to be washed and carded; carding, done with teasles, removed stray objects from the fleece. Linen was made from the grasslike stems of flax, which were soaked and beaten until the fibers separated, after which they were similarly spun into thread. After being woven, wool was dyed with natural mineral or vegetable dyes (the chemical dyes we now use were only invented in the nineteenth century). Red, yellow, brown, and blue were the principal colors for wool. Linen was also sometimes dyed, though it was more common to bleach it white in the sun.

Clothes were normally changed once a week, at the same time as people took their weekly bath. Medieval people are often depicted as grimy and unwashed, but this is a misconception. The Saturday bath was a long-established tradition in the monasteries, where the monks washed so that they would be fresh for Sunday service. Also on Saturday they were given their weekly shave, both the chin and the top of the head. By the Carolingian period, and indeed throughout most of the Middle Ages, the Saturday bath was also a tradition for the rest of the population, who wished to be sweet-smelling and clean after the week's work, whether they went to church or used the holiday for socializing. The monks considered bathing and shaving oftener than once a week a luxury. Because they were deliberately trying to keep their minds on higher things, they wanted to avoid the pleasant sensation of relaxing in a hot tub more than was strictly necessary for cleanliness.

The peasants would not have objected in principle to such a luxury, but it was a long, slow process to boil up enough water in kettles over open fires to bathe an entire family, even though they used small wooden tubs, and the fuel thus used could not be used for cooking or for heating the house on cold nights. Weekly baths for the peasants were a compromise between what they would have liked and what they felt they could afford in time and energy. The aristocracy, without these constraints, bathed much oftener. Charlemagne had large baths built at his palace at Aachen, apparently on the model of the Roman baths. They were fed by thermal springs and therefore were hot all the time. He often invited his friends and relatives to join him for a dip; his biographer said that his baths would hold up to a hundred people at a time.

Developments in Manorialism

So far I have talked about common people and aristocrats as though these were simple and straightforward categories; in fact, the Carolingian period is marked by having an enormous number of different social and legal categories. It is perhaps easiest for us to try to draw distinctions between those with more wealth or less wealth, and those with more power or less power, but the people at the time who wrote about social structures drew the main line between those who were servile and those who were free. This distinction had certainly been important in the ancient world, but, as already seen in Chapter 4, it had broken down to some extent in the Merovingian period, and by the Carolingian period there were enormous gradations in the amount of freedom or the amount of servitude one might have. The picture is even more complicated because of the great amount of regional variation, with different definitions and categories of status in different areas. Even within one area, people might be treated differently depending on which "law" they personally were considered to be under: Frankish, Lombard, or whatever.

There were still some people who could only be considered slaves, usually employed in their lords' households. There were serfs of various descriptions, called by a bewildering variety of terms, owing varying sorts of dues and services. There were people who had commended themselves as serfs out of need for support or protection, who still retained freedoms beyond those of born serfs. There were some who had been freed by their masters but still owed certain servile dues. The issue was further complicated because certain plots of land were considered "servile," apparently because they had originally been among the plots granted to slaves or serfs, but by the ninth century these had free peasants living on them. In other cases, serfs lived on plots of land that were called "free." In the face of all these complications of social and legal condition and differences in dues, it is perhaps not surprising that landlords started drawing up the polyptyques as surveys in the vain hope of getting everything sorted out.

The polyptyques show the world of the manor, where serfs or peasant tenants worked for their lord or landlord. The manorial system however was far from universal, and there are plenty of indications in the sources that a great many peasants lived in small villages without any overlord. The very structure of the manor varied from place to place. Although in the polyptyques land was often enumerated using the term *mansus*, the amount of land that theoretically could support one peasant family, by the ninth century some relatively wealthy peasant families controlled more than one *mansus*, and in other cases a *mansus* might support two or three families.

Sometimes, as when the lord of a manor was a monastery, the lord might be quite distant. In such cases, if the duty of the manor was to produce a certain number of cartloads of grain each year for the lord, the peasants received very few directives as long as the grain arrived regularly. In other cases, the lord lived virtually in the middle of the peasants. His house was finer than theirs but he wore clothes like theirs and ate food and used tools like theirs, for the clothes, food, and tools used by the lord were made by the same members of the village who made such things for their own families or their peasant neighbors. Some lords possessed more than one manor and often moved around during the year, traveling between their different estates, eating up the produce owed from each before moving to the next.

Economically, the manor played an important role because it was a system that could readily be used to produce goods for market. A lord with large estates could recognize the possibility of producing enough agricultural surplus to make it worthwhile to sell to a town, even if each peasant *mansus* only produced a tiny bit more than what it needed to feed the family on it and pay the lord his dues. The grain, chickens, cheeses, and the like that many peasants had to pay were not simply hoarded by the lord but turned into cash at market. Thus the slow growth of the towns was helped by the manorial system, because the lords made available the food that the town needed to buy.

This was of course rather difficult on the serfs, whose labor was being used to make town growth possible and to make profits for the lords, without their getting anything out of it themselves. Free peasants, however, were able to take advantage of the establishment of regular markets by organizing themselves and selling their own produce, without going through an overlord. And even the peasants on manors benefited to some extent, because it was to the lords' advantage to invest in new equipment, such as the new, heavier plows that were just starting to become common. Lords had the capital to buy such things, which the peasants might not have been able to afford on their own, and although from the lords' point of view the purpose was to grow food for market more efficiently, the peasants also benefited, because they were able to use the better plows on their own strips of land to grow more food for their own families.

Increased agricultural production in turn freed part of Europe's population to worry about things other than food, such as education. One must realize that over 90 percent of the adults in Europe were probably still growing food full-time, but the better climate, the better technology, and the better market system gave Europe a little breathing room in which to pay attention to other issues.

The Revival of Learning

Where the term "Carolingian Renaissance" is perhaps most justified is in the "rebirth" of classical learning. Since the second or third century, spoken Latin had been rapidly growing further and further from written Latin. In the eighth and ninth centuries certain scholars and educated men recognized this and put a firm stop to the slide in formal Latin which had resulted. Interestingly, the lead seems to have been taken by Anglo-Saxon monks who had come to the Continent from England. The reason is probably that the Anglo-Saxons, who spoke a language related to Old German, always recognized that Latin was a different, foreign language that had to be learned, whereas those who had grown up speaking French, Italian, or Spanish, the "Romance" languages (so-called because they were related to the language of Rome), did not make a clear distinction between their own spoken language and Latin.

At any rate, Charlemagne's court became a center of classical education. Priests, who were supposed to know Latin, came there from all over the empire to be educated in the correct forms. Even the aristocrats at court learned Latin, and they liked to show off by carrying out conversations in Latin or writing elegant poetry in the classical style. Since most of the people at court were also fluent in both German and French, they would be considered well educated in languages even by today's standards. Charlemagne himself, as well as being able to read and speak Latin, was very proud of knowing a little Greek. He could not write, however, because he had been an adult before he took up his education. The small muscles of his fingers had not been trained early enough to use a pen. (These are the muscles that kindergarten children now train using fat pencils and wide-ruled paper.) The king's biographer, however, told the charming story of how Charlemagne used to keep a stylus and tablet under his pillow and practice secretly if he woke up in the night. Although he never attained the ability to write the elegant letters used by his scribes, the king did at least develop a striking "signature" or monogram, composed of the letters of his name put together in a stylized arrangement.

The Latin of Charlemagne's court was not precisely the Latin of Cicero. New vocabulary had been added to describe objects and institutions unknown in classical times. The sentence structure had been simplified. However, the case endings, which had fallen off, were restored, and many classical words whose meaning had almost been forgotten were revived. Latin was its own language again, neither a dead tongue nor just another version of French or Italian. Although it was a language that had to be learned formally, it was definitely a living language, one in which an Italian scholar and an Anglo-Saxon scholar could readily communicate, and it was the normal spoken language within the monasteries. Latin continued to be a living language until the sixteenth century.

Many priests were brought to Charlemagne's court to study, but Charlemagne also directed that each cathedral establish a school, where men training for the priesthood would be properly educated. In the Carolingian era, most cathedrals were becoming organized as the joint responsibility of the bishops and of the priests who were permanently attached to the cathedrals. This body of priests was called a cathedral chapter. The bishop and the cathedral chapter shared spiritual authority in the diocese; the bishop kept his position at the head, but he also had to grant autonomy to the chapter in some areas. The schools were normally established under the immediate direction not of the bishops but of the chapters.

The revival of interest in classical learning in the ninth century survived, with some difficulty because of the wars and invasions discussed below, into the tenth century. In the tenth century, indeed, there was even a revival of interest in mathematics and science, which had not been studied at Charlemagne's court. This was, however, a very tiny revival, most of it attributable to one man, the scholar Gerbert, who became pope (under the name of Sylvester II) in 999.

Gerbert spent some time in his youth in Spain, which was then under the control of the Muslims. The Arabs had remained much more interested in Greek science and mathematics than had the Latin West, and Gerbert found much to interest him. He seems to have been the first Christian to use the Arabic abacus, which was based on nine buttons for the numbers one to nine, plus a zero, the "cipher" (from the Arabic word *alsifr*, meaning "the void"). The abacus made not only addition and subtraction much easier than they were with Roman numerals (try adding a column of Roman numerals and see how fast you become hopelessly confused), but could also be used, by the means of various formulae Gerbert worked out, to do multiplication and division. The very first use of Arabic numerals in the Christian West seems to have been in the tenth century, probably by one of Gerbert's pupils, although Arabic numerals did not replace Roman numerals for general purposes until the fourteenth century.

Books and Writing in the Ninth Century

As well as reviving classical Latin, Charlemagne's palace school popularized a new form of handwriting. At this time, of course, six centuries before the printing press and a thousand years before typewriters, everything, including books, had to be written by hand. The palace school developed and began using a new form of handwriting, or what we would call printing as opposed to cursive, which was very clear and easy to read. They used it for everything—books, charters, legal agreements, and letters. This style is now called "Caroline miniscule" (Caroline from the same root as "Carolingian," miniscule because it was made up of what we would call lowercase letters, rather than capitals). Before the development of Caroline miniscule, western Europe had used various "cursive" scripts, that is scripts written without taking the pen off the page, the way that one now does handwriting. These cursives were fast and sloppy, hard even for the people of the time to read (just as now many people's handwriting is hard to read, even sometimes for themselves). Caroline miniscule was slower to write, but this was well worthwhile because it was so much easier to read.

Caroline miniscule quickly became popular throughout the empire. In part, people just liked to copy the fashions of the court, to show that they too were up-to-date. But this particular script was spread especially through new copies of the Bible. Since all books had to be copied by hand, no two copies of any book were the same. Each one had its own

The upper example is a passage from the Alcuin Bible, written in Caroline miniscule c. 800. Starting with the capital D, the next words are *Dixit wero d[eu]s*. Compare this legible script with a sample of Merovingian cursive, below.

set of misspelled words, passages left out by accident or mistakenly written twice. (Try copying even one page of text, see how many mistakes you make, and then imagine trying to copy a book as long as the Bible.) This variety was considered especially deplorable in the case of the Bible, which was supposed to be the word of God, yet might well be marred by the cumulative mistakes of generations of sleepy or lazy scribes.

Determined that there should be a good, error-free copy of the Bible, Alcuin, the Anglo-Saxon head of the Carolingian palace school, gathered together the oldest copies of the Bible that he could find and compared them, sentence by sentence and passage by passage, trying to decide for each passage which were the real readings and which the scribal mistakes. (This is still the method that modern scholars use in trying to produce an edition of a work that exists in various versions.) He then had a complete copy of the "correct" text of the Bible made in the new Caroline miniscule script, as accurately as possible, and used this as a model. All new Bibles, for the various churches of the empire, were to be made by copying from this model. Thus both the corrected Bible text and the handsome Caroline script spread throughout the western Continent.

It is interesting to note that it was the royal court, not the bishops, much less the pope, who took it upon themselves to correct the Bible. Distinctions between church and state, which we tend to take for granted in the United States, would be hard to explain to people of the ninth century. The Carolingian kings did much more to spread Catholicism (often at the point of the sword) than did the popes, who had very little authority and indeed often had to call on the Carolingians for protection against their enemies. The pope's major influence on the revival of a good Latin education for the clergy was in sending Charlemagne a collection of pronouncements of church councils, which included material on Christian instruction; but this collection had been nothing more than an antiquarian curiosity until Charlemagne rearranged and reworked it and made it into the law of his kingdom. It is striking that the papal court continued to write in the old cursive styles until the eleventh century, long after all of Europe north of the Alps had adopted Caroline miniscule. The popes very rarely wrote to the northern churches in the tenth and early eleventh centuries, and when they did the northern churches must have been quite mystified as to what the letter said. The Carolingians consciously thought of themselves as reviving Roman ideas and learning; they found all the old Latin treatises they could, usually written on papyrus that has crumbled away in the thousand years since then, and made new copies of them. But the Carolingians, as well as reviving classical education, also thought of themselves as reviving the Biblical kingdom of David, in which the king was also his people's link with God.

Caroline miniscule had the twenty-three letters of the Roman alphabet then in use, comprising the twenty-six we now use, *minus j, v,* and *w* (*i* and *j* were then just different forms of the same letter, as were *u* and *v*, and *w* was still a "double *u*"). A modern person, looking at Caroline miniscule, will find it surprisingly readable, much more so than the handwriting of the later Middle Ages. Even if one does not know Latin, one can still spell out the words. The reason for this is that Caroline miniscule is the basis of modern printing (what you are reading in this book). Centuries later, when men of the Italian Renaissance were looking for the oldest copies they could find of classical works, of books and treatises written by the Romans, they found the handsome copies made in the ninth century. Not realizing that these copies were Carolingian, and thinking that they were actually Roman, the Italians decided that Caroline miniscule was "Roman handwriting" and immediately began imitating it themselves. As books began to be printed in Italy, men of the Renaissance made sure that the printing presses used what they thought were "Roman letters," and thus ninth-century script was revived to become the basis of most printed books until today.

Ninth-century copies lasted much better than earlier copies because they were written on parchment. Papyrus, which had been in common use earlier, will simply not last in the damp climate of most of Europe, but parchment will. The word "parchment" is now used just to mean heavy paper, but real parchment is sheepskin. (This is why sometimes a person will say "get one's sheepskin," meaning "get one's diploma.") Paper was not known in the West until the fourteenth century, and so making any sort of permanent copy required having parchment and hence sheep.

The preparation of parchment was a skilled and complex art. The sheepskin was scraped very smooth and thin and often bleached white, so that it was much more of the consistency of heavy paper than of leather. Nice rectangular pieces were cut out to be made into books; a single copy of the Bible would require a whole flock of sheep. The odd-shaped pieces left over after the rectangles were cut out were not thrown away but used for letters or for legal agreements. A common problem was holes in the parchment, especially those made by blow-fly larvae, a parasite that had infected the sheep while it was still alive. For Bibles, scribes would try to find pieces without holes, but most other books had holes scattered throughout them. When the scribes reached the holes they would just write around them.

Parchment was tremendously expensive, because it required first raising the sheep and then killing them and preparing the skin. Therefore, it would not be used for jottings or rough drafts; rather, these were made on a wax tablet, using a stylus. The wax could be wiped smooth and used over and over. Charlemagne kept a wax tablet, not parchment, under his pillow. Old parchment books that were not wanted anymore would be taken apart and the parchment reused. Sometimes the writing would be scraped and bleached off and the new texts written on the parchment. Sometimes the old pages would be used in the binding of new books. Even though there are very few complete ninth-century books left in existence, there are plenty of individual pages, found in the bindings of later medieval volumes.

Because of the expense of the parchment, and the slowness with which new books were made if one wanted an accurate copy, books were extremely valuable. There was no such thing as a bookstore; new copies of a book were only made when someone wanted them. A person who owned twenty books was considered to have a large library. Usually one added new books to one's collection by borrowing a copy and then either copying it oneself or having someone else do it. Monasteries usually had the biggest libraries, and many monks spent much of the day copying. Although monasteries were often willing to lend a copy, they wanted to be sure of getting it back; thus the monks wrote curses in the front against anyone who borrowed a book but did not return it. Because the easiest access to learning and books was in the monastery, people who in later centuries would go to the university (there were no universities yet) became monks in the Carolingian era.

The Monasteries

The revival of learning in the Carolingian era was accompanied by a revival of monasteries. Charlemagne and his son, the emperor Louis the Pious, deliberately set out to make the Benedictine Rule *the* rule in all the monasteries of their empire. This rule, which had spread during the seventh and eighth centuries because it set out a reasonable and eminently holy form of life, was now imposed from above for the first time. Monks who had called themselves religious men but who lived more or less like laymen were forced to reform their way of life. Every monastery had to have enough properly trained priests to say the mass correctly. Again it is interesting to note that here the emperors saw no division between church and state, and they considered it a royal duty to establish and maintain the purity of "their" monasteries.

Although many of the newly reformed monasteries were destroyed by the Viking invasions, as discussed on pages 162–64, the concept of Western monasticism as being Benedictine monasticism was firmly established in the early ninth century and not really challenged until the thirteenth century. A standard of monastic purity was established, and although it was often difficult for monasteries to meet this, especially when concerned with simple survival, the standard was still the goal. Even throughout the most difficult times of the late ninth century, a few monasteries kept this standard alive, and some new monasteries were founded.

The most famous of the new monastic foundations of the late Carolingian period was the monastery of Cluny, founded by the duke of Aquitaine in 909. Here the monks lived apart from lay society, uninfluenced (at least theoretically) by their powerful neighbors. The monks followed a complex liturgy, spending most of their day in reciting the psalms, praying, and saying mass. They considered themselves to be fighting the devil with the massed attack of their prayers. In the tenth century and much of the eleventh, the organized liturgy and the strict obedience demanded of these monks were considered to represent the holy life of the apostles.

Most of the monks at Cluny, or for that matter the other Benedictine monasteries of the time, were men who had first entered the church as young boys. These boys were called "oblates," from a Latin word meaning something that has been "offered." They were "offered" to the church by their parents as precious possessions, usually when they were about

Interior of Palatine Chapel at Aachen, Charlemagne's northern capital, c. 800.
The interior of the chapel, including the pavement, remains in its original state.

age six. Oblates were brought up by a "master of the boys," who oversaw
their education, trained them for the monastic life they would soon lead,
and tried to keep them in line; boys who were supposed to grow up to
be monks were just as rambunctious as a group of modern boys in boarding school.

The boys slept in their own dormitory, with a night light, and if they
had to go to the latrine in the night they were supposed to first wake

the master of the boys and get his permission and then take another boy with them. The reason for this was that the monks wanted to make sure that there were no opportunities for older monks to make homosexual advances to the boys, or, even more importantly, to ensure that no outsider could think there was homosexuality within the monastery. Monks were always on the lookout for such things, not because they were biased against homosexuality per se—they would have moved against any heterosexual encounters even faster—but because, in a chaste monastery from which all women were excluded, they wanted to make sure to suppress *any* sort of sexual expression, and homosexual liaisons were the only ones possible in an all-male world.

Although theoretically a young man could decide in his teens whether or not he wanted actually to be a monk, very few oblates would do anything else after having been brought up in a monastery. These oblates produced a population of very well educated men dedicated to the monastic life; education in the late ninth and tenth centuries was in fact essentially restricted to the monasteries (the cathedral schools Charlemagne established lost much of their importance by the second half of the ninth century).

The powerful lords of the time admired these monks and made them generous gifts. These were gifts "for their souls"; the monks were considered capable of attracting the saints' favor because of their holy way of life, and powerful men hoped that the monks would pray for them in return for their gifts. Lords who held or controlled a monastery ruined by Viking attacks, or one where the monks no longer followed a pure way of life, often gave it to a strict Benedictine house. Cluny especially received a number of such monasteries in the tenth and eleventh centuries and repopulated or reformed them by putting monks from Cluny in them. These monks then instituted Cluny's version of the Benedictine Rule at these houses, spreading this highly admired form of monasticism to other areas.

The Vikings

The revival of learning and religion that took place under the Carolingians suffered serious setbacks within a short time, with the beginning of the Viking invasions in northern and western Europe. The Vikings had already reached England in the late eighth century, and by the mid-ninth century they were raiding those parts of France easily accessible to Viking longboats. Monasteries, the Carolingian centers of learning, also had wealth that attracted the Viking raiders, and the monks were completely unable to defend themselves. They fled, carrying the relics of their saints and whatever they could carry of their books and treasure, and tried to find new places to settle. Some congregations had to flee several times, as a place they thought was safe turned out not to be.

The Vikings were a Germanic people from Scandinavia, tall, often blond, and extremely energetic. They lived in narrow farms along the sea and had always been good seafarers. They had been established in northern Europe since the late Roman Empire; the Romans had traded

Ninth- or tenth-century Norse amulet probably representing Thor.

with them for furs, amber, and walrus tusks (used as a cheaper substitute for expensive ivory). From the eighth century on, once they started using sails on their long warships (their boats had previously only been rowed), the Vikings started leaving their cramped farms every fall and raiding the rest of Europe. Scandinavia was then a land of many small kingdoms, and many of the leaders on the raids were powerful men, kings who had been exiled or failed claimants to a throne. Although the Europeans who suffered their raids described them (not surprisingly) as crude barbarians, the Vikings at home had sophisticated social and legal systems and their own form of writing, the runes. There were sixteen letters in the runic alphabet (compared to twenty-three in the Latin alphabet), all made by combining vertical and diagonal strokes that could easily be scratched on stone, bone, or wood.

England and France both have long seacoasts and excellent river systems, which have provided good commercial transportation over the centuries but also made these countries very vulnerable to attack by anyone coming from the sea in shallow ships. The Vikings came very quickly when they came, rowing up the rivers, then leaping out and fighting hand-to-hand. They fought both with bows and arrows and with battle axes. Viking war parties were accompanied by large dogs, the ancestors of Great Danes, which had none of the clumsiness and foolishness that seems to have been bred into modern Great Danes. The Viking dogs were even more feared than their masters.

It was easiest for the Vikings to attack the monasteries, carrying off the treasure, the jeweled relic cases, and the food-stores, but they also attacked cities. The cities were walled and better defended, but they too sometimes fell to the Vikings. The port of Dorestad, mentioned earlier, was sacked four years in a row, starting in 834, and never recovered the economic importance it had had under Charlemagne. In the Gallo-Roman cities, the old Roman city walls were hastily improved and strengthened. Often the cities paid substantial bribes to make the Vikings go away; in 845 Paris paid 7,000 pounds in silver, which ended the threat that year but made further attacks even more attractive to the Vikings. In these difficult times, the counts and warlords who were able to defend their people against the Vikings gained tremendous prestige; the counts of Paris who successfully defended that city at the end of the ninth century were made kings not long afterwards. All such successful battles were fought either in the open or from walled cities, for there were as yet no castles in Europe.

The Vikings, despite their well-deserved reputation for ferocity, were more than just raiders. They had always been interested in trade, and in many places they began establishing permanent trading centers. After all, you can only raid someone once, but by establishing a trade relationship you can make a profit from them year after year. The Viking trading routes took them not only into western Europe but also into what is now the Soviet Union. This branch of the Scandinavians were known as the "Rus"; they were the founders of what eventually became Russia.

The Rus Vikings established a long network of trade routes along the river systems, trading in such wilderness products as furs and slaves. They founded the city of Kiev as a trading post. Great numbers of silver coins, originating in the Muslim Near East, have been found in treasure hordes in Scandinavia. These coins came both from their trading and from the tribute they exacted in many areas. Traveling down the Dnieper River, the Vikings eventually reached the Black Sea and Constantinople. In this imperial city some settled down as palace guards, serving the emperor. The "Varangian guards," tall, muscular, and blond, were highly respected in Constantinople. Even today in ancient buildings in Constantinople (or Istanbul, as it is now called) one can find runic grafitti, saying the equivalent of "Erik was here."

The Vikings' travels took them not only throughout Europe but also west across the North Atlantic. Flourishing communities were established in Iceland, the Faroe Islands, and even in Greenland, which was warmer then than it is now. Here the Vikings established their farms, the farmhouses of which have been excavated by archaeologists, long low buildings with several wings that included both living quarters and barns. Around the year 1000 a group of Vikings headed by Leif Eriksson reached the New World. They landed in a place they called "Vinland," because of the wild grapes. This seems to have been somewhere in the Canadian Maritime provinces. The Vikings did not establish any sort of long-term colony so far from home; at most they overwintered there (though this has not kept a few enterprising merchants of New England from selling "genuine Viking objects" to tourists). Permanent colonies of Europeans in the Americas were still five hundred years in the future.

The Vikings were pagans, believing not in the Christian God but in a variety of Nordic gods and goddesses. (Many of these, glorified in Wagner's operas in the nineteenth century, are well known today.) Around the end of the ninth century, some daring monks set out to convert the Scandinavians. Many were promptly killed or enslaved, but others followed in the tenth century, and in the eleventh century Scandinavia was (at least theoretically) Christianized. Some Vikings had become Christians even earlier. In the year 911, the French king Charles the Simple had given in to Viking demands for a part of France of their own and gave them what is now known as Normandy (the word comes from "Northmen" or "Norsemen"). Here a large group of Vikings settled, were baptized, and married local French women. Their sons grew up speaking French and with at least the rudiments of Christianity. Within about two generations the Normans had become thoroughly French, but they were always *energetic* French, and they were good at sailing. Large Viking settlements were also established in Ireland, where they made Dublin their capital.

Vikings were also settling in England in the late ninth and tenth centuries, in a part of northern and eastern England known as the "Danelaw," because it was under the rule of the Danes (or Vikings). Here the Vikings settled with their families. In fact, they might have controlled even more of England had not Alfred the Great, king of Wessex in the last part of the ninth century, pushed them back to the Danelaw areas. In the tenth and early eleventh centuries, the rest of England even had to pay "Danegeld" to the Vikings, what might now be called protection money. During the tenth century, however, many Vikings were integrated into Anglo-Saxon society. Even today there are a number of Scandinavian place-names in England. The raids against the western parts of England, which continued until the early part of the eleventh century, when indeed the king of Denmark also briefly became king of England, were not raids by the Scandinavians living in England but by men sailing down from Scandinavia.

In addition to the Viking invasions, western Europe also experienced invasions by the Magyars and the Muslims. The Muslims had been well established in northern Africa since the seventh century, and they were also settled in many spots along the northern edge of the Mediterranean in the ninth century. Provence was virtually overrun and did not even have any Christian bishops for over fifty years, from the late ninth century until the middle of the tenth century. The Magyars, who invaded eastern Europe at the same time, came out of central Asia and were related to the Huns. They were indeed called Huns by the writers of the ninth and tenth centuries, who had read the histories written in the late Roman Empire. Like the Huns, they came riding on shaggy steppe ponies, raiding the villages they reached. Eventually the Arabs were driven out of southern France and Italy by the counts, and the Magyars were driven out of Germany by the kings, both in the tenth century.

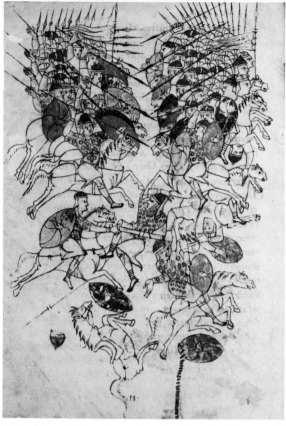

Illustration of German warriors battling the Magyars. Neither side is using stirrups.

The Carolingian Nobility

Changes in the Aristocracy

During these barbarian invasions, the noble class that would lead Europe in subsequent centuries was taking shape. Many men went from relative obscurity to great power and prestige, due to their ability to fight the Vikings or the Muslims. When the Carolingian kings began to have trouble withstanding the barbarians, and especially as Charlemagne's descendants began fighting each other, there were plenty of opportunities for upward social mobility. These avenues were of course not open to most of the population, only to those who had a fair amount of wealth and power already, but during the ninth and tenth centuries a number of people whose ancestors had served the kings and dukes became independent powers in their own right.

In the Carolingian period, as in later centuries, nobility was assumed to be a combination of wealth, power, and birth, although there were no actual criteria set out. Wealth and power came both from inherited position and from holding an important office, such as count or duke.

The counts were, as they had been for the Merovingians, the king's chief representatives in the local areas, and a duke was a rather grand version of a count, someone who controlled several counties in the same region (which region was known as his "duchy"). Someone with enough wealth and power might have his birth overlooked, especially if (as most of them did) he arranged to marry a woman who was herself undoubtedly noble, thus giving "noble birth" to his children. The descendants of men who had been counts under Charlemagne and his immediate successors became kings in the late ninth and tenth centuries, and the descendants of those who had served the counts became counts themselves.

Charlemagne consciously tried to limit the power of the counts and of his household officers, not wanting any new families to rise to power and challenge him the way his own family had risen to power and deposed the last of the Merovingian kings. Charlemagne therefore made being count strictly an appointive office and did not let any counts stay in a county for life. The counts owed him various dues, and he always made sure that they paid them and sent out representatives to check up on them. However, this changed within two generations. The counts were eager to make their offices hereditary, and Charlemagne's grandsons, distracted by invasions and civil war from close oversight of the counts, and in fact hoping to win these counts' allegiance by making them concessions, were willing to recognize hereditary control of a county. With a permanent power base established, it was only a question of time before certain counts, especially ones who had managed to marry princesses, were getting themselves elected kings.

Another change in the Carolingian nobility was that being noble was increasingly identified with being a warrior. The idea of nobility as contained in one's wealth, power, and birth did not involve one's military prowess, but by the ninth century more and more nobles took a special interest in warfare. In the Merovingian period, as noted in Chapter 4, essentially all free men were warriors, and indeed there continued to be non-nobles in all medieval armies. But, following Charlemagne's example, many of the nobles of his court marched off to war with him every spring, and, as noted previously, during the Viking invasions of subsequent generations those who could fight the Vikings successfully were the most admired.

Military equipment was also becoming increasingly expensive in the Carolingian period, more easily afforded by the nobility than by the rest of society. Better swords and armor came out of the slowly improving metallurgy of the ninth and tenth centuries, and one would not want to go to war with inferior equipment. Horses were also becoming a much more important part of the army. In part this was due to the spread of the stirrup. The stirrup had been unknown in the ancient world, and, although it was found in Byzantium in the sixth century, it only slowly reached the West. By the ninth century, however, it had become relatively common, and mounted men with stirrups to help hold them on were much more stably braced for charging or swinging a sword during battle. Horseshoes also first made their appearance in the ninth century. The Romans had not had horseshoes, instead tying sandals to their mules' feet to help protect the hoof, but these wore out or fell off quickly. Carolingian horseshoes were so expensive that a shod horse was worth twice as much as a horse without horseshoes. It was at this point that the horseshoe first developed the "lucky" connotations it still has. Soon nobles would have been embarrassed to go to war on their own feet, though most of the peasants preferred to keep their horses, if they could afford them, to pull their plows.

Marriage and the Family

More is known about noble families of the ninth and tenth centuries than the families of the rest of the population, but there were important developments going on among the aristocracy which soon influenced family structure for everyone. The most important of these changes was the beginning of the sacramentalization of marriage. Marriage was not a sacrament in the early Middle Ages; rather, it was what we might call a civil arrangement. Marriages were certainly formal or legal agreements, but they had concerned only the families, not the church. This started to change between the ninth and the eleventh centuries, so that by the twelfth century marriage was recognizably close to the modern church's idea of marriage, which it certainly had not been at the beginning of the Carolingian era.

Among the Carolingian aristocracy, mutual attraction of the man and woman was of secondary importance to political considerations. Parents often engaged their infant children; a political alliance was too important to be left to the young people's discretion. This was especially true for women. Whereas powerful young men often only married for the first time after their fathers had died and they had come into their inheritance (though they had probably had some concubines earlier), noble women were generally married off or given to young lords as their concubines by their fathers or brothers when still very young.

While surviving traditions of Germanic law mingled with Roman law to give them some protection, the status of women in this society was not enviable, whether they were daughters, concubines, or wives. Until the end of the ninth century concubinage was commonly practiced. Although it was fairly clear in Germanic usage that one could only be married to one person at a time, it was relatively common for a man to have a concubine on the side. This was a double standard, however, for married women were supposed to remain true to their husbands; no husband wanted to raise another man's children as his own. Before a couple married, they normally lived together, with the understanding that, if the man found the woman suitable, they would be married within a short while. Because the "suitability" of a wife depended to a large extent on her ability to have children, many weddings were only carried out after the woman had become pregnant. Powerful lords would normally never marry low-born concubines, but they might expect even high-born women to be "tested" before they married them. If a man decided his wife was unsuitable, he would divorce her (it was much harder for her to divorce *him*).

Some of the most important parts of the wedding arrangements, the transfer of the dowry the wife brought with her and the establishment of the amount of dower a husband would fix on his wife, were in fact negotiated by a young woman's male relatives, without consulting her at all. The dowry was a continuation of what had been the normal Roman practice of a father giving his daughter her share of the family inheritance when she married. She then gave it to her husband, whose property it became, although he was supposed to return it if he divorced her. The dower, or "morning gift," was the reverse of this—property a man gave his wife, usually on the morning after their wedding night. This property was sometimes given to the woman herself, as in Anglo-Saxon England, and sometimes to her male relatives, almost like a purchase price. The dower was Germanic rather than Roman in origin, but both dowry and dower existed side-by-side in the early medieval period.

The families of ninth- and tenth-century nobles were dominated by the men. The idea that women must be under a male protector, which had been part of both Roman law and Germanic custom, was still very strong. A woman was under her father's or brother's protection until she married, when she passed under her husband's protection. This is why much more emphasis was put on the contract between the future husband and his bride's father or brother than on any sort of emotional relationship between the couple. Much of the men's attention seems to have been aimed at increasing their power and then passing that power along to their sons. Wives were useful tools to that end, bringing in wealth of their own and often the noble blood a powerful adventurer felt he needed, as well as producing sons. There are glimpses of husbands feeling very affectionately toward their wives, but, at least on the Continent, this affection does not seem to have extended to giving them much authority. (Anglo-Saxon women may have been slightly better off.)

Women's subservient position, however, did not mean that they were badly treated. Men were very concerned about protecting their women against the abuses of other men, even if not from themselves. They may have treated their wives (from a modern feminist point of view) more like possessions than like partners, but at least they were _prized_ possessions. Germanic law codes laid down stiff penalties for various degrees of affront to a woman, with a small fine for pulling a girl's dress up to her knees, a much larger fine for pulling it up to her waist, and so on up to the extremely severe penalties for rape. Although the men seem to have been much more concerned with a shameful attack on themselves via their women than the sensibilities of the women themselves—the murder of a young woman of child-bearing age was much more harshly punished than that of an old woman—the net effect was still a restriction of the allowable amount of violence against women.

The women do not seem to have made any sort of protest against their position. A modern advocate of women's liberation would say that they needed to have their consciousness raised. The women simply accepted the form that marriage took, recognizing that, despite its defects, it was their best chance for some degree of security and even authority within the household, in what was very much a man's world. One of the few direct voices we have of a ninth-century woman's point of view, that of the noble lady Dhuoda, puts all the emphasis on her husband rather than herself. Dhuoda, an exceptionally well educated woman, who could not only read but write in Latin, is known because she wrote a treatise in the 840s to her older son, reminding him of his duties to his father and to his father's relatives. When Dhuoda wrote, her husband was not with her, having left her while he went off on campaign, taking their younger son, an infant, with him. She was, therefore, not writing out of fear of, or probably even of affection for, her husband. Nonetheless, she knew that her older son was entering a man's world, and she urged him to be true to his father and his father's relatives above all. She did not even mention her own relatives among the people for whom she asked her son to pray. Dhuoda, and doubtless the less well educated women of her time, accepted men's leading position in the world and simply tried to make the best life they could for themselves within that context.

The bishops of this period, however, were beginning to give serious thought to the law of marriage, with the idea that the mutual consent before witnesses that constituted a binding marriage was a sacrament and therefore insoluble. Though the ceremony was what we would call a civil ceremony, it still had a great deal of ritual attached, with both parties swearing to be true and exchanging rings. Though ninth-century weddings were not performed in churches or even blessed by priests, churchmen began to feel an obligation to make sure they were suitably carried out and not lightly dismissed; churchmen thus came to be allies of women.

The change in marriage which the bishops began advocating in the ninth century further helped women's position in the tenth and eleventh centuries. The bishops argued that consent to marriage had to be freely given, or else it was not a valid marriage. Although it would be hard for a girl to resist concerted pressure from her family even if she did not particularly like the man they had chosen for her, the idea of free assent became increasingly important in subsequent centuries, making it clear that one could not be forced into marriage completely against one's will. Because the bishops, quoting from the Bible, argued that a valid marriage could not be dissolved while the two partners were alive, women could no longer be dismissed lightly. Because marriage was increasingly seen as a sacrament, a man who kept concubines on the side was sinning against a sacrament, not just against his wife. This may not have changed very many men's behavior, but at least it meant that they were less casual about their liaisons. These changes in the perception of marriage, which the bishops argued on behalf of royal and noble ladies, gradually filtered down to the rest of society, even though peasant couples, long after they recognized that a valid marriage required free consent and was permanent, still often delayed the actual ceremony until the girl was pregnant.

Even during the more repressive periods, there seems to have been something of an underground women's culture of traditional folk medicine and spells, now glimpsed only dimly. The problem is that most of the treatises written on medical topics in the early Middle Ages essentially ignored women and their ailments, leaving that to the midwives, who generally did *not* write down details of their treatment. We know about such women in part because the priests railed against them when these women gave out contraceptive potions or the like; the Catholic church's view then (as now) was that sex was for procreation, not for pleasure, or merely to increase the bond between the partners, and that contraception was therefore wrong, but women of the Carolingian age paid no more attention than do modern Catholic women in America. (It is interesting to note, however, that priests at this time objected as much to potions given to *increase* fertility as to contraceptive potions; for them, birth should be in God's hands either way.)

The priests who described the old women to whom young women sometimes went for cures, contraceptives, and abortions often characterized them as sorceresses, not because they were pagans (they would have considered themselves Christian even if they only understood Christianity dimly) but because the early church had called such people sorceresses. Some of their practices were close enough to ritual incantations that there might have been some justification in comparing them to the pagan practices of Rome. We know that these old women sometimes prescribed poultices, as for burns, which were probably effective, and other times suggested charms, such as tying coriander seed to one's leg to cure infertility, which cannot have done much good. But the tendency of the people who wrote about them to revert to descriptions used by the bishops of the second through fifth centuries makes it hard to get information on what traditional herbal lore might actually have been like in the Carolingian period itself.

The Carolingian age, the ninth and tenth centuries, was a period acutely aware of its Roman legacy. This is evident in everything from priests trying to apply the strictures of the late Empire to sorceresses, to Charlemagne being crowned Roman emperor. The educational revivals were a very conscious attempt to be sure that they were keeping Rome's memory alive in the correct forms. But there was a distance between the Carolingian age and the Roman Empire that there had not been in the Merovingian age. The center of civilization had shifted north from the Mediterranean. Agricultural practices and even the variations in legal and social status were very different than they had been under the Empire. The culture of the "new Rome" of Charlemagne's court was entirely Latin, not Greek. The knowledge of classical learning was at its strongest in the monasteries, a medieval and not an ancient institution, that went from a rather disorderly variety of forms at the beginning of the Middle Ages to uniformity under the Benedictine Rule in the ninth century. In spite of the depradations of the Vikings and the other invaders, whom the monks compared to the Germanic invaders of the Roman Empire, the monasteries kept the revived classical learning alive until the foundation of the universities in the twelfth century made its wider dissemination possible. It is perhaps ironic that Christianity, widely persecuted under the Empire for its first three centuries, provided the institutions that helped carry much of the heritage of Rome into the Middle Ages.

SIX

THE HIGH MIDDLE AGES:
COUNTRY AND CASTLE

CHAPTER

SIX

THE
HIGH MIDDLE AGES:
COUNTRY AND CASTLE

THE HIGH MIDDLE AGES, the period very roughly from 1050 to 1250, is now considered to have been the high point of medieval culture. It was a period of rapid growth of new institutions, of great intellectual excitement, of a flourishing of art and literature, based in part on what had been achieved by the people of the Carolingian era but going far beyond their accomplishments. Making all this possible was a booming economy; western Europe in the twelfth century was one of the few places and times in human history when famine and starvation were *not* a constant threat. The twelfth century was also a period of rapidly growing population; and the increased population settled both on newly cleared lands and in the cities described in the next chapter.

Europe was still overwhelmingly rural, with most of the population working the soil, although the growing towns provided a market for the extra food they were able to produce as well as a place to which the peasants could move, easing the pressure which a growing population might otherwise have put on a village's available land. The centers of power for the most part, however, were not towns but castles, powerful stone structures scattered across the countryside. Interestingly, in a time when military architecture was reaching its height, most of the European countryside was more peaceful than it had been for centuries, or would be for centuries again. There was always one war or another going on, but these tended to be small and fairly local, with most military energy directed not toward other Christians in Europe but toward the Muslims of the Middle East.

The Rural Economy of the High Middle Ages

The rural economy of the high Middle Ages prospered due to a variety of factors. The most basic was an improvement in the climate. The ending of the mini ice age of the Merovingian period, which had already helped the economy of the Carolingian era, brought Europe to what is known as a "climatic optimum" in the twelfth century, when the climate was optimal for growing grain. The weather was not strikingly warmer, only a few degrees on average, but those few degrees would make the last frost in the spring a week earlier, and the first frost in the fall a week later. An extra two weeks of growing season often made the difference. (Quick-ripening hybrid plants were centuries in the future.) Even more importantly for northern Europe, the climate also became drier. Northern Europe has always been a damp area, making many of its richer soils too waterlogged for effective cultivation. With drier conditions prevailing, the heavy, highly fertile river-valley soils could be planted with crops for the first time. The resulting increase in the size of the crops made a much larger population possible than had been the case in the preceding centuries.

A More Effective Plow: The Carruca

The cultivation of damp soils was made easier by the increased use of the heavy plow, the *carruca*. This particular sort of plow had actually been invented long before, but it only became common in the high Middle Ages. The *carruca* usually had wheels, hence its name (related to "carriage" or "cart"). But its most distinctive feature was the "mould-board," designed to turn over the soil (or "mould") during plowing. At the front of the plow was a sharp iron cutter, which sliced through the soil, and behind it was a curved iron plate, the mould-board, which turned over the slices of soil as they came from the cutter. The turning over killed the weeds and facilitated drying damp soils, as moisture from below the surface was exposed to the air. Because the mould-board turned the soil over, it was only necessary to plow a field once; if a plow had a cutter but no mould-board, it was necessary to plow the field twice, with the second plowing at right angles to the first.

The advantages of the *carruca* for northern Europe were obvious, but there were also problems that made its adoption slow in some areas. Along the Mediterranean, where the climate was much drier anyway than it was farther north, soggy fields were not a problem; overdrying was. Therefore, southern Europe never used the *carruca* much. Rather, peasants there continued to use the same sort of plow the Romans had, the *aratum*. The *aratum* was not much more complicated than a forked stick, consisting basically of a point to dig through the top layer of the soil and handles with which to steer. In addition, the *carruca* was much more expensive than the *aratum*. Whereas the lighter plow could be made mostly of wood, the *carruca* needed iron for its cutter and mould-board, to withstand pressure from deep cuts through heavy soil. Whereas the *aratum* could be hitched up to a donkey (or, in an emergency, to one's wife), the *carruca* required a team of strong draft animals to pull it.

Cest li cere abanaule.

Jl a cem boir' de cere en campaigne . tenant a lecere laut Ghillain et tenant a le boie de papenghien averbaif

A *carruca*, wheeled and with a mould-board behind the iron cutter.

The type of plow used had important results for the shape of the plowed field and the organization of the village. In southern Europe, the need to crossplow meant that fields were generally square. Because a family could normally afford its own *aratum*, each family's fields adjoined that family's house or houses. Thus the social unit of the village, that group of people who acted together against outside dangers and shared a parish church, would normally be dispersed in homes separated by small fields and scattered across a fairly large territory. The village might be composed of a number of tiny hamlets, each consisting of perhaps half a dozen houses and outbuildings, where a family and their hired workers would live, with their fields immediately adjoining. (This type of village is still the norm in such areas as Périgord.) Not all southern European villages were of this type—along the sea itself people tended to huddle together in tiny walled villages for protection—but this form of village was the common result of continued use of the *aratum*.

In the north, on the other hand, where the *carruca* was widely used, fields were generally long and narrow. Because a heavy team of oxen or horses was hard to turn, it made sense to plow for some distance before trying to swing them around. (The "furlong," a rather archaic measure of distance, means "as long as a furrow," standardized at a quarter-mile.) Because both the plow, which required good metallurgy, and the team were expensive, few families could afford them on their own. Instead families had to share. This meant that the villages where the *carruca* predominated tended to be small and compact, with all the houses close together, and open fields stretching out on all sides. Several hundred people might live in a village. The men went out together with their jointly owned plow and team to work the fields.

Because the mould-board threw up a ridge of soil, and because the same furrows were plowed every year, permanent ridges ran through the fields. These, rather than fences or hedges, marked the boundaries between one man's strip of land and the next. Even today, in parts of England, when the shadows are long, one can still see the old plowing ridges under the modern fields. They are shaped like an elongated S, the curves at the end marking where the team was turned. Villagers did not own the plowed land in common, but rather each individual had holdings scattered throughout the different fields. Hence, in plowing, the first furrow or two might be one man's land, the next furrow or two another's, and so on.

Although the precise mechanism of how the land was divided in the first place is not clear, the peasants seem to have felt it right that no one have all his lands in the richest fields, nor all his lands in the worst. Because all villages practiced crop rotation by field, leaving a particular field to lie fallow once every two or three years, one would not want all of one's furrows to be in one field, or one would have no crops at all in the years that the field was not cultivated.

Even though individual furrows were in the possession of the same individuals year after year, the peasants still had to cooperate in their work. Villages normally developed some sort of council to decide when the time for the spring plowing was and when the grain was ripe, to settle boundary disputes, and the like. In the fall, after the harvest was in, the villagers would turn their animals out into the open fields to give them a chance to graze on the stubble, letting them fertilize the fields with their manure. Besides the plowed fields, most villages also possessed common pasturelands, land that was not as suitable for cultivation but could be used for animals. In some areas, the raising of livestock, especially sheep, became more important than the raising of grain. Especially in England, the increased commercial market for wool in the high Middle Ages meant that some areas, where the stony or marshy ground had never been well suited for cultivation anyway, were relegated almost entirely to sheep raising. But for most villages the animals were a side issue, peripheral to the grain.

Shrinking Forest and Expanding Fields

Besides common pasturage, the inhabitants of a village normally had common rights in the surrounding woodlands. Here they gathered wood for their fires and cut wood to build their houses; here they gathered berries and nuts in the autumn as well as wild honey; and here they pastured their pigs. But the forest was no longer the wild expanse it had been in the Carolingian period. Hunting had depleted the game to the point that many lords forbade anyone to shoot wild animals or birds but themselves. (This did not stop peasants from poaching rabbits, but at least it preserved the stags for the lords.)

In many cases the forest that had once formed a thick barrier between different villages was reduced to little more than a screen of trees. Rules had to be made forbidding people from cutting standing wood, although still allowing them to gather dead branches. The charcoal burners, who burned vast amounts of wood down to make the charcoal necessary for the iron forges, could clear large stretches of wood in a short time. In the middle of the twelfth century, when the abbot of St.-Denis, outside Paris, was trying to find long timbers for the new church he was building, it was considered miraculous that he was able to find a dozen trees that were big enough for his purposes. Almost all the mature, close-grained trees suitable for great beams, which had been growing for centuries, had already been cut down.

The woods had been diminished in large part due to the slow but steady expansion of the cultivated fields, ever since Carolingian times. Sometimes a strip of forest next to the old fields would be cleared each year, with the stumps dug out and the new land added to the existing fields. Sometimes a clearing was made in the forest a little way from the village, often with huts there as well where people could stay if it was too far to go home easily every night. Most of the villages that are now spread across the fertile fields of Europe at intervals of several miles have been there since the twelfth century, under the same names they have today.

As well as expanding the fields they already had, peasants of the twelfth century were also attacking wild and marshy areas that had never been cultivated before. New settlements were established in areas where no one had ever lived. This process is known as "internal colonization," because the peasants acted as pioneers, but inside the borders of the old, settled countries, rather than at the frontiers.

Monks often took the lead in internal colonization. The Cistercian order of monks, founded in 1098 (discussed more fully in Chapter 8), wanted to return to the "life in the desert"—the life of the Egyptian fathers of monasticism—and dense forests provided the solitude they sought. With an emphasis on manual labor, they set out to clear the trees, plow the fields, and drain the marshes. The descriptions of this clearing often took the vocabulary of warfare; they saw themselves locked in combat with trees, briars, swamps, and wild animals, with their plows and hoes as their weapons. They proved to be excellent waterworks engineers, draining the marshes and rechanneling the streams so that fresh water would come in at one end of the monastery complex, to be used successively for drinking, cooking, washing, and such "industrial" uses as powering the triphammers in the forge, before finally sweeping under the latrines and carrying the waste away downstream. Many Cistercian monasteries emphasized their flocks, because sheep did much better on newly cleared forest land than did grain, until it was possible to finish the drainage and get all the stumps out; the result was that many monasteries became major producers of wool and parchment.

Plow-Horses and Crop Rotation

With the expansion of the amount of land under cultivation, a frequent concern for the peasants was how to be able to plow the fields fast enough. There is a limited amount of time each year in which such plowing can be done. One possibility was simply to have more plows and more plow teams. But another alternative, one increasingly adopted, was to turn from oxen to horses for the plow teams. Oxen are very strong and will keep plowing indefinitely, but they are very slow. Horses will plow half again as fast as oxen, but there are disadvantages to their use. They are more difficult and expensive to raise and feed, and they could only be used for plowing for the first time once Europe invented a better horse collar.

Before the ninth century, all animals had been harnessed by wrapping something around the animal's neck. This will not bother oxen but can choke a horse if it is hitched to anything heavy. This is why the ancient world had not used horses to pull anything heavier than a light chariot.

But the introduction of a proper horse collar, which put the force on the animal's chest and shoulders, made it possible for peasants to use horses to pull the *carruca*. Another development of the high Middle Ages that also led to the increased use of horses was the spread of horseshoes. As noted in Chapter 5, when horseshoes were first used in the West in Carolingian times, they were almost prohibitively expensive. With the spread of metallurgy in the eleventh and twelfth centuries, however, horseshoes became common, and by the end of the twelfth century the iron-producing region of the Forest of Dean, in the southwest of England, was able to produce tens of thousands of horseshoes within a short time if needed for the king's wars.

In spite of their speed, horses were never universally adopted, because they were more expensive to feed than oxen. Whereas an ox can subsist without difficulty on grass and hay (that is, dried grass), and even for a short time on straw (that is, the stalks that are left after the kernels of grain are cut off), a horse needs grain. Horses do not have nearly as efficient a digestive system as do cattle, lacking their multiple stomachs that can wring every last bit of nutrition from what they eat, and therefore they need a higher quality diet. (This is also why, organic gardeners take note, horse manure is richer than cow manure, as many more nutrients pass through the horse; it is so rich in fact that it needs to be aged a year before spreading.)

A peasant using a horse therefore had to raise grain for the horse as well as for himself. Usually horses were fed on oats rather than wheat, and the spread of oat-growing across much of Europe is closely tied both with the spread of horses and with the adoption of a new form of crop rotation, called the "three-field system." During the early Middle Ages, the standard had been the "two-field system," in which one would grow grain on half one's land each year while letting the other half lie fallow, and then alternate the next year. Before the development of modern chemical fertilizers, soil would be very quickly exhausted unless it were regularly allowed to lie fallow and then have the weeds plowed back under as "green manure." Some marginal cropland even had to lie fallow two years out of three. But, starting in the high Middle Ages, it became increasingly common, at least in areas of richer soil, to let only one field out of three lie fallow each year.

There were several advantages to this practice. If two-thirds rather than one-half of all one's land were cultivated at any one given time, one would get more total yield from the same amount of land. Under this system, one-third of the land would be planted in the fall with winter wheat, another third would lie fallow, and the final third would be planted with a spring crop. This might be oats for the horses, barley as a backup for the wheat in case of a bad harvest, or peas or lentils, which would actually help the soil by putting nitrogen back in. Every year the three would rotate. This would mean that the peasant only had to work one-third rather than one-half his fields at any one time, because the winter wheat and the spring-planted crops demanded intensive labor at different times. The same men with the same plow team could thus cultivate a larger amount of land by using the three-field system. Although this system never became universal, its slow spread, usually accompanying the adoption of horses, meant that peasants could be more efficient in growing their food as well as having a greater variety of grains and legumes available.

Improvements in Peasant Status

The result of all these agricultural improvements, including the warmer and drier climate, expanded number of plow teams, and more effective cultivation due to the spread of the *curruca*, horse teams, and the three-field system, was that the average European peasant was now able to raise more food on a regular basis than he needed to feed his family and pay the rent. This did not mean the end of famine or worry, for even if crops came in well one year there was no guarantee they would the next, and there continued to be crop failures and local famines. But such things were now the exception rather than the standard (though this cannot have been much comfort to peasants forced to sell their land in order to buy food or even to abandon their homes in search of food elsewhere). The overall population grew steadily with a reliable food source. Some peasants even became relatively wealthy by selling their produce to the towns—although, as in the Carolingian age, it was the big landlords who prospered the most from the spread of the market economy.

Some areas even started to feel population pressure. This pressure was eased by rapid migration from the countryside to the cities (as discussed in Chapter 7) and by migration to new lands. As well as practicing internal colonization, often at the invitation of a lord who had large tracts of unworked land and invited peasants to come and work it in return for attractively low rents, medieval peasants moved to areas that had been thinly populated, especially Germany and eastern Europe. (It was the eastward movement of German-speaking peasants into areas with a thinly spread Slavic population, such as the region that is now Poland, that led to the patchwork of Germanic and Slavic villages in such areas from the Middle Ages to the twentieth century, a situation that was intractable to modern ideas of nationalism.)

The migration of peasants across Europe in the high Middle Ages is one of the signs of the improvements that had been made in the peasants' status since the earlier Middle Ages. Peasants were not tied to the land; in most cases, attempts to force them to stay against their will would have been useless, as this would only have been an additional impetus for them to leave. On the Continent, the long list of different peasant statuses found in the Carolingian polyptyques was reduced to only a few, although there was a greater variety in England. In France, even the word *servus*, meaning "serf," almost disappeared from the documents during the course of the twelfth century. The disappearance of this word indicates the disappearance of the once-vital distinction between peasants who were freemen but who owed rent on their lands, and servile peasants who owed all sorts of dues to the lord on whom they and their descendants were dependent in their bodies. From here on, peasants were simply peasants, men who worked the soil and owed some dues and rents.

Dues and Rents

Although the distinctions in peasant *status* broke down during this period, there was still an enormous variation in the kinds of dues and rents and the amounts that different peasant families owed. Some peasants were indeed "allodists"; that is, they owned all their land outright. This was rare, but a number of peasants had at least some allodial (or freehold) land. Most peasants, however, owed rents of various sorts for most or all of the land they worked. This was by no means as simple a situation as has sometimes been depicted. Rather, any given man might owe different rents and dues to several different landlords, even including other peasants. Because in the twelfth century financial obligations were still based on memory rather than written record, the tendency for simplification was strong, as was the tendency of the peasants to "forget" what they owed. But their dues nevertheless seem complicated, even to a modern generation raised on income tax forms.

Rents and dues consisted, as they had for six hundred years, of a mixture of money payments, payments in kind (that is, produce), and work days, days spent working on the lord's land. (Such an obligation did not necessarily mean a man had to be away from his own fields, for it was common for a peasant to send his son to fulfill his labor dues for him.) But in the twelfth century work days became less and less important. As many peasants, especially in the new villages, lived some distance from their landlords, it was hard to enforce labor dues. Even when the peasants fulfilled their obligations of work days, the receipt of such dues often involved irritation, inconvenience, and actual costs to the lord himself. The peasant laborers might not appear until well into the day, having walked from their own villages, would demand to be fed lunch, and would have to leave early to walk home before dark. Increasingly, therefore, landlords "commuted" labor dues into money rents, so that rather than having to force reluctant workers to come from some distance away to work his fields, the lord could use the money to hire laborers on the spot. Hired laborers, who needed the money and knew they would not be paid if they slacked off, were much more effective workers than people brought from some distance who would have preferred to be home working their own fields. By the end of the twelfth century, hired laborers, working for the lords and even for wealthier peasants, were a common feature; men who might otherwise have been pushed into poverty with the rapid rise in village population thus had a means to support themselves.

In the early Middle Ages, there had been certain uniquely servile dues that serfs had had to pay, as well as the various sorts of rents. These servile dues became less and less common in the high Middle Ages. They included the head tax, which involved the serf coming before his lord on his knees with a penny on his head, a practice the peasants considered very degrading. Many peasants in the twelfth century bought their way out of the head tax, offering their lord a large lump-sum payment in return for never having to go through this ritual again. As the payment represented years' worth of head pennies, the lords were happy to oblige. The other two major servile dues were a very large inheritance tax the heirs would have to pay if they were not living with their parent when he or she died (called *mainmort* in France and *heriot* in England), and a fine levied for permission to marry somebody who was not a servile dependent of the same lord (called *formariage* in France and *merchet* in England). Because these dues were collected at most once a generation, and often not then, they could be conveniently forgotten. If a lord had a longer memory than did the peasants, these dues too could be permanently bought off with a lump-sum payment.

Even if certain dues and rents were not quietly dropped, peasants were normally paying less rent in real terms at the end of the twelfth century than they had been at the beginning because rents were fixed, but prices were rising. That is, a peasant whose grandfather had owed two shillings a year for his land would still be paying those same two shillings, even though inflation had made them worth much less. A peasant whose grandparents might once have had to struggle to raise that much money would be able to pay it easily out of part of a shipment of produce to market. Once the lords realized what was happening, they tended to stop "commuting" all rents into money, which had been happening with some frequency, so that if they had been getting five bushels of grain they would still be getting five bushels. But by this time the lords had usually commuted their labor dues and had to end up paying hired laborers more each year in order to get anyone to work for them, whereas the peasants paying the fee in place of a labor due continued to pay the same low fee each year.

Conditions in England

Peasant conditions did not improve quite as much in England as they did on the Continent. Initially, in the twelfth century, labor dues decreased in England for the same reasons that they did in France, and many peasants whose ancestors had been servile were able to be treated essentially like those who were free. But in the late twelfth century, when manorial lords started trying to recover the income that was slipping away from them, many English lords began more intense cultivation of the "demesne," that land that was theirs directly, with the hope both of feeding their household well and selling the surplus to market. They intensified this cultivation in part by enforcing labor dues that had been almost forgotten.

The English lords were helped indirectly by the English common-law system, which drew distinctions between free men, who could bring suit in royal and circuit courts, whatever their economic condition, and servile men, who could not. Suits often turned on whether or not one of the parties in a case was even competent to sue, and trying to prove that a person who had sued you was actually servile was an excellent way to win a case. Since it was hard to sort out the free from the unfree, the

English tended to rely on labor dues as an indication of servility. That is, if it could be demonstrated that any of one's ancestors had owed labor dues, then one was assumed to be servile. If a man was thus judged be servile, even if he had not been paying labor dues himself, his landlord would normally leap in with the demand that he start paying such dues again at once.

Thus in England, although the same forces worked in the twelfth century as on the Continent to give many peasants free status, this process was slowed and even reversed in some cases in the thirteenth century, as many peasants who would have liked to have passed for free were instead proved to be servile "villeins." (The word originally just meant someone living in a village, though in England it became used as a synonym for "serf." Our modern word "villain," spelled almost the same but with a different meaning, is actually related, because medieval romances of lovely and wealthy lords and ladies always described villeins as coarse, ugly, and potentially dangerous; it was from there just a short step to using the word to mean a criminal.) However, in England as on the Continent, there were a very large number of free peasants in the high Middle Ages, men who owed rent but no other sorts of dues, and the English villeins looked at them as models and as goals.

Peasant Labor

The day for peasants in the high Middle Ages (as indeed for most farmers throughout history) began before dawn. A little beer and bread served for breakfast, and then they went out in the fields as soon as it was light enough to see. The particular tasks depended on the time of the year, with plowing, sowing, pruning, mowing, harvesting, and threshing succeeding each other. Because different tasks always came at the same time of the year, representations on churches of the twelve months, or liturgical books with prayers for every week of the calendar, were often illustrated with scenes of peasants at work at that month's task. Only December and January, usually represented by scenes of Christmas festivity and by someone sitting by the fire respectively, were a break in the constant cycle of work.

Farming was very labor-intensive; the only reason farmers have become a minority of the population in recent decades is the substitution of petroleum-powered machines for many tasks formerly done with human labor. And the people of the Middle Ages did not always even have the best hand tools. For example, the scythe had not yet been invented, so grain had to be harvested with a sickle. This meant grasping the heads with one hand and then slicing through the stalks with the sickle—a long, slow way to harvest a field. Threshing involved beating the grain with sticks on a smooth surface to separate the wheat from the chaff. The final step, winnowing, involved tossing the grain up in the air on a windy day and catching it in baskets, while the lighter hulls and pieces of straw blew away. Men and women both worked in the fields, at least during the busiest seasons, and children did as well. Even small children

Using a sickle to harvest grain. The woman, kneeling, gathers the grain into sheaves, and an overseer, at left, supervises.

could gather up the grains of wheat that missed the basket when their father was winnowing.

Although growing and harvesting the grain were very labor-intensive, medieval peasants were at an advantage over the people of the ancient world in that they did not have to grind the grain into flour in hand mills. There were watermills all over Europe, where the water action, harnessed by wheels and gears, drove a huge millstone around on top of a stationary stone. Grain put between the two would quickly be ground into flour. In cities such as Paris, mills were built on barges moored under the arches of the principal bridges. The windmill used wind rather than water as the driving force but could grind grain in the same way. The windmill first appeared in Europe in the twelfth century and spread very rapidly, especially in areas without rivers suitable for watermills.

A local powerful lord often tried to establish mill monopolies, so that everyone would come to *his* mills. The fee for grinding, a certain number of bags of flour out of the total, could be used by the lord to make his own bread or could be shipped to market. Peasants of the twelfth century normally did not bake their own bread. They made the dough themselves (always what we would call sourdough, because they had no little foil-wrapped packets of yeast and had to rely on a piece of dough from the last batch for the rising action), but they did not have suitable ovens in their small and simple houses and therefore took the dough to community ovens, often owned as a monopoly by the local lord. (These monopoly rights, called "banal rights," were a new development in the twelfth century and are discussed in more detail on page 198.)

Peasant houses of the high Middle Ages were usually wood-framed, with the space between the posts filled with wattle and daub—that is, a network of sticks and branches plastered over. In the thirteenth century, however, peasants began to build in stone. The floors of peasant houses were simply dirt, but householders tried to keep them tidy, sweeping them assiduously every day, so that the floor level inside a house was quickly worn down to below the outside ground level. The houses usually had only one story and two or three rooms. What we would consider normal privacy was unknown. (This may be why a "young man's fancy" was reputed to turn to thoughts of love in the spring; it was his first chance to get a girl alone after months indoors with all the relatives.) These houses did not have fireplaces, but rather a hearth in the middle of the floor of the main room, from which the smoke found its way out through cracks in the walls and roof. Cooking might be done over this fire or in a separate shed out back. Behind the kitchen was the kitchen garden, a small patch of vegetables to supplement the basic bread or bread-and-lentil diet. Because this garden was fertilized with human dung from the household, it grew very well.

This house, as well as being crowded and smoky, would have been cold and damp in the winter, but it was made somewhat cozier by the common practice of bringing some of the livestock in for the winter. They were not actually in the same room as the people, but in the other half of the house. The animals provided extra body heat, and the peasants could monitor the well-being of a valuable animal, making sure it had enough to eat. After a hard winter in which the hay ran out, the peasants might have to *carry* their ox outside in the spring and hand feed it on the new grass, but they had at least brought it through.

The Development of Castles

While the position of most peasants improved substantially during the high Middle Ages, there were also important changes taking place in the life of the nobility. Most striking perhaps is the development of castles, a new feature of the high Middle Ages that had not been found in Europe before. A castle is a combination of a strong, defensible fortress with a home for a powerful noble family. The early Middle Ages had had fortified cities as well as forts, usually only occupied in time of war, and it had had luxurious homes for the wealthy, palaces and villas, but these functions were only combined in a single permanent structure at the end of the tenth century, when the first castles were built.

Although some early castles were built of wood, the typical eleventh-century castle was made of undressed fieldstone, big and little rocks fitted together as well as possible and held in place by mortar. Originally castles were laid out in what is known as a "motte and bailey" arrangement. The "motte" was an artificial mound, with a ditch around it; the dirt from the ditch was used to build up the mound. Surrounding the motte was a large open area, the "bailey"; the whole area was surrounded by a stone wall or a palisade. Hills and ditches, topped with a few ruined fragments

The ruined motte-and-bailey castle of Great Berkhamstead. The motte is the mound at the upper right of the site, and the bailey is the open area before it.

of stonework, still show up across the European landscape, showing where motte-and-bailey castles were once located.

The heart of a castle was a "keep," a rectangular stone building of several stories with only a few windows. This was built on top of the motte. The bottom story, which had no windows at all, was used for storage. The next story, reached by an outside staircase, was the main hall, where most of the life of the castle took place. Upper stories might include a chapel, a chamber for the ladies of the castle, and workrooms. The keep could be very small, or the basic plan could be expanded into a huge fortress. The Tower of London, built at the end of the eleventh century, is a very large keep (the present windows are from the seventeenth century, however). Originally castles consisted of the keep and a few outbuildings, all located within the outer walls.

Even after castles began to grow, the original keep remained. It provided the last refuge in case of attack, and remained rough and virtually windowless, even if a more sophisticated and open set of buildings was built around it. Those who built castles entirely anew in later centuries still felt it necessary to have some sort of keep at the center. The keep was built to last, with its walls a dozen feet thick or more. Usually its walls were made by building two stone walls a short distance apart, an inner one and an outer one, and filling in the space between with stone rubble. Although most of the old keeps of Europe are in ruins today, this is not just because of the passage of nine hundred years, for they were built too sturdily to fall down by themselves. Rather, they are in ruins because at some point they were systematically dismantled; in England and France most of the big medieval castles were still defensible until the seventeenth century, when the government sent cannons to shoot against their walls, and they were finally breached.

Around the keep were located various outbuildings to serve the needs of the castle, including the kitchens, the stables, the mews where falcons were kept, weapons shops, and the like. These were constructed much less sturdily than the keep itself. They were built in the large open area within the outer castle wall, which space could also serve as a place to which people of the surrounding territory could flee in case of attack. Since castles were built after the Viking invasions, they functioned most of the time as comfortable places for nobles to live, rather than as fortresses, but they were also made to be defended at short notice.

Building castles required tremendous capital investment, especially by the thirteenth century, when kings and counts were building castles designed to hold hundreds of men. Besides the outlay for all the raw materials, stone, wood, lime (for the mortar), nails, lead, and tin, the castle builder had to pay the transportation costs for all these materials to be brought to the site (very expensive because the materials were heavy and always had to be brought at least part of the way overland), plus pay for the salaries and often food and clothing for the architects, masons, carpenters, ditch-diggers, and other laborers involved in the project. Building a castle was thus a great drain on the builder's finances, one of the principal items in royal budgets, and a tremendous boon to the local economy.

Castles were such excellent defensive structures that they were not attacked very often; it was usually not worth the effort. This was especially true as castle architecture developed in the twelfth and thirteenth centuries. By the thirteenth century, for example, castles were typically built with round rather than square towers, as they had been earlier. The absence of corners made it easier for an archer to command all the area around the tower, and it also made it much more difficult to "mine" a tower. With square towers, one method of attack had been to dig a tunnel, or mine, under one corner of the tower. This was propped up with wooden beams while the tunnelers were at work, but then the beams were set on fire, and when the tunnel collapsed it theoretically brought the wall down with it. But round towers, especially with heavy buttresses built at the base, were much harder to bring down in this way. Inside the walls, more stone buildings and towers were added in the twelfth century, and the castles the English kings built in Wales at the end of the thirteenth century had at least two concentric sets of walls, so that after the attacker had gotten through the first he would be in a narrow passage with the defenders shooting down at him from behind the second walls. (Some of the best preserved castles from the twelfth century are the ones the crusaders built in the Near East, because they were not rebuilt in the late Middle Ages, as were the castles in Europe; Krak, in Syria, is the best example.)

Well-designed castles were almost impossible to take without a long siege. The English kings of the twelfth century, who were worried that their barons would become too powerful if allowed to build their own castles, strictly regulated castle-building, only allowing a lord to begin construction after being given special permission. When King Richard the Lionheart of England built Château Gaillard in his lands of Normandy at the end of the twelfth century, he boasted that its position at the top of a series of cliffs made it so impenetrable that he would have

Dover Castle, built in England in the late twelfth century, with its square keep in the center.

been able to hold it "even if the walls were made of butter." Although this castle eventually *was* taken, it was not by frontal attack, but rather by having someone climb up from below through the drains (scarcely a savory task) and open the gates from within.

Treachery was the only quick way to take a castle. The long way was siege, with the attackers camped around a castle and hoping to starve the defenders out. Castles normally had their own wells for water and large stores of food, however, so the attackers might run out of food before the defenders did. Sieges were enlivened by the defenders sending out forays to attack the attackers and both sides using catapults to hurl stones and heavy spears against each other. (Catapults had a long history, having been used in the ninth century as cities defended themselves against the Vikings; during the siege of Paris the defenders sent heavy spears against the Vikings and laughed and said they looked like shish kebabs when several attackers were skewered together.) The attackers sometimes rushed the walls with scaling ladders, while the defenders shot them with arrows and dropped stones on them from above. In the end, most sieges were stalemates, and castles were so hard to take that by the thirteenth century a few of the strongest were never attacked at all.

The First Appearance of Castellans and Knights

The initial spread of castles in the eleventh century was accompanied by the growth of two new social groups among the aristocracy, castellans and knights. Castellans, as the name suggests, were those who controlled castles. They were nobles, less powerful than the dukes and counts who had existed since Carolingian times, but with a good deal of wealth and authority of their own. Because the counts built the first castles (the counts of Anjou in France were especially avid castle builders in the late tenth and eleventh centuries), the first castellans were the counts' appointees. Some of the castellans may have been descended from younger sons of the great nobles of previous centuries, but many seem instead to have come from more modest backgrounds and only attained their real power after they had been put in charge of a castle. Whatever their origins, castellans quickly made their position hereditary. The castles were strong enough that the castellans could be in a position to defy even the counts if the counts neglected them for long.

The other new social group to become important in the eleventh century was that of the knights. Knights, who only appeared for the first time at the end of the tenth century and became numerous in the eleventh century, were originally not considered noble. Indeed, it was not until the thirteenth century that knights and nobles fused into one social class. Originally the knights were armed retainers, men who served the counts and castellans and fought on their behalf, but they were not in any way their equals. A powerful lord always kept a group of knights with him. He paid for their armor and weapons, fed them, gave them presents such as coins or rings at Christmas and other holidays, and in general treated them as high-class servants. The word for "knight" in Latin was *miles*, *milites* in the plural (from the same root as our "military").

Ability to fight or lead an army had been admired in men like Charlemagne, but it had never been a criterion of nobility. Nobles of the high Middle Ages were distinguished, as they had been in Carolingian times, by their wealth, their power, and their birth. Knights, distinguished only by their ability to fight, tried to copy the nobles they lived among and even longed to marry noble girls, but it was not until the thirteenth century that knights and nobles became identical (see pages 195–96.

A castellan normally had a large group of knights living with him. When they got to be in their late thirties, too old to fight as effectively as they once had, the lord usually pensioned them off with some land of their own. By the twelfth century, many knights started building miniature, imitation castles on their land. After retiring, knights would marry and have children; their sons might go up to the castle to become the knights of the son of the castellan their father had served.

A knight's principal equipment was his sword, shield, and armor. Swords were fairly long and quite heavy, often requiring two hands to swing properly, nothing like the thin dueling foils Hollywood directors have sometimes put in knights' hands. Shields, carried on the left arm, were large and oval, sometimes tapering to a point at the bottom. Heraldry, an elaborate system of shield designs and coats of arms, did not come into use until the later Middle Ages. In the eleventh and twelfth centuries, armor consisted either of metal rings sewn onto a leather shirt and short leather trousers, or of a chain-mail shirt. Chain mail was much more expensive, because it required soldering hundreds of links together to form a smooth shirt. (Plate mail was not yet invented.) Armor had to be flexible, because one had to be able to maneuver, to ride and dismount, while wearing it.

Nobles and their knights usually fought on horseback after the eleventh century, as oat-growing and the availability of horses spread. From their horses they could hurl spears at the enemy. Spears were thrown overhand; it was not until the end of the twelfth century that it became common to carry heavy lances underhand, in a "couched" position, charging at someone with them in the style beloved of movie directors. The great advantage of a cavalry charge was that, even without lances, it could break up and scatter footsoldiers. For close fighting with swords, horsemen still often dismounted. Fighting from horseback was not automatically superior, especially as there was danger the horse might bolt. The Battle of Hastings, fought for control of England in 1066, was fought between Anglo-Saxons on foot and mounted Normans (the Normans had had to build special boats to bring their horses over from Normandy). The Anglo-Saxons, as shown on the Bayeux Tapestry, which was embroidered to commemorate the battle, made a wall with their shields at the top of a hill too steep for the Normans to make an effective cavalry charge against them. The Anglo-Saxons might even have won the battle if they had not already been exhausted from fighting another battle against the Norwegians just a short time earlier.

Archery always played an important part in medieval battles, but nobles and knights did not fight with bows and arrows. They certainly knew how to shoot them, using them extensively in hunting, but in battle a bow was considered a coward's weapon, because the archer could kill from a long way off, without being threatened himself. The nobles were perfectly willing, however, to employ others to use such weapons on their behalf. A church council in 1139 forbade the use of bows and arrows against Christians, but no one seems to have paid any attention.

There were two kinds of bows in common use in the eleventh and twelfth centuries. One was the ordinary bow, a long, straight stave strung with gut; it became progressively longer during the course of the Middle Ages until it became the "longbow" of Robin Hood stories in the fourteenth and fifteenth centuries. The other sort of bow was the crossbow. This was a much shorter bow, mounted crosswise on a stock like a rifle butt. Rather than drawing back the arrow on the string when one wanted to shoot, as with an ordinary bow, one drew back the string ahead of time, hooking it around a notch; the bow was then fired by pulling a trigger that released the string. Although the crossbow was much shorter than a regular bow, it was also much less pliable, and it required considerable force to bend it. In using the type of crossbow available during the high Middle Ages, the archer might put his foot on the bow to bend it while tugging at the string with both hands, or even lie on his back, pushing the bow with both feet while slowly pulling the string up to the notch. Such a powerful bow could shoot its short arrow (or "quarrel," as it was called) with much more force than could an ordinary bow, but

THE NORMAN CONQUEST

The Norman Conquest of England in 1066 was the last success-ful invasion of England in history. It began when Edward, the last Anglo-Saxon king of England, died without sons. There were, however, three men who each claimed the right to be king of En-gland. The first was Harold Godwinson, the brother-in-law of King Edward, and he was indeed elected king by the most powerful An-glo-Saxon lords. (The office of king was elective in the early and high Middle Ages, even though only the most powerful could vote.) However, Harold Godwinson immediately had to go to battle with Harold Hardrada, king of Norway, who claimed that *he* was the rightful king of England. No sooner had Harold Godwinson de-feated Harold Hardrada than he had to march across England to face the third claimant, William of Normandy.

William was the duke of Normandy, that region of France which had been given to the Vikings by the French king at the beginning of the tenth century. In the one hundred fifty years since, Normandy had become very much a part of French culture, though its dukes tended to follow their own counsel and ignore the kings. William was a cousin of Edward, the late Anglo-Saxon king, and believed that both Edward and Harold Godwinson had promised that he should be next king of England. He therefore invaded En-gland and, after defeating Harold Godwinson at the Battle of Has-tings, had his own powerful lords elect him king of England. The Norman nobles who came with him replaced the Anglo-Saxon no-bles for the most part, and for the next one hundred fifty years the king of England was also duke of Normandy. After consolidating his hold on England, William made an inventory of the property and dues of his new kingdom, called the Domesday Book, in 1086. This book is still an invaluable source of information on England in the eleventh century.

Illustration from the Bayeux Tapestry, showing Norman warriors riding into battle at Hastings. They are accompanied by archers on foot.

because it could take thirty seconds or more to load each arrow, it was much slower to use.

Fief-holding

With the appearance of castellans and knights in the eleventh century, a new form of personal relationship among the aristocracy also first appeared, that of fief-holding. A "fief" was a piece of property that a noble controlled but did not actually own; rather, he held it from another noble.

Fief-holding is sometimes called "feudalism," from the medieval Latin word for a fief (*feudum*), but it is probably better to avoid this word. "Feudalism" is not the translation of any medieval term, and, as soon as one starts to use *-ism* words, one implies that one is discussing a universal and clearly recognized system, which fief-holding was not. Perhaps even more importantly, the term "feudalism" was only invented in the seventeenth century and then used in the French Revolution in the eighteenth century as a general term for such practices as enforced peasant labor on the roads or nobles' keeping dovecots (houses for keeping doves), which the Revolution was abolishing, and which clearly had nothing to do with fief-holding. (The peasants of the eighteenth century objected to the dovecots because the doves ate their grain.) It is therefore best not to use the term "feudalism" at all when discussing the Middle Ages, and most serious scholars of the period have long since abandoned it.

Fief-holding first came into use during the eleventh century and only became common in the twelfth century. It only involved nobles or knights and nobles; it did not involve the peasants. Fief-holding was a combination of a system of land tenure with a personal relationship between the ultimate owner of a piece of land and the man who held the land from him. The person who actually owned the land, the lord, granted it, as a fief, to another man, who was known as his "vassal." In return, the vassal promised to support and defend his lord.

The vassal swore this oath of fidelity while performing a ceremony known as "homage," to symbolize that he was his lord's man. ("Homage" comes from the Latin *homo*, or "man.") In this ceremony, the vassal went down on his knees, put his hands together, and held them up to the lord. The lord put his hands around his vassal's hands, drew him up, and kissed him. Thus the ceremony symbolized, on the one hand, the vassal's dependent position and, on the other hand, the ultimate social equality between lord and vassal. (Interestingly, it was at this time, the eleventh and twelfth centuries, when fief-holding first became common, that the "attitude of prayer" which now prevails came into use. Earlier one had either prayed standing, with the arms outstretched, or else lying prone; now one knelt, with the hands clasped together, as God's vassal.)

Homage was supposed to be a lifelong relationship; the lord could only take the fief back from the vassal if the vassal broke his oath of fidelity and turned against him. There were no regular dues owed in return for a fief, other than fidelity and support against attack, although by the end of the twelfth century it was generally assumed that this fidelity included helping ransom one's lord if he were captured, as well as helping him pay for the marriage of his oldest daughter and the knighting ceremony of his oldest son (both of these, discussed further on pages 196 and 206, were expensive ceremonies). The support the vassal was supposed to provide was soon defined to mean giving forty days of military service a year if his lord needed him.

Because fief-holding was a personal relationship, it had to be renewed in every generation, although it quickly took on a hereditary aspect, with the expectation that the vassal's son would do homage to the son of his father's lord, in return for the same fief. It should be clear that this sort of relationship was quite different from the relationships between landlords and peasant tenants, or between serfs and their lords of the body. Fief-holding was a personal relationship between aristocrats, whereas the peasants were involved in economic relationships with people whose status was far above theirs. Peasants were not in any way the social equals of their lords, as vassals were assumed to be the social equals of *their* lords, and peasants held their land hereditarily, in perpetuity, as long as they paid their dues and fees regularly, whereas no dues and fees were involved in fief-holding.

Fief-holding originally began on a small and rather haphazard basis. In many cases when it first appeared it did not actually change how much land either lord or vassal directly controlled, but rather put the relationship between the two on a new basis. For example, the counts who found that the castellans they had put in their castles as their agents were becoming increasingly independent tried to persuade the castellans that they held these castles in fief, in return for fidelity. Two castellans who had quarreled over a piece of property might reach an agreement by which one agreed to hold it in fief from the other. By the end of the eleventh century, although most nobles still owned most of their land as allods—that is, outright—they were also part of a complex web of fief-holding, holding different pieces of land in fief from several different lords, and being lord in return to several different vassals. Land that one held in fief might be "sub-enfeoffed" to one's own vassal.

The result was a tangle of ownership and obligations in which even the same two men might be respectively lord and vassal for one fief and vassal and lord for another. Because a vassal was supposed to support his lord, there quickly arose the question of which lord he should support if two of his lords were at war. The answer to this particular dilemma was the development of "liege homage," in which the vassal promised to support one lord, his liege lord, against all others. But there were problems here too, for liege homage soon multiplied, with a vassal promising several different lords that he would treat *them* as his liege lord.

This tangled set of relationships was no orderly system and grew up in many different places at once. Originally it did not involve the kings at all. But the kings were quick to realize that fief-holding and homage might be valuable tools to bind the dangerously independent-minded nobles of their realm to them. In England, at the time of the Norman

EUROPE IN 1200

At the end of the twelfth century, the kings of Germany, who were also emperors of the West, controlled much of central Europe and northern Italy. France was politically divided because the areas of western France, which had once been controlled by the dukes of Normandy or Aquitaine, were now under the English crown. Kings of Spain and Portugal had pushed the Muslims to the southern part of the Spanish peninsula.

Conquest in 1066, William the Conqueror made it clear that he would not only be king of England but also lord of all its lands. He made all the barons do homage to him for all their holdings in England. Because William was able to start in England with a clean slate, he was able to persuade the Norman lords to accept their position as his vassals, but this was harder for the French and German kings, who had to deal with dukes and counts who might have been established longer than the kings and who were resistant to anything they perceived might decrease their power. Only in the second half of the twelfth century were the kings of France and Germany able to persuade the great nobles, by now accustomed to the ideas of fief-holding and vassalage, that they had actually been the king's vassals all along.

Changes in the Position of the Nobility
in the Thirteenth Century

Increases in Royal Power

By the end of the twelfth century, then, the nobles were in a quite different position than they had been two centuries earlier. With the advent of the castellans, there were many more nobles, and some things that they had long considered their prerogatives were now being challenged, especially by the growing powers of the kings. Nobles no longer could act as independent agents when they were the king's vassals, and when the judicial and military functions they had long assumed were gradually being taken away.

Whereas at the end of the Carolingian era the local lords had also been the lawgivers, the kings of all European countries increased the prestige and universality of royal law, so that by the thirteenth century local lord's courts, if they still existed, were assumed to be subservient to the central royal "supreme court," to which the lords' decisions could be appealed. Also during the twelfth century the kings increasingly fought their wars with mercenary soldiers, rather than calling on their great vassals. Mercenaries, who fought for money, were generally low-born rather than nobles, but the kings found them more reliable because they would not always come up with their own battle plans or decide to go home at the end of forty days, as might the more independent-minded nobles.

Perhaps most galling to the nobles, the kings of the thirteenth century first began to claim the right to "create" nobles who would be equal in social status to the nobles who already existed. Nobility had been something inborn, not given by the kings, and the kings could certainly not remove someone's noble position, but it could be challenged when, for the first time, kings began "ennobling" those who served them. The French kings of the thirteenth century, especially, relied on low-born men as their principal advisers, not nobles as had the kings of previous centuries, because these men, who owed everything to the king, would be less likely to show an unwanted independence. And the kings soon started granting "licenses of nobility" to these men as a reward for years of faithful service. These men in France were referred to as having *noblesse de robe*, nobility of the "gown" they wore as the king's clerks, rather than having the *noblesse d'épée*, the nobility of the sword of the hereditary nobles.

The Rise of the Knights into the Nobility

Not only were nobles' functions being taken away by the kings from above, but they were being challenged from below by the rise of the knights. Knights increasingly worked their way into the noble class during the course of the twelfth century. They had been imitating them as much as possible since the eleventh century, dressing, talking, carrying themselves like the lords to whom they lived in close proximity. And knights increasingly married the daughters of castellans. Although a castellan would naturally want a wealthy and noble wife for his oldest son, he was much less fussy over whom his daughters married. It was considered much better to marry off one's daughters than to have them be old maids in their brothers' castles, but it was often hard to find suitable husbands for them. This was because many castellans preferred to have only one son marry, having the other sons stay single, to avoid having to split the inheritance among them. Boys might also enter the church, but in the twelfth and thirteenth centuries there were very few nunneries and thus few opportunities for girls in the church. There were always more noble girls seeking husbands, therefore, than noble young men seeking wives.

The problem was made even worse because the church at this time forbade anyone more closely related than sixth cousins to marry, and, since the castellans of a region had all been marrying members of each other's families for generations, it was hard to find *anyone* who was a social equal who was not too closely related. An unrelated knight might therefore seem like a desirable match to a noble father desperately searching for a son-in-law, especially since such a tie would also increase the ties binding a retired knight to his lord.

A castellan's daughter was usually no older than fifteen or so when she married a knight of thirty or forty, but this sort of discrepancy was readily accepted; most twelfth-century marriages involved husbands much older than their wives. Such a knight's wife, though young, would be considered a noble lady in her own right. She therefore gave a distinct "tone" to her husband's little imitation castle, and, even more importantly, gave noble birth to their children. Thus, by the end of the twelfth century, castellans and knights, once distinct groups, had become socially and biologically one. There were certainly gradations within the nobility—those more wealthy and powerful and those less so—but by the thirteenth century the terms "knight" and "noble" meant the same thing, which they certainly had not 250 years earlier.

While the knights had been rising in status during the twelfth century, the castellans had also been increasingly defining themselves by the military functions that had once exclusively characterized the knights. Part of this seems to have been a product of the Crusades, when, starting at the end of the eleventh century, "Christian" fighting was described as something desirable and glorious. The coming-of-age ceremony for young noble boys came to be known as "knighting." (There is confusion in

195

*Changes in the
Position of the
Nobility in the
Thirteenth Century*

THE CRUSADES

There was only one successful Crusade, the first, launched in 1095, which captured the city of Jerusalem from the Muslims in 1098 and created a Kingdom of Jerusalem, modeled on French ideas of kingdoms, counties, and fief-holding. However, the crusading ideal was very strong throughout the twelfth and much of the thirteenth century and was still being invoked in the seventeenth century. Crusading combined an opportunity for adventure and booty with a promise of salvation for those who went, thus combining pilgrimage with war. It was also an extremely expensive expedition and an extremely dangerous one.

The Second Crusade was launched in 1147, after one of the outlying counties of the Kingdom of Jerusalem was recaptured. King Louis VII of France went on this Crusade but was able to do nothing. After the city of Jerusalem itself was recaptured in 1187, the kings of England, France, and Germany all went on the Third Crusade in 1189, but this Crusade also ended unsuccessfully. After the soldiers of the Fourth Crusade ended up being diverted to Constantinople, a Christian city that was theoretically their ally, and sacking it in 1204, the heart went out of the crusading movement. Crusades continued to be preached and expeditions launched, but none had any success, and it is not even agreed how to number the thirteenth-century and later Crusades.

modern English between the two meanings of "knight," between the armed retainer, the *miles*, on the one hand, and a young man who had just "come of age" on the other, but medieval French and German clearly distinguished the two concepts, using two different terms.) This ceremony initially consisted of simply giving a boy his first sword and spurs of his own, but by the end of the twelfth century it had become an elaborate business. It was the culmination of eight years or more of training and might involve days of feasting and exhibition fighting and dances. Since a boy's father had to pay for all this, he was often glad to be able to call on his vassals for help with the expenses (especially since they were usually invited to the festivities).

The increasingly military view nobles took of themselves made it easier for them to fuse with the upwardly mobile knights. In the thirteenth century, when nobles decided for the first time to create firm criteria of nobility, they decided on the knighting ceremony as the best criterion. To keep just anyone from being knighted, they started to insist that one could only be knighted if both one's grandfathers had been. Somewhat ironically, however, the knighting ceremony, intended to separate nobles from non-nobles by its very elaborateness, had become so expensive that many young nobles who would have liked to be knighted came from families that could not afford the ceremony. A new title was therefore invented, the "esquire," for someone who could and should have been knighted but had not been. It is interesting to note that earlier, when there had been an enormous gulf between nobles and the rest of society, there had been no need for criteria to define nobility. Only after the nobles had begun to lose some of their functions and authority and after the socially mobile had penetrated their ranks did the nobles find it necessary to define themselves, to keep any more people from calling themselves nobles, and, just as important, to keep themselves from losing their noble prestige.

The Nobles' Decreasing Wealth

The nobles' position became especially precarious in the thirteenth century, at least for some members of the group, because they had become much poorer than they once had been. There are many reasons for the gradual impoverishment of the nobles during the twelfth century. To our eyes, of course, they still seem very wealthy, much more so than the peasants, but in their own eyes they had lost much of what they had once had. In part the nobles were trapped by fixed income in a period of rising prices. As already mentioned, peasant dues and rents were fixed in perpetuity, but the things the lords had to buy with that money were increasingly expensive. The nobles also had new expenses they had not had in the eleventh century. New developments in castle architecture meant that every self-respecting castellan had to remodel and add to his castle every generation. The increasing availability of luxury trade goods, as discussed in the next chapter, meant that a noble had more to spend his money on. One of the most expensive undertakings of the twelfth century was the crusade, for a lord going on this expedition needed a great deal of equipment and enough money to last several years if needed. And, due to generations of dividing the inheritance and making gifts to the church, most nobles inherited less than their fathers or grandfathers had had. The result was that by the end of the twelfth century many nobles were short on ready cash and might have to pawn some of their property if leaving on crusade or paying for a knighting ceremony.

A castellan going into debt would borrow money in the hopes that a few years of economizing would allow him to save enough to repay the debt (the same happy belief people have today while running up the balances on their credit cards). But repayment was always more difficult than the noble had hoped. By the end of the twelfth century, monasteries were frequently advancing nobles cash, and every town had bankers willing to make large loans. Such loans were only made with a substantial piece of property as collateral, and unless the noble or his heirs repaid the loan within a certain period of time, they lost that property for good. By the thirteenth century some noble families had lost almost everything except their claim to be noble, including their castles. Meanwhile, some knights, or even some merchants, had taken the opportunity to buy up such property and install themselves in the castles. The most powerful nobles were able to become money lenders themselves and thus profit from others' difficulties, but below the highest ranks there were a great number of rising and falling fortunes within the aristocracy in the high Middle Ages.

However, the nobles were not helpless in the face of higher expenses and shrinking incomes. The castellans, especially, sought to increase their incomes by selling more and more of the produce of their estates at market and by increasingly demanding what are known as "banal dues." These were monopoly rights, which a castellan demanded in the region around his castle (his castellany), not because he was the landlord of the peasants of the region (he would only be the landlord for a few of them), but because he felt he had rights within an area he called his *bannum*. Such monopoly rights included the monopolies on mills and ovens, mentioned above, as well as toll bridges and market stalls. Banal rights did not extend to taxing everyone in a region just because they lived in that region, but the tendency was certainly in that direction. It indicates a new sort of idea of one's obligations, that one might owe certain things because of where one lived, the same concept we have now, rather than owing certain dues based on one's personal and family history. The establishment of banal rights, however, was only open to the more powerful castellans; the less powerful and wealthy did not have these opportunities to increase their income.

Life in the Castle

The life of a castle in the high Middle Ages was symbolically the life of a family, even though most of the people who lived in the castle were not actually related. Most castles, or at least the small and medium-sized ones, only had one married couple, the lord and lady of the castle. They

Stokesay Castle, in England, is typical of the many small castles that dotted Europe in the twelfth century.

were in effect the parents of all their knights and servants. These knights and servants were almost without exception men; the cooks, stablemen, chaplains, falconers, and dog-handlers, as well as the knights, were un-married men. The only women were a few handmaidens for the lady and her own unmarried daughters, plus possibly the lord's mother and his sister, if she had not married. These women had their own room on an upper floor of the castle. The different people who lived in a particular castle, whatever their social status, identified themselves with that castle, against all inhabitants of other castles, including those with the same social status. They had none of what today would be considered class consciousness.

The major activities of the castle were the same as those of any large country house throughout history: estate management and the oversee-ing of the farm. Although in the twelfth century the castellan himself rarely participated directly in agriculture, he had plenty to supervise. All lords had demesne land, which they worked directly, as well as land they rented out to the peasants. On the demesne land the lord had to make the decisions; when to sow, when to harvest, which crops to grow, how much to pay the hired workers, how many plow teams to use, and a myriad of other details. If some demesne land was located a distance from the castle (as it frequently was), the lord had to have an overseer there and then periodically check up on him. For the rented land he had to be sure that all the rents he was owed were properly paid. Some of the work on the demesne land was always done by men who lived in the lord's castle. The castellan was therefore not as far from the agricultural concerns of his peasant tenants as his castle walls might have suggested.

In the twelfth century, everyone in a castle, except the unmarried women, lived together in the great hall. They ate on trestle tables, and at night they cleared the tables away and set up beds on the floor. The lord and lady had by far the best bed, set on a dais at the end of the hall. It was curtained, which gave them a measure of privacy the other people in the hall did not have, but they were still very much a part of the hall. During the course of later centuries, much of the change in architecture of the castles, and after them the great country houses, was influenced by the gradual retreat of the lord and lady's bed: first to an alcove, then to its own room, then to a room at the end of a corridor, and so on. By the seventeenth century, a whole series of rooms led from the main hall to the lord's bedchamber.

Women in the Castle

The lord and lady had children of their own as well as being the sym-bolic parents of several dozen or even several hundred men. Girls were brought up at home and were trained in castle management almost from the time they could walk. The lady of the castle was its chief executive, being responsible for making sure there was enough food put away in the storerooms for everyone's needs, supervising the preparation of meals and the baking of bread in the castle oven, arranging to buy or weave cloth for everyone's clothes, overseeing the servants, keeping the knights from fighting each other. The castle's heavy set of keys hung on her belt. If the lord were away, his wife assumed even more duties, including, if necessary, defense of the castle from outside attack. Because a girl who married the lord of a castle would have to take over these duties immediately, and because noble girls normally married in their teens, a girl growing up was supposed to help her mother from the time she was very small. As part of their training, girls had to acquire a great deal of practical knowledge and also learned a little reading and writing (usually not in Latin but in the regular spoken language, whether French, German, Italian, or Spanish), as well as simple arithmetic.

Although a castellan's wife was theoretically subject to him, there are plenty of examples of women—both women in the stories of the time and historical ladies—who were much more formidable than their husbands. They might incite their husbands into actions they never would have dreamed of on their own. One woman named Juliana, an illegitimate daughter of King Henry I of England, directed the defense of her castle when she and her husband rebelled against the king. When the king, her father, besieged the castle, and it became clear that she could not hold out for long, she invited her father in for a conference, speaking to him as a dutiful daughter, but holding concealed a crossbow ready to shoot him. But her shot when wide and the king had her seized. Impressed by her audacity even though bitterly disappointed in her treachery, King Henry restricted Juliana's punishment to having her jump off the castle walls, wearing nothing but a shirt, into the bitterly cold waters of the moat, from which she was pulled, soaking and frozen, but not repentent.

The Training of Young Noblemen

Boys received their early education at home, along with their sisters, but they often received their training in fighting elsewhere. When boys were seven or eight, their parents decided for them whether they would go into the church or grow up in the secular world. If they were to enter the church, they would leave home to be trained in a monastery or in a cathedral school, as described in more detail in Chapter 8. On the other hand, if the parents decided that their sons would be trained as knights, they were also sent away from home, to be trained in someone else's castle. Often the count of a district had the heirs of his castellans all come to his court to be trained together. Other times a boy would be trained at his uncle's castle. His mother's brother was preferred to his father's brother; a maternal uncle was not a threat, but a paternal uncle was always a potential rival to his own father, a dangerous person to be entrusted with the heir to a birthright he might want to claim himself.

A boy's training typically took place in the company of other boys his age. Together they learned to ride, starting with ponies and working their way up to the massive warhorses. They fought first with wooden swords and shields, before moving on to real weapons, which at first had the edges blunted. By the end of the twelfth century, battles between mounted warriors usually entailed a charge, each warrior carrying a heavy lance, underhand in the "couched" position. The lance was steadied with the right arm and aimed at the shield of the warrior riding in the opposite direction, with the intention of knocking him off his horse. High saddles and stirrups helped the riders keep their seats. Boys practiced by riding at the "quoint," a small suspended hoop through which one would try to thrust the point of one's lance.

As well as learning military techniques, noble boys also learned more reading and writing than their mothers had taught them, maybe a little Latin, the intricacies of hunting and falconry, and such gentlemanly acts as singing, dancing, and playing musical instruments. Just as the lord of the castle where they were being trained was in effect the father of all the boys under him, the lady of the castle was both their symbolic mother and the lady whose favor they practiced winning with fine manners and pretty compliments. Boys also learned to play chess, which became quite popular in Europe during the high Middle Ages. The game seems to have come originally from India and to have evolved over the centuries, but by the twelfth century it was essentially the same game we play now, and fancy carved-ivory sets were highly prized. The boys were amused in the evenings by jugglers and tales of King Arthur, either told by story-tellers or read out from the books of popular literature that began to appear at the end of the twelfth century. Their training was long and often arduous, but the boys had much to enjoy and were by no means cut off from their relatives. They went home and visited their families fairly frequently, just as modern boys go home from boarding school for the holidays.

A combination of good manners, civilized accomplishments, and handsome appearance, called "courtliness," was the goal. Courtliness as a concept seems to have originated in reading Roman authors, many of whom advocated "civilized" behavior. During the tenth century, when men in the church were reading classical authors, such courtliness became an ideal for the bishops, but by the twelfth century it was an educational goal for members of the nobility as well. Although such a goal was never fully realized, young nobles of the high Middle Ages, trained in courtliness, had much more restraint in their personal interactions, less coarseness in their habits, and better table manners than did their predecessors of the early Middle Ages.

After a young noble's training was complete, he went through an elaborate dubbing or knighting ceremony, as mentioned on page 195. In the eleventh century, when dubbing began, it was a simple operation, the girding-on of a boy's first real sword to show he was a man. By the thirteenth century, however, the ceremony had become extremely elaborate. All his family's friends and relatives were invited for festivities that might go on for days. There was also a strong religious element in knighting by this time. The young noble sat up in prayer all night before his official dubbing, and the handle and guards of his sword, which might indeed be inset with a saint's relics, were consciously equated with the cross. It is significant of the high-medieval nobility's attitude toward both war and religion that they thought the two could be combined. The theory was that, under the guidance of God, the young noble would use his fighting skills to protect churches and the weak and poor from their enemies.

Once dubbed, a young noble was supposed to be a man, ready to take his place in society and to fight for Christianity, but in practice he often found himself with little to do. Back home from his warrior training, he was in the awkward position of being an adult without any of an adult's rights or responsibilities, for until his father died he could not be the lord of the castle. Until the thirteenth century, fathers even discouraged their sons from marrying, because a castle could only have one married couple as the symbolic parents of all the castle's inhabitants. The only exceptions were if a family controlled more than one castle, in which case the heir might marry and settle in one, or if he were able to marry an heiress and take *her* castle. There was a special medieval Latin term, *juvenes,* or "youths," meaning young knights and nobles who had finished all their education and training but had not yet come into their inheritance and responsibilities. The term did not strictly describe one's *age,* for some men were *juvenes* into their forties, but rather one's status or position.

The *juvenes* provided the great mass of crusaders in the twelfth and thirteenth centuries. Both the great expeditions now numbered as Crusades (the First, Second, and so on), as well as the many expeditions to the Holy Land mounted in the years between, were made up mostly of young knights and nobles. These expeditions promised salvation for their souls and offered the possibility of making their fortunes. After the first generation or so of crusading, however, it became clear that a great many crusaders—in fact the majority—never came back, drowning in shipwrecks on the way, being killed by the Saracens, or dying of disease. Many fathers who did not like to have their sons underfoot in the castle were still very upset at the prospect of their going to the Holy Land, probably never to return; such fathers might give their sons advances on their inheritance as an inducement to stay.

The *juvenes* also made up most of the converts to the new monastic orders discussed in Chapter 8. Although noble parents preferred that their sons be monks rather than be dead on crusade, they still often reacted in the same panic-stricken way if the heir announced he was going to join a monastery as if he told them he was going on crusade. Indeed, in some ways conversion to monasticism *was* comparable to death—at least death to the world—for sons in the cloister could not inherit or carry on their fathers' lineage. Young men with a sincere religious vocation might receive the same stiff opposition from their parents that college students of the last twenty years or so have received in announcing that they were going to join a commune or the Hari Krishnas.

If the *juvenes* did not go to the Holy Land or become monks, they often amused themselves by fighting in tournaments. Tournaments appeared for the first time in the twelfth century, as substitutes for the open warfare that was becoming increasingly banned or at least difficult. Although tournaments were condemned by bishops from the beginning, they were always enormously popular; the only drawback to fighting in one was that it was hard to be buried in consecrated ground if actually killed. And people *were* killed in twelfth-century tournaments with some frequency, even though that was not the purpose of the exercise. The pageantry and formal conventions depicted in Hollywood movies were not found in the twelfth century (although late medieval tournaments did become much more elaborate). Rather, the main form of fighting was the "melée," a free-for-all on horseback. The warriors fought, theoretically, with blunted weapons, but there were few other regulations to govern the fighting, which was not even confined to a particular area. The fighting might range over several square miles and go on all day.

The result was something more like a small war, with few rules other than those against deliberately killing or maiming someone. The men of the count of Flanders once came to a tournament announcing that they had come to watch, not participate, but once everyone else was exhausted they saddled up and quickly took a number of prisoners, which everyone agreed was an excellent trick. The taking of prisoners, who would have to pay a ransom, was the main purpose of these tournaments. Although the amount of such ransoms was not overly large, typically being a man's horse and armor, a skillful fighter could do very well for himself on the tournament circuit.

It is interesting to note that in the high Middle Ages, as in the previous six centuries, war was considered a glorious and worthy occupation, especially for the upper classes, but one that was becoming much more difficult to practice at home. The tournaments and especially the Crusades provided outlets for the military activities of young men who were caught between believing that success in battle was a glorious goal and having it drummed into them that they should not kill the defenseless, or even Christians who defended themselves.

In the twelfth and thirteenth centuries, while the Crusades were still going well, the Christian church came as close as it ever did to stopping fighting between Christians. A sign of its success was the popularity of the Knights of the Hospital and the Knights of the Temple (Hospitallers and Templars), military orders that started in the Holy Land. The knights who belonged to these orders lived almost like monks, under a rule and a master, but instead of spending their days copying books, working in the fields, or praying, they fought the infidel and protected pilgrims. The combination of warfare and a monastic lifestyle was an uneasy one, without much potential for universal application, but that it was successful at all indicates how far the church had come. (Interestingly, in the fourteenth century, as will be seen in Chapter 9, Christians were back at open war with each other in Europe again.)

Choosing Prospective Partners

If a young noble survived tournament and crusade and did not become a monk, he typically came into his inheritance after a few years or more of being a *juvenis*. That is, the oldest son would come into his inheritance; younger brothers might be *juvenes* indefinitely, or at most be given some land to hold in fief from their older brothers, unless they found heiresses of their own. Now, perhaps in his thirties, the heir would get married and settle down, marrying a girl often only half his age. His wife was expected to be of at least the same social class, and indeed many a young man dreamed of marrying a woman of a more distinguished background than his. A young man might choose his own wife, or his parents might have selected a wife for him earlier, while the girl was still much too young to be married. In either case, it was assumed

Thirteenth-century betrothal document of a lord and lady, showing their family trees.

that both families would have to agree to the match. Although one would not have to marry someone one found disgusting (the literature of the time often portrayed parents who tried to marry their children to repellent spouses, but such parents were always described as wicked parents), personal attraction was not the chief criterion for choosing a mate.

In modern America, we tend to be shocked at the idea of arranged marriages or of being sure of marrying within the right social group, but in fact these elements are still very much part of society. Parents who send their children off to college do so with at least some thought that their children will meet their future husbands or wives at college. Although we do not assume, as did the knights and nobles of the twelfth century, that someone from a wealthy family must marry someone from another wealthy family, we do assume that spouses should have a similar educational background. A marriage between a Ph.D. and a high-school dropout today would be considered nearly as shocking as a twelfth-century marriage between a knight and a peasant's daughter. And, in spite of advances against discrimination, a young person today bringing home someone of another race or religion can still cause plenty of upheaval.

The Marriage Ceremony

Although mutual attraction was not the principal reason for an aristocrat to choose his or her spouse, the idea of falling in love and getting married as a result did begin to appear in the literature of the twelfth century. Knights and ladies of the stories met each other during various adventures and overcame great difficulties to be married (although, in these stories, the young lovers were always of suitable status to have married each other anyway). Even in an arranged marriage, the people of the twelfth century assumed that spouses would be affectionate toward each other; one was *supposed* to love one's husband or wife.

By the twelfth century, marriage, which had once been a purely secular contract (as noted in Chapter 5), had become sacred, and the pledging of troth was considered a sacrament. Interestingly, it was a sacrament that the priest did *not* administer. Rather, the man and woman performed it themselves in the act of swearing their oaths to each other. This actual sacrament, however, did not take place without a lot of preliminary negotiation. Before the wedding ceremony, the bride's and groom's families had to agree on the amount of the dowry the girl would bring with her and determine the amount of dower her husband would settle on her.

Roman law had stipulated that a bride bring a dowry with her, and Germanic custom had added to that the dower or "morning-gift" a husband brought to his wife. Both dowry and dower, as noted previously, had been important throughout the early Middle Ages. In the high Middle Ages, on the Continent, the dower was becoming less important, being reduced to some presents (such as jewelry) rather than an actual share of the husband's inheritance. It was stipulated, however, that even an insolvent husband's creditors could not take the wife's dowry; although she had given it to him, it was to remain inviolate to support her if she was widowed. In England, where the system of dower never died out, a rough third of a husband's wealth was settled on his wife for her to live on after he died.

Although in the United States prenuptial agreements have traditionally been quite rare, at least for first marriages, they were the norm in the high Middle Ages among the aristocracy and townspeople. Unless the bride had already been widowed, negotiations did not involve her directly but were carried out between the husband-to-be and the bride's father or brother. After all the financial arrangements had been made, the wedding ceremony itself, the sacrament, was short and simple. In the high Middle Ages, it took place not in church but on the church porch. There the bride and bridegroom promised, in front of witnesses, to stay with each other and be true to each other all their lives. As a symbol of this promise, they exchanged rings.

This oath was the heart of a valid marriage. In fact, such an oath created a valid union even if there were no witnesses. Since without witnesses it was often very difficult to determine if oaths *had* been exchanged if one party denied it later, one was legally supposed to have people witnessing. But even if the couple exchanged their vows illegally, in private, they would still be validly married (that is, they could not marry anyone else), even if they had to do penance for marrying in secret.

After the brief wedding ceremony—that is, the oaths and the exchange of rings—the wedding party, consisting of the couple, their families, and their witnessing friends, all went inside the church. Here the priest, who had not even been out on the church porch for the exchange of vows, blessed the new couple, and everyone heard mass. Even today, although church weddings are held entirely inside the church, Catholic weddings still have two parts, first the wedding ceremony itself and then the separate nuptial mass. After the mass, there was feasting and dancing for the entire wedding party, very much like the modern wedding reception. Noble fathers were expected to put on a very elaborate party, at least for their oldest daughters, just as fathers today are pressured to pay for a big reception.

But there was still one final thing necessary for a valid marriage, the "carnal copulation" as it was called. A medieval couple was not validly married until the marriage had been actually consummated, and indeed many husbands held off transferring the dower to their bride until the next morning. (Couples living together today, who have promised each other to stay together indefinitely and have consummated their union, might be surprised to learn that, by medieval standards, they are validly married.) Because one of the principal purposes of marriage was the production of heirs, the new couple was supposed to start the process as soon as possible. The wedding party took it upon themselves to get them underway, usually tucking them into bed together. Even after leaving them alone, friends and relatives tried to help out by singing naughty songs below the window or yelling useful suggestions through the door. (This too has modern analogies; many people today find it hilarious to try to locate a honeymooning couple at their motel and perhaps learn the telephone number of their suite so they can call and give them helpful comments.)

Both husband and wife in the high Middle Ages were expected to be true to each other. The double standard that earlier centuries had taken for granted might still be in place, but it was no longer accepted or taken for granted in the same way. Before marriage, although young ladies were supposed to be virginal, it was assumed that young men would have several amorous adventures, perhaps with women of a much lower social status, women whom they would never marry themselves but to whom they might make rich gifts that would give them importance in their villages. If a noblewoman was widowed, she was supposed to remain chaste, whereas a noble widower, it was expected, would take a concubine. But at least while husband and wife were still alive both were expected to remain faithful, and now general noble sentiment, not just the bishops, urged chastity on the men. When the English king Henry I lost his one legitimate son in a shipwreck in the early twelfth century, leaving him over twenty illegitimate children but no royal heirs, it was agreed that this was a judgment on him for not staying at home where he belonged.

Annulments

Once married, one was supposed to be married for life. The church had begun objecting to divorce in the ninth century, and, once marriage came to be a sacrament in the eleventh century, there was no changing one's mind. A divorce would be the dissolution of something sacred and thus impossible, as indeed it still officially is in modern Catholicism. The only possibility was an annulment, that is, an official declaration that one had not actually been married in the first place.

If either the husband or wife was already married to someone else, then of course their wedding could not be valid, but other grounds for annulment were more complicated. If the couple could prove that they had not in fact exchanged oaths or had not actually proceeded with "carnal copulation," then they were not married, but these were hard to prove, especially if one person wanted an annulment and the other person did not. At the end of the twelfth century, the French king Philip II took a strong dislike to his new bride on their wedding night and started first thing in the morning trying to get an annulment, claiming that the marriage had not been consummated. But proceedings dragged out for years because the new queen insisted to the contrary that it *had* been consummated, that she remembered perfectly, and that it was not the sort of thing one could mistake. If witnesses could attest that a couple had indeed exchanged their vows and if there was little doubt that their marriage was consummated (for example, if they had had children), then one or the other might still try to claim that they had only exchanged oaths under duress, because a promise that was not given freely was not a real promise and thus did not count.

But the most common grounds for annulment or divorce in the high

Middle Ages was the "discovery" that the couple could not have been validly married in the first place because such a marriage would have been incestuous. This was based on the church's definition of "consanguinity," of how closely people could be related and still marry. As already mentioned, at this time the church forbade marriages between people related more closely than sixth cousins. When this definition of consanguinity was first promulgated widely, in the tenth and eleventh centuries, nobles seemed to take it seriously. As discussed above, the nobles' desire to find marriage partners to whom they were not already related helped facilitate the knights' entry into noble ranks.

By the end of the twelfth century nobles began disregarding such prohibitions, marrying third or fourth cousins to whom they knew they were related but keeping it secret from the priest who was going to bless the new couple. If the couple later decided for other reasons that they wanted to get a divorce, they could "discover" that they had been living in sin all along. In the middle of the twelfth century, the French king Louis VII (father of King Philip II, just mentioned), who had married his third cousin, "discovered" that they were third cousins only after she had still failed to produce a male heir when they had been married nearly fifteen years. (She remarried, however, and bore a son to her second husband within the year, indicating that a lack of male heirs had not been *her* fault.)

Even if a couple had not known when they were married that they were related, the fact that the number of one's relatives increases exponentially for each generation that one traces one's ancestry, meant that a determined couple could probably find a common ancestor without great difficulty. In essence, the church's prohibition of broadly defined "incest" meant that noble couples could practically obtain divorce on demand. At last, in order to end this practice, a church council in 1215 officially changed the definition of incest, so that only marriages between people related more closely than third cousins were forbidden.

The high Middle Ages was a period during which society had become well enough ordered that it was possible, for the first time in centuries, to try to work out such apparently minute details as what constituted incest and indeed to enforce them. The greater agricultural productivity of the period gave society the opportunity for some people to go into such areas as legal studies, theology, and long-distance commerce, as detailed in Chapters 7 and 8, rather than agriculture. It also gave society a respite from fear of famine, which made it possible for certain people to give their attention to other details of society than simple survival. In sharp distinction to the ancient world, however, many of those who devoted themselves to such activities did so in nonurban settings such as the monasteries.

The castles that sprouted across Europe in the high Middle Ages are one of the most visible symbols of medieval culture. The men who lived in them certainly gave much of their attention to training for warfare, to stories of King Arthur, to hunting, chess, and courting the ladies. But they were also acutely aware of their dependence on continued agricultural productivity. The big manors often took the lead in raising food for market, and the castellans were able to maintain their position, even in an era of declining rents, by exercising new banal rights over such things as the increases in trade and milling. The nobles also produced many of the leaders of the church and the intellectual lights who will be discussed in Chapter 8. The high Middle Ages was one of the few times in history when both the lords and the peasantry found themselves in relatively secure and economically advantageous positions.

SEVEN

THE HIGH MIDDLE AGES: TOWNS AND TRADE

c. **950**	Trade routes with Jewish merchants first appear
c. **1000**	Urbanization begins in Italy
c. **1100**	Urbanization begins in France
c. **1100**	The office of *podestà* becomes common in Italy
c. **1120**	Invention of the astrolabe
c. **1150**	Communal government becomes common in France
c. **1180**	Establishment of major trade fairs
1193	First mayor of London
c. **1200**	Bridge House Trust established in London
c. **1250**	Champagne trade fairs begin to decline in importance
1252	Florentine gold florin first minted

CHAPTER

SEVEN

THE HIGH MIDDLE AGES: TOWNS AND TRADE

URBAN CULTURE WAS REVIVED in the high Middle Ages after a lapse of some six centuries. Although the cities of the period between 1050 and 1250 were not nearly the size of ancient Rome, and although, outside of Italy, the major part of society and government remained rural, the revival of the cities was an essential and highly visible part of the changes from the early to the high Middle Ages. Today we may find it easier to think of the Middle Ages in terms of castles and peasant farmers, but cities with elected town councils, international trade fairs, and a growing banking industry were just as much a part of high-medieval civilization. Tournaments may be more colorful on the big screen today than urban self-government or the wool industry, but the latter were at least as important to the people of the time. The cities grew as a result of trade and commerce; manufacturing and commercial enterprises, which had not been major parts of the European economy for centuries, acquired new importance in the high Middle Ages. Unlike the city-states of the ancient world, medieval cities outside Italy did not dominate their countryside politically. In northern and western Europe, the castles rather than the cities were the chief political centers, but the cities were increasingly the economic centers.

The Growth of Medieval Cities

Almost without exception, the growing cities of western Europe were the same cities that had once been Roman provincial capitals. This is both because the Roman cities had been located in the places that were naturally suited for cities (for example, at rivers and crossroads), and because throughout the early Middle Ages much of the commercial activity that persisted (with the exception of the "northern trade" discussed in Chapter 5) was centered on the old Roman cities, which thus provided a good basis for commercial expansion. Long-deserted streets once again had houses built along them, and new walls had to be constructed as the city grew far beyond the original Roman walls. The urban culture that revived in the twelfth century has continued without further break and for the most part in exactly the same places, which are today the cities of modern Europe.

A twelfth-century city was of course not nearly as urbanized as a modern city. Many of the houses had large garden plots behind them, and cows and vineyards were common within the city walls. There are probably nearly as many people in a modern suburban shopping mall on the last weekend before Christmas as lived in twelfth-century London. But these medieval cities had a distinctly urban culture and organization, recognizable as such even to twentieth-century city dwellers, and it would have been recognizable to the citizens of Rome. The medieval cities still exist at the heart of almost all European cities. It is rare for city buildings (other than some churches) to have lasted eight hundred years, but the narrow, crooked streets are still in the same places they have always been. A European city's "old town" today, usually less than a mile across, includes both the Roman city and all the additions made in the twelfth and thirteenth centuries. These towns, small enough that one could walk across them in fifteen or twenty minutes, were designed for pedestrian traffic, and wise city councils have recently begun making these ancient centers of the modern towns pedestrian-only zones.

Although a medieval city was very small by modern standards, usually no more than ten thousand people, it was still divided into several sections. The bishops, who had maintained their residences in the shrunken Roman cities throughout the early Middle Ages, still retained control of the oldest part of a medieval city, that tiny area walled during the late

Medieval walls surround the town of Baützen in eastern Germany.

Roman Empire. Here a bishop had his cathedral and his palace, and here the cathedral canons lived, those priests who helped in cathedral services and administration of the diocese. (Canons are discussed in Chapter 8.) The bishop's part of town is often called the *cité*, reflecting the fact that religious buildings and religious government were always a major factor in medieval cities.

Besides the *cité*, there were at least three other parts of town, and often more, each called a "burg" and typically having its own walls. Every important monastery had its own burg, with a small residential and commercial district, as well as the abbey church and cloister, within its walls. The count had a burg of his own around his castle, from which he eyed the bishop with suspicion; since bishops and counts controlled more or less identical regions, though the former theoretically had spiritual authority and the latter secular authority, each considered the other a principal rival. In most cities in the twelfth century, bishops and counts worked out formal agreements by which certain areas, certain activities, and certain types of crime within the city would be in the bishop's jurisdiction, and the rest under the count's. The bishops, for example, normally maintained their authority over local churchmen.

But the biggest threat to the position of both the counts and the bishops came from the new inhabitants of the cities, the merchants and the artisans. Because they had their own burg, separate from that of the bishop or count, they are sometimes called "burghers." It is interesting to note that separation of a city into separate functions is often still visible today. In France, for example, the twin city of Clermont-Ferrand, which still has a wide, fairly empty area between the two halves, was originally two cities, a bishop's city and a count's city, built next to each other. Even in modern London there is still a distinction between the City, as the medieval merchant's town and the center of modern British finance is called, and Westminster, the medieval center of government and still the site of the Houses of Parliament, a short distance up the Thames River from the City.

Whereas in the ancient world most city dwellers (outside of Rome itself) had been directly involved in agriculture, going out from the city during the day to work in the fields, in the high Middle Ages most of the people who were not directly attached to the churches or the count's castle were either employed by the merchants and involved in trade, or the artisans, who spent their days engaged in a craft, such as shoemaking or silversmithing. The cities were growing rapidly in the twelfth century; much of the population consisted of former country-dwellers who had migrated to the city, taking up new ways of life when they arrived. The merchants and the artisans might share a burg within a city or each group might have its own. The merchants' burg (which was sometimes known as a *wik*) included taverns and inns for travelers and warehouses where trade goods could be stored. The artisans' burg was commonly divided among the different crafts, each having its own street—for example, the street of the butchers, or the street of the wool dyers.

Urban Self-Government

From the time that towns first began to grow, the merchants and the artisans were involved in a struggle for self-government against the bishops or the counts or both. The autonomy of most high-medieval towns, as well as their (reasonably) democratic form of government, are in many ways parallel to the government and structure of the *poleis* in ancient Greece (see Chapter 2). However, medieval towns were not modeled on the *poleis*, of which the burghers were unaware. And there are several important differences between the cities of the high Middle Ages and the city-states of Greece. In Greece, there had been no central government, which meant that each *polis* was politically independent; although this was to some extent true in medieval Italy (where the theoretic central government was in the hands of the emperor, in Germany), in other parts of medieval Europe the cities always had to consider the king. Even more striking, in Greece the citizens who ran the *poleis* had been warriors, philosophers, and gentleman farmers, men who left trade and commerce to "foreigners," whereas in the cities of medieval Europe urban self-government was the government of merchants and artisans.

Business people like to be governed by those of their own kind—not that they want to avoid government regulation per se (after all, regulation can be very useful if it holds down competition), but because they want the regulation to be predictable and sensitive to their concerns. From the middle of the twelfth century on, the inhabitants of most cities tried to establish "communes," governments of and by the merchants and artisans. The counts, who had their capitals in the cities but their main power in rural areas, were easier to persuade to accept a commune than were the bishops. (Interestingly, although a commune was a self-governing body, the people who formed them did not believe in self-government as an abstract principle; usually one of their first acts was to try to extend control over the surrounding countryside.)

A commune might have any of an enormous variety of governmental forms, but it was always a self-government by (at least some of) the men who lived in the city, what we would call a republic. While the older cities were trying, with greater or lesser success, to establish communes, "new towns" also began to be established during the twelfth century, which had self-government from the beginning. These were not real cities but rather large villages, where the powerful man who controlled some uninhabited land invited people to come and settle it and pay him rent, using the promise of communal government as an attraction. These new towns still exist throughout northern and western Europe. They are usually named Villeneuve or something similar, although at seven or eight hundred years old they are no longer new. These "new towns" can easily be recognized because they were usually laid out scientifically, on a rectangular grid, with plots assigned to the different settlers. This is in contrast to the older villages and towns, which had virtually no straight streets except for the two or three most important, having instead a complex network of twisting streets that developed as the population grew.

Whether a commune was established at an old city or granted at a new town, the local inhabitants were intensely proud of their local government. City governments had seals, which served as symbols of their corporate identity and usually depicted the city walls or gates. City walls were much more than lines of defense; they were also symbols of city unity, of wealth and power, and very real ways of assuring that no one brought goods in or out without paying the appropriate tolls and taxes. Just as the inhabitants of a castle, from the most powerful to the lowest servant, identified themselves much more with that particular castle than with people who filled a similar social role at another castle, so city dwellers thought of themselves as residents of a particular city first and as members of a particular social group which might also be found in

Aristocratic families in medieval Italy built defensible towers on their town houses, like this one in Perugia.

other cities secondly, if at all. This sort of civic pride was especially marked in Italy.

Some cities were quickly successful in establishing self-governing republics, especially in Italy, where the bishops and the nobles found it easier to join the merchants than to fight them. In other areas, however, the attempt to set up a commune led to prolonged struggles, with the count often joining the merchants against the bishop (especially if he were paid a large sum). The French kings were quite willing to support communes in return for a fee, although they never allowed a commune in their own capital of Paris. By the end of the twelfth century, most cities had worked out some sort of compromise between the different parties, with the commune a third governmental voice besides the voices of the count and bishop. The settlement of the worst of the disagreements between them meant that it was possible for them to join forces on such projects as building a new city wall, enclosing cathedral, castle, and the different burgs all within one wall for the first time. Such walls of the early thirteenth century enclosed what are now considered the "old towns" of modern European cities.

Italian cities grew and acquired self-government before the cities of northern Europe. Under the Roman Empire, Italy had been more highly urbanized than the rest of Europe, and it never completely lost its urban culture during the early Middle Ages. Whereas in the north, by the eleventh century, power was quite firmly in the hands of rural castellans, in Italy powerful men were settling in the cities in the same period.

In northern Europe in the twelfth century there was an important distinction drawn between those who inherited power and wealth and those who acquired it by trade and commerce, but this distinction never had much meaning in Italy. While new men came to power by shrewd trading, buying and selling, the longer-established Italian families participated in trade with equal enthusiasm. Different powerful urban families in Italy had the same sort of rivalry with each other that castellans of northern Europe had with other castellans. A powerful urban family might take over an old Roman theatre or amphitheatre and make it into a warren of fortified homes. Even today, in cities like San Gimignano, one can see the high towers that noble families erected, so that they could look down on their neighbors (who, however, were soon building rapidly to surpass them in height). From these towers the Italian nobles could, if pressed, hurl stones on their rivals for power.

The Organization of Urban Communes

In all high medieval cities, in Italy and elsewhere, the desire for self-government led to the same sorts of questions that had arisen in ancient Greek city-states: how to determine citizenship and how to choose the rulers. As in the ancient world, medieval cities did not extend citizenship to all residents but only to those who had resided there a long time (or, in some cases, who had been born there) and owned a certain minimum of property. Women were still excluded from citizenship, even though, as indicated later, they played an active role in a city's commercial life.

Every city defined citizenship in its own way. In Italy, the citizens, however defined, were called *boni homines*, or "good men." These citizens elected
a council, which did the actual day-to-day governing. The members of
the council, called consuls, were usually from the most powerful local
families. They served as judges or magistrates as well as legislators; the
medieval cities did not have the same belief as does modern America that
legislative and judicial functions ought to be separate.

The urban republics did not originally have what we would call an
executive branch of government—that is, a mayor or city manager.
However, during the course of the twelfth century, most of the communes decided that it would be more effective to have one person at the
head of government, even if he still had to rule through the council.
There was a fear that competition between the different consuls would
lead to civil discord, if there was not one man over all of them, and that
committees would be much less efficient than a single head. Therefore,
during the twelfth century, most communes went from being governed
purely by a council to being governed by a mayor as well.

The idea of a mayor is now so commonplace that it may be hard to
grasp how innovative the idea was in the Middle Ages. The word comes
from the Latin *maior*, meaning the most important or major person; it had
been used, for example, in the early Middle Ages as the title of the
person who headed the king's household, the "mayor of the palace." In
some twelfth-century cities the first mayor was elected by members of
the council. In other cities, the king or count who gave grudging assent
to the establishment of a commune also appointed the first mayor, though
with the understanding that he would work with the commune's elected
representatives. In London the first mayor, who took office at the very
end of the twelfth century, was chosen for life, but later the custom grew
up of having the mayor of London elected for only one year at a time
and chosen by all the citizens of the city, not just by the council.

In Italy, where most of the cities had mayors from the beginning of
the twelfth century—well before the cities of France and England—the
office of mayor developed into something quite different than it did in
the north. An Italian mayor was called a *podestà*, from the Latin *potestas*;
the term meant someone with power. Because Italian cities usually experienced a great deal of fighting among different factions, it seemed
better to bring in an outsider to manage the city than to choose someone
from one or another of the various factions. The *podestà* therefore was an
outsider, in fact a professional with expertise in city management, who
was chosen by the consuls as their ruler.

A *podestà* was given a great deal of power and discretion, including
most judicial functions. But he only ruled the city for one year. At the
end of the year, the consuls examined his books and his decisions, to be
sure that he had been competent, had used sound judgment, and had
not embezzled city money. If his record was good, he would be very
richly rewarded and sent on his way with a positive recommendation for
his next city. Although a man could not be *podestà* for a particular city
more than once in his lifetime, he could make a career of being *podestà*
for a succession of Italian cities, starting with small ones and working his

Oltrado di Tresseno, podestà of Milan (1233).

way up to the wealthiest. If a council's examination showed that a *podestà* had been incompetent or corrupt, however, he would be severely fined or even executed. The *podestà* system, which varied from city to city because each was independent, was the principal system of urban government in Italy from the middle of the twelfth century until the end of the thirteenth.

Although a city as a whole was typically governed by a council and a mayor or *podestà* during the twelfth century, there were a number of other governing bodies within the city, with authority in certain areas or over certain types of activity. As noted on page 213, bishops maintained their authority over all the priests of a city; in addition, both bishops and the major abbots might have jurisdiction over all men living immediately next to their churches. The upkeep of a bridge or the city walls might be entrusted to a board of governors specifically appointed for that purpose. In London, for example, the maintenance of London Bridge was extremely important, for it was the only easy way across the Thames for miles. The bridge had originally been built of wood by the Romans, and it was repaired and rebuilt several times over the succeeding centuries. After the bridge was rebuilt in stone at the end of the twelfth century, the Bridge House Trust was organized to administer it; this same Trust is still responsible for the administration and upkeep of the bridge in London today.

Activities of City Government

Whereas many Americans are only vaguely aware of their city government today, the city council was a source of intense pride in the Middle Ages. Different cities competed with each other to see which could have the finest town hall, the symbol of their government. This could include the great council chamber, judicial courts, and rooms for clerks and records, as well as apartments where many of the government leaders lived.

Members of a modern city council would find many similarities in a meeting of a medieval city council. As today, government then was primarily concerned with setting standards to protect general health, safety, and welfare. City governments still have to decide if a new sewage system is required, if Main Street needs to be dug up and completely repaved, if additional firefighters or policemen are necessary, and, if so, where to find the money. All these concerns had parallels in the twelfth century. Medieval city governments, however, also had concerns that do not trouble American city councils, such as deciding which system of weights and measures to adopt, whether or not a traitor should be executed, and (in Italy) whether to go to war with another city. An important concern for all medieval city governments was also making sure that there was enough grain stockpiled to feed their population in case of an emergency; towns thus almost always had municipal grain warehouses.

Establishment of regulations against fire and pollution were always important tasks for medieval city governments. Fire was a major fear, for most houses were built of wood, or at least framed in wood, constructed of posts and beams with plaster over a meshwork of small branches woven between the posts. Only the wealthy could afford stone houses. Wooden houses would burn very rapidly, especially since originally they were thatched; thatching was a relatively inexpensive but long-lasting form of roofing that was very common in the countryside. City governments tried to force the citizens to replace their roofs with tile or slate (the roofing materials of almost all town houses in Europe today), because even a few sparks could ignite old, dry thatch. The houses were built so close together that a fire, once started, was very difficult to control.

There were no organized fire stations or brigades in the Middle Ages, but in many cities a large barrel of water was kept on every corner. The inhabitants of that block were legally responsible for making sure that the barrel was always full and ready; they were fined if it was found empty. If a fire did break out, everyone was supposed to turn out to fight the blaze. They used the water from the fire barrels and then, if necessary, formed a human chain to bring water from the river. These precautions kept most fires limited, but with all their efforts most medieval cities were burned at least in part once or twice a century. Only the stone churches might be left after a major blaze.

Besides fire, the other major concern for medieval cities was pollution. They naturally did not have the automobile exhaust that forms the smog layer today over such cities as Los Angeles and Denver, but already in the late thirteenth century the frequent use of coal had begun to cause the chokingly thick fogs over London that have more recently made such an effective background for eerie movies and mystery stories. This coal was either surface-mined or "sea-coal," which had been washed up on shore from underwater seams. (The famous London fog is now fortunately gone, due to modern prohibitions on coal-burning in the London area).

All medieval cities had plenty of pollution to guard against or be concerned about; it is inevitable whenever a large number of people live close together. Wood fires in the buildings in a twelfth-century city kept a steady haze in the air. In some areas, where wood was scarce, both village and town dwellers burned peat, which was even smokier. Peat is partially carbonized plant material (a very early stage in the formation of coal) found mostly in boggy areas; it can be dug up like turf and used for fires, but one needs a great deal of it to equal the fire one would have with wood or coal. In the eastern part of England, in Norfolk, so much peat was dug out of the marshy river bottoms during the Middle Ages that the rivers spread out into lakes, which are still there today (the "Norfolk broads"). The use of gas or even efficient and clean-burning wood stoves was centuries in the future.

The smell of smoke was not the only form of pollution in the air in a medieval city. With either no sewage system or, at best, the remains of the Roman system, there was a constant odor of human waste. Although strict rules and stiff fines kept people from actually throwing refuse in the street, there were privies behind every house, and privies never smell like flush toilets. There were also no municipal garbage collectors, though citizens were required by law to band together and hire men to collect garbage regularly and carry it out of town. (Some cities' councils set the amount these collectors could charge.)

Sanitation was actually better in the twelfth century than it was several centuries later, in the early modern period, when overcrowding made real estate too valuable to allow for backyards and privies, and houses normally had cesspools in the basement. But the best efforts of medieval city councils could not keep the air smelling pure. Animals in the streets only made the problem worse. As well as dogs, which still foul modern sidewalks, cities contained a great many horses, free-ranging chickens, and cows and pigs kept in the backyards along with the privies. These animals sometimes got loose, creating further nuisance or even danger. In the first half of the twelfth century, the oldest son of King Louis VI was killed while riding through Paris, when a pig shot out of an alley and caused his horse to fall on him (the pig was referred to as a *porcus diabolicus* in accounts of the time).

Water pollution was another major concern. Without filtration plants and chlorination, getting pure drinking water was always a problem. Diseases like typhoid are carried in contaminated water and can devastate a city, just as smallpox and other diseases can be spread by personal contagion. Medieval cities were always considered less healthy places to live than the countryside, even though the excitement and opportunities of the city made people want to continue to live there (just as many people today would never dream of leaving the city, in spite of the higher crime rate). Some cities still had Roman waterworks systems, with pure water piped in from miles away. The main Trevi fountain in Rome, supplied by aqueducts from the time of the Empire, continued to be the city's major source of drinking water throughout the Middle Ages (the present-day sculpture on the fountain is however from the seventeenth century). But most cities had to rely on wells and local fountains, where house-holders came to fill up their jugs. Wells could easily be polluted if disease got into the ground water, or even if an unscrupulous person dropped a contaminant into the well. City councils were virtually paranoid about having the city wells poisoned; one of the easiest ways to destroy some-one was to start a rumor that he had poisoned the wells.

Cities were normally built along rivers, and drinking water was also sometimes taken from the rivers on the upstream side. The upstream side of town also provided fish and eels, an important part of the urban diet. But water could not be taken from the downstream side, which suffered from what can only be called industrial pollution (much to the dismay of cities downstream). The butchers produced vast amounts of blood, fat, and bits of bone, all of which went in the river, and the tanners dumped into the river the harsh chemicals they used as well as the fat and fur their chemicals removed from the hides. These two trades were by law located on the downstream side of the city, in a quarter that was there-fore always considered less desirable than any other. (The butchers' area was called "the shambles" in England, meaning a slaughterhouse and meat market; when we say today that a place is a shambles we are really saying it is a scene of bloodshed and destruction.)

Venice, which was built on the water, with canals instead of streets, had to be particularly severe in its regulation of water pollution. The medieval canals were actually cleaner than they are now; the tide came in twice a day to scour them out (the tide's action is now much less effective because of the silting in of the bay, and the multiplication of industries on the edges of the lagoon has certainly not helped), and Venice's government moved all polluters (such as the tanners) to the mainland and laid down strict penalties for dropping the smallest object into the canal.

Urban crime was not the problem in the high Middle Ages that it had been in the ancient world and would be again in the late medieval and modern periods. This is partly because the small size of the cities meant most people knew each other, and it was much harder for a thief to disappear anonymously into the crowd. Medieval cities also did not have the drug addicts who make up a large proportion of modern urban crim-inals, or the handguns that make crime in American cities relatively easy. Yet even a small city offered some anonymity, especially when trade brought a constant stream of strangers through, and cities were the usual refuge of runaways in the high Middle Ages. Crime, especially petty thievery, was a constant low-level concern. There were not yet police forces in the modern sense (these were only developed in the nineteenth century), but the commune hired guards who roamed through the streets at night, alert for break-ins and fights. Bishops and counts normally employed guards as well, and different groups of guards might quarrel over who had first spotted a criminal, because those who captured him often got some share of any fine he had to pay.

A captured criminal was tried very quickly, often the next day in the case of minor offenses, with the strongest presupposition of guilt. Someone wrongfully arrested might have real difficulty in proving his innocence. Penalties depended on the crime, ranging from fines, to mutilation, to death. Murder was a capital offense, and the murderer was hung at a gallows set up at the edge of town. A multiple offender might also be hung for repeated thefts. Not all city governments had the right to impose capital punishment, however; when the courts approved the establishment of communes in many French cities, they only granted the communes the right to "low justice," for ordinary crimes, keeping the right to "high justice," for capital crimes, for themselves. Someone who had committed a lesser offense would be sentenced by the city magistrates to pay a fine and often would be put in the pillory as well. Here he would have to sit all day in the square, his hands and feet secured, facing the mockery of other citizens. Pillorying was a common punishment for polluting the streets, letting the fire barrels leak unrepaired, or cheating on weights and measures.

The Guilds

The most important governmental institution within a city, besides the council itself, was the guilds. Guilds were organizations of men who followed the same trade or pursued the same craft, and they regulated many of the details of the daily working life of their members. There were ties between guild government and city government, because in many cities each guild chose its own representative on the council, even though in other cities the citizenry as a whole elected the consuls. But more important than their role in urban politics, the guilds were in charge of much of the economic functions of a city. Although the mayor and council might establish weights and measures and decide on the opening and closing dates for trade fairs, most setting of standards and quality regulation were carried out by the guilds.

Guilds were organizations of and by the masters, those who had their own workrooms or shops. There were separate guilds for separate trades or crafts, with the guild of the tanners, of the goldsmiths, of the bakers, and so on. Although in modern America most trade unions are for "blue-collar" workers (steelworkers or plumbers, for example), in the twelfth century there were guilds for every occupation, including lawyers and magistrates. Medieval guilds were not really analogous to modern trade unions anyway, because there was none of the modern distinction between labor and management; the masters who ran the shops and employed the workers were the leaders of the guilds. Every medieval city had a somewhat different collection of guilds, and there was only rarely cooperation between guilds in different cities; the shoemakers of one town, for example, considered the shoemakers of the next town not their friends but their principal rivals.

Ypres Cloth Hall, built during the thirteenth century (destroyed 1914).

The masters of the guilds established standards for the guilds' products and determined membership criteria. Although becoming a master was the goal of most guild workers, only a few could do so. A master would have started as an apprentice when he was between the ages of seven and ten. Apprentices learned the craft from the bottom up, starting with simple tasks and working up to the more difficult. The masters gave them the dirtiest jobs but also fed and clothed them. Sometimes apprentices worked in their own parents' shops, sometimes in someone else's.

After an apprentice had grown up and learned his craft, he was known as a journeyman. Journeymen were the principal employees and workers. Although a small shop might have only one journeyman, or even none, large shops had a half dozen or more. They worked in a room that was both workshop and sales room, in a building fronting the street. Large shuttered windows opened to the street; they stood open during the day to admit light, air, and prospective customers. The master and his wife lived upstairs over the shop.

If a journeyman had learned his craft well enough that he wanted to establish his own shop, and either inherited a shop from his father or had enough capital saved to buy one, he would have to satisfy the masters of the guild that he was competent to join them. To do so, he had to produce a "masterpiece," a superb shoe or gold cup or whatever, depending on the guild. This would demonstrate his mastery of the craft. Although in modern usage we use the word "masterpiece" to mean the finest piece of work of someone's lifetime, originally the term meant that the work demonstrated complete competence, even though the master might go on in later life to produce something even finer.

All the masters of a particular guild would have their shops on the same street or on adjoining streets. They agreed on prices for the finished product, which meant that someone wanting to buy something could go to any shop and pay the same amount. The only reason to choose one shop over another, besides friendship with the master, was that one shop produced goods of a higher quality; therefore, the masters competed with each other to produce the finest goods they could at the established price. (Even today in Europe a few trades are run almost like medieval guilds; all French bakers in a particular city, for example, charge the same price for bread of the same weight.) As well as setting standards and prices, medieval masters also tried to regulate the price of the raw goods they needed, entering into agreements as necessary with the masters of the import guilds. They also set the level of wages they would pay to the day-laborers many guilds employed, men who did menial tasks (carting and carrying, cleaning up, and the like) but were not involved in the craft itself enough to become journeymen.

The guilds were more than economic groups; they also functioned as religious groups. Because the members of a guild generally all lived near each other, the parish church of that quarter of the city became the church for that guild's members. The masters and journeymen would consider such a church *their* church (which caused conflicts if several guilds shared a parish church). In the twelfth century there were great numbers of parish churches in close proximity, many of which in succeeding centuries have been torn down or taken over for other purposes. Although most urban parish churches were dedicated to a local saint, often a Merovingian saint, the particular saint of each guild would also have an altar of his or her own, and, by the thirteenth century, often a stained-glass window. Different guilds had different saints, usually with some connection to the craft; St. Sebastian, for example, who had according to legend been executed by a firing squad of bows and arrows, was the patron saint of archers and arrow-makers. By the fourteenth century, when towns began performing plays based on the Christmas story or other biblical stories, different guilds sponsored and often performed in these plays, frequently in competition with each other. Religious and civil organizations were thus very closely tied.

The Urban House

Because real estate within a city's walls was always valuable, urban houses were smaller, or at least taller in proportion to their width, than houses in the countryside. They were built with their front doors opening immediately onto the street and covered the whole lot from side to side, usually adjoining the neighbor's walls on either side. Originally city houses were just somewhat more cramped versions of houses in country villages: that is, built all on one level, with a fire burning in the middle of the floor in the main room, and a thatched roof. But city houses quickly began to be built three or four stories high, to take best advantage of the limited square footage on the ground.

At the same time as burghers, under pressure from the city councils, began replacing their thatch roofs with slate or tile, they also began having real fireplaces in their houses. The development of fireplace technology in the twelfth century, accompanying improved quarrying and stoneworking techniques, was a great step forward. By the end of the twelfth century, every self-respecting castle had proper fireplaces and chimneys, and by the middle of the thirteenth century all but the poorest city dwellers had them as well. A masonry fireplace with chimney was

A twelfth-century merchant's house in Cluny, France. The wide, arched opening on the right originally led to a workshop and retail store.

(and is) very expensive in materials and labor to build properly and was the single most expensive item in the construction of a medieval house. Burghers considered a fireplace well worth it, however, because the fire burned more efficiently, not being subject to drafts in the middle of the room, and, even more importantly, the room was not always smoky.

In the well-to-do household of a master craftsman, the big room on the first floor served as both workshop and retail store. When the shutters were opened in the morning, the workmen were practically in the street. The private living and sleeping rooms were upstairs, however, at least one flight away from the noises and smells of the street. The major room, what we would call the living room, was the "solar," so called because the sun was supposed to come in during the day (the sun might never reach down the narrow streets to ground level windows). The solar served as both living and dining room, with trestle tables set up for every meal. A large household, with a number of apprentices and journeymen to feed, would have to have two sittings; the family was fed first and the servants and employees second.

Originally the kitchen was a shed out back, half open to the elements. But with the improvement in fireplaces by the thirteenth century, the kitchen moved into the house, usually to the second floor, the same story as the solar. The fireplaces of the two rooms were set back to back, sharing a chimney. The kitchen had a wide hearth on which a fire was always kept burning, even in the summer. Soup might be kept simmering there all day, and, on the rare occasions when the household could afford a roast, the fire was stoked high to cook it.

A thirteenth-century kitchen had a good collection of pots, casseroles, and bowls, made from wood, pottery, and increasingly from iron. (Some scholars think that anemia, especially among women, was less common from the twelfth or thirteenth century on than it had been earlier, because increased use of iron pots resulted in more dietary iron.) The spice cabinet of a burgher's house was guarded as assiduously by the mistress of the house as was a castle's spice cabinet by its lady. The cabinet was always kept locked, except when she was actually taking out spices or putting in a new stock. Kitchens had mortars and pestles, where the spices were ground for use. A large house might have a fish tank in the corner, where fish could be kept alive to assure complete freshness when they were eaten; fish, rather than meat, was prescribed for Fridays and for the many fast days in the church's calendar. (The amenities that seem like kitchen essentials in a modern American house—the range, the refrigerator, the dishwasher, even a sink with running water—were unknown in a medieval kitchen.)

On the third and fourth floors of an urban house were the bedrooms for the household. In the thirteenth century, the master and mistress of a well-to-do house had their own bedroom, no longer sleeping in the same room as their servants (although the lord of a castle probably still did so) as they had in earlier centuries. Theirs was the nicest room and the best bed in the house. The bed consisted of a straw-filled mattress, supported on a network of rope, and topped with linen sheets and wool blankets. In the winter they kept warm under a feather comforter, made from feathers carefully saved, often over several years. The rest of the family and the journeymen, if they lived with the family, also slept on the third floor, but the servants and the apprentices had to climb the last steep stairs or the ladder to the top floor, which was always the coldest.

A town house was sparsely furnished by modern standards, although burghers and their wives quite consciously tried for what they considered comfort. There were no carpets; floors were spread with rushes. Oiled parchment covered the windows, which at least kept down the wind although it also cut down the light. Embroidered hangings decorated the walls. The furniture was made of wood: tables, benches, chairs, and the boxes and wardrobes in which clothes and personal possessions were kept. Boxes were made of planks nailed together side by side, and they were always subject to warping, which resulted in splitting and gapping. Iron bindings and linen or leather wrappings were used without notable success in an effort to keep the planks from warping apart; the invention of tongue-and-groove construction at the end of the Middle Ages was the final solution.

Aside from its kitchen utensils, a medieval household had very few of the "things" that make modern housekeepers have to fight constantly against disorder. Newspapers and junk mail were centuries in the future, so houses were not overwhelmed, as are houses today, by a continual influx of paper. Most houses had no books, and ornamental knickknacks were too expensive to be common. Children's toys were few and did not include small plastic pieces to shatter underfoot. People owned very few clothes. Keeping a house tidy was therefore not very difficult.

Keeping it clean, on the other hand, *was* a real challenge in a period before detergents and commercial cleansers. Mud and worse came in from the street every time someone stepped in. Paving of city streets only started in the twelfth century, and then only involved the most important streets. All sorts of bits of food, insects, and rodents could hide in the rushes on the floor. Once bedbugs got into a mattress they were almost impossible to get out again. Open fires, smoky oil lamps, and tallow candles left a greasy layer of grime on the walls and furniture. Conscientious housewives fought a daily battle against filth and the insect kingdom.

If keeping a clean house was a problem for a wealthy urban housewife, life was much more difficult for the urban poor. These included people who had moved to the city looking for opportunities that were not there, people employed as day-laborers or in other menial positions, and many of those in low-status service industries such as launderer. With housing much more expensive in the city than in the country, poor families could not afford their own houses. They often ended up renting a room in a larger house, where a whole family had to live entirely in what would have been just one bedroom for a wealthier family. The houses for the poor were the last to have fireplaces, and several families had to share an unsatisfactory cookshack. Disease naturally always spread most rapidly in the poorer sections of town.

The clothing that men and women wore in medieval towns was somewhat different than that of earlier periods, especially for the men. Whereas in the ninth century the basic garment for men was a tunic, knee-length or longer, worn over leggings (see Chapter 5), trousers had been invented and become very popular by the thirteenth century, at least in the towns and among the fashion-conscious. Trousers are something we take so much for granted that it may be a surprise how novel they were in the high Middle Ages. There had been breeches (or underpants) since the beginning of the Middle Ages, and leggings too had a long history, but it was new to combine these into one garment. Trousers were dyed bright colors and worn very tight, to show off a man's legs; his tunic was very short for the same reason. Whereas until the twelfth century men had normally worn beards, and indeed spoken in scorn of "beardless youths" whose whiskers had not yet grown in, by the end of the twelfth century all men of fashion were clean-shaven, or as clean-shaven as possible given the quality of the available razors.

Women's clothing had changed less; it still consisted of an ankle-length tunic, belted at the waist. While the men were proudly showing off their legs, no modest woman would dream of showing hers. Women even wore their hair covered, under a wimple, when they went outside. Both sexes wore soft leather shoes. Generally they wore the same clothes all week, changing when they took their weekly bath. Pajamas were unknown; everyone slept naked.

Medieval cities, like the cities of the ancient world, had bath-houses, where anyone might bathe for a small fee. Many entrepreneurs found a bath-house a profitable business; there were thus a number of bath-houses, most of them small, scattered through different neighborhoods (unlike the great bath-houses of an ancient city). Bathing, besides being a chance to get clean, was a good opportunity to relax, meet friends, or make new acquaintances. Men's and women's bath-houses were supposed to be kept separate, either by having separate pools or by having the men and women admitted at different hours. In practice, however, there was a great deal of mixed bathing, of greater or lesser naughtiness. (The modern British slang term "stews," meaning a house of prostitution, has its origin in the word for bath-house, a place where one soaked in hot water until "stewed.")

The other ubiquitous public buildings, besides the baths and the parish churches (discussed on page 224), were the hospitals. These were run not by private individuals but by bishops or abbeys as charities. In the thirteenth century some private individuals established hospitals, but they were still run by the churches. Medieval hospitals were originally open to anyone who needed help or shelter. The sick, the destitute, the aged who had no families to take care of them, unwed mothers, unwanted babies, those blind or crippled, even travelers needing a clean place to spend the night, all appeared on hospital doorsteps. They were cared for in large wards, furnished with rows of chairs and beds. The hospitals did not charge for their services, but anyone who could afford it was expected to make some sort of gift.

As long as the cities were fairly small, and as long as there were no plagues or major famines to tax their resources, the hosptials functioned very well. They naturally did not have anything we would consider modern medicine. The chief method of caring for the sick in the high Middle Ages was to keep them warm and clean and fed, supplemented with various herbal purgatives and powders; this was actually better for the patients than the enthusiastic use of powerful drugs, such as arsenic and mercury, which came into vogue at the end of the Middle Ages and in the early modern period. With the growth of cities and the subsequent increase of hospital business came the founding of new hospitals, which usually specialized in a clientele as early hospitals had not; by the end of the thirteenth century, there were separate hospitals for the sick, the aged, and foundlings.

The workday in a medieval city, as in the medieval countryside, went from dawn to dark, with a break for a nap in the summer during the hottest part of the day. (This is the origin of the noon closing that is still the rule in France and the Mediterranean countries.) Because candles and lamps were expensive and did not provide nearly enough illumination to work by, all work was done by natural light and thus started at sunrise. Although the workday was long by modern standards, people had off at least one day a week, Sunday, and often more. By the high Middle Ages the proliferation of saints' festivals meant that there was, on the average, at least one other day off a week. (Although there was no need to work on festival days, one also did not get paid.)

Scattered through the year were also several important holidays, on

Detail of Giovanni di Francesco's *Race of the Palio in the Streets of Florence* (c. 1400). The Palio, a festival centered on horse racing, began in Siena, but became so popular that most Italian cities had a Palio by the end of the Middle Ages.

which everyone might be off work for days. Christmas and New Year's were the biggest, but most cities also had their own urban festivals. In Siena, the big festival was the Palio in August. This included all sorts of live entertainment, eating, fireworks (from the fourteenth century on), and bullfights, but the principal entertainment was the horse race. The race was run right through the city (like a modern Grand Prix), and the excitement, pageantry, and betting were all spectacular. The Palio was so successful that by the late Middle Ages most Italian cities had one, and Siena, which still runs its horses through the streets today, was up to three a year.

Women in a Medieval City

Women were outnumbered by men in the cities of the high Middle Ages. This was because much of the urban population was composed of immigrants from the countryside. Young men felt much more confident in setting out for the strange and even dangerous world of the city than did their sisters. Even though single women could earn a living, there were many more opportunities for men. Cities were also not considered a healthy place for young children, because of the danger of contaminated water and the ease with which infection could spread; one need not know about bacteria to be able to recognize contagion. Therefore, even married women might stay in the countryside when their husbands went to town.

Officially women were only second-class residents of a city. They could not participate in town government, and a women's financial affairs were supposed to be under the direction of her father or brother if she were single or her husband if she were married. In practice, however, women had a fair amount of autonomy in medieval cities. They ran their households, buying the food, arranging for the construction of new furniture, hiring and firing the servants. Because they kept the family purse, they actually had direct control of much of the money that was supposed to be their husbands'. Sermons of the thirteenth century were full of warnings to housewives not to spend the housekeeping money on jewelry, gold belts, or makeup; the warnings would not have been so frequent or so pointed if the women had not been regularly spending money on luxuries for themselves.

Indeed, besides the housekeeping money, well-to-do urban housewives controlled a certain amount of capital directly. In the prenuptial agreements most couples drew up, the amount of money a woman inherited from her family and would manage directly was specified, as well as the money that went to her new husband as a dowry. If her husband died first—which was common, because men tended to marry much younger women—she was assured in many regions of receiving at least one third of his assets as well as getting back her dowry. Freed from the direction of father or husband, widows often proved themselves shrewd money-managers.

Even while their husbands were alive, medieval urban women worked behind the scenes to influence them. Few men would take on a new apprentice or invest in a risky enterprise without their wives' approval. Humorous stories of the thirteenth century are full of references to women who "wore the trousers in the family" (the term came into use at the same time as the garment). And indeed, among the artisans, women were often equal partners with their husbands. Women could even become guild masters. Most of these women masters were the widows of masters, but some were single women (usually a master's only child) who had learned the trade from their fathers. These women masters trained apprentices, employed journeymen, and participated in decisions about wages, prices, and standards, just as the male masters did.

Women could also earn their own living, hiring themselves out as cooks, as waitresses in the inns, as servants to the wealthy, as laundresses, or as prostitutes, always an important trade in a medieval city. Becoming a servant girl was usually the first choice of a poor girl coming from the countryside to try to make her living in the city. A higher proportion of houses in a city employed servants than did country houses, and a girl in her teens might hope to meet a nice man and save up enough in a few years for a suitable dowry. The concept of equal pay for equal work had not yet occurred to anyone, which made it harder for women to make a living than men, but being a servant at least meant one was guaranteed food and lodging. Prostitutes in the twelfth century were tolerated, although they were also the targets of determined preaching that urged them to reform and become honest housewives. By the thirteenth century some towns even had special houses, set up as charities, for retired prostitutes. Whatever their occupation, urban women were often better educated than men in reading, writing, languages, arithmetic, and music. (This was especially true in northern Europe).

Trade in the High Middle Ages

Although the craftsmen and the merchants within a particular city were sometimes treated as separate groups, in fact there was no sharp line between them. While some guilds, such as the butchers and bakers, sold most of their products locally, virtually all guilds manufactured products that might be sold outside the city to nearby villages or to villages some distance away. This meant that, although there was uniformity in price and quality of a guild's products within a city—the masters felt that competition among them would ruin them all—guilds of different cities making the same product were in fierce competition with each other. Something as ordinary as shoes could be the source of vicious acrimony if a shoemakers' guild found cheaper or better shoes from elsewhere appearing on the local market. (The protectionist impulse of modern industries already existed in the Middle Ages.)

Trade, which had only been a minor component of the economy throughout most of the early Middle Ages, became a facet of everyone's life by the end of the twelfth century. Rural manors no longer had to be self-sufficient; they sold their excess grain and used the money to buy goods of a higher quality or a greater variety than could be manufactured at home. Short-distance trade brought such local staples as grain and vegetables a few miles into town, and long-distance trade transported silk and spices thousands of miles from Asia; there were all sorts of variations in between. Products traded over long distances had to be lightweight and valuable for their size to be worth the trouble. Some products came enormous distances before reaching Europe, especially silk. This originated in China (the Chinese jealously guarded the secret of silk manufacture) and came by camel across the Himalayas, through what is now Pakistan, and across the Middle East, before finally reaching the eastern end of the Mediterranean. This long and arduous route had already been established in antiquity, and it was a very busy one in the high Middle Ages. Marco Polo, the Italian explorer, followed it all the way to China in the thirteenth century.

In general, bulky products such as grain, relatively heavy in proportion to their value, were only traded short distances, because transportation was always difficult and expensive before trains and interstate highways. Europe's river system did make transportation of bulky items by barge feasible, where overland transport would have been prohibitively expensive. For example, Paris was directly downstream from the fine vineyards of northern Burgundy and received most of its wine from there. In the thirteenth century, a friar passing through the Burgundian city of Auxerre commented that the people of the area had almost completely given up grain growing, devoting themselves instead to wine grapes.

The trade in wine is a good example of how growing trade could affect both peoples' fortunes and the local economy. New vineyards were often established through a system known as "complant," in which both the landlord and the peasant who worked among the vines would contribute to the planting of new vines and would both share in the profits. Under the complant system, the landowner provided the land and bought the rootstocks, tools, and stakes necessary. The peasant contributed his labor, planting and tending the vines until they became established. Once this was done, and the vines began producing grapes, the landlord and the worker shared equally in the profits. This method gave workers without the capital to buy land or equipment a chance to become involved in the lucrative wine business, and it gave the landowner a good return on a previously unused piece of land. The best winegrowing areas of Europe quickly expanded their production of grapes through this complant system in the twelfth century.

The same areas were good for wine grapes in the Middle Ages as are today: Italy, the Rhine valley, and Burgundy, Bordeaux, and the Champagne region in France (though the drink we call champagne was only invented in the seventeenth century, after advances in bottling technology made it possible to carbonate beverages). Areas such as England, which had always had trouble growing wine grapes, gave up the effort with relief, once it was possible to bring barrels of wine down the Seine on barges and then transfer them to ships to cross the Channel. (It should be noted, however, that the continuity of cultivation and production from European vineyards was broken in the nineteenth century. After an outbreak of phylloxera, a disease that destroys grapevines, the French vintners had to send to California for cuttings from the rootstocks there,

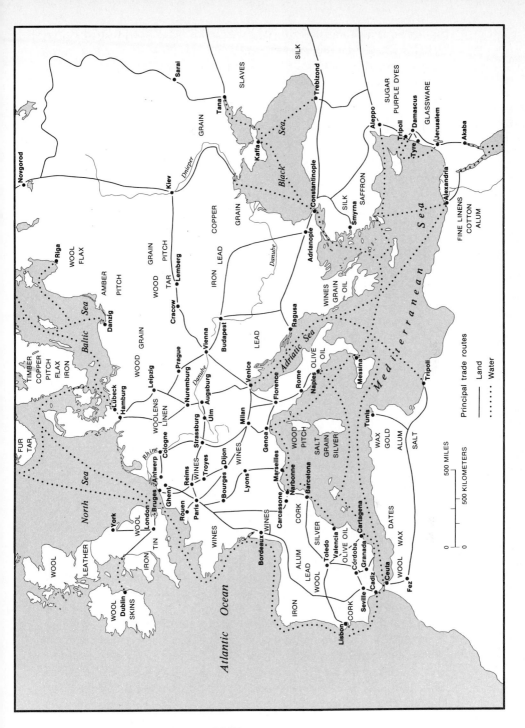

PRINCIPAL TRADE ROUTES OF EUROPE, c. 1200
Trade goods ranging from wool to luxury spices from Asia to salt and wine were
traded across medieval Europe. In the high Middle Ages, Italy and the Flemish
region around Bruges and Antwerp were the most heavily commercialized areas,
and the major trade route between these two regions ran through Troyes, heart
of the Champagne fairs.

recovering famous varieties that had themselves been brought from France as cuttings a generation earlier.)

Medieval wine was always drunk young because bottling had not yet been invented. Made and stored in barrels, wine came close to being vinegar within the year. This meant that the new wine in the fall was always anticipated with great eagerness. At Paris, the wine barges from Burgundy tied up under the bridges, and the citizens hurried down to the river to taste the new vintage and to carry some home. The Parisian guild of longshoremen held a monopoly and charged high rates for unloading barges, but the longshoremen would allow someone to buy and unload a barrel or two for personal use. To avoid paying unloading fees, therefore, many wine merchants sold the wine directly from the barges. The Parisians only allowed a wine merchant to sell from his boat for a space of three days, but if his wine was new and good, he would have little trouble selling all his cargo by then. In the major wine-producing regions, there was great competition as to which vineyard's wine would be first to reach the market, where it could command premium prices. In some parts of France, the counts exercised what they called a "wine-ban" (see the discussion of "banal rights" in Chapter 6, pages 183 and 198). This meant that the count could sell the wine from his vineyards at the local markets for a full week before anyone else could sell their new wine.

Initially, when trade began to revive in the tenth century, most international trade was carried on by Jews. There had always been Jews in Christian Europe, and there was little out-and-out discrimination against them in the early Middle Ages, but they were always treated as outsiders. With a religion that emphasized education, and with closer ties to the Jews in other areas than to many of their Christian neighbors, the Jews were in a good position to take the lead in long-distance trade. They held on to this prominence until late in the eleventh century, when they were joined by Italian merchants.

The most important trade routes were dominated by the Italians in the high Middle Ages. Different Italian cities were in fierce competition with each other. Venice was the first to come to prominence and retained a dominant position throughout the Middle Ages. Founded by people fleeing to marshy islands in the lagoons from first the Lombards and then the Muslims, Venice had an organized, independent city government by the ninth century. With no place to grow its own food on the salt marshes, it relied from the beginning on trade. The Venetians traded salt from their marshes and glass made from their sand across a progressively wider area, starting with Northern Italy but by the eleventh century reaching throughout the Mediterranean and east to Constantinople. Venice was the first of the western cities to establish its own trading houses in Constantinople.

Constantinople (the modern Istanbul) was a city of proportions completely unknown in the West, with over three-quarters of a million people, an opulent imperial court, a circuit of walls twelve miles long, and a great church, Hagia Sophia, which, when its thousand lamps were lit at night, could be seen twenty miles out to sea. The traders of Venice brought luxury goods unknown in the West from Constantinople but also provided that great city with goods it needed. Originally this meant raw goods such as salt or iron, but by the twelfth century Constantinople was avidly buying woolen textiles from Europe. The Venetians, knowing the eastern Mediterranean well, also provided most of the ships to transport crusaders on the sea route to the Holy Land (at a handsome profit, of course).

Part of the increase in trade involved improvements in transportation. Overland transport remained primitive in the high Middle Ages and was avoided if other methods were available. This is because it was much less energy-efficient than water transport. The Middle Ages had no fossil fuels to draw on, as we do, and had to rely on human and animal power. A horse walking beside a river can pull a barge weighing much more than the heaviest wagon it could pull on land, because the water does not offer the resistance that must be overcome on land. Wagons or packs lashed to horses or donkeys were the only means available for carrying goods on dry land.

Although the roads remained unpaved (except where the old Roman roads were still in use), guidebooks to the different routes began to appear, including information on inns and tolls. These were initially put together for the benefit of pilgrims rather than merchants, but they were useful for both. Enterprising local lords often instituted tolls at bridges or crossroads in their castellanies, claiming that this was a "banal" right to which they were entitled; equally enterprising merchants tried to find new routes around these. Although there were no particular technical advances in carts or packs, men of the twelfth century did try to breed sturdier pack animals.

There were, however, steady improvements made in ship technology. Shipbuilders enjoyed a great deal of wealth and autonomy; no local lord or even commune dared pressure them too much, for their craft was essential to the economy. On the rivers, barges predominated—wide, flat-bottomed boats that could hold a large amount of cargo and still go up shallow rivers. On the Mediterranean, galleys predominated—sailing ships with pointed prows—which could be used fairly interchangeably for commerce or war. Galleys could either be rowed or sailed; most were outfitted with a complex arrangement of sails and oars that could be modified for any contingency. Galleys had to be fairly small to be able to enter small harbors. The need for increased cargo space meant that more ships were built, rather than larger ships, which has been the modern solution. Modern superships, however, are restricted to a very few deep-water ports, where their cargo is unloaded and then carried by train or truck to its ultimate destination. In the Middle Ages, because land transportation was so much more expensive than water transport, the goal was to bring the galley as close to the final destination of its cargo as possible.

Ships preferred to stay within sight of land if possible—scarcely surprising considering how small their ships were and how treacherous the Mediterranean can be—but if necessary they could navigate by the sun and stars, as they had essentially the same navigational instruments as did ships in the "age of discovery" of the sixteenth century. The astrolabe had been invented in the twelfth century. This instrument was used to measure the angle of the sun and stars from the horizon and thus could be used to determine one's latitude. It was considered an exciting enough innovation that the famous French philosopher Peter Abelard named his son Astrolabe. The magnetic compass and maritime charts became common in the thirteenth century. Although the men of the thirteenth century saw no particular reason to venture down the coast of Africa or out across the Atlantic, as did later navigators, they did send their galleys out of the Mediterranean through the Straits of Gibraltar and up the coast of France to England.

Markets and Trade Fairs

In addition to the shops of its resident craftsmen, every town had a market to which people from the surrounding countryside, and sometimes farther away, brought goods for sale on a regular basis, usually once a week. Whereas normally only the members of the merchants' guilds could sell goods, during a fair anyone who wanted could set up a booth. In the center of town would be a large open square, the marketplace, in which farmers could park their wagons or set up stands. Markets were organized almost as rigidly as were crafts shops within the city; those selling oxen would always be on the same side of the market, those selling fruit and vegetables on another, and so on. Although the markets were originally open-air, by the thirteenth century some cities built covered markets, to make commerce easier for both buyers and sellers in inclement weather. Such covered markets also provided a place where a seller might store some of his goods from one week to the next.

Farmers' markets were held once a week, markets for less perishable goods, brought from further away, less often. There was a complete range of sizes and types of markets, from the market where a peasant might come to sell a cart of turnips, to the market where one could buy a goldfinch in a cage or a trained falcon, to the large market for the merchant wholesaling bales of cloth. By the late twelfth century, the latter type of market had evolved into great trade fairs. In England, for example, seven or eight of the towns of East Anglia had, in addition to their weekly markets, an annual one-week fair in which buyers and sellers came from as far as Italy. At a few regional centers, wholesale trade went on more or less permanently.

The term "fair" here does not mean a carnival with merry-go-rounds, although there always was a festive spirit and plenty of entertainment available on the side. Rather, medieval fairs were places where traders from far away, local merchants, and townspeople would gather to buy, sell, and place orders. The two most commercialized areas of Europe in the high Middle Ages were, on the one hand, Flanders and the Low Countries (in the part of Europe that is now Belgium, the Netherlands, and the northernmost part of France), an area that specialized in wool and fabrics; and, on the other hand, Italy, the import point for the goods

Section of the town of Troyes where the Champagne fairs were held. Although the present buildings date from the end of the Middle Ages, the street plan has been the same since the twelfth century.

of the East. The greatest trade fairs, therefore, took place roughly half-way between Flanders and Italy, southeast of Paris in the Champagne region.

There was a cycle of six trade fairs in Champagne, held at four different cities, which among them covered the year. The cycle started with a fair at Lagny in January and February, than came a fair at Bar-sur-Aube in March and April, a fair at Provins in May and June, the "Hot Fair" at Troyes in July and August, which was the biggest fair of the year, then another fair at Provins in September and October, and finally the "Cold Fair" at Troyes in November and December. Many merchants would simply pack up their goods at the end of one fair and move on to the next, though those coming from a long distance away, such as Italy, might only attend one fair a year, usually the "Hot Fair" at Troyes.

A trade fair, in Champagne or elsewhere, would be set up in the central square of town and spill into the surrounding streets and sometimes even out of town. Some of the sites of the important English fairs, such as St. Ives, were small towns most of the year, but during the Easter fair their population swelled to that of a midsize city. Goods were sold from stalls and shops, and entertainers and food sellers moved through the crowds.

A fair was a tremendous boost to the local economy while it was in town, just as modern American cities benefit from the influx of dollars from a major convention or from the Super Bowl. Those bringing goods to the fair had to rent booths or halls to display their wares, rent rooms to stay in if they did not set up tents outside of town, and buy their food and drink locally. Those coming to buy also rented rooms, bought their dinners, and paid for entertainment ranging from jugglers to prostitutes. There were always local people ready to gamble with the merchants for their profits.

The city government also benefited. In England, where many of the fairs were "owned" by a local bishop or monastery who was also the landlord for many of the local people, he made it a condition of leasing that the tenants move out of their front rooms during the week of the annual fair so he could rent them to the merchants. Bishops and city governments charged tolls on the bridges for those bringing their goods into town and charged fees for weighing and checking measures. The governments of the Champagne cities charged sales taxes on all transactions.

Concern for public safety and for honest dealing intensified during a fair, keeping the local government busy. Each of the cities where fairs were held appointed "Keepers of the Fair" who were responsible for keeping order, preventing merchants from building dangerous fires, fining people for allowing garbage to pile up, and making sure there was no cheating on weights and measures. At Troyes, where the counts still wielded a good deal of power, one Keeper was appointed by the local nobles and one by the local burghers. The Keepers oversaw sergeants who guarded the roads and patrolled the booths and halls. They also kept the master set of measures against which all the merchants' sets of measures would have to be calibrated. They acted as magistrates in special courts that judged anyone who committed a crime at the fair, including thievery, assault, and selling defective or underweight goods. The principal penalties levied by these courts were fines, which went to the city government.

Towns where fairs were held advertised that merchants coming to their fairs would be safe from violence and unfair competition, and the Keepers enforced this protection. Thieves were pursued across France if they tried to flee. Someone who intentionally sold defective merchandise might be barred from all future fairs. If it was determined that the brigands who had set on a merchant caravan had come from a particular city, then that city itself would be held responsible for damages until the brigands could be caught. If the city did not make suitable restitution, all its own merchants might be excluded from the fair.

An enormous variety of goods were traded at the Champagne fairs. These included the chickens and pigs that would be sold at any weekly agricultural market. But the most important transactions were in cloth and spices. The textile industry was revolutionized in the high Middle Ages by the spread of the horizontal or treadle loom, replacing the vertical loom of the ancient world and early Middle Ages. It took up much more space than the vertical loom, and thus was not nearly as well suited

A horizontal loom in a relief from the bell tower of the cathedral of Florence. The seated woman is holding a shuttle.

for the manufacture of cloth just for the household, but it could produce much larger pieces of cloth faster and more efficiently and thus provided the basis of commercial textile production.

Cloth manufacture was also greatly assisted by the spread of the watermill. The Middle Ages was much more energy-efficient than was antiquity, and the watermill was their equivalent of an electrical generating plant. Watermills, as noted in Chapter 4, spread rapidly between the sixth and the ninth centuries, freeing people from having to grind grain by hand. In the eleventh century, rural England, as revealed by Domesday Book, was thick with watermills that were found on every stream with enough power to turn a wheel. In the twelfth century, such wheels were connected to hammers for use in the fulling of cloth, a washing and beating process that would have been exhausting for humans but was easy for water-powered, wheel-operated triphammers.

By the thirteenth century, many Flemish cities had turned into virtual factories for the manufacture of cloth. Much of the raw wool came from England, where some soil that had never been very good for grain made excellent grazing. The monasteries of northern England, which by the late twelfth century had large herds of sheep, sent their fleeces to the fairs every year. These monasteries also provided a market for local peasants who owned only one or two sheep, not enough to make it worth their while to take the fleeces to the fair, but who could make some money selling the wool to the monks. The monks in turn make a profit reselling these fleeces along with their own. Flemish merchants crossed the Channel every year to the East Anglia fairs to buy up bales of wool, which they brought back to be spun and woven into cloth. Much of the cloth returned the next year to England, where it was bought by English merchants and by the king, whose need to keep a large royal court suitably clothed made him the single biggest buyer of cloth at the East Anglia fairs.

Cloth manufacture was a "cottage industry" in certain northern French and Flemish cities but was organized on a scale far larger than what the term implies today. Individual families were given wool to be carded, or carded wool to be spun, or spun wool to be woven, or woven cloth to dye, or dyed cloth to be fulled (fulling involved washing the cloth, to shrink it and make it thicker, followed by hammering to make it flat again). As they finished carding each bale, or dyeing each woven cloth, and so on, the entrepreneur who oversaw the cloth manufacture would pay the workers and pass their produce on to the next family for the next step. The wool entrepreneurs were capitalists who paid their cottage workers by the piece to encourage them to work quickly, but refused to pay them for substandard work to keep quality high. The textile cities were always jammed with carts carrying bales of wool, yarn, or cloth from one place to another; newly dyed yarn or fabric hung from the fronts of buildings; and the fields outside of town were covered with newly fulled cloth spread out for drying. (For an example of a cloth hall, see the photograph of Ypres Hall on page 223.)

There were seventeen principal French and Flemish cities that produced most of the commercial wool cloth for northern Europe. These seventeen formed a trading league, a "Hanse," agreeing that they would maintain very high standards and avoid undue competition by all selling their first-quality cloth only through the Champagne fairs. "Seconds," however, could be sold locally. Each city specialized in a certain color or a certain kind of finish, the secret of which was carefully guarded. Each city also had its own size for a finished bolt of cloth. All the bolts from that city were supposed to be precisely that length; just to be sure that they were, inspectors at each fair measured them as the merchants were setting up their stands. Most of the cloth, already dyed gray, brown, or dark blue, was bought up in large quantities by other merchants at the fairs, to be taken home and resold at a profit. Some wool cloth was sold undyed, however, principally to certain Italian firms, who took it home, dyed it rose or scarlet by jealously guarded processes, and then brought it back to the fairs to resell at a premium.

Wool was the principal cloth sold at the fairs; it was indeed the most important cloth for the clothes of all members of society throughout the Middle Ages. The fairs also sold some silk, always a luxury item, some cotton, which was first introduced into Europe in the twelfth century and was not yet very common, and a fair amount of linen. Linen was used for sheets and sacks as well as shirts and undergarments. Hemp, used for fishing nets, ropes, and bowstrings, was also sold at the fairs. (Polyester, nylon, and rayon are modern inventions and naturally were not available.)

Besides cloth, spices were the other major item sold at the fairs. Spices came from southeast Asia by a long series of sea trips and overland caravans, finally reaching northern Europe via Italy. The Italian traders brought their spices by heavily guarded ships and transports to Champagne, where merchants from all over Europe bought them. Pepper was the queen of spices, with a value that may be difficult for modern Americans to comprehend, accustomed as we are to thinking of it only as the "dark stuff" in the other shaker beside the salt. Pepper was valuable enough that prices of many other goods might be calculated in peppercorns. It was so expensive that spice merchants were set up to sell as little as one peppercorn at a time. Unscrupulous merchants might try to stretch their stock by mixing in tiny balls of clay, a practice that the Keepers of the Fair, other spice merchants, and buyers all watched for assiduously. Besides pepper and the other spices used in cooking—cinnamon, cloves, and the like—spice merchants also traded in alum and dyes, which were used in the tanning and cloth industries.

In addition to cloth and spices, the Champagne fairs also traded an enormous variety of raw materials and finished products. Armorers and weapons-makers always sent representatives to the fairs to buy iron from Germany, steel from Spain, tin from England, and lead and copper from eastern Europe. Leather workers bought skins and hides and sold saddles, leather jackets, boots, and sheaths for swords. Wines, cheese from Brie and Roquefort (already highly prized), ivory from Africa, horses, and even precious stones were all bought and sold at the fairs. Although merchants came to Champagne from all over Europe, they could communicate with each other because they all spoke some form of "trade" French. French was the international language of trade, the *lingua franca*, as it still is today the international language of diplomacy.

Banking and Investment

Perhaps surprisingly, the currency used in this trade was not international. Every country, and indeed most major cities, had their own coinage. This meant that every fair had to have a large contingent of money changers, men who determined the relative value of all the different currencies and changed the money that people brought with them for the currency demanded by those from whom they wanted to buy. By the twelfth century, most exchange was no longer in the large silver coins of Carolingian times, much less in gold coins. Most coins were copper, often small and rather undistinguished looking; even those that were supposed to be silver were usually heavily mixed with other metals (with the exception of the English silver penny). The multiplication of such coins indicates how thoroughly the money economy had been revived;

there would not have been so many small coins in circulation had not all sorts of minor transactions, which might have been handled by barter a century or two earlier, become monetary exchanges. The use of small coins of low value, however, did make it difficult to carry out large transactions, a problem that Florence overcame for its own trade routes with the introduction of the gold florin in the middle of the thirteenth century.

The money changers originally worked in the open, on benches, with the different coins spread out before them; the modern word "bank" comes from the same root as "bench" (the two are even closer in modern French, where *banc* means bench and *banque* bank). Besides changing money, these bankers quickly began making loans as well. For example, a merchant arriving at the fair would take out a loan to cover his living expenses while there, and then repay the loan at the end of the fair out of his profits. Longer-term loans were also possible. Someone who wanted to make a large purchase could borrow money to do so and arrange to pay off his debt in several installments, to the banker or to his firm.

At the end of the twelfth century, banking had grown well beyond money-changing benches, and many banking firms or houses were established. These granted loans and mortgages just as do modern banks. A peasant at the end of the twelfth century whose crops had failed could take out a mortgage on his property rather than having to sell outright to buy food, but if he could not keep up his payments the banks could and did foreclose, leaving the peasant landless anyway.

Part of the reason that Europe's revived commerce was able to flourish with a quite nondescript currency was that, increasingly, transactions were being handled through bookkeeping and credit. Although we do not tend to think of checks and folding money as instruments of credit, they are actually just that, having no intrinsic value; medieval bankers operated systems of credit which, although much more convoluted, had a similar net result. The wealthiest and the most prominent banking houses were Italian, generally based on an extended family, with representatives at all the international trade fairs and capitals of Europe.

The English kings very quickly began taking advantage of the opportunity to take out loans at the East Anglia fairs. When the kings were slow to repay, the bankers stopped advancing them money, but the king then simply demanded that the cloth merchants give him the bales he wanted in return for a promissory note. The merchants soon dreaded seeing the royal agents coming through the crowd, for they could not very well refuse the king, yet they knew it would be a long time, if ever, before they saw their money. By the middle of the thirteenth century, the English king was *eleven years* behind in his payments to the cloth merchants at the St. Ives fair.

Banking houses made investments of their own and made loans to those who wanted to invest. One of the most profitable investments available in the high Middle Ages was merchant caravans. If one could travel to where a certain valuable commodity was available, such as the end of the spice route in the Near East, and then transport it to where it could be sold for much more money, such as the Champagne fairs, then one could clear a substantial profit. However, one person rarely had the capital to outfit an entire caravan, including transportation costs, living expenses on the road, and the price of hiring guards. A caravan could also be a risky undertaking, because of the ever-present dangers of bandits and shipwreck, as well as the possibility of being undersold by a competitor.

The solution was to spread out both the risks and the profits in some sort of contract or partnership system. Various systems were used, but the most popular was the *commenda*. This system was very common among Italian merchants especially, from the twelfth century onward. A number of investors, some of them merchants and some burghers with no intention of leaving home, would advance larger or smaller amounts of capital toward outfitting a merchant ship or caravan. If the enterprise was successful, they would all share in the profits. Many investors tried to reduce their individual risk by putting small amounts of money in a number of different ships, hoping at least some of them would come in with handsome profits.

The urban revival of the high Middle Ages can in some ways be seen as a revival of Roman cities, because medieval cities were almost invariably located on the sites of old Roman cities. But the cities of twelfth-century France were very different from those of Gaul under the Roman Empire. The biggest difference was their independence, their ability to be self-governing, for Roman cities had served as capitals for magistrates carrying out orders from Rome. And although no city in western Europe was as big as ancient Rome had been in its heyday (including medieval Rome itself), most of the medieval cities quickly grew larger than the Roman provincial capitals that had once occupied the same spots. Like Roman cities, or for that matter cities of any period, medieval cities served as commercial centers where farm produce, locally manufactured goods, and luxuries from far away could all be bought and sold. But technical improvements in weaving and milling made many manufactured goods cheaper or better than they had been under the Empire, and the growth of banking made exchange and credit both more complicated and more readily available.

If there had been time machines in the twelfth century, and a twelfth-century townsman had been transported eight hundred years back, to the fourth century, he would not have recognized the Gallo-Roman settlement that stood on the same spot as his city. However, if he had instead been transported eight hundred years forward, to the twentieth century, he might have found much he recognized. The automobiles and electric signs would of course seem bizarre, but a twelfth-century man in a modern city of France or Italy would at least recognize the language being spoken, would find many of the churches that he knew still located in the same places, and would even, in some parts of town, be able to walk down the same streets. There was a clean break between the urban culture of the Roman Empire and that of the high Middle Ages, but medieval urban culture has continued without any further breaks down to the present day.

EIGHT

THOUGHT AND RELIGION IN THE HIGH MIDDLE AGES

c. **1000**	Hermits first appear in Italy
c. **1030**	Rebuilding of churches in Roman-esque style begins
1046	German emperor reforms the papacy
c. **1050**	Augustinian "canons regular" first appear
1073	"Investiture controversy" breaks out between pope and emperor
1098	Foundation of the monastery of Cîteaux
c. **1100**	Schools and schoolmasters begin to be common
c. **1100**	Abbey church of Cluny completed
1115	Cistercian order begins to spread
1122	Settlement of initial stage of investiture controversy
c. **1150**	Bologna becomes the major center for study of law
c. **1150**	Gothic architecture first appears
c. **1170**	Wandering preachers become common
c. **1180**	Aristotelean thought begins to reach the West
1200	University of Paris gets royal charter
c. **1200**	Flying buttresses invented; Gothic architecture widely adopted
1209	Albigensian Crusade
1215	Fourth Lateran Council recognizes Franciscan and Dominican orders
1226	Death of Francis
1260	Expectation of the end of the world
1274	Death of Thomas Aquinas
1276	University of Paris issues list of condemnations
1290	Edward I expels the Jews from England
1300	Date of Dante's *Divine Comedy*

CHAPTER

EIGHT

THOUGHT AND RELIGION
IN THE
HIGH MIDDLE AGES

AS ALREADY SEEN in Chapter 7, there was much more to the high Middle Ages than castles and peasants. The growth of cities and commerce were also accompanied, as this chapter will indicate, by the foundation of the universities and by new attempts to define and follow the religious life. The power of reason has probably never again been so highly esteemed as it was in the twelfth and early thirteenth centuries. Professional lawyers, modern bureaucracies, and rambunctious undergraduates all began with the foundation of medieval universities. The universities, although they quickly started preparing people for secular careers, began as church schools, and applying new forms of reasoning to religion was one of their principal activities. Other religious strands, however, were also strong in this period, including a radical rejection of all property, fervent preaching to the masses, and the construction of churches taller than any buildings attempted again until the twentieth century.

The Growth of the Universities

Universities were an invention of the high Middle Ages. The modern college or university is organized in a way first established in the twelfth and thirteenth centuries. The ancient world had had private schools and tutors, informal gathering places (such as the Groves of Academe) in which people could meet and discuss intellectual topics, as well as some men who offered to impart "higher wisdom" for a fee, but these were not universities. A university is a permanent, organized school, with a set

245

curriculum, employing teachers who have to meet certain minimum standards of competence, teaching students advanced subjects, and eventually granting them diplomas to show their mastery of these subjects. This is how we perceive universities today, and this is how universities were first organized in the twelfth century. Medieval universities also had the same combination of intellectual ferment and young people letting off steam, in a brief period between childhood and adult responsibilities, which is found in colleges and universities today.

The universities grew out of cathedral schools, and even today many university officers (for example, the chancellor, the provost, or the dean) have the same titles as officers in a cathedral chapter. All cathedrals had had schools attached to them since Carolingian times if not earlier, although these had been less important than the monasteries as educational centers in the late ninth through early eleventh centuries. These schools were designed especially to educate young men to be priests, and all young nobles whose parents wanted them to join the cathedral chapter, with perhaps the hope of becoming bishop some day, started in the cathedral schools. But other men, who did not intend to become priests but still wanted to learn Latin and some history or philosophy, also attended these schools. Still, the association between being a student and being a priest remained strong throughout the Middle Ages. The origin of the universities in fact lay in the banding together of masters of several different schools, monastery schools as well as cathedral schools, but the latter came to predominate.

University students of the twelfth and thirteenth centuries usually had no intention of becoming priests, but they still were considered ecclesiastics in issues of law and discipline. The churches that had recently worked out agreements with the local counts or kings on immunity from secular justice for the clergy tried to extend the same immunity to cover university students. This meant that students would be punished for infractions in ecclesiastical rather than secular courts. Most students were in what were called "lower orders." In becoming a priest, there were seven grades or orders that one rose through, and priesthood was only the last one. Men in the lower orders were still free to marry. This is why, even today, academic gowns look like priests' robes. This is also why in the Middle Ages women, who could not be priests, also could not be university students.

The evolution of the universities took place slowly and informally during the twelfth century. In the first half of the twelfth century, there appeared teachers who wandered from place to place, taking students for a fee; such itinerant teachers had existed in classical times but had not been seen during the early Middle Ages. Peter Abelard was the best known of these. Other teachers who were associated with cathedral or monastery schools began taking extra students in the same way. The reputation of particular teachers spread by word of mouth; those who seemed to have the most exciting insights into philosophical questions gathered large groups of students around them. Both large and small towns had schools, and their reputation varied depending on which teachers happened to be teaching there. There was a tremendous interest in education, but there were no Barron's Guides or college catalogues to steer one toward a particular university.

By the thirteenth century, things had become somewhat more organized, although perhaps not by modern standards. The major universities of France, England, and Italy were all founded by the end of the thirteenth century (the German universities were only founded in the fourteenth and fifteenth centuries). Different universities were well known for their specialities, so someone wanting to study a particular specialty would know where that subject was best taught. Then as now, however, a university always offered courses in a variety of topics at the under-

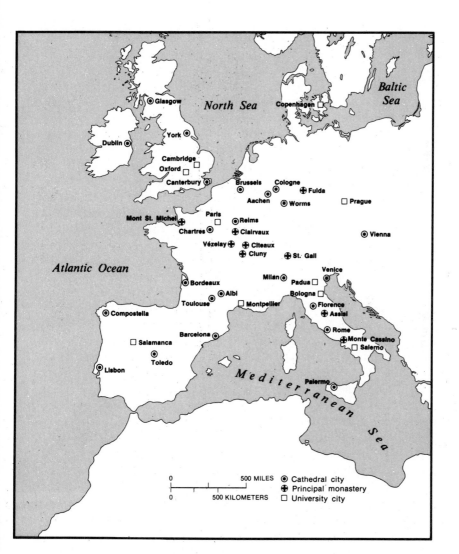

PRINCIPAL RELIGIOUS AND INTELLECTUAL CENTERS OF EUROPE, c. 1300
The political capitals of Europe were rivalled in importance by the university cities and the religious centers. Both the cathedrals and the principal monasteries served as foci of pilgrimage and religious inspiration.

graduate level, even if at the graduate level it only offered one or two courses of professional study.

Different universities excelled in different areas. The University of Paris was the center for studying philosophy and theology. Bologna, in northern Italy, was the chief center for the study of law, both secular and canon (or church) law. Roman law, which had been rediscovered at the end of the eleventh century, was an especially important topic of study there. Salerno, in southern Italy, and slightly later Montpellier, in France, were the two great medical schools. English students and teachers, some of whom had been at Paris before the wars between the French and English kings made education there difficult, founded Oxford University in the late twelfth century. Oxford seems to have developed as a university because the town was an important judicial center, where a great deal of ecclesiastical litigation went on, and the schools there started attracting students interested in law. Cambridge was founded as a breakaway from Oxford not much later.

There were no universities specializing in what we would call science, in biology (other than medicine), chemistry, or physics. This is because in the high Middle Ages there was very little interest in experimental science. Practical knowledge in such areas as architecture, the engineering techniques required for the construction and operation of mills, or agricultural practices, was certainly valued but was not considered part of the business of universities. In the realm of pure inquiry, basic knowledge of how the world functioned was obtained through observation and reasoning, rather than through experimentation, and was considered to be a branch of philosophy. What we would call the classics were also a part of philosophy; ancient literature was studied together with ancient philosophy and theology. History was another branch of philosophy, though not yet a particularly important branch, and contemporary or popular literature was considered too lightweight to be a part of a university education.

Because students from all over Europe would go to the university where their special subject was being taught, the student body was an international one. This is why what we call a university was called a *studium generale* in the Middle Ages, a place where people in general, from all over, could come and study. At Paris, in the streets of the Left Bank, which have been packed with students for eight hundred years now, there were students speaking all the different dialects of French, Anglo-Saxon, Celtic, German in its various dialects, Italian, Spanish, Catalan, and Provençal, and even occasionally Greek. Language study (other than the study of Latin) was not a university subject in itself, any more than slang and dialects are studied at modern universities, because ordinary spoken language was not a learned subject. The students certainly could learn each others' languages if they wanted. But the ecclesiastical roots of the university and the practical necessities of such international student bodies mandated that the principal language of communication be Latin. Latin was a living language, one that could be understood by scholars from every country, and all classes were held in Latin, even though the students used their native languages to joke or argue with each other.

In spite of the many differences between the medieval and modern universities, a thirteenth-century student would instantly recognize a twentieth-century university as such. (He might, however, have a little more trouble with the small liberal arts college, which is actually a uniquely American institution, with nothing comparable in Europe even today.) He would certainly recognize students and their combination of unprecedented freedom and intellectual excitement. Medieval university students, like modern students, often found that their brains were treated seriously for the first time in their lives and therefore combined a great deal of hard intellectual work with their carousing. Medieval students, like modern students, often stayed up too late, drank too much, argued with their landladies, were viewed with suspicion by girls' fathers, and wrote home to their parents with plausible stories of why they had to have more money at once.

The University Course of Study

Although medieval universities did not have the modern framework of freshman distribution requirements, majors and minors, electives and all the rest, there was still a curriculum through which the student was supposed to proceed. Medieval university students started younger than modern students, probably closer to age fourteen than eighteen, and most completed their studies with bachelor's degrees by the time they were twenty. But to proceed through to a doctorate was a much longer process, as the degree implied a comprehensive knowledge of *all* fields of knowledge, and men took their doctorates only in their forties.

Even though a medieval university, like a modern university, put a great deal of emphasis on independent study by the masters, its principal purpose was teaching and learning. The information students were supposed to master was conveyed in lectures. The word "lecture" comes from the Latin word meaning "to read," and originally lectures were precisely that, the lecturer reading from the text and commenting on it, while the students followed along in their copies. It is important to note that the "text" from which the lecturer read was not the same sort of thing as the modern textbook. A "text" now usually means a book that has been written expressly for students, that digests information from a variety of sources into one easily readable package. The "text" of the Middle Ages, on the other hand, was the actual *text* of the laws, if one were studying law, the actual theological pronouncements of popes and councils, if one were studying theology, and so on. This sort of detailed primary material, rather than some simplified synthesis, was the text the lecturer read out and commented on in every class.

Because all students needed to have copies of the text, long before the invention of the printing press, all books had to be copied by hand. A student might go through his university career only acquiring a few books. A student could borrow another student's book and copy it himself, but it was more common to have it done professionally. Small bookshops sprang up around all the universities, turning out copy after copy of the most frequently used books and making individual copies of the more unusual ones if a student brought one in. Since it took a long time to copy a book by hand, they were extremely expensive, and many students economized by buying their texts a chapter at a time. Errors invariably crept into these handwritten copies, especially as they were usually done under a deadline. Various shops advertised that *their* copies were freer from errors than their competitors'. In following along as the lecturer read aloud from the text, the students caught and corrected the errors in their own copies.

They would also write in the margins the comments and explanations, called "glosses," which the lecturer gave. For the Bible and a few other basic texts, there very quickly developed a so-called "ordinary" gloss, that is, a series of comments and explanations that seemed fairly definitive; therefore, a lecturer might read the gloss or commentary as well as reading the text, rather than giving his own comments. Students could soon buy copies of the texts with the glosses already written in the margin, so they would not have to take their own notes.

In going through a text closely and minutely, a student would essentially memorize it. They may have had only one or two books, but these they knew extremely well. Besides taking his students through a text word by word, a lecturer also engaged them in a series of questions and answers that assumed they had the body of the entire text ready in their minds. The posing of questions took the form of what is called the "scholastic method" (the word "scholastic" means something to do with schooling). The scholastic method consisted of posing a question, then answering it by bringing out various pieces of text that seemed relevant, using reason to reconcile the different elements, and finally arriving at an ultimate solution. The combination of selecting the correct phrases of text from the hundreds of pages one had memorized, and then working out an answer by the use of reason, was the medieval method of arriving at answers in all disciplines, including science and medicine, but it was at its best in philosophy and theology.

An example of a theological question might be, "Is it the will of God that man commit sins?" or even more basically, "Does God exist?" The plainest answer, yes or no, was of course already considered to be known, but to say "yes" or "no" was not the point. Rather, the student would have to bring up many relevant quotations from the Bible and from the pronouncements of popes and councils, including some that on the face seemed to lead to the *opposite* answer than the one he would eventually reach. This showed both how much he had committed to memory and his ability to use reasoning and logic to bring a coherent answer even out of apparently contradictory statements. An example of a more complicated question might be, in church law, "If a man has fornicated with a certain woman, should he be allowed to marry her sister?" In these questions the answer, yes or no, might not be as immediately obvious as it was for many theological questions, and in fact the scholastic method was used to find answers to questions no one had asked before.

After studying for a certain amount of time at the university, one became a *bachelor*. The term is still used with the same meaning; one who had received his first university degree. But this was only the beginning; a student aspiring to real scholarly status then went on to become a *magister* (or master, also a term still used with the same meaning), someone who had mastered a certain subject area. As a final "master's exam," he had to spend the day on the cathedral steps, answering any and all questions posed to him by all comers—particularly the masters of the school itself—to prove his command of the field. He was like a guild master after this in that he was treated as an equal by the other masters and was able to teach undergraduates. In fact, the modern word "university" comes from the Latin *universitas*, the term used in the Middle Ages for any guild or commune. University charters were grants of rights specifically to the *universitas* or guild of the masters.

Although most universities were under the direction of the masters, there were often guilds of students as strong as the faculty guild. The term "student union," which today usually only means the student union building, a place to buy hamburgers and watch television, originally meant something much closer to a labor union. At some universities, such as Bologna, the student guild was so strong that it essentially ran the university, issuing regulations to the faculty. These included the requirement that lecturers start and stop their lectures precisely on time, not get behind during the semester, and not leave town without express permission of the students. At other universities, the students were not as strong but the faculty had to accept the determined supervision of the bishop. At Paris, for example, the bishop felt himself responsible for keeping tight control of what had after all originally been his cathedral school.

Most people never got past being a *magister*, but there was still one final degree, that of *doctor* (the modern "Ph.D." still means "doctor of philosophy"). After a number of years as a master, a doctoral candidate began a final round of study, emerging with a degree that meant he had not only completely mastered a field but was qualified to teach it to other doctoral candidates. The word *doctor* itself means "teacher." By the middle years of the thirteenth century, the different European universities all recognized each others' doctorates. That is, if someone had been made *doctor* at one university, other universities would recognize him as such. This now seems self-evident, but it was a big step forward (even now, universities will only recognize degrees from other "accredited" universities).

Careers for University Graduates

In the high Middle Ages, as now, there were a variety of reasons for getting a university education, from pure desire to learn to career advancement. By the thirteenth century, when the universities were fairly well established, law and medicine had both been established as professions, which they had not been earlier in the Middle Ages, and these required a university degree. The litigiousness that is found in modern society—the tendency to sue one another with great frequency—was already found in the late twelfth century, and those suing found the services of a professional lawyer necessary.

A bachelor's degree was also virtually a necessity for those wanting to serve in the court of a king or great lord. These notables always hired several clerks to draw up their charters, keep their records, translate old histories from Latin into French, and the like. Earlier, the clerks serving great lords had all been priests (the word "clerk" is just a variation of "cleric"). But by the thirteenth century many of these clerks were only in minor orders; they were not priests but instead university graduates. Lords in the thirteenth century were proud of having large numbers of both clerks and lawyers attached to their retinues.

The papacy was the biggest single employer of clerks in the twelfth and thirteenth centuries. The popes, who had been virtual nonentities in the tenth and early eleventh centuries, had become by the middle of the twelfth century the undoubted heads of Christendom. This initially turned out to be more of a disadvantage than an advantage, because it meant that anyone with any sort of question, quarrel, or legal case that even vaguely involved religion appealed to the popes in Rome for help. Any court case could be stopped cold by someone announcing that he was appealing to Rome. Monasteries that wanted simple confirmations of their possessions, a bishop and a count who were disputing their relative authority in a certain village, law students who had thought of a particularly complex legal situation and were wondering how it would be adjudged

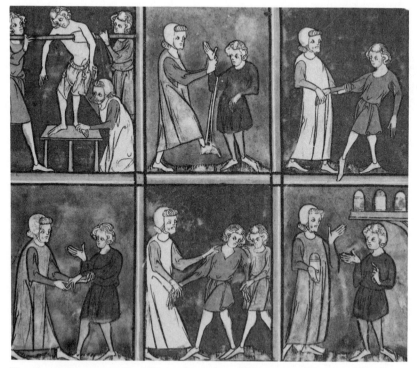

Treating dislocations. From Roger Parma's twelfth-century *Treatise on Surgery*.

THE INVESTITURE CONTROVERSY

Throughout the early Middle Ages, the popes had a vague moral authority as heirs to Saint Peter, chief of the apostles, but very little real authority over the churches of the West or over the practice of Christianity. This all changed in the middle of the eleventh century, due, somewhat ironically, to the interference of the king of Germany, who was to become a chief opponent of the pope's in later generations.

During most of the tenth through thirteenth centuries, the kings of Germany also held the title of emperor, in conscious imitation of Charlemagne. (In the late twelfth century, they started calling themselves "holy Roman emperors.") In 1046, King Henry III came to Rome to be crowned emperor; ever since Pope Leo III crowned Charlemagne in 800, it had been agreed that one had to be crowned by the pope to be emperor. He found not one but three different men who all claimed to be pope. Each belonged to a different faction in the city and was largely interested in the practical advantages of holding the papacy. Shocked, and doubtless also desirous of being crowned by one unquestioned pope, Henry deposed all three and had one of the German bishops he had brought with him elected pope instead.

The German bishops who became pope in the next decades set out on an ambitious program to make sure that only chaste, well-qualified men became priests and bishops, and that bishops were freely elected by the local clergy and Christian laymen rather than buying or simply seizing their offices. This effort at purifying the church succeeded so well that by 1073, the man who was then pope, Gregory VII, had come into open conflict with the emperor, the son of the man who had overhauled the papacy in 1046. The heart of the quarrel was the emperor's practice of appointing all German bishops himself and "investing" them with their symbols of office. The pope said that the emperor must immediately give up control of the bishops (whom the emperor had been using as administrators in Germany). This "investiture controversy" quickly went beyond the narrow issue of bishops' symbols of office to become a quarrel over whether the pope or the emperor was the ultimate authority in a Christian empire.

Officially, this particular quarrel was settled in 1122, but the underlying issue could not be settled. It led pope and emperor into repeated quarrels and even open warfare during much of the twelfth and thirteenth centuries, especially convulsing Germany and Italy. The pope finally defeated the last strong emperor in the middle of the thirteenth century, but by that time the pope's own spiritual authority had been eroded by two hundred years of conflict.

by church law, all wrote to the pope. The halls of St. Peter's were always jammed with people from around Europe who had come to plead their case in person.

At first the papacy was overwhelmed by the flood of appeals to Rome. With no good record-keeping system and a clerical staff that did not know how to handle what we would now call a mountain of paperwork, the papal court was in danger of grinding to a standstill. Someone writing to Rome might wait several years for an answer. Someone going in person had to be ready to make large bribes in order to get a good position in the months-long line of those awaiting a decision. Enterprising forgers set up near St. Peter's, offering letters purporting to be from the pope, sealed with lead seals indistinguishable from the pope's own. Even though the penalty for forgery was death, enough people who did not want to stay in Rome for years turned to the forgers so that they did an excellent business.

The only solution was the establishment of the first modern bureaucracy in the West. The papal bureaucracy was established in the second half of the twelfth century and was functioning nicely by the thirteenth century. The enormous numbers of incoming letters were classified, answered, and filed with commendable speed by an army of clerks. Most legal cases referred to Rome were simply referred back to the local bishops, so that the pope's own legal decisions would be reserved for the biggest cases. The European kings quickly imitated the papacy in establishing their own bureaucracies, to keep track of their various rights, dues, taxes, and legal decisions. These bureaucracies provided lucrative and honorable employment for men with a university bachelor's degree. Even someone who wanted eventually to become a *doctor* and a university professor might find it to his advantage to serve in a royal or papal court for a while before doing his doctoral work.

Knowledge and Reason in the High Middle Ages

Someone who was a *doctor* not only trained doctoral candidates but also wrote books distilling the knowledge of his field. Some of these books in turn became texts used in classrooms. A very common form of scholarly writing was the *Summa*, in which the author brought together the "sum of knowledge" (hence the term) in his field. A number of men wrote *Summae* in theology, combining not just what the Bible and the church fathers said about God and His relations with man, but also what ancient Greek and Roman philosophers had said on the subject. These *Summae* were compiled using the same scholastic method of questions and answers which was used in the classrooms.

A medieval *Summa* is by modern standards dry as dust, a whole series of questions, arranged by topics and subtopics, each one treated by quoting pieces of text and drawing logical distinctions. But a *Summa* was never intended to be light entertainment. It was an attempt for one brain to encompass an entire subject and set it out so others could follow and learn, and that was considered to be exciting enough in its own right.

The most famous of the medieval *Summae* was that written by Thomas

Aquinas (d. 1274), who held the Dominican chair of theology at the University of Paris. Although deeply influenced by previous *Summae*, it was still a very original integration of religion and philosophy. He wrote it entirely on his own, not under commission from the church hierarchy. But it was such a complete statement of Christian theology, and did such a thorough job of reconciling faith and reason, the Old and New Testaments, pagan and Christian thought, Aristotle and Plato, that it was later accepted as *the* definitive statement of Catholic theology, and indeed continues to be in the Catholic church today.

As the above suggests, in the high Middle Ages, especially the twelfth century, there was no gap perceived between religion and reason. The issues of the Bible versus science (for example, creationism versus evolution), which sometimes convulse school boards and churches today, would have had no meaning in the twelfth century. Medieval men believed that God had given them a brain capable of thinking and reasoning, just as He had given them the revelation of divine purpose through the Bible and divinely inspired church fathers. Therefore, the answers that one reached through reason or through revelation ought to be the same answers. There were thus no taboo topics for thinking or reasoning; any aspect of religion was considered appropriate for an application of reason.

People of the twelfth century started with the assumption that God knew everything, and that, according to the Bible, God made man in His image; therefore, man too ought to be able to grasp all knowledge. The limits of man's knowledge were only due to the fact that the human brain was finite, whereas God's thought was infinite, or else due to obstacles to thought which had come from original sin. Although modern science also does not accept limits on what man may try to know, it tries to reach this knowledge in a very different way than did men of the twelfth century. Modern scientists start with the assumption that the senses only have access to a small amount of information; the purpose of science is therefore to perform experiments to increase the amount of information available.

Whereas a modern scientist is concerned primarily with explanations of specific phenomena and only secondarily with where these phenomena fit in a cohesive world picture, a medieval philosopher was trying to construct, through reason, a coherent overall explanation. Whereas a modern scientist faced with a scientific question performs an experiment to see what will happen, the medieval philosopher would have tried to think and reason his way to the answer. If he had reached an answer using reason that seemed contradictory to a clearly understood answer reached by revelation, then he would have concluded that his logic was somewhere faulty and gone through it again. But if the answer given by revelation was murky, or seemed to bear more than one interpretation, he would consider it quite appropriate to use the answer reached by reason as a guide to clarify the deeper meaning behind the apparent obscurity.

In spite of the emphasis on reason over experimentation, it should be pointed out that there were also a few men in the high Middle Ages who *were* interested in experimenting, and thus are considered the fathers of modern science. The most famous of these was Roger Bacon, a Franciscan friar who lived in the second half of the thirteenth century. He believed that an understanding of mathematics was the basis of all other understanding. He wrote extensively on optics and on astronomy, both of which he approached from a combination of mathematics and experimentation. Bacon even did experiments on frozen food, putting dead chickens outside in the snow to see if the flesh would last longer than that of dead chickens kept inside. But he was unusual in his time; most thinkers of the high Middle Ages were more interested in the powers of reason than in setting up experiments.

Initially, in the twelfth century, it was very hard to tell whether the answer one reached through reason *was* contrary to Christian faith because there was no single statement of orthodox theology. There was only the huge hodgepodge of statements by church fathers, popes, and councils, plus quotations from the Bible; many of these statements had serious differences with each other. It quickly became clear that these statements, even if taken as authoritative, could not be sufficient in themselves, because of these very contradictions. Peter Abelard first pointed out the inherently contradictory nature of these authorities in the first decades of the twelfth century, deliberately putting side-by-side statements which contradicted each other even on what might have been thought simple and self-evident theological questions. He ended up being condemned and having to retract, not for pointing out that there were contradictions, which was indisputable, but for implying that all the authorities were *wrong*, or that only he, cleverer that anyone else, could deal with the issues.

Still, his method of putting contradictory authorities next to each other became the scholastic method, discussed previously, only a few years later. But now reason and authorities *together* were supposed to reach the truth. When the church finally did reach a definitive statement of Christian theology, that of Thomas Aquinas, it was through precisely this method of arguing and reasoning. Even in the twelfth century, however, when faith in man's reasoning was at its height, it was assumed that there were a few areas in which unaided reason might not be able to reach the final answer. This was because man was "fallen," and as well as making him sinful this had made his brain defective, so that sometimes reason could not take him all the way. In some areas, then, revelation was a shortcut to understanding, and in others it took man to areas where reason alone could not have taken him. But twelfth-century thinkers still wanted to *understand* what they already believed, and they thought that the Greek philosophers of antiquity, although hampered by having missed Christian revelation, still showed how far man could go with reason alone and therefore had a great deal to offer Christian philosophers.

By the late thirteenth century, however, there were beginning to be doubts about the ability of the human mind to attain all knowledge. There were also questions raised for the first time about the wisdom of having all areas of thought and belief wide open for reasoning and debate. In modern society, in spite of our belief in science and technology, few people would agree that all the answers are attainable if we just applied enough reason and logic. Some of this pessimism about human reason was already present in the late thirteenth century. At the same time, there had been an enormous increase in the number of books one might read or study, and some sectors of the organized church began to doubt if all of them were suitable for impressionable young minds.

In the high Middle Ages, philosophy was considered by far the most exciting field of study because it concerned the basic questions of the nature of man and the world around him, including what we would now consider the disciplines of history, science, literature, and so on. (This is why advanced degrees in most fields are still called Ph.D.s.) It was difficult for reason and logic to go very far in the early twelfth century, when only the rudiments of Greek philosophy were known. But in the final decades of the twelfth century, a great deal of Greek thought, especially the treatises of Aristotle, began to be introduced into the West, and the use of logic and philosophy took off.

Reading Aristotle was not simply a matter of rediscovering treatises that had been misplaced, however; it was a question of importing and translating philosophy from the Muslims. Back in the seventh century, when most of the Greek-speaking world had been overrun by Islam, Greek thought had been cut off from the West, except for a few treatises that existed in Latin translations. Many Arabs had been interested in philosophy and had therefore translated Greek treatises into Arabic. At the end of the twelfth century, many of these were in turn translated from Arabic into Latin. The Spanish city of Toledo, which was still under Muslim rule, became a major center for translation. Because these philosophic works were reaching the West after having been translated twice, from Greek to Arabic and then into Latin, they often arrived somewhat garbled. Worse, many works that purported to be by Aristotle were actually by someone quite different, or were genuine Aristotle but accompanied by an Arabic commentary that the translator did not distinguish.

The result of all this was that an enormous variety of Greek, Arabic, and even Hebrew philosophy, plus garbled mixtures of all three, arrived in a great indigestible mass in Western thought in the late twelfth and early thirteenth centuries. Much of this new thought was actually openly antithetical to Christian beliefs. It was one thing to say that the human mind could understand God and another to maintain the eminence of human reason in the face of an enormous mass of philosophy that seemed to interpret God very badly.

The initial reaction, however, was tremendous excitement at the opportunities to look at things in new and previously undreamed-of ways. It took three generations before the church hierarchy decided things were getting out of hand. In 1276, the bishop of Paris issued a long list of "condemnations," of ideas, philosophies, and books that should no longer be presented to beginning students. The upper-level students, those who already had their bachelor's degrees, would still be allowed to read them, but they were to be kept away from the undergraduates, who it was assumed did not have the wisdom and maturity to distinguish truth from error. In practice, many teachers ignored the bishop and went on using these texts anyway, and in other cases undergraduates who might never have read a book if it was assigned now sought it out eagerly, since it was forbidden. But the condemnations do show that the belief in the unlimited rights and abilities of human reason was decreasing in the late Middle Ages; the twelfth and early thirteenth centuries were an eminent Age of Reason, but this was no longer true in later centuries.

New Forms of Religious Life in the High Middle Ages

One aspect of the religious life of the high Middle Ages, then, was the intellectual excitement that accompanied the revival of philosophy and the rise of the universities. But there were actually many other threads in medieval religion. One of the most important was the continuing search for a pure and holy form of life, one that would imitate the life of the apostles, specifically in the monasteries. This had of course always been the goal of monasticism, but in the eleventh, twelfth, and thirteenth centuries this goal was pursued with more enthusiasm than it had been since the end of the Roman Empire. In fact, especially after abbots decided in the early twelfth century that their monks should not leave the cloister to go study in the schools and universities, the monasteries were alternatives to these schools, providing alternative ways of life and alternative ways of seeking the knowledge of the divine.

In the late ninth and tenth centuries, most western European monasteries had been concerned simply with survival. At a time when the monasteries on the river systems that connected with the Atlantic were being raided by the Vikings, the ones near the Mediterranean raided by the Saracens, and the ones on the eastern side of France and in Germany raided by the Magyars, there was little leisure to worry about purity of monastic life. Even if a house was not sacked, it was often difficult to maintain a community of monks and their regular discipline in the chaotic conditons of the period. Several monasteries did in fact do so, as discussed in Chapter 5. The most famous of these was Cluny, a monastery where the holy life was defined in terms of a liturgy that took almost all the monks' day in a round of psalms, prayers, and masses.

By the first decades of the eleventh century, the most difficult period was past, and Benedictine monasticism flourished throughout the high Middle Ages. At these houses, as in the early Middle Ages, most of the monks were from noble families and had joined the monastery as boys, when they were seven or eight years old. Here they grew up schooled in the rigorous monastic life. After the general upheaval of invasions and civil wars had subsided, many of the deserted or dilapidated monasteries were refounded and the Benedictine Rule was established in them once again. The restoration of old churches had gone so far by 1033 that a monk who lived then said that, in that year, the 1,000th anniversary of the crucifixion and resurrection of Christ, Europe seemed to be putting on a "new white robe" of recently constructed or rebuilt churches. (In the Middle Ages churches were whitewashed and hence were white. Interestingly, several centuries later, someone reading this monk's passage totally misunderstood it and thought it meant that people believed the world would end in the year 1000. This is completely wrong. As can easily be seen by reading texts written in the year 1000, it never occurred to anyone at the time that the world would end soon. Unfortunately, this idea, long since disproved, clings on in popular romances.)

In the eleventh century, at the same time as traditional monasticism was being reestablished, certain men were also experimenting with new forms of the religious life. Hermits began to be found in Europe's woods and wild places. Although there had been a great many hermits around the Mediterranean basin in the late Roman Empire, there had been very few (outside of Ireland, discussed on pages 137–38) ever in northern and western Europe. The bishops of the eleventh century were not quite sure what to do with these earnest, unwashed men living in the wilds by themselves, or in groups of two or three, and claiming to be following the life of Christ's apostles. The usual solution was to try to get them into a monastery, or to have several hermits group together and form a monastery of their own, with a rule and an abbot. A monastery was at least something the bishops knew how to treat.

New Forms of Monasticism: The Cistercians

New monasteries began to be founded in the eleventh century. These followed the same Benedictine Rule that most monasteries of western Europe, including Cluny, had been following since the eighth or ninth century, but they interpreted this rule somewhat differently. The new monasteries often tried to incorporate the radical rejection of property practiced by the hermits. Although Cluny and the other Benedictine monasteries practiced common property—that is, the monks had no possessions of their own—the monasteries as entities were sometimes quite wealthy. The monks might refer to themselves as "poor men," because they had no individual property, but because of the generous gifts the monastery had received from laymen over the generations, the monastery itself might own large expanses of land and rich ornaments. The abbey of Cluny was one of the biggest landowners in Burgundy by the early twelfth century, and in the same period Westminster Abbey, in England, had an estimated 60,000 acres of demesne farm. Some of the new monasteries of the eleventh century, deciding that this was not the real life of the apostles, set out instead to live a deliberately poor life.

The most famous of these new monasteries was Cîteaux, founded in 1098. The first monks of Cîteaux deliberately sought out the marshy area where they built their church because it was wild and deserted. They wanted to be "in the desert," in conscious imitation of the first Egyptian monks, and although northern Europe did not have sandy wastes it did have plenty of thorn-grown and marshy land. (The name Cîteaux itself comes from the same root as "cistern"; like a cistern, the monastery's location was full of water.) Unlike the Cluniacs, who had had peasant tenants work their fields, the Cistercian monks intended to labor with their own hands. They made manual labor, rather than the liturgy, the chief focus of their day. This is both because Benedict had talked about manual labor in his rule and because they wanted to humble themselves, as Jesus had told His followers to do.

Life was never easy for a new group of monks who wanted to follow this sort of life. Many were young men who had been trained as knights but had decided to give it all up for a life of religion. Most of the members of the new monasteries of the eleventh and twelfth centuries in fact were young men who had "converted" to the monastic life in their late teens or early twenties. Cîteaux forbade its churches to take "oblates," the young boys, offered by their parents and brought up to be monks, who were the backbone of more traditional monasteries. Instead, the young knights of the eleventh and twelfth centuries who became recruits for monasteries like Cîteaux often went off into the wilderness to become monks in the face of strong parental opposition. Their parents, far from intending them for the religious life, had brought them up, paid for their military training, gotten them ready to take a prominent place in the world, and now were shocked to see them giving it all up.

These young knights and nobles who took off to the marshes to become monks and hermits are in many ways comparable to the groups of

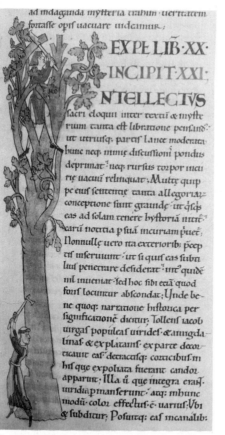

In this twelfth-century manuscript illustration, a Cistercian monk and a peasant team up to cut down a tree. The form of writing in the twelfth century was still fairly close to Caroline miniscule (see p. 157).

American college students of the 1960s and 1970s who, although they had scarcely seen a cow in their lives, decided to form communes and live by organic farming. Although living off the land may seem straightforward (just work hard in the healthy outdoors and eat the high-fiber, all-natural food one grows), in fact farming has always been extremely difficult and complicated, as any farmer can tell you. Enthusiastic new monks of the eleventh and twelfth centuries would all meet in the wild spot they had chosen, bringing with them a few hoes and sickles, a couple of loaves of bread, and some cheese. It would take them only a few days to eat all the food they had brought, to become soaked sleeping outside in the rain, and to have it occur to them that, even if they could build a monastery with their bare hands and grow a crop of grain, it would be at least six months until the grain ripened, and they did not even have any neighbors from whom they could beg food in the meantime. At this point, a certain number of would-be new monks always gave up. But a surprising number persisted, many more than the number of young people of the modern middle class who would have persisted in a commune under such conditions. This is because the young aristocrats-turned-monks genuinely believed that this was what God had commanded them to do, and although they quickly realized that they were foolish not to have made better preparations, they also believed that, having make the commitment to be monks, it was too late to back out. Salvation for them was more important than physical comfort and convenience.

In spite of early difficulties, Cîteaux and other monasteries of the Cistercian order grew and flourished in the twelfth century. The order was organized much more rigidly than the Cluniac order, which could scarcely be called an order at all in the eleventh and early twelfth centuries, being comprised simply of those monasteries that followed Cluny's version of the Benedictine Rule; some had their own abbots, and others recognized Cluny's abbot as also being *their* own. The Cistercian order, on the other hand, was composed of a hierarchical series of daughter-houses. A monastery founded by monks from Cîteaux was Cîteaux's daughter-house; this house in turn would have daughter-houses of its own. Each house had its own abbot, but the first abbot was chosen by the mother-house, which maintained authority over the daughter-house even when he was gone.

The growth of the Cistercian order was almost like the growth of a chain of franchise restaurants. Each group of monks who founded a new Cistercian monastery built their church just like Cîteaux's and followed a set of rules and regulations just like Cîteaux's. Every year each abbot was supposed to visit all the daughter-houses founded from his monastery, checking to make sure that no irregularities had crept in, and once a year all the abbots of the entire order met at Cîteaux in a large meeting, called a chapter general, in which policy was discussed and abbots who had slipped up were disciplined.

The austere life of the Cistercian monks—living in the wilderness, working with their hands, eating a strictly vegetarian diet and not a lot of food at that, wearing simple robes, worshiping in bare and simple churches that had none of the stone sculpture and stained glass of other churches of the time—seemed tremendously holy to people of the time. Many young men left home to become Cistercian monks, and men who did not want to become monks themselves still flocked to the abbey gates to make presents of their property. The appeal of the holy life was especially strong in the twelfth century because this was the period in which the church gave final form to the idea of Purgatory, a place neither heaven nor hell, to which people would go who had neither been good enough for heaven nor bad enough for hell. It was an uncomfortable place, certainly, with many of the same punishments as hell, but it was not permanent, and, best of all, one could shorten one's stay there by having holy men pray for one.

All this caused a surge both in enthusiastic converts and in material gifts and thus presented a problem to the monks. Enthusiastic converts they could deal with, making them novices, giving them a year before they actually took their monastic vows so that they could decide if they really wanted to spend the rest of their lives working in the fields, sleeping under insufficient blankets, and eating coarse brown bread and a few vegetables, all in the name of holiness. But it was harder to know what to do with gifts from laymen, especially when the gifts consisted of toll bridges, of houses in town, of watermills, even of war horses and hunting dogs, all the things the monks had hoped they were leaving behind.

If the abbot tried to explain that this was not what he wanted, the donor would be insulted. ("So my gift isn't good enough for you, huh?" one can hear him saying, or "Since when are you in a position to be so picky and choosy?") Essentially forced to accept property of a sort they had not wanted, the monks grew wealthy in spite of themselves. The deserted, swampy land the monks took over because no one else wanted it proved to be excellent agricultural soil once it was cleared and drained; the Cistercians became highly proficient waterworks engineers. The poverty and the rejection of society were taken as such signs of holiness that society rushed to associate itself with the monks and make them rich presents. In effect, the Cistercians' own success worked against them, and they had to be continually vigilant to avoid being hopelessly compromised.

Canons and Preachers

Meanwhile, at the same time that both old and new forms of Benedictine monasticism were flourishing in the high Middle Ages, there also appeared several new nonmonastic forms of religious life. The most successful were the canons regular. The term "canon" by itself merely means something to do with the church, as in "canon law" (it has nothing to do with cannons and cannonballs). Used to describe a person, the word canon refers to a member of a group of priests who served a church together. As noted in Chapter 5, all cathedrals had a chapter of priests, or canons, associated with them, consisting of priests who assisted the bishop in administering the diocese and carrying out the service in the cathedral. Many other churches also had canons, usually a very small group, who among them acted as priests for the church.

In the eleventh century, it started to be common for these canons to have a rule, and hence to be considered "regular" canons. (The term comes from *regula*, the Latin for "rule.") As priests, they were already supposed to be unmarried—although it was only in the twelfth century that rural parish priests stopped having live-in concubines, if not indeed wives. But regular canons went much further than this standard. Their rule, the Augustinian Rule, was not the monastic rule; it was based on a letter St. Augustine had supposedly written in the fifth century. But in practice it had many similiarities to the Benedictine Rule. Regular canons lived in common, sharing all their income and property, unlike ordinary priests or cathedral canons, each of whom had his own personal income. Canons regular had an abbot or prior over them and had to obey him, rather than coming and going as they pleased. Although their way of life was similar to that of many monks, regular canons were very different in that their purpose was preaching and administering the sacraments to the lay public, whereas monks tried to withdraw from the world and pray for it from behind the cloister walls.

Only shortly after the first houses of canons regular began to appear, there began to be houses of canonesses, women who lived togther, sharing their property, following a strict rule. However, other than the actual wording of their rule, it is very hard to tell the canonesses from the Benedictine nuns. Whereas the canons administered divine service in their churches for the good of the laity, canonesses could not do so. As women they were forbidden to become priests (this is still the case in the Catholic church). And they were also not supposed to preach to the general public, instead remaining within their cloister, even though preaching was becoming an increasingly important part of religious life.

The emphasis on preaching was quite new in the twelfth century. It was based on the idea that even ordinary people, leading ordinary lives, could be holy, but that they first needed to be educated. This was to be done by every means from telling them stories of the life of Jesus to pointing out explicitly whenever they had committed a sin. In the twelfth century, there began to be wandering preachers in the West for the first time in seven hundred years, men who moved from town to town, living by selling what they once had owned and by begging, preaching in every town they reached. They had read the Bible, and it was quite clear to them that this life of wandering preaching was precisely what Jesus had followed; thinking of themselves as His apostles, they determined to do the same. Good preachers were received enthusiastically. An especially fervent preacher often left town accompanied by a crowd of well-to-do followers, both men and women, who had decided to leave all for Christ. Even though most returned home shamefaced in a day or two, it is clear that the call to give up one's wealth struck a responsive chord in the relatively wealthy burgher class.

Two centuries earlier, such voluntary poverty, the willingness to give up what one had painstakingly acquired, would have made no sense. But

This small Romanesque church at Avenas, France, is typical of those built in villages and small towns in the twelfth century. It is still in use today.

there was enough wealth around in the twelfth century to make money seem banal, even degrading. When wealth had been very scarce, in the early Middle Ages, it had been something special, something ennobling, and a person building a church or making a reliquary box in which to put a saint's bones would have felt he was insulting God and the saints if he did not put gold and jewels and fancy ornamentation all over it. But when commerce and urban society reawakened, as detailed in Chapter 7, wealth became something one could attain by work, slippery dealing, and clever balancing of the books, not something rare and almost magical. Under such conditions wealth was no longer considered an attribute of the holy. In modern society we have a very similar attitude. Even though people who do not have much money are envious of those who do, there is a strong feeling that someone good and virtuous and wealthy should want to give all his money away in ways that would benefit his fellow man, and that God would be insulted, not honored, by a jewel-encrusted church. (The United States, founded by Puritans, is more prone to this attitude than Europe; many American tourists, including Catholics, who often are accustomed to worshiping in elaborate churches at home, are shocked at the elaborateness of some European churches.)

In the twelfth century, bishops were not sure how to react to wandering preachers. On the one hand, it was certainly commendable for people to preach the word of God to the general public. On the other hand, one never knew what these people might be saying; they could be spreading all sorts of theological errors. The fact that the preachers usually refused to listen to the bishop when the bishop thought it appropriate to scold or warn them did not help. Normally, bishops used the same strategy with wandering preachers that they had already tried (with moderate success) with the hermits, which was to try to make them settle down and become monks. Some groups, such as the followers of a man named Waldo or Valdes, called the Waldensians, refused to settle down. Both men and women who had joined the Waldensians traveled extensively, preaching and encouraging people to lead holy lives. The Waldensians spent much of the twelfth century skating along the edge of orthodoxy, almost being condemned several times. In many cases the wandering preachers' tendency to make pointed remarks about the sinfulness of the wealthy, among whom they explicitly included the bishops, put additional strains on their relations with the church.

The Friars

The difficulty for the organized church was that the bishops thought poverty and preaching were excellent ideas, but only if carried out in an organized context, not practiced freelance. An institutionalized form for these activities first appeared at the very beginning of the thirteenth century, with the establishment of the friars. The term "friar" comes from the Latin *frater*, meaning "brother," and the friars were groups of men who lived like brothers, sharing their goods, obedient to a rule and to the church hierarchy, but still engaged primarily in wandering preaching. There were two orders of friars, both recognized officially by the pope in 1215—the same year that he announced that after this there would be no further foundations of new religious orders. The two orders of friars were headed by men named Francis and Dominic and were called, appropriately enough, the Franciscans and the Dominicans. Both were dependent directly on the pope.

The Dominicans, sometimes known as "friars preacher," were always especially concerned with education. They believed that if people became heretics if was often because they did not know any better, and that good education and preaching would solve the problem. Dominicans quickly became established at the universities as well as preaching to the general public; Thomas Aquinas, mentioned on page 254, was a Dominican. Although the Franciscans, also known as the "friars minor," also believed in preaching (Francis himself went to Egypt to preach to the Turks in the hope of converting them from Islam), they were distinguished above all by their radical rejection of property. Francis wanted to go far beyond the idea of "individual poverty," practiced at all monasteries, where the monks had no separate possessions of their own. He wanted the Franciscans *collectively* to be poor, to reject all gifts of all sorts except enough food to last the day. He did not even want his followers to store up an apple for the next day. To be sure his friars did not become wealthy the way the Cistercians had done, without meaning to, he even forbade them to touch money.

Francis's rejection of property was only possible in a society that had become increasingly urban and oriented toward monetary profit. It was possible to live by begging in the cities as it would not have been in the countryside. The changing attitude toward money, that it was an at-tribute of materialism and not of holiness, mentioned above in connection with the twelfth-century preachers, was intensified in the thirteenth century. Francis also seems to have had a better idea of the misery real poverty actually entails than did many of the monks of the twelfth century, who, while living fairly simple lives, had never had to worry about having a place to sleep or having enough food to stay alive; and Francis wanted to embrace that poverty. By adopting the life of the poorest of the poor, Francis was deliberately humiliating himself, trying to do penance, willingly enduring suffering in the name of God.

While Francis was alive, his friars followed the path he had chosen for them. He was a charismatic figure who attracted huge crowds wherever he went. He felt a strong sense of brotherhood with nature and was said to have preached to the birds as well as to people, but he was much more than a flower-child. In trying to imitate Jesus's life as closely as he could, and in trying to practice absolute poverty and humility, he was unique, even in an age of great religious fervor. Stories of his great humility were told about him after his death. One famous collection of such stories, called the "Little Flowers," includes such incidents as a time when he and another friar were walking toward the house where they would spend the night. It was dark and very cold, and they were very hungry, and the other friar remarked how good it would be to be inside by the fire. To that Francis replied, "What would indeed be best of all would be if they don't recognize us when we arrive, and throw us out in the snow, and beat us with clubs as thieves, because then we will know the real meaning of suffering hardship for the love of Christ."

The Franciscan friars, unlike some of the wandering preacher groups with whom they had similarities, were an all-male group. Saint Clare, who was smitten with the same admiration for Francis and his holy way of life as were many men, persuaded Francis to start a "secondary" order of Franciscan women. This order (known as the "Poor Clares" in her memory) was much more like a traditional order of nuns than it was like the Franciscan friars. The nuns had to stay in the cloister, rather than wandering, begging, and preaching, and were indeed forbidden, out of fear of their "delicate" nature, from practicing the absolute poverty of Francis's male followers. In the following decades, however, both men and women joined what became known as the "tertiary" Franciscans, a rather disorganized group of people who did not take actual vows but tried to follow Francis's precepts in the context of ordinary life by doing such things as caring for the sick.

Francis was enormously admired, but (not surprisingly) no one seemed capable of living up to his example. Without his leadership, the Franciscan order started changing almost immediately upon his death in 1226, when he was only in his forties. Enormous numbers of would-be friars, burning with sincere desire to follow Francis's example but without the long-term commitment necessary for the harsh life of a Franciscan, flocked to join the order. Laymen who had tried unsuccessfully to give their property to the order while Francis was alive soon prevailed upon his successors to accept it. Francis's rule was soon "glossed"; that is, it had

St. Francis preaching to the birds. From a thirteenth-century manuscript.

explanatory notes added, such as that his prohibition of touching money meant that friars had to have a representative touch it for them! (Francis, fearing that this might happen, had ordered his rule *not* to be glossed; this passage was the first one glossed, with the explanation that what he *really* meant was that only "correct" glosses should be added.) The Franciscan order soon changed into something scarcely distinguishable from other monastic orders of the day. Franciscan friars became involved in education, as were the Dominicans; Roger Bacon, mentioned above, was a Franciscan. In its transformed condition, the Franciscan order was a perfectly valid form of religious life, but it was not what Francis had intended.

However, some members of the order, especially those who had known Francis personally, refused to go along with this development. Calling themselves "Spiritual" Franciscans, they formed a break-away sect, insisting that Jesus had owned no property, Francis had owned no property, and that they would not either. The question of property within the church was a somewhat touchy one in the thirteenth century. The papacy had become extremely wealthy, but all the groups that considered themselves to be seeking real holiness rejected property, at least to some degree, and the self-righteousness of the Spiritual Franciscans touched a raw nerve. But this splinter group really got into trouble by becoming associated with a "millennarian" heresy, the Joachites (discussed on page 268). Prolonged association with the heretics made everything the Spiritual Franciscans said seem heretical, and in the fourteenth century a pope declared that Jesus *had* indeed owned property, and to maintain otherwise was heresy.

Heresy in the High Middle Ages

Heresy was an issue in the thirteenth century, which it had not been in the early Middle Ages. In the first centuries of Christianity there had been a great many heresies, and, as noted in Chapter 3, many aspects of Christian doctrine were worked out in direct response to them. But after the end of the Roman Empire communication had been poor enough that people usually did not know what people in the next city believed, and the central organization had broken down enough that there was no one, except for the bishops of each area, to check on the correctness of belief. When most of the population was pagan, or still semi-pagan, simply trying to Christianize them was the chief concern, without worrying unduly over the details of a purported Christian's belief. It should be pointed out that a heretic was not just someone who did not believe in orthodox doctrine. Someone who had never heard of Christianity or who was an adherent of a different religion would be considered a pagan or an infidel, rather than a heretic; Muslims and Christians at the time of the Crusades called each other infidels. A heretic was someone who *ought* to know correct Christian teaching but had willfully rejected it.

It has always been difficult to tell the heretics from the "real" Christians, because Christian heretics have always argued that *they* were correct, and that it was the others who were the real heretics. Throughout Western history, heretics and orthodox Christians have always agreed up to a point, so that from an outsider's point of view it might sometimes be difficult to tell them apart. The only way to really distinguish between the heretics and the orthodox is to look at the aftermath: the orthodox are, by definition, those who won. Whereas in the early Middle Ages people had believed in a variety of forms of Christianity without realizing that they were doing so, in the twelfth and thirteenth centuries education and communication had greatly improved, and the revived papacy was making a conscious effort to define what really was orthodox Christianity, and to make sure everyone followed it.

Millennarianism

There were a great many different heresies in the twelfth and especially in the thirteenth century. The Joachite heresy, with which the Spiritual Franciscans became involved, was "millennarian," which meant it looked toward the end of the world. Whereas nobody thought the world was going to end in the year 1000, as noted on page 258, a great many people expected it to end in the year 1260. This was due to the writings of a man named Joachim, who himself spent a life of perfect orthodoxy. However, after his death, people reading some of the things he had written decided he was predicting the end of the world. He had tried (as many people have before and since) to calculate the age of the world by counting years and generations in the Old Testament. He decided that there had been 1,260 years from Adam and Eve to the birth of Christ. These 1,260 years were for him the era of the Old Testament, or of the Father. Logically, then, he took the next 1,260 years, from the birth of Christ to 1260 A.D., as the era of the New Testament, or of the Son, with the Third Age of the Holy Spirit to come next.

Because Joachim died long before 1260, it is not clear exactly what he expected to happen in that year, but, when the year did arrive, a great many people were expecting Judgment Day. Flagellants appeared in Europe in great numbers—that is, people who walked from town to town, flagellating (or beating) themselves and each other in order to try to drive out their sins and purify themselves before it was too late. In every town, they called on people to repent and come with them. The bishops were even less sure how to react to the flagellants than they had been to the barefoot wandering preachers. Christianity had always called on people to repent of their sins, but it was startling, to say the least, to have a band of wailing men and women in rags, beating themselves with whips and staves, stagger into town and then leave again the next day, accompanied by many local citizens. For the most part, the bishops just hoped that when the year 1260 was over things would quiet down.

The year passed and the world had not ended—in spite of repeated prophecies of its end, the world has, so far, stubbornly continued. There are several reactions to this sort of failure of prophecy. (Even today, people are still intermittently predicting the end of the world, and their reactions are still the same.) One can sneak home and try to pretend he has never believed it anyway, or that some strange fit must have seized him; this was the most common reaction in 1261 (and still is). Another possibility is to redo one's calculations, deciding that the prophecy was correct but that one had somehow gotten the wrong day or year, that the world is still about to end, even if slightly later than originally thought. The problem here is getting anyone to listen next time. Another reaction is to decide that God decided not to destroy the world after all, once He saw all the people preparing for the end and realized there were some truly good people left after all.

A final reaction, quite common in 1261, was to decide that the world really *had* ended, or at least had begun to end, but that only a few people were wise enough to notice. This is actually not as bizarre as it sounds. Christian millennarianism has generally been based on the Book of Revelation, the last book of the Bible, which is open to dozens of possible explanations but does strongly suggest that the end of the world will take place over a certain period of time, that it will not be a single thunderclap but a long series of painful events. It was easy in 1261 to describe anyone who disagreed with this interpretation as one of the beasts or serpents of which Revelation is full, to see the wars that then, as now, kept men unhappy and occupied as the wars that Revelation showed leading up to the final battle. Bishops who had, after consideration, accepted flagellants repenting of their sins as odd but orthodox could still not be expected to agree with being called seven-headed beasts of the Apocalypse, and starting in 1261 the Joachites began systematically to be prosecuted.

By then there had been a radical change in the church hierarchy's attitude toward heresy. In the twelfth century, when heresy had first become an issue again after being virtually forgotten for centuries, the first reaction to heretics had been to try to persuade them of their error. First the Cistercians and then the Dominicans had preached to heretics, urging them to come back to the "true way"; however, it was difficult to persuade people to come back to the true way when they were convinced they were already following it, and that those trying to persuade them were following the way of error.

The Albigensians and Their Brutal Repression

In the late twelfth century, the preachers came across a group that proved especially tenacious in holding onto its beliefs. This group was the Albigensian heretics, who not only refused to give up what they thought was the real religion but proved very successful in converting others. After over a generation of trying to convert the Albigensians, popes finally decided that they were a spreading cancer that must be cut out if the body of the church were to survive. At the beginning of the thirteenth century, therefore, the popes began using systematic violence against the Albigensians.

The Albigensians, so called because they were found in great numbers around the town of Albi in southern France, are also known by many other names. They called themselves Cathars, from the same root as "catharsis," meaning a purging or purifying. The organized church also sometimes called them Manichaeans, as there had been a heresy in the Roman Empire called the Manichaean heresy, and this new group was considered to have similar beliefs. They were also sometimes called Bogomils, or followers of the "Bulgarian" heresy. This is because Cathar beliefs actually do seem to have reached western Europe from Bulgaria; they were related to the beliefs of the Zoroastrian religion, which was not even a Christian religion.

The basic Cathar belief (like that of the Zoroastrians) was that the universe was the battleground for a never-ending struggle between God and the devil, between good and evil. There is of course a great deal of this in Christianity, but orthodox Christianity holds that God is stronger than the devil and will ultimately prevail, whereas for the Cathars there was no ultimate victory expected. Christianity held that, because God created the world, it was basically good (though fallen from grace), and that at the Resurrection people would arise in the flesh, even if in *purified* flesh. The Cathars, on the other hand, thought that the world was the devil's creation, not God's. Therefore for them the purpose of existence was to free oneself from the taint of the earth. Gradually they would do without more and more physical comforts. Finally, when they had almost freed themselves of the world, they would become known as *perfecti*, or perfect ones. The Waldensians, mentioned on page 265, also used the term *perfecti* for those who had attained the highest levels of religious knowledge. The *perfecti* could be either men or women. They preached to the unconverted, ran schools for young people and for those who wanted to be schooled in the faith, and at some point they would ideally starve themselves to death. The Cathars were, like all heretics, grossly misrepresented by their enemies. Their gradual purification, for instance, was described (incorrectly) as a warming-up ritual for blatant sexual orgies.

Catharism became enormously popular in Italy and southern France. Peasants, townspeople, even bishops and counts all joined the sect. They still considered themselves Christians but thought that finally they understood the *real* message of Christianity. The friars who tried to persuade them they were wrong were, to the Cathars, just the devil's representatives in disguise, trying to lure them back into the world of evil. Finally, in 1209, the pope launched the Albigensian Crusade against them.

It shows the change that had taken place in the crusading ethos in the last century that, rather than going to fight the infidel in the Holy Land, Crusaders were going to fight people in southern France who called themselves Christians (for the Crusades, see Chapter 6). The northern French entered into the Crusade with great enthusiasm. Here was an opportunity for winning spiritual rewards and also collecting booty much more easily than going to the Holy Land and probably dying of disease or shipwreck on the trip. The difficulty in southern France, which had not been a problem in the Holy Land, was how to tell the Cathars from the orthodox Christians, when one had captured a city held by the Cathars. Simon de Montfort, leader of the Crusade, resolved the problem simply and ruthlessly. "Burn them all," he said, "the Lord will know his own." (Even today it is not a good idea to tell Simon de Montfort jokes in southern France.)

The bloody Albigensian Crusade, which decimated cities and ravaged the countryside, looks to us like a horrible perversion of the Christian ethos, which indeed it was. But it was based on the singleminded idea that the end justifies the means, that maintaining pure Christianity was worth violently cutting out the cancer within it. The same sort of attitude is often found today. The United States has for decades supported absolute dictators, in spite of their purges, repression, and secret police, and funded guerrilla warfare, in the name of freedom, peace, and democracy. Marxist-Leninist thought explicitly approves the use of any and all methods against counter-revolutionaries or class enemies. The Albigensian Crusade was deplorable by any standard, but one should realize that it came out of a basic human response, not something unique to the Middle Ages.

After the Crusade was over, Dominicans came again into southern France, but this time to establish an inquisition, the first western Europe had known. The inquisition tried to make sure the Cathar heresy did not break out again, by quizzing people closely about their activities and beliefs and those of their neighbors. The inquisitors were looking for anyone who did not adhere to orthodox Christianity; they began medieval Europe's first systematic persecution of the Jews. But their principal targets were the Cathars.

Those caught practicing Catharism were given a final chance to repent. But if they clung stubbornly to Catharist beliefs or, even worse, gave them up and then went back to them, they were burned at the stake. Burning had been a standard response to heresy in the late Roman Empire, and although no one had been burned for six centuries or so, once heresy became an issue again in the twelfth century burning also revived. The Middle Ages had enough respect for tradition and the practices of the early church that it turned to accounts of early Christian heresies when dealing with its own. Burning is a horrible way to die, but at least theoretically it served a good purpose for the heretic, as well as setting an example for other potential heretics: by giving the heretic a dose of hellfire on earth, it was believed that burning might free him from having to stay in hell eternally, and might even make it possible for his soul someday to be saved.

Thus the late thirteenth century, a period when there started to be restrictions put on what might be taught in the schools, was also the period in which heresy and orthodoxy were firmly separated. Because the Jews were clearly not orthodox Christians, the official church hierarchy ceased to tolerate them, as it had in the early Middle Ages. Several kings, starting with Edward I of England in 1290, officially expelled the Jews from their kingdoms. This was also, interestingly enough, the period in which homosexuality, which had been tolerated throughout the early and most of the high Middle Ages, first began to be widely persecuted. The willingness to accept variations in ways of life or religious practice, including tolerance of the Jews, which had been relatively common in the twelfth century, was rapidly diminishing.

Persecution certainly did not end heresy, however, or even variations in orthodox Christianity. Scholars continued to argue and debate theological points, while maintaining their orthodoxy, at the same time as heretics of all descriptions, convinced that *they* had the truth and everyone else was wrong, continued to flourish, though increasingly underground. Through all of this variation remained the conviction that there really was only one Truth. In modern America, by contrast, the most widespread view has recently been that no one has all the Truth, or that the dozens of denominations are all sufficiently close as to make adherence to any given one a matter of strictly individual preference. Although this sort of humane tolerance certainly appears to be more like Jesus's version of Christianity than does religious persecution, it is unfortunately *not* the result of rereading the New Testament so much as it is the result of most people not caring very much about religion anyway. It is deeply ironic that throughout history, including now, those who claim to take most seriously a religion based on love have been the most intolerant.

New Forms of Church Architecture

The many changes and developments in education and religion in the high Middle Ages were accompanied by changes in church architecture. The Middle Ages built well and built to last. Many medieval churches are still solid after eight hundred years. Even now, most of the churches in western Europe, the places where people go to Sunday school and have weddings and funerals, were built in the Middle Ages.

Although masonry and stone sculpture had been highly developed in the Roman Empire, these skills were essentially lost in the early Middle Ages and had to be reinvented in the high Middle Ages. Some churches of the early Middle Ages were made out of old Roman temples, such as the Pantheon in Rome, but most had to be built from scratch as Christianity slowly spread across Europe. The churches of the fifth through eighth centuries were built on a very simple plan, one possible even for those without great masonry skills. They were essentially small rectangles, with an altar at one end; the wall at the altar end (usually the east end) was build as a semicircle, enclosing the area behind the altar, which was known as the choir. A central aisle ran the length of the church, with secondary aisles on either side, separated from it by a row of pillars. This is the "basilica style" of church. Roofs were flat or sometimes made in a simple barrel arch. Stones were rough and undressed. These churches could be built by little more than a dedicated group of people to find and carry the stones, plus a moderately trained architect to lay out the walls and direct the building. These churches tended to be small and dark inside, because the architects did not want to risk the structural integrity of the walls by putting in large windows.

In the ninth century there was a brief flurry of church rebuilding, at the same time as the revival of education and religion under the Carolingians. New crypts were dug to which the bodies of sainted bishops and abbots were moved, and these crypts were ornamented with wall paintings and with stone sculpture done after Roman models. Sometimes the churches were decorated with elaborate frescoes. Much of this seems to have been directly influenced by the Byzantines, who had not lost the architectural skills that had been nearly forgotten in the West; it is thought that the Carolingians hired Byzantine architects and artists. But by the late ninth century this rebuilding period was past.

Romanesque Architecture

There are very few churches now left from the early Middle Ages. The men of the eleventh and twelfth centuries thought of them as too small and too dark, and they tore most of them down and rebuilt, starting in the very late tenth or early eleventh century, at the same time as old, ruined monasteries were being refounded with new groups of monks in them. Rather than simply trying to shore up what was there, bishops and abbots hired professional builders and set out to make larger, airier churches than what had been there before. Architecture began to be a highly skilled profession in the eleventh century, and good craftsmen were sought out and well paid. They built so well that, in much of the European countryside, the churches built in the late eleventh or twelfth centuries have never been rebuilt again; at most they have been added to and emended.

Interior of the abbey church of Vézelay. The central aisle is divided from the side aisles by pillars topped by elaborately carved Bible scenes.

entire old church would be torn down, the only part left being the crypt below ground (often a Carolingian crypt). If new suitable tombs for the saints had been built in the ninth century, the architects did not want to disturb them again. The old church had been built on two levels, the crypt below and the main church above. When the high Middle Ages rebuilt, they often only rebuilt the upper, main church, making it tall and airy, while retaining a low, dark crypt with only one-quarter or even one-tenth the floor space of the church above.

As part of this building program, many new churches were also built where there had never been churches before. Most villages in the countryside first got their own parish churches during the twelfth century, as bishops tried to improve the religious life of the people of their dioceses by making the sacraments more directly accessible. More parish churches meant that people no longer had to travel miles to church in order to baptize a new baby or just to hear a sermon.

The architectural style of the eleventh and most of the twelfth century is now called "Romanesque." It was not called anything in particular at the time; it was just the style in which churches were built. The Romanesque style is called "Norman" in England because it arrived in England after the Norman Conquest. Romanesque was not qualitatively different from the style of preceding centuries; it was still based on square towers and barrel arches, with the churches made of rough fieldstones rather than smooth blocks of quarried stone. But Romanesque churches were much larger, higher, and lighter than the churches of the earlier centuries. Big Romanesque churches had a central aisle and then lower aisles running parallel to it, down each side. Increasingly churches were built in the shape of a cross, with a transept forming the arms of the cross. Since both the transept and the main aisle had barrel arches, architects had to work out ways to make these arches intersect.

The Romanesque style could be used for buildings both very large and very light. Although the walls remained thick and solid, and the windows small by later standards, the architects arranged them cleverly to take best advantage of the angle of the sun. At the abbey church of Vézelay, built in the twelfth century, for instance, the windows are designed so that the sun hits the floor all along the center aisle on the summer solstice, and illuminates the elaborately carved capitals of the pillars along the northern aisle at the winter solstice. The largest example of a Romanesque church, the abbey church of Cluny, was completed in the first years of the twelfth century and was over one hundred feet high from the floor to the top of the arch. It was the longest church in Christendom throughout the Middle Ages; when St. Peter's basilica was built in Rome in the sixteenth century, it was deliberately made a few feet longer than Cluny. (Cluny unfortunately is gone, taken down systematically at the time of Napoleon. A transept alone is left, still impressive in its size.)

In Romanesque churches the aisles were divided from each other by pillars, and the head of each pillar, the capital, was highly decorated. The large area over the front door, the tympanum, was also decorated with stone sculpture. Indeed, Romanesque stone sculpture is the most characteristic attribute of the style. It is perhaps not terribly realistic by the standards of either Rome or the late Middle Ages, but it has tremendous life and vitality. The tympanum was usually a representation of Christ, sometimes with angels, sometimes with apostles, sometimes with a depiction of the Last Judgment. The capitals on the pillars were scenes from Bible stories or from the lives of the saints. Their purpose was to make it possible even for those who could not read to see religious stories illustrated.

Although some of this art fits modern notions of the inspirational, many of the sculptures were grotesque, a few even obscene. This grew out of the idea of "opposition," that seeing how grotesque worldly things could be would direct the mind to higher, purer topics. These sculptures are highly decorative even now, and they must have been especially flashy in the Middle Ages, when they were brightly painted. The Cistercian order deliberately rejected Romanesque sculpture in their churches, saying it only distracted the mind from pure topics rather than reminding one of them, and the Cistercian churches of the twelfth century are simple basilica-style churches, built without transepts, large windows, or any decoration. But the Cistercians were a minority among church-builders. Good stone sculptors were eagerly sought and were very proud of their work, which they often signed.

Although weathered from the passage of centuries, much Romanesque sculpture still survives. That which has been destroyed was for the most part deliberately destroyed; the stonemasons of the twelfth century tried to choose stone that would last for centuries. In France, most of the destruction is due either to the seventeenth-century Wars of Religion or to the eighteenth-century French Revolution. In the Revolution, the country officially went atheist, and enterprising young men with hammers were able to collect so much per head for knocking the heads off religious sculptures and statues. In England, the Dissolution of the monasteries under Henry VIII in the sixteenth century and the civil wars and the short-lived Puritan commonwealth of the seventeenth century had a similar effect, as both deliberately set out to destroy anything seen as too Catholic. Romanesque sculpture survives best in those churches, like Autun, where men of the late Middle Ages or early modern period decided it was ugly and plastered it over, so that it was hidden during the most destructive periods, waiting to be rediscovered.

The New Gothic Style

In the second half of the twelfth century, a new architectural style was developed. Then it was called the New Style; now it is called Gothic. The terms "Romanesque" and "Gothic" are actually products of the Re-

The cathedral of Notre-Dame of Paris. Flying buttresses support the choir, on the right.

naissance. Certain men of the Renaissance looked at Romanesque churches and assumed they had been built by the Romans. After all, like Roman buildings, they did use the rounded arch, although the similarities really stop there. The men of the Renaissance therefore called this "Roman style." (These were the same men who thought ninth-century Caroline miniscule was Roman handwriting; see Chapter 5.) Even though the name is wrong, it has stuck; modern architectural historians, however, have at least termed the style of the eleventh and early twelfth centuries "Romanesque," rather that Roman, to distinguish it from real Roman architecture. The same men of the Renaissance, looking at buildings built from the late twelfth century on, in New Style, concluded that since this style came after "Roman" style it must have been the style of the barbarians who invaded the late Roman Empire. They called it the "Gothic" style, after the Goths who sacked Rome in the fifth century. Although these men of the Renaissance were seven hundred years off in their calculations, and though the New Style of the late twelfth and thirteenth centuries has nothing to do with the Goths, the name has remained.

Gothic is distinguished from Romanesque in particular by having pointed rather than rounded arches. Churches with pointed arches could be built higher, and long narrow windows made it possible to let a great deal of light into the church. These churches were built with smoothly-quarried stone, not fieldstone. Architects of the twelfth and thirteenth centuries experimented with the structure's limits: how many windows they could put in, how tall they could build a church without having it collapse. Gothic churches, like the castles being built at the same time (see Chapter 6), required tremendous capital investment and could keep scores of workers profitably employed for years.

Notre-Dame of Paris, one of the early Gothic churches constructed in the second half of the twelfth century, began to shift disconcertingly by the time its walls had been up for twenty years. The architects responded by devising and adding flying buttresses, which later builders in Gothic almost all used. These were arched supports built onto the outside of the walls, designed to support the walls and keep them from bulging outward of their own weight. With the invention of the flying buttress, the architects started trying for even new heights. Beauvais, the tallest cathedral ever attempted (and never actually finished, because it really did overreach the technology of the time), still survives in part; its vault is over 150 feet from the ground, high enough for a fourteen-story building under it.

The windows in the walls of Gothic churches were big enough for some spectacular stained glass. The art of stained glass was highly developed in the twelfth and thirteenth centuries, producing colors that craftsmen in later centuries have not been able to duplicate. Individual pieces of colored glass, sometimes with outlines of figures painted on them, were put together between strips of lead to form pictures and tell stories, much as the capitals had in Romanesque architecture. The Ste.-Chapelle in Paris, built in the mid-thirteenth century, has walls almost entirely of glass. Unfortunately, the Ste.-Chapelle is almost unique in still having its high-medieval windows. Notre-Dame lost most of hers in the middle of the eighteenth century, when an architect commissioned to "update" a church that seemed unnecessarily antique had them smashed and replaced with plain glass! And modern air pollution is destroying much of the thirteenth-century glass the cathedrals have left.

The Gothic cathedrals were decorated with much more realistic stone sculpture than had been used on Romanesque churches. Starting in the first decades of the thirteenth century, stonemasons produced the most realistic-looking sculptures that had been produced in Europe since the Roman Empire. The saints on the facades of the churches were modeled after real people and had individual faces and personalities.

The main problem with Gothic architecture as opposed to Romanesque is that is was extremely expensive and time-consuming to build so large and so high. Although almost all of Europe's churches had been built or rebuilt in the Romanesque style in the eleventh or early twelfth centuries, only wealthy religious communities could afford Gothic. This means that the churches of the small towns and countryside in Europe are still largely Romanesque. Hiring large professional crews was very expensive, although the church might ask the local townsmen to contrib-

Chartres cathedral is decorated both with twelfth-century carvings (left) and with much more realistic carvings from the thirteenth century (right).

ute to the cost; for example, guilds often paid for windows in a Gothic cathedral, each window representing a particular guild's saint. Moreover, Gothic churches took at least two generations, and sometimes two centuries, to complete. Work might start well but then come to a stop for years while the church saved up money again. New architects hired to start up a stalled project carried on in whatever style was current at the time, which means that no Gothic church has an overall homogeneous style.

Whereas Romanesque architects believed in safety first, building much more sturdily than they actually needed to, Gothic architects believed in trying to see if something would work, and as a result their churches are not as solid. Gothic churches bombed in the two world wars were destroyed, yet several Romanesque churches received direct hits but still survived. But for the most part Gothic architects stayed just within the

Interior of Beauvais cathedral (choir end), built in the thirteenth century. It was the tallest cathedral ever attempted.

range of the possible. Today, most urban churches in Europe are Gothic, having been in place since the high or late Middle Ages.

Even today, accustomed as we are to skyscrapers and football stadiums, it is startling to enter one of the big cathedrals such as Notre-Dame of Paris. For people of the high Middle Ages, accustomed to buildings no more than two or three stories tall, it would have been even more awe-inspiring and impressive. A big cathedral, made to hold ten thousand people—the total population of many cities—was designed so that it still retained its spiritual integrity even with a noisy crowd inside. The very height of the building swallowed up the noise and made it insignificant. Tourists in Paris today who deplore the tour groups in half a dozen languages and the offers to see the treasure for twenty francs, wishing that *they* were the only tourists in Notre-Dame, should at least be reassured that crowds speaking every known language and booths selling snacks and trinkets have been part of the cathedral since the day it was built.

Such buildings required breakthroughs both in architecture and in stoneworking. The stone-cutters were professionals, men who were able to cut smooth, square stones with what we would consider quite primitive tools; they marked all their stones with special marks (which can still be seen on several churches), so that they would be sure to get credit at the end of the day for all of *their* stones. The architects had even more professional pride; starting in the thirteenth century God was sometimes portrayed as an architect Himself, laying out the universe with a compass and calipers. The geometry and trigonometry the architects needed seems to have come, like much thirteenth-century philosophy, from the Arabs. They laid out their cathedrals based not on absolute measurement (such as feet and inches) but rather on proportion, so that the height was always a certain multiple of the width, and so on. All the proportions were based on certain multiples of a unit with which the architect started, combined in ways that they guarded as professional secrets until the end of the Middle Ages. Rather than using tape measures, the architects set out the dimensions of all parts of the cathedral geometrically, from the basic square, marking them out on the building site by means of cords and pegs, and then constructing wooden models on the ground that could be hoisted up and used as frames for the stonework.

The complicated technical knowledge of how to build a cathedral can be compared to the complicated reasoning of the scholastic method. In the universities and in architecture, the goal was the greater glory of God and the approach of the ordinary man to the holy. The men of the high Middle Ages, while recognizing the enormous gap between themselves and God, still were very optimistic about their ability to begin to bridge it. Students hurried to the universities, and cathedral chapters competed to hire the best cathedral architects.

By the end of the thirteenth century, some of this initial optimism had passed off. The organized church was beginning to doubt the value of wide-open intellectual inquiry, at the same time as architects realized that there were indeed limits as to how high one could build a cathedral, and as cathedral chapters realized that their new cathedrals would probably not be finished for several generations. But in the meantime, the combination of religion with reason and practical achievement, which marked the high Middle Ages, had given birth to the cathedrals that still dominate the skylines of Europe's cities, and to the university system that still continues around the world.

NINE

THE FOURTEENTH CENTURY

c. **1280**	Cooler climate brings less reliable harvests
c. **1290**	Invention of the mechanical clock
1315–1317	Disastrous harvests in much of Europe
1338	Beginning of Hundred Years' War between France and England
1347	Black Death first reaches Europe
c. **1350**	Paper begins to replace parchment
1358	Jacquerie breaks out in France
c. **1360**	Gunpowder begins to be important
1378	Ciompi rebellion in Florence
1379	Beginning of Great Schism of the papacy
c. **1380**	Municipal brothels become common
1381	English Peasants' Revolt
1400	Chaucer finishes *Canterbury Tales*

NINE

THE FOURTEENTH CENTURY

THE FOURTEENTH CENTURY, the beginning of the period now known as the late Middle Ages, was a much grimmer period than the high Middle Ages. In its wars and disasters many historians have seen parallels with the twentieth century. It was the time of the Black Death, of the beginning of the Hundred Years' War, and of the Peasants' Revolts. On the other hand, it was also an extremely creative and stimulating age, a time when both eyeglasses and gunpowder were invented, a time of literary flourishing with authors like Boccaccio and Chaucer, a time when mechanical clocks first began to affect people's lives.

Agricultural Setbacks

Underlying all the disasters of the fourteenth century was economic collapse. There were many factors involved, but the most basic was a worsening of the climate, which made it harder to harvest good crops reliably. Because of this, even if the population had ceased to grow, the shrinking food supply meant that Europe was increasingly overpopulated. The change in the climate began in the late thirteenth century, with what modern historians now call the onset of a "mini ice age." Although it was a relatively small shift in the climate compared to a real ice age, it was enough to shorten the growing season and make a destructively early frost a common fear rather than a rare event. The improvements of the climatic optimum of the high Middle Ages (see Chapter 6) were thus reversed. Heavy storms, especially hailstorms, began to appear with some frequency in the middle of the summer, destroying crops long before they had any chance to ripen. The worst famine of the Middle Ages happened between 1315 and 1317, as a series of disastrous harvests led to mass starvation in a Europe that suddenly found itself seriously overpopulated.

Europe's population had been growing rapidly for over two centuries. It has been estimated that England's population, for example, was three or four times as high in the early fourteenth century as it had been in the late eleventh century. As long as new fields could be put under the plow every year and the crops brought in reliably, this was not a problem. The occasional devastating flood or hailstorm of the twelfth century had been a local occurrence, and a badly hit village could buy food from elsewhere. But, by the end of the thirteenth century, crop disasters were hitting much wider areas, and it was growing harder to find someone with extra food to sell. This growing scarcity of food in bad years was naturally accompanied by rapid inflation in food prices; by the fourteenth century, a peasant family that might earlier have been able to buy its food for a short period could no longer afford to do so even if food were available.

There were no new fertile fields waiting to be cultivated, as all the good land *was* cultivated already. Indeed, by the end of the thirteenth century, many peasants were trying to grow grain on very marginal tracts of land, including the lower slopes of the Alps, which have never been suited for growing grain. The more marginal lands were quickly exhausted, and even the feeble grain-growing capability of the Alps was restricted by the new advance of the glaciers. Thus less land was available for crops by 1300 than there had been fifty years earlier, even aside from the fact that all cultivated land was producing smaller and less reliable crops.

The result of all these factors, even when there was not famine, was a general level of malnutrition in the fourteenth century. Very few people always had enough to eat, and in the first great famine many peasants were forced to start selling off their land. Soon many had no choice but to wander from town to town, begging for enough food to keep themselves alive, and scavenging chickens out of backyards or bread out of bakeries if given a chance. The arrival in town of the beggars, carrying their bowls and staffs, became a cause of real trepidation. "The poor," who had been a group to be pitied and helped in the high Middle Ages, became a group to be feared in the fourteenth century. Although the worst of the overpopulation problem was grimly solved in the middle of the fourteenth century by the loss of a third of the population to the Black Death, as discussed later, this was scarcely a comfortable solution.

It is interesting to note that by the year 1300 the European idea of "the poor" was quite similar to ours, or for that matter to that of the Roman Empire: that is, people living at the edge of starvation, caught in a desperate cycle with no clear way to escape, relying on the generosity of others just to stay alive. In the middle of the twelfth century, by contrast, "poverty" had been something different, something that a person might seek out voluntarily, usually for religious reasons, rather than something from which one would urgently want to escape. The wandering beggars of the twelfth century were usually not the desperately poor but rather pilgrims who had deliberately put off their fine clothes for a trip of penitence. Peasant families going through difficult times could hope that their situation would improve in a year or two, rather than knowing they were permanently trapped in poverty. Plenty of people in the high Middle Ages had had little property, but there were opportunities in the twelfth century for anyone willing to work hard and usually enough food to go around. These opportunities were gone in the fourteenth century.

Many monasteries in the eleventh and twelfth centuries had institutionalized the biblical command to "give to the poor," but since there *were* very few poor people in the countryside in the sense that Jesus had meant (urban poor with no property or income), rural monasteries had to find "token" poor people. These token poor were kept at a monastery year round, with the monks buying their food and clothes; they were available on Maundy Thursday to have their feet washed, and received coins as ritualized gifts "to the poor." For that matter, many monasteries thought of *themselves* as the "poor," for after all the monks had no individual property; they used this definition when reminding their wealthy neighbors that they were supposed to make "gifts to the poor."

But in the fourteenth century monasteries that wanted to help the poor, as most of them sincerely did, had no trouble finding genuinely needy people. As noted in Chapter 8, the friars in the thirteenth century had already associated themselves with the urban poor, and by the fourteenth century poverty-stricken individuals and families were found both in the cities and in the countryside. They were desperately trying to survive without any of the elaborate system of welfare, Medicaid, food stamps, or Social Security which it is now too easy to take for granted.

The Black Death

The Outbreak of the Plague

General malnutrition left the European population weakened and especially susceptible to infectious diseases. (The human body is able to resist infection better if strong and well fed, which is why famine and disease have always arrived together.) Thus, when the Black Death reached Europe in the middle of the fourteenth century, the population was not in a position to resist it, and this plague killed between a quarter and a half of the people of western Europe within two years. The cities were especially hard hit; some took two centuries or more to return to the population levels of the end of the thirteenth century. No system of hospitals, medicine, quarantine, or prayer could cope with a disaster of such magnitude. Several times as many people died in Europe of the plague as died in either World War. In the speed and thoroughness with which the Black Death devastated western Europe, perhaps the only modern parallel would be our fears of nuclear holocaust.

The Black Death was caused by one or several variations of the plague bacillus, primarily bubonic plague. It is a disease spread by fleas carried principally by rats, but any other mammal can be a carrier. The bacteria had been around for centuries, but only at a low level. After the great outbreaks of the sixth century, bubonic plague had essentially disappeared from the West. In the early fourteenth century, however, a new and more virulent strain seems to have appeared somewhere in central Asia. From there it spread to China, the rest of Asia, the Middle East, and North Africa. In 1347 it hit Constantinople, and in that same year an infected Genoese ship brought the plague to Sicily. Within the next year, half or more of the urban population of Italy died. One can map the spread of the disease across Europe like ripples from a stone dropped in a pond. From Italy in 1347, the plague reached France in 1348, Scandinavia in 1349, and eastern Europe in 1350. Its effect was immediate whenever it arrived; in 1348 in Paris eight hundred people died a day. By 1351 the bacillus seems to have become somewhat less virulent, but the cold and damp of northern Europe meant that the pulmonary complications that often attended the plague could be fatal even if the initial infection was not.

It actually was possible to survive the plague, if one were in reasonable health, as long as one caught one of the less virulent forms of bubonic plague and not the closely related but more deadly pneumonic plague. In some cities, almost everyone may have been infected and developed at least some symptoms. Since cold weather limits flea activity, outbreaks were the most intense in late summer (the same season that pet dogs and cats today get the worst fleas). Those who had caught the plague and recovered from it would usually not succumb again. This meant that none of the cycles of the plague that followed in the succeeding centuries were quite so devastating. However, the children who had been born since the last outbreak would be extremely susceptible, especially because children have fewer natural defenses to all infectious diseases. A long period between plague outbreaks only meant that the next one would be worse. Thus it took a very long time for Europe's population to reestablish itself. There were outbreaks every generation or so throughout the late Middle Ages and Renaissance and during the whole early modern period, up to the eighteenth century. (Even now, the bubonic plague is still with us, endemic among rodents in the Sierras, though it is a relatively mild strain.)

Results of the Black Death

The Black Death had a tremendous impact on Europe even aside from the destruction of a third of its population. The buoyant optimism that had marked the high Middle Ages was gone for good. There cannot have been a family that did not lose at least one family member to the plague—if indeed the entire family was not wiped out. The loss of children would be a blow especially hard to take. Psychological depression was the norm from the middle of the fourteenth century on.

The situation was made even worse by the blind and quite understandable panic that set in. This panic led to a very rapid breakdown of government and society's institutions. The men of the fourteenth century, even without understanding bacteria, certainly recognized the contagious nature of infection when they saw it. (They also recognized the role of fleas in spreading it; pet dogs and cats were usually slaughtered at the beginning of an outbreak of plague.) As soon as the plague first appeared in town, much of the rest of the population would flee, abandoning friends and responsibilities. Towns, universities, and royal courts were all abandoned repeatedly in the late fourteenth and the fifteenth centuries, whenever a new outbreak of the plague occurred. The bodies of the dead were left unburied in the streets.

Those fleeing might in fact already be infected, as there was close to a week between infection and the appearance of symptoms with bubonic plague; this meant that those trying to escape the plague might instead be spreading it to a new town. Many cities, realizing what was happening, locked their gates, refusing to let anyone new in or anyone back in who had once gone out, even if they stood below the walls and screamed and cursed and pleaded. The only really safe place to flee was the countryside, away from the population centers where the closely packed houses allowed the plague to spread like wildfire. The hills became full of terrified families, clinging together and armed with bows, shooting on sight anyone who came within a hundred paces.

Even after the worst of the plague was over, a deep morbidity of thought and perception lingered. This is perhaps most evident in the new forms that tombstones started to take. After the mid-fourteenth century, it became increasingly common to depict the deceased on his tomb, not as he looked when he was alive, but how he would look when some days dead. A partially decayed corpse, carved in stone, often complete with worms, was supposed to make the viewer think of death and contemplate his sins. This was called a *memento mori*, or reminder of death. Several royal French tombs of the late Middle Ages were made on two levels, with the royal couple depicted alive on the top level, fully clothed and kneeling in prayer, but depicted as naked cadavers on the lower level. In

Tomb of Cardinal Jean de La Grange. The tomb was built on two levels: the cardinal appears clothed and sleeping above, and as a decaying corpse below.

other cases, the deceased might be depicted as sleeping (as had been common since the early thirteenth century), but the tomb would also include scenes of mourners overcome with debilitating sorrow.

In some cases, this constant reminder of death, from such symbols and from outbreaks of the plague itself, led to a hedonistic, live-for-today attitude. Per-capita wealth increased essentially overnight with the plague, since there were many fewer people, especially in the cities, among whom wealth was divided. The immediate result was a great increase in per-person spending on manufactured and luxury goods, as people hurried to have as good a time as possible before their inevitable deaths. Many people turned against the organized church, which had shown its inability to deal with the plague; the prayers and elevation of relics that had worked against earlier disasters had been ineffective, and priests had fled the cities as rapidly as anyone else. Some people even took the plague as a sign that God, if He existed, did not care about humans one way or the other. The debauched partying and celebrating that broke out in the aftermath of the plague had a decadent and morbid air; parties were held in the graveyards, and the elegant came dressed as skeletons.

On the other hand, there was also an increase in personal piety, because turning against the organized church did not necessarily mean turning against Christianity. Many people felt that God was punishing His people for their sins, and those who survived felt they had been given a last precious opportunity to reform and repent. In the plague years, this repentence once again often took the extreme form of flagellation, as groups of people went from town to town, beating themselves and each other, wailing and preaching the end of the world (and probably in some cases spreading the plague). The plague years saw more flagellants than had been seen since 1260 (see page 269). Once the first wave of the Black Death had passed, however, repentence took calmer forms. There was a great deal of increase in such "good works" as the foundation of chapels or hospitals, as well as in the number of people who went on pilgrimage. The pilgrims in Chaucer's *Canterbury Tales* were following a route that attracted hordes of pilgrims every spring in the late fourteenth century.

Although there were no new great monastic orders or orders of friars founded in the fourteenth century, as there had been in the twelfth and thirteenth centuries, there were plenty of new small orders, often very local, based on the attempts of rather ordinary people to lead simple and holy lives. Many would try to continue their ordinary occupations during the day but live an almost monastic life at home, or perhaps would devote themselves to care for the sick. Women especially began living together in small groups in the cities, making their living through such occupations as weaving or taking in laundry, sharing their goods with each other, reading the Bible together, and wearing white cowls like nuns.

These new religious groups were only marginally governed by the church hierarchy. The late medieval church had become quite rigid, and there was no room in the ecclesiastical structure for these groups. The bishops were not sure what to do with them because unregulated religious activity outside of the church organization was heresy by definition in the late Middle Ages, but these people were usually so self-evidently pious that there was no reason to prosecute them. The usual answer (not particularly successful) was to try to get all such groups to adopt a formal rule and to persuade the groups of women to put themselves under the spiritual direction of a priest.

Although withdrawal from the crasser concerns of society in order to live pious lives was certainly an important reaction to the plague and its aftermath, a more disruptive but also widespread reaction was to turn to violence. With the structure of society and morality broken down, people became violent much more readily, and the local lords who had once tried to impose law and order were either gone or incapable of enforcing it. In England, for example, even though the population was at least a third lower in the 1350s than it had been just a few years earlier, the absolute number of homicides seems to have doubled. In the Italian cities, poisoning and assassination became so common that even when a pope or duke died of natural causes there were always rumors of foul play.

Anyone who might be considered a scapegoat for the plague was viciously attacked. The Jews, who were tolerated much less graciously in the late Middle Ages than they had been earlier, were sometimes accused of starting the plague by poisoning the wells. The kings had to step in several times to protect the Jews from vicious accusations and threats of retaliation, even though the medical schools all quickly issued proclamations saying that there was no way that the Jews could be responsible. In spite of this, in some towns, especially in Germany, thousands of Jews were rounded up, tortured to extract false confessions, and burned. (The Jews were not forced into ghettos until the sixteenth century, but they still tended to congregate in their own quarters, which made it easier to round them up.) In many places the Jews, who had played a major part in the commercial life of medieval cities, dwindled sharply in numbers or had to go underground, not to regain their position until the seventeenth century.

Another result of the plague was a series of attempts by the cities to regulate anything that might help the disease break out again. Regulations against filth in the streets, already strict, were strengthened. Many cities shut down their bathhouses, fearing they served as centers of infection. In other cities, people avoided the bathhouses in large enough numbers that they had to close down anyway. Regular bathing, which had once been universal, declined sharply. Those who worked in the fields, becoming covered with mud and sweat, were still forced to bathe, although they increasingly did so at home. But the upper classes, who did not become covered with filth in their daily activities, began to pride themselves on *not* bathing. Whereas between the ninth and thirteenth centuries it had been a sign of luxury to be able to afford to bathe as often as one wished, even once a day, in the late fourteenth and fifteenth centuries it was a sign of luxury to wash only one's hands and neck. Queen Isabella of Spain, Christopher Columbus's patron, said proudly at the end of the fifteenth century that she had only had two baths in her life, one when she was born and another the day before she married

Ferdinand, and that she hoped to have only one more, when she had died and was being laid out for burial.

The Regulation of Prostitution

The cities also began to regulate houses of prostitution, due in part to the same belief that if something were regulated it could be made more healthy. Prostitution, unlike bathing, showed no signs of dying out by itself. It had been tolerated in the cities of the high Middle Ages, neither encouraged nor really discouraged, but treated as a necessary evil. Prostitutes had rights just as any other woman had; in most cities the penalty for raping a prostitute was the same as for raping a citizen's wife (although one might wonder if this was always enforced). It was assumed that unmarried men, single or widowers, would want to have some sort of sex life, and prostitution was considered preferable to the corruption of virgins or adultery with married women. The church's main reaction to prostitution had been to try to encourage the women to repent and give up their profession. Both the churches and private donors sometimes founded "Magdalene houses" (named for the biblical Mary Magdalene, who was supposed to have been a repentent prostitute). These provided a place to live and food to eat for prostitutes who wanted to try to reenter society. Although there probably were some young women who genuinely repented of what they had been doing, in many cases these Magdalene houses provided a useful retirement home for older prostitutes, or a "halfway house" for women who had taken up the profession because they felt they had no other marketable skills but had not yet given up hope of getting married and having a family once they had accumulated some money. Many prostitutes were country girls or girls from small towns, from very poor families, who came to the cities hoping to make a living.

Starting in the late fourteenth century, many cities established municipally licensed brothels, forbidding freelance prostitution. If all the brothels were together in one place, it was assumed, it would be easier to keep an eye on them and to hold down public disorder. Therefore an official "red-light district," as it would now be called, was created; the fourteenth century called such a district a "hot street." It was always difficult to choose an appropriate place for the municipal hot street. Residents of different areas always had reasons why *their* area would be unsuitable. It was generally agreed that brothels should not be placed too close to churches, schools, markets, or the residences of "honest" people (just as there are ordinances in every American city regulating where bars may be located). Prices were set for the municipal brothels, regular health inspections were established, and the women were paid a minimum wage. Prostitution could be a very profitable trade for the women, once price competition was limited and they did not have to pay much of their income to procurers and protectors. Magdalene houses continued to exist, however, providing places for any prostitutes that changed their minds. Municipal licensing and regulation of brothels continued until the sixteenth century, when renewed health concerns and the new puritanical attitude, due in part to the Protestant Reformation, led to houses of prostitution being officially (at least) banned and shut down.

Witchcraft and Medicine in the Late Middle Ages

With the worsening of the general health of the population, due to malnutrition and infectious disease, young children were especially prone to ill health. In the late thirteenth and fourteenth centuries, it started to be relatively common for mothers of sickly children to resort to what would now be considered witchcraft. Although such practices were present throughout the earlier Middle Ages as well, they seem to have become much more prevalent as mothers became more desperate. We also know more about witchcraft in the late Middle Ages because we know more about *everything* in the period, for it had become much more common to write things down than it had been in earlier centuries.

Witchcraft and Folk Medicine

A belief that recurred constantly in the countryside was that a baby who cried all the time and did not seem to grow at all was not one's *real* baby but rather a changeling, left by demons who had somehow managed to switch babies between birth and baptism, after which the real baby would have been safe. (Even today, mothers with colicky or unresponsive babies must wonder, at least in passing, if this rather unlovable child is really theirs or if there was a mix-up at the hospital.) Certain old women knew the secret spells to make the demons come back for the demon child, leaving one's own healthy baby in its place.

There were also certain saints who were considered to be especially concerned for sick children, and mothers would consult these saints. One of the most popular saints in this regard in southern France was St. Guinefort, a rather unusual saint in that he was not a human but a greyhound. An old folk tale, which occurs throughout Europe and parts of Asia in several forms, was attached to the holy greyhound. A dog (Guinefort) was told by his master to guard a sleeping baby. Suddenly a wolf (or snake or monster) sprang at the cradle. The valiant dog fought desperately, finally killing the beast, but in the struggle the cradle was knocked over and the baby tossed into the corner. The master then returned, saw the cradle empty and the dog's mouth all covered with blood, and went into a rage, killing the dog he thought had eaten his child. A moment later, however, he found his baby safe in the corner and saw the dead wolf. Realizing what had happened, he sorrowfully buried his faithful dog. The place where Guinefort was buried was supposed to be especially conducive to healing children.

From the point of view of the organized church, the problem with St. Guinefort was that greyhounds could not be saints; several bishops tried to stop what they considered very misguided appeals to St. Guinefort. This had little effect, however, since many women continued to believe that Guinefort could help them; his aid was still being sought at a special fountain in southern France into the twentieth century.

In the thirteenth and fourteenth centuries, the organized church la-
belled as witches the old women who knew the spells to call the demons
who had left a changeling baby and who knew the rituals that would
please St. Guinefort. However, being a witch was not a particularly wicked
thing to be; witch-burning and witch-hysteria did not come until the
seventeenth century. Although witchcraft was considered to be a form
of paganism, in practice there was very little difference between the
witchcraft of the time and some approved Christian rituals. One should
not think that pagan practices had gone underground with the rise of
Christianity or had continued as a separate tradition. Rather, there was
a gradation of practices between learned religion and folk religion, both
of which were considered to be Christianity, and although folk religion
had more of what might be considered pagan rituals, one cannot draw
any sort of clean dividing line. After all, the mothers who went to St.
Guinefort would have been perfectly orthodox if the helper they considered a Christian saint had been a human rather than a dog.

The continuous nature of the gradation between folk religion and that
of the organized church becomes more evident when one looks objec-
tively at the actual ritual activities performed in each. Mainstream, learned
Christianity included many signs and rituals: the sign of the cross, the
lighting and extinguishing of candles, the correct sequence of words said
over the bread and wine at the altar. There was no easy way to distinguish these rituals from the sprinkling of salt and the lighting of candles
at the head and feet of a changeling baby. Although church leaders
themselves found these distinctions clear, they realized that they would
be less clear to the uneducated. They thought that the witches who
taught mothers the magic ceremonies and the women themselves were
terribly misguided. In calling on saints who were not really saints, according to the organized church, they were instead getting a response
from demons. To traffic with demons was to endanger their souls, and
mothers, trying to make their childrens' bodies healthy, were considered
to be putting their salvation in peril. As long as one did not wilfully seek
out the company of demons, in the full realization of what one was
doing, one was not actually a heretic, but bishops and preachers were
still very concerned about witchcraft and tried to persuade people to turn
instead to correct Christian practices and recognized saints.

The Beginning of Modern Medicine

Another area in which folk practices and practices approved by the more
learned often overlapped was in medicine, which in much of the Middle
Ages was scarcely distinguishable from magic or witchcraft. The basis for
much medieval medicine was the belief that similar *appearance* of two things
meant that they were related *functionally* as well. For example, if there
had been kidney beans in Europe (there were not, as kidney beans are
New World), it would have been universally agreed that they were good
for diseased kidneys. The basis for this was a perception that since the
world had been created by God, for the benefit of man, He had consciously created analogies in appearance as hints to His creatures. All

A Caesarean section, performed by a midwife. From the *Life of Caesar* (1375).

sorts of herbs were prescribed for various ailments based on their physical structure, as well as on past experience. Although we may think of this as quaint or backward, it is still a well-established belief in much of the world today; because rhinoceros horns are long and pointed and hard, men in many countries take powdered rhinoceros horn to make themselves potent and virile.

One of the results of the Black Death, however, was an overhaul of the medical system, which could perhaps be considered the beginning of modern medicine. In the high Middle Ages, when most people had been (relatively) well nourished, and there had been few epidemic diseases, medicine had not been particularly scientific. Most people who became sick either got well by themselves (with—or in spite of—the aid of herbs prescribed by apothecaries or old women) or died, but they died singly, not in large groups. Wounds were cleaned and closed and broken bones set by surgeons, who might also serve as barbers. The apothecaries who prescribed herbs usually were spice merchants as well. Besides these rather unprofessional "health providers," there were the real doctors, but these highly educated men had had little contact with what we would consider real medicine.

The doctors trained in medical schools in the thirteenth and early fourteenth centuries had mostly studied texts, especially those in Greek and Arabic, rather than patients. A doctor coming out of medical school would be able to recite a catalogue of herbal cures and healing practices without necessarily knowing if any of them would work. A "proper" medical education had involved much more theory than practice. The underlying theory had been that of the "four humours," derived from the ancient Greeks. The healthy body was supposedly based on a balance between blood, phlegm, yellow bile (from the liver), and black bile (from the spleen). If someone was not healthy, doctors tried to restore the correct balance—for example, by bleeding someone to get rid of excess blood. These "four humours" were supposed to correspond to the "four elements" of the universe: earth, air, fire, and water.

When the plague hit, however, this sort of theory was useless, and the doctors knew it. The surgeons were not able to cure people with much more success, but at least they had a better understanding of the practical conditions under which the plague broke out and of its symptoms and progress. The immediate result was a professionalization of the surgeons, and the coming together of what had been two separate groups, the doctors and the surgeons, as the doctors began for the first time to put real emphasis on practical anatomy. "How to" anatomy books began to be written for the first time, to supplement the theoretic texts; some were even aimed at a popular audience. In the aftermath of the first outbreak of the Black Death, many doctors persuaded municipalities to establish boards of public health, with authority over quarantine, clean streets, and the like. Some municipalities began to hire doctors, at high salaries, specifically to treat plague victims.

The Peasantry after the Plague

The immediate result of the plague on the condition of the peasantry was to force many of them back into the serfdom that had been nearly gone in the West for two centuries. Although the cities lost many more people in the plague than did the countryside, a great many peasants moved into the cities to take advantage of the new opportunities that had opened up. The result was that the countryside was left relatively unpopulated. Some villages were completely deserted and never inhabited again. In fact, Europe's rural population has probably *never* been as high again as it was in the early fourteenth century. Because of this, the landlords started imposing draconian new rules to hold on to their peasants. Their land was useless to them unless they had someone to work it, preferably at a wage they wanted to pay, not the wages the peasants were asking in a seller's market.

The landlords' measures were relatively successful in eastern Europe, where serfdom was imposed for the very first time in the fourteenth century, and in England, where the small size of the country and the fact that it was an island made it hard for the peasants to escape. In western Europe, however, after a difficult decade or two, the peasants seem to have ended up somewhat better off. Even in England, repeated attempts to set the wages of agricultural laborers at a low level were routinely ignored. The landlords, desperately needing labor, were willing to pay high wages to lure each other's peasants away, rather than working in concert to suppress them. Peasants were able to demand, and get, an end to all labor dues.

Peasants who felt that the newly imposed servile obligations were intolerable were able simply to run away anywhere there was a nearby city where they could hide. Traditionally, someone who eluded discovery for a year and a day was able to relax, knowing he was now free. "City air makes one free," according to a popular saying of the time. (The peasants living in the cities were hiding both from rural and urban landlords, for many cities—not wanting to lose the peasants they needed to provide the city's food—had extradition treaties.) In the countryside, because there were fewer peasant families competing for the resources, those left were able to eat better than they had for some time, and the well-to-do among the peasants were able to buy up the land of those who had died or moved to the cities and thus establish solid holdings. A deep measure of dissatisfaction remained, however, both in England and on the Continent.

Another cause for peasant unhappiness, especially in England, was the tendency of landlords to try to appropriate the peasants' land and use it for sheep. When lords realized they did not have enough peasants available for grain-growing, and that with the collapse of prices in the grain market, due to loss of population, their own profits were falling anyway, many decided to turn to sheep-raising, which required less human labor. In England there was always a good market for wool, to be turned into textiles sold across Europe, an international market that was not as subject to fluctuations as was the local market for grain. With greater or lesser success, landlords began attempting in the late fourteenth century to take away the grain fields that peasants had always rented from them and turn them into pastures. In some cases, peasants were forced off land that they and their ancestors had farmed as long as anyone could remember. This increase in livestock raising did mean that there was more meat available (especially mutton), and at a cheaper price, in the late Middle Ages than there had been earlier, but peasants forced off their fields could hardly have been expected to appreciate these improvements in townsmen's nutrition.

In the same way, people who worked in manufacturing found both new opportunities and new restrictions after the plague. The increased demand for luxury manufactured goods meant that laborers could, at least in theory, demand higher wages. Weavers, miners, and blacksmiths, to name just a few, found higher demand for their services, especially as there were fewer of them. However, at the same time, those who employed them began imposing regulations to keep them from leaving in search of better living conditions elsewhere, and began working them harder, to try to keep up with the increased demand for their goods.

The increasing dissatisfaction, which involved both peasants and the lower social classes of the cities, led to the first organized class revolts the Middle Ages had seen. There had been risings on individual manors, of course, of peasants protesting or rebelling against intolerable conditions, but in the second half of the fourteenth century peasants or the urban poor began grouping together in uprisings that spread across entire areas or even countries. The first such outbreak was the Jacquerie in France in 1358, so called because it was a revolt of "ordinary Jacks" against new dues imposed in the wake of the plague and new requirements that the peasants help rebuild castles and walls destroyed in the Hundred

THE HUNDRED YEARS' WAR: FRANCE AND ENGLAND IN 1360
At the end of the first phase of the Hundred Years' War, after the English victory
at Poitiers in 1356, the French had to agree to English control of most of southwest France.

Years' War. This rebellion, which included peasants, urban laborers, and
renegade soldiers, only lasted two weeks, but it was a harbinger of many
more rebellions over the next two centuries. Twenty years after the Jacquerie, in 1378, the Ciompi rebellion of oppressed textile workers broke
out in Florence. In an industry that was increasingly shifting to luxury
textiles, these workers demanded to be paid for a certain minimum number of bolts a year when the entrepreneurs, producing fewer bolts but
making more per bolt, tried to reduce their wages. The biggest rebellion,
however, was the English Peasants' Revolt of 1381. All these revolts had
a similar pattern of early success—bloody attacks on those the rebels
considered their tormentors, random violence, and looting—followed by
a brutal suppression by the local aristocracy and execution of the leaders.
In the aftermath of the revolts, however, conditions were always quietly improved.

The peasants' and workers' revolts of the second half of the fourteenth century indicate the rise of a new attitude within society. Medieval man had always taken it for granted that it was natural that society be divided into more and less privileged orders. Such a division, at best, was seen as the necessary result of man's sinful nature. It may be difficult for modern Americans, raised in a self-consciously egalitarian and democratic society, to realize how deeply ingrained in Western civilization was an acceptance of differences in status based on birth. Not just those of the upper strata but those of the lower strata had accepted such divisions as inevitable. They could no more easily be changed than could the rising of the sun in the east. Individuals certainly tried to move to higher levels, but they only wanted to better their own situation, not overthrow the structure of society. Stratification of society by birth had been part of classical society, and although Christianity taught the equality of man before God, it was a spiritual equality, not a social equality.

Perhaps the medieval acceptance of differences of birth can be better understood by realizing that modern America, opposed to privilege though it is, readily accepts differences based on wealth. The fabulously wealthy in our society, or at least the most visible of that group—movie stars, rock stars, and sports stars—are admired and treated with deference and awe even while many of their fans wish *they* had that much money. There is always a tension in modern America between thinking that it is not right that certain people should have so much money, and wanting to find out all the juicy details of the lives and habits of the wealthy. Any suggestion that all Americans should be economically equal, that everyone's money should be taken away and then redistributed in equal amounts to everyone, is considered scandalous, communist, and worse by working-class America. In the same way, in classical and medieval times, the great majority of the population, those managing to make a living but never getting rich, would have rejected the very concept of everyone being politically equal.

But this acceptance of differences began to break down in the late Middle Ages. Questioning this stratification of society began, interestingly enough, not with the lower classes but with the political philosophers. Returning to the old idea that a division between men was inevitable, that there was no other option in a sinful world, some suggested that if Adam and Eve had *not* sinned everyone would have been equal. In England by 1381, some of those who read the political philosophers were reaching the conclusion that social stratification was a sin in itself. A poem began making the rounds, "When Adam delved and Eve span [the past tense of "to spin"], / Who was then a gentleman?"

However, when the English Peasants' Revolt broke out, its aim was not a new form of social structure; rather, it was an attempt to return to the "good old days," to conditions that the peasants felt had always been theirs by right but had recently been taken away. It was a very conservative rebellion by modern standards. The peasants believed that the king was their friend and would protect them, and that their recent oppression had only come about because the king had been kept from finding out the situation by wicked counsellors. Even though the king turned against the peasants, after their ringleaders (more radical than the peasants as a whole) had captured and killed the archbishop of Canterbury and used his head as a football, he was in fact not insensitive to their plight. Although heavily-armed aristocrats cut down the rebellion, lords who would not have wanted to make concessions in the face of a bloody uprising quietly made some of the concessions the peasants had demanded once the rebellion was over. Over the next one hundred fifty years, peasant conditions slowly improved, as short but violent rebellions ended in defeat for the peasantry but were followed not long afterward by various concessions.

Family Life in a Late Medieval City

The family of a late medieval urban household was essentially the same as a modern family: It was organized around a married couple and their children. However, the number of people living together was larger than the number of people we would consider typical, for every well-to-do family had servants who lived with them, possibly apprentices and journeymen, and often such incidental relatives as widowed mothers, destitute cousins, or orphaned nephews. Because the high mortality of the fourteenth century meant that most people married more than once, there might be children from several marriages in the household, as well as perhaps some of the husband's illegitimate children. The basic unit was still the conjugal family, however, even if it had more "extra" people in the household than would be typical today. One did not have an extended family sharing one roof (such a pattern was indeed very rare throughout the Middle Ages), although, especially in Italian cities, brothers might live in adjoining houses in a block or section of town inhabited primarily by their relatives. This extended kindred usually functioned as a unit in the political factions that were found in all late medieval Italian cities (For a further discussion of the extended Italian kindred, see Chapter 10.)

As in the high Middle Ages, most town houses were fairly small, and much ordinary life was carried out in the streets. This was especially true in southern Europe, where the warmer climate made outdoor life possible almost year-round. In Italy, many people were entertained in the early evening by going to hear public storytellers. These people set themselves up on platforms and told long, involved stories, including love stories and lives of saints, but especially tales, like that of Roland and Charlemagne, that were based on high medieval French epics. Sometimes they added puppets to act out the different characters. Every night they told the next installment of the tale and passed their hat at the end. Six hundred years before television, family members of all ages loved these continuing sagas.

In the thirteenth and the early part of the fourteenth centuries, city couples married relatively late, with the wife usually at least twenty and her husband in his thirties if not forties. This seems to have been due in part to the difficult economy and overcrowding, which made it hard for any couple to be ready to support themselves as a family unit. Delayed marriage may also have helped reduce the birth rate. But all this changed in the aftermath of the plague. Couples in northern Europe started marrying much younger, with the brides about fifteen and their husbands in their twenties. (It is actually hard to say precisely how old people were, because until the end of the Middle Ages most people did not bother to keep close track of their ages.) In part the earlier age of marriage may have been the result of new opportunities opening up for those who had survived, to take the places of those who had not. In part, too, it may have been due to a new attitude that it was not worth putting off something that one wanted because it was not at all clear that one would survive long enough to do it at some supposedly more auspicious time.

In the fourteenth century, a marriage contract was a necessary part of betrothal. In northern Europe this contract spelled out both the dowry that the bride brought to her husband and the dower property that he settled on her. (The Romans had had only dowries, from the bride to the groom, and so dowers, from the groom to the bride, were much less common in southern Europe, where revived Roman law dominated in the late Middle Ages.) Although a bride gave all her personal property, her dowry, to her husband when they were married, he was required in England to settle on her at least a third of the property that *he* brought into the marriage or acquired during it, so that she would not be destitute if he died before she did.

A woman selling bread to a customer. Merchants' wives in fourteenth-century northern Europe usually operated the shops jointly with their husbands, while some women operated their own shops.

Once a marriage had taken place, whatever the legal details worked out in the marriage contract, husbands and wives seem to have shared in determining how their money was to be spent. There was a good deal of partnership and equality between husbands and wives in a fourteenth-century city of northern Europe. Shops and crafts were usually run jointly, with the wife often as knowledgable concerning the craft as her husband. Officially only widows or single women who had been emancipated by their parents could enter into legal contracts on their own, but married women's consent was still required for all deals made on their behalf by their husbands. Such women seem in fact to have strongly influenced their husbands' investments of their own money. Last names appear for the first time with regularity in the fourteenth century (in the early and high Middle Ages most people had had only one name), and women were free to keep their own names, although some preferred taking their husbands'.

Although most working women acted as partners with their husbands, some, depending on their own family background and training (if, for example, they had learned quite a different trade from their fathers), might run their own businesses. In Paris, the one hundred official guilds included six that were *only* open to women, such as the guild of the makers of elegant hats and wimples or the silk-weavers. Women were most commonly found in the food and textile industries, but no crafts were closed to them, except for political office, the priesthood, and in some cities the retail merchants' guild; women could and did act as brewers, moneychangers, and the like.

Because a late medieval city was even more unhealthy for small children than a high medieval city had been, infants were rarely raised in the city, except by the poorest women. Everyone who could afford to sent their new babies to the countryside to be raised in their first months by wet nurses. These were country women who, having just had babies of their own, were producing milk and could earn a tidy wage by putting someone else's baby on the other breast. (Formulas and commercially prepared baby foods were centuries in the future, and babies do not do well on cows' milk alone, which is an adequate diet for calves but not humans.) There was also an element of fashion in having someone else nurse one's baby, because that meant that fourteenth-century townswomen could keep the small breasts that were considered attractive and sexy at the time, rather than having them enlarged by nursing.

Families were very fond of their children, however; putting them out to nurse should not be seen as an attempt to get rid of them. Once children returned to their families at age one or two, they were pampered and spoiled shamelessly. Having children was an expensive undertaking in the late Middle Ages, as it is now, but it was an expense families gladly undertook if they could. Generally the wealthier the family the more children it had. Although some of the poorest families, who could not afford to raise their infants, took them to foundling homes, and the illegitimate children of servants might similarly be left at these "Hospitals of the Innocents," such foundlings usually quickly found a home with another family, who adopted such a child both because to do so was considered a holy work and because they just liked having large numbers of children around. The large families were usually the result of a conscious decision to have numerous children (if not the result of combining the households of a widow and widower who had remarried). Women did not simply have large families because they had no birth control, for in fact both birth control and abortions were available (the old women and witches who knew about how to cure changelings also knew about birth control, and their techniques here were quite practical).

Medieval women were just as overcome with grief when their children died as modern women are. Fourteenth-century children died much more frequently than modern children, especially in the cities, where, in spite of the care in sending children out to wet nurses, many died before age six of malnutrition or the gastrointestinal diseases spread by a contaminated water supply. The plague hit young children especially hard. But seeing one's friends' children die or having had older children die would not have made it any easier for a couple when they lost a child.

Despite such tragedies, many children survived and were brought up. Children spent the first five or six years of life at home (once they had returned from their wet nurse), after which, in northern Europe, both boys and girls were sent to school. (In Italy, as will be seen in the next chapter, only boys went to school.) There was no official age at which one was supposed to start school, for school was not obligatory, and in the fourteenth century most people did not keep very close track of their age anyway. People knew approximately how old they were, but such things as majority did not turn so much on specific age as they do now; regardless of age, one usually had to be emancipated by one's parents, officially freed of parental authority, to act without them.

After a few years of school, children started to learn a craft or trade, usually their parents'. Both girls and boys were instructed in the trade. When parents died, their legitimate children, both boys and girls, were expected to share equally in the inheritance. The girls' shares usually became their dowries, which they took with them to their husbands. If (as commonly happened) both husband and wife had been married several times, inheritance could be very complicated, as the assets of each separate "bed" had to be separately calculated and the children of that particular union given their share of their parents' inheritance. By the fourteenth century a number of people also made wills, in which some amounts of money could be distributed separately from the general inheritance of one's legitimate children; many fathers made provision in such wills for illegitimate offspring.

The fourteenth century was a period of great mobility (like the twentieth century), with people moving into or out of the city due to new opportunities or fear of the plague. Both boys and girls often left the area where they had grown up to get married or to follow their trade in a more conducive setting. Parents, then as now, liked to keep track of their children, which was hard to do without a regular postal service. Such a service was still several centuries in the future, so families of the fourteenth century had to rely on sending messages by someone who was going to another town anyway. A merchant traveling to a nearby city on business could often pick up some extra profit by offering to take and deliver personal letters for a few pennies each. We still have some fourteenth-century letters, in which the writer sends greetings to all friends and relatives and begs to hear from them in return. In an age without telephones or real mail service, one's relatives must often have seemed very far way.

Northern cities of the late fourteenth century had a quite relaxed attitude toward morality, accepting things that would have been considered scandalous a century earlier. For example, many well-to-do married women openly had lovers. Couples who were kept from marrying because they were too closely related, or because one was already married to someone else from whom he or she was now separated, might set up permanent housekeeping together. Some of this was doubtless due to the greater hedonism that followed the plague, but even conscientious, hardworking people seemed to feel that they had better things to do than judge their neighbors' morals. In this light, the town councils' actions in setting up municipal brothels may be seen not as an acceptance of prostitution itself, but rather the acceptance of a lesser evil. Official "hot streets" were an attempt to regulate sex outside of marriage, to make brothels available so that men need not feel compelled to corrupt married women.

Cities and Commerce in the Fourteenth Century

There were changes in the commerce of the fourteenth century compared to that of the high Middle Ages. Some of these changes were the result of the double blows to the economy first of overpopulation and then of plague, and some were just the sorts of changes and developments that any dynamic economy experiences over time. In the fourteenth century, Italy lost the commercial preeminence it had enjoyed since the eleventh century. In part, this was due to the fact that Italy, the most urbanized part of Europe, was hit hardest both by the plague and by the violence and warfare that broke out in its wake. But it also was a result of shifting markets.

The strongest commercial growth of the fourteenth century was in the north, as exemplifed by the foundation of the Hanseatic League. This was a league of trading cities in northern Germany and on the Baltic, who agreed to work together for their mutual benefit rather than competing with each other. They established ports at different cities where any member of the Hansa could dock and unload. The goods they shuttled back and forth across the Baltic and North Sea were primarily the raw goods that much of Europe no longer had ready access to but that were still available in Scandinavia and Russia: rye, timber, tar, honey, wax, and furs. Spices, salt, and salted herring were also important cargoes for the Hansa.

At the same time, the industrial centers of Europe were shifting. Northern France and the Low Countries had been the center of cloth manufacture in the high Middle Ages, as noted in Chapter 7. In the fourteenth century, however, this most important industry of the European economy was becoming less concentrated, as both England and Italy became important weaving centers. England's growth in textile production came especially at the expense of the Flemish cities. English wool, shipped as fleeces across the channel, had been the basis of the continental textile industry, but increasingly the English kings put stiff export duties on this valuable raw product. Much of the English expenses of the Hundred Years' War were financed by taxes on English wool. The kings also limited the number of continental ports to which English exports could be sent. English cities began producing their own high-quality cloth, which was competitively priced against the continental cloth.

Weaving also became an increasingly important part of the economy in Italy, especially in Florence. Italy had long had important dye works and had worked in silks, but in the fourteenth century it also took the lead in cotton manufacture and even in manufacturing wool cloth for the southern and Asian markets. Though Italy's production of bolts of cloth decreased in the late fourteenth century, the decrease was not as steep as in Flanders, and profits were kept from declining too rapidly both by putting more emphasis on luxurious, high-priced cloth and by getting as much as possible out of the workers. It was the overworked textile workers in Florence who started the Ciompi rebellion in 1378, as noted on page 296.

The old textile manufacturing cities fought back against this new competition with greater or lesser success. They began finding other sources from which to buy their fleeces, especially Spain, which was rapidly expanding its sheep farming. By concentrating on opening new markets in Germany and around the Baltic, many Flemish cities were able to continue selling their textiles at a good profit in spite of the increased competition. In many cases those actually working in textiles took control of their towns away from the merchants. In Ghent at the end of the fourteenth century, the weavers and the fullers were the two principal guilds; the other fifty-nine guilds were all lumped together for political purposes (the butchers, brewers, carpenters, and so on). Bruges, however, which had been the leader in both manufacturing and shipping, slowly declined in importance in the late fourteenth and fifteenth centuries, never to recover its eminence (this is why Bruges is now a popular tourist spot for those wanting to see a late medieval city; its economy was never again healthy enough to allow for large-scale rebuilding).

City governments in the fourteenth century became increasingly complicated. One of their principal concerns (as for modern cities) was to try to raise enough money for municipal needs, and governments had to be fairly inventive to accomplish this. There was not yet anything comparable to modern property taxes; it was only in the fifteenth century that city governments first attempted to inventory and assess the wealth of the different households within them. Sales taxes and fees for such things as toll bridges made up a fair proportion of municipal income. Florence had a graduated income tax (a third of the population was too poor to pay taxes and was officially exempt), but not all cities had the necessary organization for such a system. Several Italian cities instituted a program called a *Monte*, in which citizens were invited to buy shares in the public debt; the shares paid about 5 percent a year. (The modern analogy is government savings bonds, which citizens buy to help the state and also to earn interest.) If Italian citizens of the fourteenth century did not buy these shares in large enough numbers, some cities simply forced the wealthier citizens to buy them, promising that they could get their money back as soon as the current fiscal crisis had passed (sometimes they even did).

Cities also developed fairly complicated local judicial systems. In England, all the cities were supposed to be governed by the same laws; in Italy, each city had its own. But regardless of the country, local courts dealt with such matters as litigation over debt, broken contracts, and trespass; the recording of land transfers; and prosecution of crimes. In spite of the growing sophistication of the legal system, the blood feud, with its code of private vengeance, still reigned in some areas, especially in Italy. Until the middle of the fourteenth century an Italian who had been murdered was laid out on his bier unwashed, with clotted blood still on him, as an incentive to his kindred to extract vengeance from the murderer and his family. In practice, however, most townsmen would have preferred not getting drawn into the spiralling violence of a vendetta. They supported legislation to put the prosecution of such crimes in the hands of the impersonal state, and to limit the number of people at funerals, to prevent the formation of a frenzied mob ready for revenge.

Inventions in the Fourteenth Century

The fourteenth century, in spite of all its difficulties, was a very lively and inventive age. The growing sophistication of the legal system, mentioned above, was just one of many institutional and mechanical innovations. Some of the inventions of the fourteenth century were fueled by the Hundred Years' War; the concentration of resources that a war causes always leads to new discoveries in areas related to defense or destruction. Some of the inventions were the result of the labor shortage caused by the plague; more efficient ways had to be found to do many things that relied on human energy. Some of the inventiveness was doubtless the result of the greater movement of people during the period, resulting in more rapid exchange of ideas.

The Mechanical Clock and the Changing Concept of Time

One of the most notable inventions of the late Middle Ages was the mechanical clock. It had actually been invented in the final decade or so of the thirteenth century, but it was only perfected in the fourteenth century. A clock is a mundane object to us today, but in the fourteenth century it revolutionized both how people perceived and how they used time. In order to have a mechanical clock, one needs to have all the hours of the day the same length. This seems obvious to us, but, throughout the classical and medieval periods, different hours had been different lengths. Hours of the day and of the night, of the summer and

Clock with a single hand, for telling the hours (c. 1410).

of the winter, had been shorter or longer than each other, depending on the season of the year. The astronomers of Babylon had divided the day into twenty-four hours, a system that has now been in use for four thousand years, but how those hours were measured changed drastically in the late Middle Ages. Before then, there were by definition twelve hours of day and twelve of night. When the sun came up, it was automatically 6:00 A.M., and when it set it was 6:00 P.M., and noon was halfway between. During the winter, when the sun was only up for a short time, day hours had to be very short to squeeze twelve of them in between sunrise and sunset, and night hours were correspondingly very long. Each hour was assumed to be composed of sixty minutes, which naturally had to be longer and shorter as well, but medieval men did not worry too much about minutes.

In fact, before the invention of the mechanical clock, the chief way of telling time was not even precise to the hour, but only to the three-hour interval. Churches all rang their bells eight times a day, corresponding to the eight ecclesiastical "offices" (at strict monasteries, the monks celebrated them all; at lax monasteries they might sleep through the night ones). Matins was held at midnight, Lauds at 3:00 A.M., Prime at 6:00 A.M. (dawn), Tierce at 9:00 A.M., Sext at noon, None at 3:00 P.M., Vespers at 6:00 P.M. (sunset), and Compline at 9:00 P.M.

Because the person responsible for ringing the bells had of course no wristwatch or alarm clock to tell him when to do so, exactly when the bells were rung varied even in the same place at the same time of year. Good bell-ringers prided themselves on being able to tell how far the night had progressed by watching the stars, or on not dozing off and forgetting to ring Prime until the sun was well up. In a cathedral city, the bell-ringer at the cathedral had a special weight of responsibility, because all the parish churches in town were supposed to wait to ring their bells until the cathedral bells had started ringing, to avoid the unseemly spectacle of bells being rung at different churches at all hours of the day and night. (Some monasteries, however, to prove their independence of the bishops, would deliberately ring their bells at different times.)

All this changed in the fourteenth century, with the invention of mechanical clocks. Considering that all the cogs and wheels were made of wood and were thus subject to warping, the early clocks were remarkably accurate, as long as the weights that drove them were wound up properly. Since clocks could be synchronized, two churches or even two towns could now keep the same time. (This was never universal practice until the nineteenth century, when the advent of railroads and railroad schedules forced towns to adopt a uniform "railway time," though in some American towns there long persisted clocks with two faces, one with railway time and one with local—or "real"—time.) Clocks were very expensive (and much too bulky to be pocket watches), so private individuals did not own them originally, but most communes had a clock, and churches put them in their towers (as modern banks, the temples to today's god of money, still do).

With a town clock it was possible to make and keep appointments, to meet for business purposes at a certain hour. Again, this is something we take very much for granted, but it would not be easy without clocks. With clocks, one can plan one's time and arrange to be heading for an appointment just at the hour, but when the only formal timekeepers were the church bells, one could at best agree to meet when Tierce was rung but would spend the morning working with no way of knowing how long until Tierce. By referring to the municipal clock, one was able to use one's time more efficiently in any sort of enterprise, such as commerce, that involved agreeing to meet with other people. Still, the measurement of time was not nearly as precise in a fourteenth-century town as it is now, for the clocks only had hour hands, not minute hands (though they also included dials showing phases of the moon and the rotation of the zodiac). In the countryside, for most purposes, one still did not need clocks; one began working in the fields as soon as it was light enough to see and continued until dark.

Double-Entry Bookkeeping

Aside from the clock, the fourteenth century was also the period of another commercially significant "modern" invention: double-entry bookkeeping. This is the system in which one keeps one's financial records with separate entries for debits and credits. Although it seems self-evident to modern accountants, it was a step forward for the merchants and traders of the time, especially in Italy, where commercial ventures were always complicated. It enabled them to have a better idea where they stood at any one time, to start having clearer records of the capitalist enterprises they had been pursuing for the last two centuries. Better accounting was especially useful in a time of more precarious profits.

One difficulty with double-entry bookkeeping is that, if one is making money in an improper fashion, it shows up much more clearly. The biggest concern of those making money, especially the bankers, was in avoiding the appearance of usury. The term "usury" now is just used to mean excessive interest, but in the Middle Ages the term meant charging any sort of interest at all on a loan. The Old Testament quite clearly forbade charging interest to one's brother, and the church took this literally. (The Jews also took the same prohibition to heart, but since they

Genoese bankers of the late fourteenth century. This illustration is from a treatise on the seven vices.

did not consider the Christians their "brothers," they were able to lend at interest to them without sinning, which helped establish many Jewish families as important moneylenders.) This prohibition created real problems, because one cannot carry on commercial enterprises without some form of credit, and no one will want to loan money unless they can get some sort of return.

The fourteenth century developed many inventive ways to get around this difficulty. One of the simplest was to keep two sets of books, the public ones, which would show no interest charged, and the private ones, which showed the *real* gains. Or one could write a loan with no official interest but a "penalty" if the loan were not repaid on time, with it fully understood on both sides that repayment would be "late" and therefore require a penalty (generally about 1 percent a month). Italian bankers also were able to work out complicated systems in which a loan made in one place and in one sort of currency would be repaid in another place, and in another currency, with the differences in exchange rate yielding the (unofficial) interest.

However, even if the bankers who practiced usury might have been able to fool the church officials, they knew they could not fool God. From their writings it is clear that they thought of God in the same sort of credit relationship in which they stood in relationship to their customers. For every usurious loan they made, they were going deeper and deeper into debt to God, a debt they often tried to pay off with sudden and spectacular charitable bequests to churches (which must have been intensely frustrating to a banker's heirs who had hoped to inherit it all).

Eyeglasses and Paper

Another major invention of the fourteenth century was that of eyeglasses. Alhtough it might seem very anachronistic to us to imagine the knights, ladies, and friars of the late Middle Ages wearing glasses, many of them did so. Glasses were tremendously expensive by modern standards and not very effective. Although it had required major technical advances in glassblowing and cutting to make eyeglasses possible at all, the technology was still far short of the plastic lenses, ground to correct individual astigmatism, that we take so much for granted today.

Even crude glasses were a tremendous advantage to those who needed them, especially those in the church who spent much of their time reading and writing. Many medieval manuscripts, especially legal treatises and textbooks, were written in very small letters that are almost impossible to read today without a magnifying glass, due to the desire to economize on costly parchment. The eyestrain from using such texts must have been considerable. Although the prevalence of contact lenses enables some of us to hide it, over half the well-educated population of the United States needs glasses today, and all those people would have had to grope their way through life before glasses were invented in the late Middle Ages.

Some of the worst eyestrain problems were also alleviated in the fourteenth century by the replacement of parchment with less valuable paper as the chief writing material. Although the Romans had used papyrus, made with reeds from Egypt, parchment had replaced papyrus once the rise of Islam cut off the West from the Mediterranean basin. As discussed in Chapter 5, parchment was sheepskin, very carefully cleaned, scraped, and smoothed, with neat rectangles cut out of the middle of the skin for book pages and the oddly-shaped pieces left used for letters or for legal records. Parchment was much too valuable to be used for random jottings or scratch paper; wax tablets were used instead for such purposes, as they could be wiped clean and used over and over.

But in the fourteenth century paper manufacture developed to the point that it was cheaper than parchment, and of a high enough quality that one could make books out of it as well as using it for odd notes. Books were henceforth copied using much larger handwriting—although, because deciding to write something down was no longer the major decision it once had been, people also began to write much more sloppily. Medieval paper was made entirely or almost entirely of cotton rags; its spread depended on the establishment of regular importation of cotton in the thirteenth century. Being all-cotton, it was of much higher quality than most modern papers, which are made of wood pulp, often with a high acid content, and deteriorate easily. (Hold a piece of expensive modern paper up to the light. It will probably say "25% cotton," well below medieval standards.) Although medieval paper did not have the durability of medieval parchment—it was more susceptible to water and insect damage—it was made to last much longer than the high-acid wood-pulp papers of today; paper from the late Middle Ages is often now in better condition, six hundred years later, than a yellow and disintegrating twenty-year-old paperback.

Architectural Changes

The men of the fourteenth century also made innovations in architecture. Many of the great cathedrals begun in the thirteenth century were still being slowly constructed in the fourteenth. Although there were no major technical breakthroughs, the architects of the time were able to work out ways to make the windows of the churches much wider, allowing more stained glass. This is the style known as "perpendicular" in England, because it was necessary to put a thin support of stonework straight up through the middle of the window to compensate for having the actual sides of the windows much farther apart.

Gunpowder and Cannons

A final invention of the fourteenth century was gunpowder. The Chinese had long had gunpowder, but, with few exceptions, they had used it for such peaceful purposes as fireworks. It took the West to develop all sorts of ways to use gunpowder to kill people. Handguns were still in the future in the fourteenth century, but cannon technology made great strides. A cannon is essentially a metal tube, at the bottom of which one puts gunpowder, with a stone or metal cannonball on top. One then lights the gunpowder with a fuse, and theoretically the explosion sends the cannonball flying out the front of the tube. If the cannon itself is weak, however, the exploding gunpowder may blow up the whole cannon.

Engineers and metallurgists worked diligently in the fourteenth century, improving the technology of cannons to make them both safer for the people firing them and more dangerous for those at whom they were aimed.

Cannons could be used very effectively against both cavalry and infantry charges in a pitched battle. Although they were slow to load and fire and were extremely inaccurate, a few dozen cannonballs fired along the ground could rip through charging ranks of men and horses with devastating effect. An army making a stand on a hill with its cannons ready was probably not even worth charging by the end of the fourteenth century. Although late medieval battles were still fought largely by archers and pikemen on foot and mounted knights wielding swords and lances, every army had to have cannons as well.

Cannonballs proved especially effective against castles. As noted in Chapter 6, it had been almost impossible to capture castles after the late twelfth century, except by treachery or occasionally protracted siege. But the spread of gunpowder changed that. Several cannons lined up outside a castle wall, hurling cannonballs against it for a few days, would eventually make a breach through which the attackers could pour (dodging cannon fire from above). The result was a change in how castles were built in the late fourteenth and fifteenth centuries. Less powerful lords, of the sort who had previously been castellans, gave up making their homes defensible at all, feeling it was not worth the effort and probably impossible anyway. This is the time that gracious and elegant châteaux

These fourteenth-century windows in Kenilworth Castle were made for large panes of glass. With the advent of gunpowder and cannons, castles were no longer built as defensive fortresses.

or country houses, with large windows, began to be built in place of or next to earlier castles. Some castles, such as Kenilworth in England, retained their imposing twelfth-century keeps but made new additions of rooms with large, traceried windows, which were very attractive but could not possibly have been defended from attack.

Those who still had the resources and the need to construct large fortresses did so in a new way, making the walls twice as thick as even the earlier thick castle walls, to be able to withstand cannon fire. However, the walls were also built much lower than they had been before. Because both attackers and defenders had cannons, the attackers had to set up some way back from the fortress walls, which meant that aiming was difficult. The defenders hoped that a low wall would be harder to hit than a high one, and that most cannonballs would either fall short or sail harmlessly over, landing in the big empty center of the fortress. There the cannonballs could be gathered up and shot back at the attackers. Thus the towering castles which had dominated the European rural landscape since the twelfth century had a very short period of preeminence, for by the fifteenth century defensive stoneworks had taken on a very different look than the lofty towers and battlements of a twelfth- or thirteenth-century castle. Already in the late fourteenth century, castles had started to become what they are now, objects of fantasy and nostalgia, more than practical military structures.

In some ways the fourteenth century seems very "modern" to the eyes of someone of the twentieth century. Urban couples, working together as partners, sent their children to school and hoped they might continue to the university. They drew up legal contracts, prosecuted people who did not pay on time in court, and kept sophisticated records of debit and credit. They were governed by clocks, wore eyeglasses, worried about the outbreak of war, and lived under a constant cloud of mass death striking without warning. Yet to see the late Middle Ages as "modern" is to miss the point. Rather, much of the kind of life that we take for granted today was taking something like its present form in the late Middle Ages. The fourteenth century is not "modern" so much as the twentieth century is a reflection of the fourteenth.

Yet there are fundamental differences between the late Middle Ages and the twentieth century, even aside from all the technology that accompanies electricity and gasoline-powered automobiles. A late medieval person's world was narrow, extending no farther than Europe, and in many cases no farther than the town walls. In spite of increased literacy, books were still so scarce and expensive that very few people had ready access to them. Even though there were a tremendous number of different forms of religion available, a certain number of them were considered heresies, and adherence to them could lead to death. During the fifteenth and sixteenth centuries much of this began to change, as will be seen in the next chapter. The printing press made dissemination of ideas far easier, and the beginning of the great age of exploration opened the rest of the globe to the Europeans. The distinctively Western civilization was formed during the Middle Ages, but only in recent centuries has it had an impact on the rest of the world.

THE END OF THE MIDDLE AGES

c. **1400** Slavery begins to be common in Italy
1415 John Hus burned at the stake
1417 End of the Great Schism of the papacy
1425 *Monte delle doti* established in Florence
1427 First Florentine *catasto*
1431 Joan of Arc burned at the stake
1453 Constantinople falls to the Turks
1453 End of Hundred Years' War between France and England
1454 War of the Roses begins in England
1456 Gutenberg prints first Bible from moveable type
1485 War of the Roses settled in England; Henry VII becomes king
1492 Columbus reaches western hemisphere

CHAPTER
TEN

THE END OF
THE MIDDLE AGES

THE FIFTEENTH CENTURY is usually considered the final century of the Middle Ages. When Columbus reached the New World at the end of this century, in 1492, a new era of European expansion began. With the Protestant Reformation of the early sixteenth century, the unity of western Christendom, which everyone had taken for granted even while the heretics were claiming that *their* version of Christianity was the one true form, was irrevocably broken. The invention and spread of the printing press made the dissemination of new ideas much more rapid.

The fifteenth century itself was an age of tremendous luxuries and of grinding poverty. The differences between rich and poor were much more pronounced than they had been in the high Middle Ages. Even though the rural peasantry were probably better off than they had been in much of the fourteenth century, there was a great deal of urban poverty. There was also a higher level of urban violence than there had been in previous centuries. The upper levels of society, meanwhile, were building great palaces and following elaborate social rituals. This was the age of chivalrous display, of the great tournaments in which the knights wore plate mail and silk robes. (Hollywood producers like to put such scenes into movies purportedly set in the twelfth century because they are spectacular.) It was also the age of the Italian Renaissance.

The Italian Renaissance

The term "renaissance" has been misused enough by the popular press that it needs to be defined. The Italian Renaissance, it must be noted immediately, did not come *after* the Middle Ages. Rather, it is just an-

313

other name given to the late Middle Ages in Italy. When one speaks of "the Renaissance," one is describing the late fourteenth and the fifteenth centuries. It is a period that lasted in Italy from the first outbreak of the Black Death in the middle of the fourteenth century until the great wars between France and Italy at the beginning of the sixteenth century.

The term "renaissance" means "rebirth" (we use the French word in English; the Italians called the period *rinascimento*). The reason that the period is referred to as a "rebirth" is that Italians of the time who were interested in literature and learning believed that they were taking part in a rebirth of classical language and culture. They were tremendously interested in Greek and Latin (that is, classical) literature, which they studied avidly, and tried to recreate the lives of the Greeks and Romans in their own lives. They even wore togas when possible and addressed each other in Latin.

It is interesting to note that this looking back to an earlier age as the "golden age" was a new development in the late Middle Ages. In the high Middle Ages, most men had thought of the present age as the best one yet, but in the wars and plagues of the late Middle Ages no one thought that way. Rather, powerful men of England and France dreamed of a past "age of chivalry" and tried to recreate it, wearing jewel-studded armor and putting on King Arthur parties. Italian scholars dreamed of recreating the world of Greece and Rome.

Although these Italian scholars thought of themselves as reviving a classical literature that had been forgotten for centuries, in fact most of the Latin literature they studied had never been forgotten at all; it had been copied by monks throughout the early Middle Ages and made part of the curriculum at the University of Paris in the twelfth and thirteenth centuries. It is true, however, that this literature was not widely known in Italy in the high Middle Ages. This was because Italian universities concentrated on law and medicine, rather than classical studies or philosophy, and because the Italians of the twelfth and thirteenth centuries had been much more interested in commerce than in literature. But just because this literature had not been read widely in Italy before the end of the fourteenth century did not mean that it had been lost.

In the fifteenth century, however, Italian scholars did start to read a great deal of *Greek* literature that had not previously been known in the West. Although much Greek science and philosophy had reached the West in the late twelfth and thirteenth centuries, as discussed in Chapter 8, university scholars of the time had not been particularly interested in Greek drama. Also, much of this Greek science and philosophy had reached the West in somewhat garbled form, having been translated from Greek into Arabic and from Arabic into Latin. However, in the second half of the fifteenth century, a great deal of Greek literature began to reach the West directly, as Greeks fled to Italy from the fall of Constantinople.

The city of Constantinople had been threatened by the Muslims for eight hundred years. After it was sacked by Latin Crusaders in 1204 (see Chapter 6), it had been recovered by the Greeks, but the city finally fell to the Turks in 1453. (This is why this city, now called Istanbul, is the capital of modern Turkey.) Many Italians learned to speak and read Greek, which had previously been an unusual accomplishment. They could now read Greek philosophy and science in much better texts than had previously been available, but these did not interest them nearly as much as did the literature and drama. Those Italians who were interested in classical literature and were intensely proud of their ability to read Greek called themselves "humanists." It must be stressed that this term had nothing to do with "humanity" or "rights of man." As they used it, the terms humanist or humanism simply referred to an interest in the classics.

One of the principal concerns of the humanists was to try to find the earliest possible texts of the literature that fascinated them; therefore, a number of them traveled around to Europe's monasteries, looking at their old books. Here they found a great many copies of Latin works, which monks had made in the ninth and tenth centuries. Because the papyrus copies from which the monks had worked had long since crumbled away, the parchment copies of the ninth and tenth centuries were the oldest copies of these works in existence. They were written in Caroline miniscule, a clear, upright script (see Chapter 5), which the Italian humanists mistakenly thought was Roman handwriting from the first century A.D. The humanists took these manuscripts home from the monasteries, copied them out themselves, and then, to the great vexation of modern scholars, often threw the ninth-century manuscripts away.

Caroline miniscule made a deep impression on the Italian humanists, because of their belief that it was actually Roman handwriting. They knew from inscriptions on stones that the Romans used large, straight capital letters, but they thought that now for the first time they had discovered both Roman handwriting (as opposed to the chiseled inscriptions) and Roman lowercase letters. They immediately abandoned the form of handwriting they had been using and started instead trying to copy ninth-century handwriting. For capital letters, they used the (real) Roman capitals (which we still use), and for lowercase letters they used Caroline miniscule.

When printing presses were first set up in Italy in the late fifteenth century, they used this same script as their model. This is why, as mentioned in Chapter 5, modern printing looks a great deal like Caroline miniscule. Because it was hard to write quickly using the upright letters of the ninth century (the ninth century had not been interested in writing quickly but rather in accuracy and readability), the humanists developed a second form, basically similar but with the letters slanted so that they could be written more easily. This is the origin of modern italics (the word "italics" originally meant "Italian-style").

The scribes of the ninth century had followed classical usage in terms of spelling, grammar, and the like, but in the following centuries, medieval Latin, still a living language, had undergone a good deal of change in both style and spelling. For example, the classical *ae* dipthong had become an ϱ in the twelfth century and simply an *e* in the thirteenth. The humanists, trying to recover pure, classical Latin, ended up stultifying and ossifying the language, driving out all the terms medieval Latin had acquired to describe a world very different from the ancient world. The Italian reverence for classical Latin ended up killing Latin as a living language by the sixteenth century.

One should not hold it too much against the humanists that they thought that manuscripts written in the ninth century were actually eight hundred years older, or that (as discussed in Chapter 8) they thought that the churches built in the eleventh and twelfth centuries had been built by the Romans or the ones from the thirteenth century by the Goths who invaded the Roman Empire (we still speak of these styles as Romanesque and Gothic, respectively, due to the influence of the humanists). After all, they did not have available to them the great amount of historical method and scholarship we have now. However, one should also not take them too much at their word that they were bringing about a rebirth of something long forgotten, for Latin literature had been alive in the West and Greek literature in Byzantium throughout the Middle Ages.

Renaissance Art

Whereas Renaissance interest in classical learning was not nearly as novel as the humanists wanted to think, in one area the Italian Renaissance *was* a remarkable period of innovation, and that was in art. Here they were not rediscovering anything old but rather breaking new ground. New techniques were invented for frescoes, or wall paintings. The rules for perspective were worked out for the first time by Alberti in the first half of the fifteenth century. (Roman wall paintings had used perspective, but the rules seem never to have been explicitly set out, and the technique itself was forgotten in the Middle Ages.) Realistic portrait painting began to be prevalent for the first time in history. Most fifteenth-century art depicted religious subjects, as most medieval art had done, but there also began to be a number of portraits done of secular people, as well as a great many pictures representing classical themes. The stonemasons of the twelfth and thirteenth centuries who had decorated the Gothic cathedrals had often used real people as their models for religious subjects, and painters of the Renaissance often did the same thing.

The Renaissance was a great age of church-building in Italy, and the new churches were decorated with large and elaborate paintings. These new churches were built in a style that is now called "neoclassical," a self-conscious attempt to build something approximating the architecture of Greece and Rome. (Italy had never been very good anyway at the Gothic architecture that flourished in northern Europe in the late Middle Ages. Its Gothic churches, such as the cathedral of Milan, were not the very tall and light edifices of France but rather great barnlike structures with Gothic ornamentation put on.) The demand for artwork to decorate these structures, along with the growing private demand for art, gradually created a new figure, the individual artist, known by name and reputation. Although the stone-carvers of the high Middle Ages had often been sought out for their reputation and had been proud enough of their work to sign it, they had normally worked as part of a team or crew of

Masaccio's mural *Trinity with Virgin, St. John, and Donors* (1427). He has produced
a strikingly realistic three-dimensional effect on a flat surface.

architects and builders. But the painters of the Italian Renaissance sometimes worked alone, offering to paint for whomever paid them the most.

Initially, however, someone learning to be an artist worked in a stu-
dio, like any apprentice learning a craft from the masters and journeymen. For a long time stone sculptors enrolled as members of the masons'
guild, and painters were a branch of the doctors' and apothecaries' guild
(because many of their paints were concocted from powdered substances
of the same sort that apothecaries used). Workshops turned out many
pictures as joint projects. But progressively during the course of the
fifteenth century, artists started to consider themselves more than
ordinary artisans or craftsmen and began to be proud of their
individual achievements.

Artists made a living primarily through attracting the eye of the rich and powerful. Rich men liked to have their own palaces decorated with paintings, and also liked to bestow paintings on both old and new churches as signs of their munificence. The most secure position for an artist was to be attached to a great lord's household, where his living expenses would be paid and, if he pleased his lord, he would receive many rewards and presents. Because many of the investment opportunities of earlier centuries were no longer available, as discussed on page 319, the wealthy had tended to turn from saving to spending on luxuries, and having one's own private artist was a luxury they were proud to display.

The difficulty with this arrangement was the same one that always attends being "kept": The artist served at his master's whim, under the constant pressure to produce art he hoped would please his patron, rather than doing the paintings he wanted to do himself. All successful artists had to turn their hands to a variety of endeavors; Leonardo da Vinci painted and did bronze sculpture, architectural planning, and mechanical engineering. Alberti, who first worked out the principles of perspective, wanted all artists to study mathematics. (We still use the term "Renaissance man" for someone with a number of different talents.) Although a famous artist might be lured away from one lord to another by offers of more money and more artistic freedom, most artists of the Renaissance discovered what all modern artists know, that art is a very difficult way to earn a living.

Economy and Politics in the Italian Renaissance

Although the Renaissance was certainly a period of new horizons in the area of art, it was definitely *not* a period of improvement in either social justice or the general standard of living. That is, there was neither an economic nor a political "renaissance" in the fifteenth century. The men of the Italian Renaissance knew this perfectly well (after all, they lived through it), and never tried to pretend otherwise. However, many modern historians have shown a deplorable tendency to romanticize the Italian Renaissance and to assume that, because the art of the Renaissance was so novel, it could have developed only in a favorable economic and social climate, amid a general flowering of individualism and personal opportunity.

This was far from the case. The very rapid decline in the urban population after the plague meant a lower demand across Europe for many trade goods, and Italy, whose economy was built on commerce, was hit especially hard. Even worse, most of the big banking houses of Europe were Italian-owned in the late fourteenth century, and many of these houses began to go bankrupt in the late fourteenth and the fifteenth centuries. The problem was that these banking houses had made heavy loans to the kings of France and England, both of whom went so hopelessly into debt during the Hundred Years' War that repudiation of all their debts seemed the only way out. Banking firms that had been among the most prosperous in Europe collapsed abruptly as a result. Even the governments of many Italian cities went deeply into debt, as the plague meant they had a smaller tax base to draw on even as their wars grew increasingly expensive in an age of firearms and mercenary soldiers; these governments too sometimes defaulted on their loans.

In this climate, it is not surprising that the wealthiest Italians, who had earlier invested their money in commercial ventures or in banks, felt that there was no further advantage in such investments. At the same time, the hedonistic attitude that increasingly prevailed with the repeated outbreaks of the Black Death meant that consumption of luxury goods skyrocketed. The Italian princes who started acquiring artists for their courts felt that spending their money on art made much more sense than any other use they could have made of it. Some economic historians have therefore suggested, with good reason, that the economic disasters of the fourteenth and fifteenth centuries were directly responsible for the artistic flourishing of the Renaissance.

The princes whose wealth financed the artists were primarily tyrants, men who ran the Italian cities as their private domains. As discussed in Chapter 7, in the high Middle Ages most Italian cities had been republics, governed by an alliance of their nobles, merchants, and artisans, but in the late Middle Ages the republican governments were replaced by tyrants. (The popes at Rome, though they had not replaced any republic, became in many ways similar in their policies and actions to the tyrants of other Renaissance cities.) Some of these tyrants were military men, who had been leaders of bands of mercenary soldiers, and took the opportunity when they saw it to seize power (one fifteenth-century pope had even been such a soldier of fortune). But most of the tyrants had come to power at the invitation of at least a segment of the city. There had been a good deal of unrest in the fourteenth century between the poorer and the wealthier members of society, and both sides often thought that an outsider would best represent *their* interests while reimposing order in a city where violence was becoming endemic.

Even in Florence, where the citizens prided themselves on maintaining democratic government long after other cities had abandoned it, real power was effectively in the hands of one family, the Medici, throughout the fifteenth century. Florence had been so fearful of letting in tyrants that the city had set up an extremely elaborate system of checks and balances, of multiple officers and committees, but these checks and balances worked so well that the city might have come to a complete standstill had not the Medici taken control.

The Medici were the heads of a banking house that had managed *not* to collapse when so many other bankers did (and in fact prospered due to lack of competition). Although they only became the official heads of state at the very end of the fifteenth century, previously being (officially) just members of the ruling council, no one doubted who really ran Florence. (In the same way, many theoretically democratic American cities have been run effectively by "party bosses" for long periods of time.) The rule of a tyrant is in some ways advantageous for a city; this is after all why tyrants had been invited in at all. The Medici long kept Florence free from foreign domination and were great patrons of the arts themselves. But with them, and the other great tyrants of other cities, republican government disappeared in Renaissance Italy.

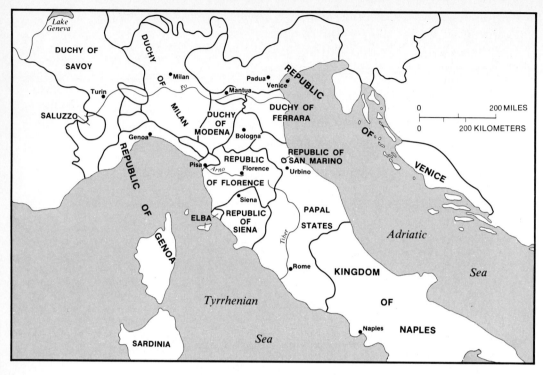

THE ITALIAN CITY-STATES IN THE FIFTEENTH CENTURY
Renaissance Italy was divided into a number of separate and independent political units. Some, such as Florence, were republics; some, such as Milan, were
duchies, ruled by dukes; Naples was a kingdom; and the Papal States, under
personal control of the pope, was a theocracy.

The governmental innovation of the fourteenth century continued in
the fifteenth century, whoever was the head of government. In Florence,
the great innovation was the *catasto* of 1427, a survey of the goods and
property of its citizens as the basis for the city's first property tax. Although the *catasto* was more interested in a family's possessions than its
members, it can also be seen as the first census. The *catasto* surveyed not
just Florence itself, a city that had shrunk to perhaps half the size it had
been a century earlier before the plague, but also all the surrounding
countryside and the other cities Florence had subjected in its wars. On
the basis of this survey, historians have recently been able to draw conclusions about family structure in Renaissance Italy that supplement the
information from literary and notarial sources.

It is interesting to note that the *catasto*, which was implemented to give
a more "objective" determination of the taxes each citizen owed, was
repealed within a few years as being *too* objective. Previously, taxes in
Florence had been assessed by district, with seven or ten assessors in
each district, who knew everybody, deciding qualitatively what everyone
should pay toward the sum which was required of that district. Assessors
took into account such things as someone having just been disabled, so
that his future earnings would be much lower, or a rich man also being

Lorenzo de' Medici (1449–1492).

very influential, so that it seemed wisest to tax him a little more than people with less property but not *proportionately* more. The *catasto* was supposed to replace all this with a flat .5 percent tax on everyone's property and assets, as long as they were above a certain minimum. Virtually everyone objected to the new assessment, however; a good 85 percent of the returns were modified after negotiation. Although naturally those with high taxes felt theirs should be lower, a few declared officially indigent actually demanded that they could bear paying a few pennies in tax, because Florence's indigents were not allowed to hold public office, the chief avenue to social and political advancement. The citizens quickly decided that, with all its problems, they preferred their old tax system.

Because literacy was high in Italian cities during the Renaissance, we know a fair amount about family life at the time and in much greater detail than for the preceding centuries. Many Italians kept personal histories of their families and their doings. There are also extensive official records in which many of the landmarks in a family's life might be noted. Today local governments keep track of births, deaths, and marriages. No Italian city kept records that were nearly as systematic as these; for example, baptismal records only started being kept in certain areas in the sixteenth century. But Renaissance cities recorded such things as "emancipation" of children—that is, the parents' formal declarations freeing children from direct parental control—and they had complex tax records. Men of the Renaissance engaged in many legal agreements, and all of these had to be drawn up by a notary, who would keep track of the transactions in which he had taken part. Men of the Renaissance were nearly as litigious as modern Americans, so there is also a great deal of information in court records.

The Italian word *famiglia*, which we might translate as "family," had two separate meanings during the Renaissance. On the one hand, it meant what we would call a nuclear family—father, mother, and children—plus the servants in a well-to-do household, plus sometimes unmarried sisters, a widowed mother, or the like, if they all lived together. On the other hand, *famiglia* also meant the lineage, the "house," that group of men descended from a common male ancestor, who by the fifteenth century usually shared the same surname. Both sorts of "families" existed side by side. The household or nuclear family was the basic economic unit, and cousins did not normally own property jointly, but the households of close male relatives were often built close together. Fathers and sons, or brothers or cousins were often business partners and usually acted as a bloc in local politics. Several important political offices in Florence always went over the generations to members of the same paternal lineage.

The city of Florence during the Renaissance was divided into fifteen or sixteen districts, each of which was a unit of local administration and taxation, and each of these districts was dominated by several powerful extended kindreds. The important people in such a district, or *gonfalone*, were the lords or patrons of a large proportion of the other inhabitants. Each *gonfalone* had its own symbol, a unicorn, or a bull, or a red lion, or a black lion, and so on. The unit of the *gonfalone*, which combined family membership with important neighborhood ties, was more important to those who lived there, rich and poor alike, than was membership in any social "class."

In Renaissance Italy as now, marriage was the center of household life. Marriage then was a much more complicated undertaking than two people meeting and falling in love. Falling in love, though certainly not precluded, was not a necessary part of a Renaissance marriage, which was usually arranged by the couple's parents. If two members of unrelated lineages had gone into economic or political partnership, it was common for them to solidify this business tie with a personal one, by marrying their children to each other. Business ties and family ties were close to being the same thing.

A woman getting married had to bring a dowry, a large sum of money to be given to her husband. As long as the man and wife both lived, this money was controlled by the husband, but if he died his widow recovered an equivalent amount from his estate, to support her for the rest of her life. It would have been disgraceful for a girl, even from a very poor family, to marry without at least some sort of dowry, and no self-respecting man would have her. Fathers were therefore required to come up with a large lump sum when they wanted to marry off a daughter.

Whereas today hardly anyone, except for the wealthy or occasionally a previously married couple, draws up a prenuptial agreement (though such agreements are now beginning to be found among the young professional class), in the Renaissance everyone had one. Such a contract would be worked out well ahead of time, though the dowry actually changed hands the day of the wedding or shortly thereafter.

The position of poor girls without a dowry in this society was a very difficult one. (Indeed, dowries have continued to be vital in some parts of the Mediterranean; girls from certain parts of rural Greece take jobs before marriage to save up enough money for a suitable dowry.) Saint Nicholas, who we today think of as Santa Claus, coming down the chimney to leave presents for good girls and boys, was portrayed in the Renaissance as coming down the chimney (not just on Christmas but anytime during the year) with sacks of gold to provide dowries for poor but honest girls. Unfortunately, unlike Santa Claus, the Renaissance Saint Nicholas could not be counted on to put in regular appearances. In his honor, wealthy citizens sometimes grouped together to form Saint Nicholas societies to provide dowries for such unfortunate girls. Such societies also might commission stained glass windows or paintings of the saint for the local church. He was usually shown as dropping bags of gold into the laps of poor but honest girls who had fallen asleep by the fireplace. It is significant that the gold went into their *laps*, because a dowry would safeguard their chastity; a girl without a dowry often had no alternative to becoming a prostitute in the municipal brothel.

In Florence, the city government decided to set up its own fund to provide dowries. In 1425 it established a municipal investment fund for this purpose, called the *Monte delle doti*. (The idea of a *Monte*, or municipal investment fund, had begun in the fourteenth century, as discussed in Chapter 9, but its use to establish dowries was new in the fifteenth century.) Fathers could enroll their daughters in the *Monte* when they were born by paying a small fee; when the girl was married, the *Monte* would pay her husband her dowry, an amount much more than what her father had originally invested. The city government hoped to be able to run the *Monte* profitably, because there were always more girls whose fathers were paying in for them than there were girls whose dowries were being paid. If the girl died in childhood or never married, her father did not get his money back. Also, the government had the use of the money for fifteen years or so. There were different categories in which a father could invest. If he had only a very small sum, he could enroll his daughter for a small but decent dowry, whereas if a father were wealthy, he could put in a large sum with the intention of receiving a very large dowry.

The city of Florence ended up having more and more of its municipal budget run from the *Monte delle doti*. Just as Social Security, originally a small and separate program, has become a major part of the income and budget of the United States federal government, so the Florentine government found that borrowing from the *Monte* to pay other expenses was the fastest way to raise money. If they realized that the *Monte* was shrinking too fast, that there might not be enough in it that year to pay out the dowries that were owed, then they would bring in new money quickly by offering better and better returns for new fathers' money, to entice fathers who might otherwise not have bothered to invest in the *Monte* to give the government their florins. This was an easy way to make money in the short run, but of course it only created worse problems in fifteen years when much bigger dowries had to be paid out. The Florentine *Monte* and government eventually collapsed completely in the middle of the sixteenth century, but it is indicative of how important dowries were in the Renaissance, as important to society as retirement pensions are today, that Florence was able to run its government from a dowry fund for so long.

An urban woman arranging to be married was supposed to be a virgin. In this respect the cities of Italy were much more puritanical than the countryside, where it was fairly common to "test the goods," and many peasant couples were not married until the bride was pregnant. Italy also seems to have been more puritanical than the north, where urban girls had much more freedom. In order to keep a girl pure for marriage, she was always closely chaperoned whenever she went out, and married when young, before she had had a chance to get into trouble. No one cared whether or not her husband was a virgin.

If a husband discovered on his wedding night that his wife was not a virgin, he could repudiate her and keep the dowry. This was not as easy as it might seem, because the girl and her family would normally claim that she *was* a virgin, and the case would then proceed through the courts, both sides trying to produce legal proof of how virginal or not the girl actually was. If the court decided the girl really had been a virgin, a man might repudiate her anyway, but this was rare, for in such cases the court would usually order him to repay the dowry and also make a financial settlement to ensure her a life income, since at this point no one else would be likely to marry her. Usually economics overcame the husband's initial distaste if things went this far, and he decided to stay married to his bride anyway, though one must wonder how happy such a marriage would be.

When a couple was married, it was a popular custom to hold a *charivari*, in which their friends and neighbors would stand outside the house where they had been bedded together, blowing horns, ringing bells, and telling the passersby all about it. This was especially popular if a man were marrying a widow. The couple found this as acutely embarrassing as a modern couple would. Although the cities passed repeated laws forbidding the practice, the new husband often had to resort to bribing his friends to make them stop.

Within marriage the husband was the absolute master legally; he did not even give his wife a share in his wealth. Florentine law did not recognize community property, and a woman whose husband left her would get her dowry back but nothing of what her husband had acquired while they were married. However, wives had a fair amount of autonomy in their daily lives. When their husbands were out of the house, as they were most of the day, young wives were unsupervised for often the first time in their lives. Husbands worried about their wives taking lovers in such a situation; if the neighbors suspected something was going on, they might hang horns or other symbols over the house door and make unmerciful fun of the deceived husband. Court records indicate that many a young man, seeing and being attracted by a pretty young wife, tried to sneak into her house, in the hope that once he was there she might prove willing. A wife in such a situation could be badly compromised if no one believed that the man had sneaked in uninvited. To restore her honor she could have him prosecuted on charges of attempted rape, but in the Renaissance, as now, the normal defense of accused rapists was that they had been invited.

Food and Clothing in the Renaissance

A Renaissance family ate two meals a day; a late breakfast, around ten in the morning, after people had already been up and at work for quite a few hours (almost like a coffee break rather than breakfast, except that they had no coffee yet), and dinner in the mid- or late afternoon. Breakfast consisted of bread with fruit or jam, and dinner consisted of soup and pasta, plus cheese and vegetables. Except for rich families, most people could only afford meat once a week. Pasta was ubiquitous, however, for the hard winter wheat that grew best in Italy's hot climate was much better suited for pasta than it was for bread. It was made into many of the same forms it takes in Italian cuisine today (ravioli, spaghetti, rigatoni). One must realize, however, that Renaissance Italians had no tomatoes from which to make tomato sauce, for the tomato is a New World vegetable.

The basic clothing for men in the Renaissance was a short, loose tunic, usually belted, worn over tights designed to show off the legs. In Florence the official (though certainly not real) equality of all citizens was demonstrated by everyone wearing the same kind of hat, called a "citizen's cap." Women wore dresses with tight bodices and high waists, cut rather low over the bosom, and long, full skirts. Both sexes wore cloaks to keep them warm. Women grew their hair long but generally wore it pinned up. Men wore their hair at shoulder length or a little shorter and were almost always clean-shaven.

Women, especially young women, were often accused by moralists of the Renaissance of dressing like harlots. (The older generation has always thought of the younger generation's clothes as too provocative or too revealing.) They also wore heavy makeup. They plucked their eyebrows and used hot irons to curl their hair. Unlike now, when the goal is to be tan, in the Renaissance the goal was to be white. The reason for this change is that most people, working for a living, had to spend a lot of time in the sun, and only the elegant could afford to stay inside; now, when most work is inside work, only the rich can afford to be outside getting tan during the day. In order to attain the desired whiteness, Italian women used powder and even special bleaching lotions, which they rubbed on their hands at night.

Children in Italian Cities

Children born in Renaissance cities were, like the children born in the cities of the high Middle Ages, normally sent out of town to a wet nurse to be raised for their first two years or even more. After this they were brought back to town, to parents they had rarely if ever seen. The term for such a wet nurse was *balia*, and parents looking for a good *balia* were warned to be sure to choose a woman of good moral character, because children were assumed to take in a woman's characteristics along with her milk. In practice, however, parents were much more concerned that the *balia* be healthy and strong than that she be highly moral. The *balia* would have had a child of her own quite recently, which was why she was producing milk. A woman whose baby had just died was considered an ideal *balia*, because she would not be tempted to give her baby the milk her employers thought belonged to theirs. In some cases a woman might never let her breasts dry up after her own child was born, producing milk for years for a succession of other people's children.

Acting as a *balia* was an important addition many peasant women who lived near the Italian cities could make to their household finances. A woman might make enough as a *balia* for an urban mother that she was able to hire a *balia* herself (of even lower social status) for her own child. Although an urban child was normally sent out of town to its *balia*, a baby born to a well-to-do couple who owned a slave woman with a baby of her own might have that slave woman be the nurse; in such cases, *her* baby was simply sent to a foundling home. (For a discussion of the reappearance of slavery, see pages 330–31.) If the child was returned to its own parents before the normal two years had lapsed, it was usually because its *balia* had unexpectedly become pregnant and therefore stopped producing milk (contrary to popular belief, nursing will not prevent pregnancy indefinitely).

The house a two-year-old child returned to after having been weaned by its *balia* was often large and full of people. Older brothers and sisters, unmarried aunts and uncles, stepbrothers and stepsisters filled the household. Many Renaissance men married more than once, as widow- or widowerhood occurred frequently, and the children of a first marriage were raised by the second wife along with her own. Some men even brought home illegitimate children to be raised, and there might be the illegitimate offspring of the master and one of the maids or slaves in the house as well. As well as being surrounded by members of his or her own household, a Renaissance child lived very close to a large group of cousins, for powerful families often took over a city block, with brothers and cousins and their families all living as neighbors, often overseen by a white-haired and iron-fisted grandfather.

Children were identified very much as part of this paternal kindred, more so than was their mother. Women were always to some extent caught between the physical and family units which constituted urban "houses," for they were born into one house but spent their adult lives in one or more other houses, whereas a man remained part of the same "house" all his life. As mentioned on page 323, if a man died his wife recovered her dowry, and if she remarried she took her dowry with her, but she left behind any children she might have had by her first marriage, in the care of her father-in-law or brother-in-law.

Small children seem to have been fairly well treated, to judge by the chubby little cherubs that were the artist's ideal, and by the frequency with which moral preachers found it necessary to tell mothers not to kiss and fondle their children too much or to spoil them with too many presents. Children played with dolls, or toy birds or animals. Both boys and girls wore a simple tunic without much under it. Although parents intermittently decided it was good to "toughen" a child by feeding him or her chewy meat or by making the child sleep in the cold with few blankets, small children, with the run of the house and plenty of playmates—and, if they were lucky, with a doting mother—seem to have enjoyed themselves greatly.

Discipline, however, arrived when the children, especially the boys, were about seven, for this is when their education began. The ideal, rarely achieved, was for a father to teach his own sons. Powerful merchant fathers were often off traveling for long stretches of time, might be exiled from their city for various offenses or political disagreements, and usually had little time or inclination anyway, and smaller local merchants or craftsmen were generally much too occupied with simply making the family living to concern themselves directly in the formal education of their sons. Therefore, education usually had to be turned over to someone else. A well-to-do father would hire a tutor for his sons, but most boys went to the public school run by the city. These schools were for boys only in Renaissance Italy; girls were educated at home or in a convent. In the Renaissance, girls became nuns much more frequently than they had in the high Middle Ages, so education in a convent was often a first step to entering one. Parents still had to pay for a boy's education, even if the city organized the school and arranged for the teachers.

Boys started by learning reading and writing, then learned mathematics and accounting, and typically were apprenticed to a shop or a bank by the time they were in their teens. Schooling for everyone was interrupted by the periodic outbreaks of the plague. Schoolmasters whipped boys for misbehaving or not learning their lessons; much later many boys still recalled particularly harsh schoolmasters with horror. Because those fathers who took their own sons' education in hand were equally harsh, believing that a boy was made a man by such treatment (this belief still rules in the modern armed forces), being educated at home was no advantage to the naughty or the slow-witted.

The wealthiest fathers hired private tutors to teach their children at home. Young Piero de' Medici, for example, was able to write to his father in Latin from the time he was seven years old. His father, the most powerful man in Florence, stayed in town during the summer while the rest of his family was out at their country villa, and Piero wrote him regularly, to let him know how the family was doing and to show off his education. Through the formal Latin a very recognizable little boy appears:

> "So far Lucrezia [his older sister] has had all she asked for," Piero complained in one letter. "I, who have always written in Latin to give a more literary tone to my letters, have not yet received that pony you promised me." A little later that summer, Piero wrote again, "I fear that some misfortune has happened to the pony. I think of it night and day, and until the pony comes I shall have no peace." But his persistence was finally rewarded. At the end of the summer he wrote again, "I cannot tell you, Magnificent Father, how glad I am to have the pony, and how much his arrival encourages me to work hard. He is so handsome and perfect. I send you many thanks for such a fine gift, and I shall try to repay you by becoming what you wish."

The father's iron hand in education (tempered though it might be by such indulgent gifts) was only a part of the father's general rule over the household. A father's authority over his children was absolute until he either died or emancipated his children. Children who had not been formally freed from parental control never had full legal status while their parents lived. Whereas in modern America children automatically become adults at eighteen or twenty-one, passing a certain birthday was not enough in Renaissance Italy. Rather, a father had to "emancipate" his children, appearing before a judge to formally free them from his control. (This is the same word used to describe freeing slaves, and children under a Renaissance father's authority had scarcely any more independent power than a slave.)

Although emancipation often took place at such turning points as a son's betrothal, probably in his late twenties, a child could also be emancipated very young, in his early teens, or might continue under his father's authority until his father was quite old and he himself a father and middle-aged. Daughters were usually emancipated when they were married, but sometimes their fathers only emancipated them years later. Even then, they did not enjoy the same legal rights as emancipated men, as authority over them passed to their husbands. The idea of having a formal emancipation came from Roman law, which, after its rediscovery in Italy in the late eleventh and twelfth centuries, was increasingly applied to many different aspects of law and government in Italy. In northern Europe, where Roman law never had as great an impact, formal emancipation never became as important an issue.

Violence in Renaissance Cities

Renaissance Italy was a violent society, even more so than modern America. At night no one who could help it moved outside of their heavily barred doors. In Florence curfew was imposed at sunset, and after that no one except the municipal police was supposed to be in the streets. If one had to be out, one had to have a special pass to avoid being arrested. The city gates were locked to prevent anyone coming into town from the outside, and the curfew and the roaming police were supposed to keep thieves and murderers down. Even so, violence was a constant, and many women slept with their small children in bed with them as obstacles to would-be rapists. One was not safe even at home, for great technical advances had been made in poisons, and poisoning by family and friends was a constant concern, especially for the powerful.

Renaissance cities, like modern states, considered violence an assault on the honor and social organization of the state as well as on the individual. The legal penalties were very severe for a number of crimes, both with the intention of deterring criminals and for the purpose of restoring the state's honor. In Venice, for example, there was a rapidly escalating series of punishments laid out for those guilty of robbery, depending on the value of what the robber took. Stealing something worth less than a lira was punished by a whipping, but the punishment for stealing something worth ten lire was having an eye put out, and for stealing something worth more than forty lire the penalty was death. All second offenders were also hanged, no matter what the value of what they stole. As now, grim punishments did not decrease the level of crime; they only encouraged criminals to be more inventive to avoid being caught.

Even religion was sometimes very violent in Renaissance Italy. The most outstanding example was the meteoric rise and fall of the preacher Savonarola in Florence in the 1490s. He preached sermons of fire and brimstone to rapt audiences, castigating both worldly pleasures and the organized church. "The clergy make mock of Christ and the saints," he cried, urging the Florentines to break with Rome and turn Florence into a "republic of Christ." He called on the citizens to turn away from lives of debauchery and to burn both fripperies and the unrepentant sinners themselves in huge bonfires. Games, fancy clothing, and dirty pictures were all relegated to Savonarola's fires. He enlisted children into a "vice squad" to spy on adults, including their own parents. His hold on the Florentine imagination, although strong, was short-lived; he himself was burned at the stake in 1498 as a heretic.

Several factors contributed to the high level of violence. Most important was the constant recurrence of the plague, which came through Europe every decade or two from the late fourteenth through eighteenth centuries. Florence, which had had roughly 100,000 people in the first half of the fourteenth century, shrank to 50,000 after the first outbreak of the Black Death, and never passed 75,000 again until centuries later. The sight of so much death made the value of human life much lower, and those who lived through the plague often became both hedonistic

DOMINVS PHLIPPVS HISPANVS DE SCOLARIS RELATOV ISTORIE, THEVCROI

Pippo Spano, leader of a band of mercenary soldiers.

and reckless, feeling that they might as well take what they wanted in the short time they had left, regardless of the consequences. Another factor was the high level of poverty; the poor and dissatisfied, surrounded by wealth in which they cannot share, have always turned to violence more frequently than the better off. In Florence, for example, the tax rolls show that a rough third of the population was below the poverty line and officially exempt from taxes.

The decreased value put on human life in the Renaissance is also demonstrated by the reappearance of slavery in Italian cities. Slavery had ceased being a major factor in the West by the ninth century and had disappeared by the eleventh century, before reappearing four hundred years later. In the overwhelmingly agricultural economy of the early Middle Ages, there had been agricultural slaves, but it had become easier and more economical, as discussed in Chapter 4, to use serfs rather than slaves in the field, and the last slaves had been domestic slaves. When slaves reappeared in Italy in the fifteenth century, it was again as household workers or as artisans, making useful handcrafted goods for their masters. And, as mentioned on page 326, a slave woman might serve as a *balia*.

These slaves were for the most part non-Italians obtained by trade in the Mediterranean from the Muslims. Slaves were treated fairly humanely, or at least were treated no worse than could be expected in a society where street violence was endemic and schoolboys were instructed with the beating-rod always ready. Many wealthy merchants had a child or two from their slave girls, and these children were raised at home. But the ready acceptance of slavery by the Italians of the supposedly enlightened Renaissance (it was after all sanctioned by the Roman law they studied so closely) foreshadows the massive enslavement and exploitation of other peoples by the Europeans in the expansion and colonialization of the sixteenth and seventeenth centuries.

Northern Europe at the End of the Middle Ages

The Cities

The end of the Middle Ages was quite different in northern Europe than it was in Italy. There was increased violence and increased gaps between the very rich and the very poor in the north as along the Mediterranean, as well as a nostalgic looking-back to a rather inaccurately portrayed "golden age" of the past. But the north remained much more rural, and thus developed in different directions than did highly urbanized Renaissance Italy.

In the north, as in Italy, cities were much smaller at the end of the Middle Ages than they had been in the thirteenth or early fourteenth centuries. The plague, famine, wars, and general economic collapse meant that cities did not really start to grow again until the sixteenth century, after two hundred years of population stagnation. There is some indication, however, that English and Flemish towns began to experience economic recovery slightly earlier than Italian towns, perhaps in the final decades of the fifteenth century.

The northern cities of the late Middle Ages, like those of Italy, tended during the fifteenth century to lose the republican form of government most of them had acquired in the twelfth and early thirteenth centuries. (One must keep in mind that their "democracy" was not rule by the people in general but rule by a select minority—they thought of their government as democratic, and it certainly had democratic elements, but we might instead call such a government an oligarchy.) Although we, living under a democracy, tend to think of democratic government as very modern, and as something that evolves naturally out of earlier forms, in fact democracy has been tried a number of times throughout history, as favorable circumstances arose, and just as naturally abandoned as circumstances changed and the bulk of the citizenry found it too difficult or inconvenient to concern themselves with government any longer.

Northern cities did not acquire tyrant-princes like those of Italy, for northern countries (unlike Italy) had centralized governments that would have prevented such absolute local one-man rule, but they did increasingly fall under the control of just a few families. In the Low Countries, the guilds that had governed the cities from the twelfth through the fourteenth centuries became closed, hereditary castes in the fifteenth century, impossible for new residents of the city to enter. In England city government, which had originally been open at least theoretically to all citizens, became a closed corporation, as only members of certain families were allowed to become mayors or even members of the municipal council.

At the end of the Middle Ages, the cities of the north, which had once been independent, were drawn under the influence of the increasingly powerful central governments. In England, from the fourteenth century on, all the important towns sent representatives to Parliament, the organization that governed in conjunction with the king, especially by agreeing to taxes. Taxes were assessed on places, such as the towns, rather than on individuals, with the town itself responsible for raising the money. In the same way, a king going to war would demand a certain number of soldiers from each town, especially as war became increasingly a matter for infantry soldiers rather than for the nobility.

Northern cities, like the Italian cities, had to deal with the problem of

A fifteenth-century hospital.

urban poverty, for which it was clear in the fifteenth century that there was no easy solution. Even people with regular employment in a low-status job could not possibly earn enough to support a family and certainly not enough to save up and start over elsewhere. Many municipalities had taken over the local hospitals, just as they had taken over regulation of the houses of prostitution, and so the hospitals, which once had been run by the churches, were now run by the secular government. In the fifteenth century these municipally run hospitals, which continued to be a principal source of urban charity as they had been in the high Middle Ages, first started making distinctions of the sort we now make, between the able-bodied and those unable to support themselves, with charity going only to the latter. Medieval hospitals had taken all comers, from a religious impulse, but fifteenth-century hospitals used criteria of municipal expediency (such as a desire to hold down the number of tramps and beggars) to decide who was worthy of charity. The able-bodied considered "not worthy" could often find temporary work by going at dawn to one of the "hiring" squares every city had, where an employer who wanted a strong back for virtually no wages would hire workers by the day. But life for the urban poor at the end of the Middle Ages was the dead-end it has remained until the twentieth century.

The Rural World

The rural peasantry at the end of the Middle Ages were freer than they had been in the middle of the fourteenth century—or would be in the sixteenth century. As noted in Chapter 9, peasants were given concessions in the aftermath of the popular revolts that began in the second half of the fourteenth century, and the process continued over the next hundred years. When landlords were unable to enforce low wages in the aftermath of the plague, they leased out more of their land to peasant tenants, rather than having to pay increasingly high wages for workers on the demesne. Many peasants were able to amass fairly large landholdings and become major suppliers of wool and grain to the markets.

By the fifteenth century the cash economy, which had been flourishing in the cities since the twelfth century, had reached the level of peasant villages. The records of land transfer which many manors kept show a high level of peasants buying and selling land for cash in the fifteenth century. In some places, peasants were able to make quick fortunes through such rural "industries" as quarrying, lead mining (especially in England), or cloth manufacture. Peasants paid their rents almost entirely in cash, rather than in produce or the "work-days" that earlier had been a symbol of servitude in England. On some manors, landlords allowed "rebates" of rents for new tenants as an incentive to have them stay, but somehow the level of rent never rose to what was supposed to be its official level, and the landlords were soon faced with *all* their tenants withholding something from their annual rents. In practice, then, the rents of the fifteenth century, already fairly low compared to the fourteenth century, were actually even lower than their stated level.

However, especially in England, some of these gains were counterbal-

A Flemish farm in winter. From the *Breviarum Grimani.*

anced by the landlords who turned their tenants off their land in order to create sheep pastures, a process that had begun in the fourteenth century but intensified at the end of the fifteenth century. During the English popular revolts of the sixteenth century, peasants demanded a return of their rights of the "good old days" of the fifteenth century.

The aristocracy remained a rural rather than an urban force in northern Europe. Some of the most powerful nobles, the dukes especially, became tremendously wealthy, and some duchies stretched for hundreds of miles. But most of Europe's elite was much less wealthy and could not in any way consider themselves the dukes' social equals. Whereas daily peasant life remained much as it had been in the previous century, that of the rural aristocracy, and in consequence that of persons of the merchant or craftsmen classes who dealt with them, was in the process of change.

It was during the fifteenth century that "the gentry" took form, a group of people who did not hold the high titles of the dukes and counts and did not own castles, yet who were much wealthier than the rest of the population, usually being landlords, local administrators, and judges. They were tied together by an intricate network of marriages. They took the title of knight or esquire (the latter meaning someone who was qualified to be knighted but had not been; the esquires eventually far outnumbered the actual knights). The gentry continued in England to form the backbone of government and refined society until the nineteenth century, if not indeed the twentieth.

The gentry built themselves elegant houses, no longer, as mentioned in Chapter 9, even trying to build defensible castles. In England, stone was increasingly replaced by brick as the main building material for expensive country houses. Although some knights put battlements and drawbridges on their houses, such features were decorative rather than functional. Those who could not afford stone or brick, or who lived in areas where these were unavailable, built large country houses in the "half-timber" style, in which a house was framed with wood but the space between the timbers was filled in with plaster, over a backing of wattle. These are the "black and white" houses still seen both in England and on the Continent. (They were originally not black and white but brown and tan; in the nineteenth century, especially in England, many people decided black and white was more attractive and accordingly dyed the timbers and whitewashed the plaster.)

The same impulse to emulate great warriors without being actually warlike led to the final flourishing of "chivalry." The knights loved to participate in tournaments, some of which went on for days; great dukes always organized tournaments for such important events as marriages or birthdays. The church, which had originally opposed tournaments as warlike exercises probably leading to pointless loss of life, lifted the ban (which had never been particularly heeded anyway) in the fourteenth century. Plate armor had by now been developed, primarily as a result of the spread of gunpowder and the invention of portable firearms. It was hoped that a bullet would glance off a slanted, highly polished breastplate, and by covering the entire body with armor, it was intended that no chink be left for a bullet to penetrate.

Guns, however, had no place at a late medieval tournament. Nor did maces, the weapons that armored knights used in real battle to try to crack open each other's armor. Weighted down by extremely heavy armor that had been designed to withstand gunfire, the knights were raised by pulleys onto the backs of massive horses (the ancestors of modern Clydesdales and Percherons) and then charged at each other with their lances, in a style of fighting that had scarcely changed since the late twelfth century. With so much armor on, they were protected from any serious damage from their opponents' weapons, but a fall from such a height could be crippling for someone wrapped in metal. Therefore, the late Middle Ages developed very deep, secure saddles, so that only the worst horseman would be likely to fall off. With unhorsing no longer a criterion for winning or losing, tournament participants turned increasingly to judging and the awarding of points for technical merit and artistic expression (very much like the judging for modern figure skating).

Tournaments of the late Middle Ages were extremely opulent affairs, with the knights and ladies all wearing bright silks, staying in silken tents, and displaying elaborate coats of arms. Flamboyance was used both to prove and to show off one's social status. Heralds inspected the coats of arms and the "proofs of nobility" of anyone who wished to take part before he could be formally admitted. Participants in the jousts made extravagant vows of tasks they would undertake if they won.

The "chivalric orders," like the Order of the Garter in England or the Order of the Star in France, both founded in the middle of the fourteenth century, became extremely influential in the late Middle Ages. These particular orders were founded by kings, but a great many powerful princes founded their own "orders" in imitation. People would be invited to join these exclusive clubs in recognition of their prowess, religious generosity, or ceremonial service to women. Some governments considered their secret meetings a political threat, but they were less political entities than opportunities for men to gather together, showing off their best clothes and best manners, and take part in ceremonies often modeled after literature. (Their relationship to the earlier crusading orders, such as the Templars, was slight.)

Little Moreton Hall, England, a half-timbered "black-and-white" manor house built by a member of the new "gentry" class at the close of the Middle Ages.

Chivalric literature also flourished in the fifteenth century to a degree previously unknown. The stories of King Arthur and his knights, which had been growing since the twelfth century, were grouped together into long, coherent narratives for the first time. The English writer Thomas Malory, who lived in the second half of the fifteenth century, put the King Arthur stories into the form that they are usually met with today. Here is the Round Table, the highly refined treatment of women, the desire to undertake impossible (and often pointless) tasks just for the glory of them, the willingness to fight on any pretext, the rather uneasy fusion of the Christian quest for the Holy Grail with warlike escapades and adventures. These stories were tremendously popular, and the knights of northern Europe loved to have parties in which everyone came dressed as a different figure from Arthur's court.

These stories were written down in languages that can be read today, with reasonable success, by someone who knows only modern languages. That is, French and German had evolved to something fairly close to the modern form of these languages, and, even more striking, so had English. Modern English is a fusion of a Germanic language (Anglo-Saxon) with the French that the Norman invaders spoke in 1066. The fusion took a long time to happen because for several centuries the upper classes continued to speak Norman French, while the lower classes spoke Anglo-Saxon. (In some areas that had been less thoroughly Normanized, Anglo-Saxon persisted at all levels of society.) To be well educated in thirteenth-century England, one had to know both French and Anglo-Saxon.

By the fifteenth century, however, the languages had finally joined into one. Modern English has almost as many words as modern French and modern German put together, because English kept *both* Norman and Anglo-Saxon terms. We use the French phrase for elevated conversation, the Anglo-Saxon one for earthy speech, or use two words for different aspects of the same thing where both French and German have only one, such as "swine" for the animal and "pork" for the meat (like the French *porc*—which refers both to the animal and to its meat—and unlike the German *Schweinfleisch*, or "swine-flesh").

A Noble Household at the End of the Middle Ages

Noble households at the end of the Middle Ages were organized around ceremony and display. They tended to be large, including over a hundred people and often several hundred, and the gentry tried their best to imitate, on a smaller scale, the lifestyle of the most powerful nobles. The household consisted of much more than the family and servants; it also included companions to the family, management officials, secretaries, and bodyguards. The kings had counts who filled at least some of these roles living with them, the counts had castellans living with *them*, the castellans had members of the gentry living with *them*, and so on, so that each big household included a social spectrum, starting with the status of the master of the house and working down to the lowest levels. Households usually had at least some boys and young men who were being trained there; at the end of the Middle Ages, service in a grand household was the other major route besides the church or the legal profession for upward social mobility.

The household was attached to the family more than to the house itself, for all the most wealthy, and even some of the gentry, owned several different houses. When a noble family traveled, the household traveled with it, a few members of an advance party going ahead, but most of the hundred or two hundred people traveling together. They made an impressive spectacle and they knew it. The lord and lady rode with their closest companions and armed retainers around them, and behind them came the housekeepers and servants, with carts carrying essentially all household necessities, including clothing, bedding, kitchen equipment, liturgical books, musical instruments, and carpenter's tools. Households that could afford glass, which was just becoming popular in the late Middle Ages, took the panes out of the windows and carried them along. The idea was that, wherever they stopped, the household with its ordinary practices and rituals could be reconstructed around the lord.

The armed retainers who accompanied a great household on the move or accompanied their lord on the few occasions when he went to war were not permanent members of the household. Rather, unlike the knights of the high Middle Ages, they had their own houses and families and often careers, only coming up to the big house for special occasions. By the end of the Middle Ages, the lords no longer granted these men fiefs, such as the vassals and knights of the castellans had received in earlier centuries (see Chapter 6). Rather, the lord paid these retainers an annual fee in return for their service as needed. The word "fee" in fact comes from "fief," but this payment was very close to what we today consider a "retainer fee," an amount of money paid someone to have them ready at hand, and quite different from the high-medieval fief.

Some of the most important members of a great household were the administrators, but they were fairly few in number and often not even there. These were the men who looked after the lands and rents from which the household derived its income. For the most part these were men of gentry status, trained as lawyers. The peasantry of the fifteenth century now primarily paid for their land in money rents, as noted on page 333, and a lord's administrators spent full time overseeing both the peasant tenants and the lord's own lands, on which hired laborers raised crops or livestock.

The steward was the chief administrator of the lord's estates and as a result was often gone from the house, though he and a few clerks and servants often showed up to consult or report. By the end of the Middle Ages, the steward had taken over many of the duties that had once belonged to the lord himself. The most important of these duties was officiating at the manor court, where he settled disputes between tenants or prosecuted them for failure to pay rent. Other important administrators included gamekeepers and rent collectors. Sometimes the lord received the rents himself from his rent collectors or, for the lands lying

closest to the house, from the peasants themselves. But the grandest
households even had treasurers to receive and tally the money.

These administrators were the backbone of a great household because
they were responsible for its financial base, but much more in evidence
were the servants and companions who made a household grand and who
dispensed its hospitality. Everyone wore a badge or livery to identify
them as part of the household, and these were worn with pride. Ceremony attended every action, from eating, to going to bed, to going to
mass. Symbolic emblems, colors, and rituals were everywhere.

The lord of a great house ate at a table by himself, unless he had
exalted company, for no one else was of high enough status to share his
table. The men who carved his meat and poured his wine were members
of the gentry themselves, except in the smallest households. Another
gentleman, with servants to help him, oversaw the lord's bedchamber
and clothes. Even the daily service at the household chapel was made
grand by an organ and a full choir.

Lords could only afford to keep enormous households at the end of
the Middle Ages because a great many people wanted to be part of such
a household and because the lord did not have to pay them a salary, as
would the modern head of such a house. The gentry who served at table
and oversaw everything from the bedchamber to the stables had personal
incomes of their own, so they were not working for money, only for the
honor. Servants were paid, but only token sums, more gift than salary.
Even the fee for the armed retainers was a small sum, since their services
were not needed most of the time. However, the lord did provide the
food and livery as well as a place to live for everyone who lived with
him, as well as dispensing hospitality both to visitors and to the poor. It
was evidence of a man's wealth and glory to have crowds of people in
the house, either permanently or visiting, to have great quantities of
food and wine served at every meal, and to feed the poor at the back
door with the leftovers.

The grandest display of hospitality was at Christmas, which at the end
of the Middle Ages was a continuous celebration for the entire "twelve
days of Christmas," from Christmas Day itself until Epiphany (January 6).
Feasting went on continually, with great lords, accompanied by the most
important members of their households, traveling back and forth between each others' houses to be fed and entertained. On one day of the
twelve, all the peasant tenants were invited in for a meal. Traveling bands
of minstrels and players put on "mummers' plays," and the choirboys of
a household put on a nativity play in the chapel. Christmas carols were
both sung and danced to. On New Year's Day people exchanged presents, and in many households a "lord of misrule," chosen from the
household staff (often a boy), became lord for the day. He sat at the
high table, did comic imitations of his lord's voice and manners, made
everyone bow before him, and issued ridiculous orders. This was a chance
for everyone to let off steam, to say things to the "lord of misrule"
they could never have said to their real lord, and to relax for a short
time the order and ceremony of the household. In a subtle way,

the practice of having a lord of misrule also reinforced the real lord's authority, by making the very idea of someone else ruling appear ridiculous.

The house in which such ceremony took place was quite different from the castle of the high Middle Ages. As noted on page 310, the spread of gunpowder and cannons made it useless to try to build castles anymore, except for great forts, so the late medieval manor house was no longer defensible, though it still often had decorative towers and battlements. The original castle plan, consisting of a great chamber where everyone slept and ate, with storage rooms below and a few smaller rooms upstairs (see Chapter 6), was long gone. There was still a great hall, but it no longer served as combination living room, dining room, and bedroom for the entire household; therefore, it was smaller than the hall of a castle had been. Many of its original functions were now scattered through the many other rooms that manor houses now had.

A manor house of the end of the Middle Ages was usually built around a rectangular courtyard. Usually two of the sides were taken up with lodgings, rooms where most of the members of the household slept. The idea of private rooms (actually semiprivate, for all but the most important household officials shared their rooms) would have seemed very odd in the high Middle Ages, when the emphasis was on the community between members of the household, symbolized originally by everyone sleeping together in the hall, or at least in a few large chambers. But by the fifteenth century it was part of the grandeur of a house to have separate rooms for every two to four people above the lowest servants. These lodgings opened directly into the courtyard, and the ones on the second or third stories had their own stairs. This plan for lodgings has continued at the colleges of Oxford and Cambridge (not surprisingly, since many of the colleges were constructed by men who themselves lived in late medieval manor houses).

On the other two sides of the courtyard were the grander rooms, which opened into each other as well as into the courtyard. There was still a great hall, used now primarily as a dining room when everyone ate together, though the tables were taken down between meals so that it could be used as a living room as well. Though not as large as high-medieval halls, it was still too large for comfortable conversation, so in the late Middle Ages it became common to have a "parlor" opening off one side (the word is from the French, meaning a room where one talks). This had a lower ceiling and its own fireplace, to make a cozier and more private place. Nearby was the household chapel.

At one end of the great hall were three archways. One led to the room where wine and beer were poured out and from there down to the cellars, another led to the pantry, from which bread was dispensed (this room also became the room in which the household steward entertained the stewards of visiting lords), and the third, the center one, led to the kitchens. Late medieval kitchens were built with very high roofs, to reduce the heat and smoke. Most cooking was still done on open fires, and a large household had several fireplaces around the walls of the kitchen. A separate brick oven was used to bake the bread.

The calendar illustration for the month of June from *Les Très Riches Heures du Duc de Berry*, a highly prized book of hours from the early fifteenth century. Such devotional objects were treasured by members of the aristocracy. For each of the twelve months, *Les Très Riches Heures* alternated scenes from aristocratic life with scenes, as here, from the lives of peasants. The sun's progress through the yearly zodiac is charted in the lunette above.

   When dinner was served, servants from the kitchen carried it triumphantly through the long passage that usually separated kitchen and hall and then through the archway at the great hall's end. In the most elaborate houses there was a musicians' gallery over the arches, from which trumpeters began to play at the moment the food arrived. Usually the lord, at the high table at the opposite end of the hall, watched his food approach, carried in great state. He took up his spoon and knife before anyone else could start eating. Forks were invented in Italy in the fifteenth century, but they were initially used only to transfer food from the platter to the individual plate, not for eating. They were not adopted at all for a long time in northern Europe and only reached England in the seventeenth century.

In many cases, however, the lord was not actually in the hall. The lord's bedroom had fairly early retreated from the great hall, originally into an alcove at the end of the hall, but soon up a flight of stairs, to become the great chamber. For more private dinners, the lord now often ate in the great chamber rather than the hall. This did not mean more informality, for there was at least as much ceremony in the great chamber as there had been in the hall. But now the servers, after carrying the food from the kitchen and through the hall, had to continue up the stairs at the end to the chamber, where tables were set up next to the lord's bed. After the food had thus traversed several hundred feet, and after it was ceremoniously carved and served, it may often have become quite cold.

In many late medieval houses, the great chamber was the extent of the lord's retreat from the rest of the household. But in others the lord's bed was moved out of the great chamber and into a smaller room behind it. This was called the closet, a word that now only suggests a place to hang clothes or store the broom but was then an intimate room in which the lord slept and had his most private conversations. The closet was also a room for the lord's private devotions, and it often had a small window opening onto the upper level of the chapel, so that he could hear service on those occasions when he did not want to go down himself.

Some manor houses (and rebuilt castles) from the end of the Middle Ages have a "double" plan: two courtyards, two great halls, two great chambers, even two kitchens. (Windsor Castle, the English royal family's residence outside of London, is like this.) The reason for such an arrangement was so that one structure could accommodate two separate households. For example, if the castle belonged to a king or very great duke, who was rarely there, he would have to have his own set of accommodations waiting for him and his household to move into when he came, and his constable, who normally lived there, would stay in the other set of separate accommodations.

War at the End of the Middle Ages

Although war had been a constant concern in the castles of the high Middle Ages, it seemed very far away in the elegant manor houses of the fifteenth century. Yet wars were at least as common as they had been three centuries earlier, if not more so; they simply no longer involved the lords' residences, or even always the lords themselves. There were still large contingents of heavily armed and noble knights in every army, many of them younger sons of great lords who were making the army their career. But many of the gentry were no longer interested in the glory that war had promised for centuries; staying at home in peace seemed much more attractive. Increasingly the mass of late medieval armies were infantrymen.

Portable firearms were invented at the very end of the fourteenth century and became fairly common in the fifteenth century. These were weapons for footsoldiers, not for knights; they were difficult to aim and control standing on solid ground, much less on horseback. These "arquebuses" had a great fascination but were not yet efficient weapons. Given more attention were the cannons, which were enormous in the fifteenth century. One, nicknamed Monster, weighed over five tons, and must have slowed down its army markedly, for it had to be dragged from place to place on a sled. All kings and great dukes spent huge sums on their cannons, and the best were so remarkable that they were given individual names, such as Mad Margaret, Lion, or Dragon.

Much more efficient than firearms was the crossbow. This bow, as discussed in Chapter 6, could shoot its short arrow, or "quarrel," with more force than a shot from an ordinary bow. This was especially true because in the fifteenth century most crossbows were fitted with a crank or winch that allowed the archer to bend an extremely stiff metal bow he would never have been able to bend with his unaided strength. Although it took a while to crank up a crossbow, it was still less time than it took to load an arquebus, and the bow was much more accurate.

Most infantrymen of the late Middle Ages had pikes or halberds, both vicious steel thrusting weapons on the ends of poles. The pike was simply pointed; the halberd had an axe-head on the side as well. These weapons made the sword obsolete for massed fighting among infantrymen because they both had a much longer reach for thrusting than any sword. The heavy, two-handed sword, which had been especially popular in Germany, was the first to go because it had to be whirled around one's head for full effectiveness, and a pikeman could thrust during the whirl. Thinner swords persisted, however, but by the sixteenth century they were used mainly in duels between members of the gentry.

The Swiss, who had become at the end of the Middle Ages the best mercenary soldiers in Europe, usually were pikemen. They were professional in a way that most infantrymen were not, for they were well trained and well disciplined; even today, the pope is guarded by a contingent of the Swiss Guard, as popes have been since the end of the Middle Ages. The Swiss soldiers were extremely proud of their position and showed off with ostrich feathers in wide-brimmed hats, full sleeves slit to show brightly colored undertunics, and other flourishes of apparel. Such professional fighting men considered themselves, and were widely considered to be, the epitome of virility. Paintings from the end of the Middle Ages show all professional soldiers, not just the Swiss, in swaggering and sexually aggressive poses, with prominent codpieces and suggestively held swords. The idea of an army of professionals in khaki, camouflage, or navy, standing in smart but anonymous rows, was still far in the future.

The Swiss were professionals, but the great mass of infantry at the end of the Middle Ages were men who either did not want to be in the army or should not have been, or both. In all the nations of western Europe, England, France, Spain, even the individual small states that made up Germany and Italy, the princes had a theoretic right to the military service of all male citizens. But in practice only a tiny percent ever served. Because the governments had no idea who all their citizens were, much less their addresses or birth dates, it was impossible to have anything like the modern military draft. Rather, kings and princes had to send out recruiters. Frequently these men simply went around from town to town, trying to bully and bribe people into joining the army.

Citizens were always ready with excuses: they were the only support of a widowed mother or of six tiny children; in the last war citizens from their town had fought so well that the king had promised they would never have to fight again; they were lame and would be useless in battle. Legal petitions flew toward the royal supreme court as quickly as the recruiter moved through the towns. For those who could afford it, one common way out of the army was to pay someone else to go in one's place. To try to entice people into the army, recruiters promised fat paypurses, but clever townsmen had heard that one too often before. The end result was that most armies were made up of the slow-witted who could not think of an excuse fast enough or actually believed the stories about military pay, of criminal elements that the rest of the townsmen wanted to get rid of anyway, of restless young men who wanted to get away from familiar settings on any terms, and of the very poor and very subservient pressured by their masters to go in their places.

Not surprisingly, such troops made terrible soldiers. They deserted in droves, caught diseases and died, did not know how to handle weapons, and seemed incapable of turning the random individual violence that some had long been practicing into the organized violence that an army requires. Their commanders considered them scum and referred to them as "cannon fodder" and "worm food." If they fought well, they received no awards or commendations; when they died they were shoveled into mass graves. This disregard for human life in the armies of the time indicates that in the fifteenth century warfare was starting to resemble much more closely the warfare of modern times than that of the Middle Ages.

Religion at the End of the Middle Ages

Religion at the close of the Middle Ages was no longer the rather optimistic search for holiness it had been in the high Middle Ages. As already seen in Chapter 9, the helplessness of the organized church in the face of the plague led some to reject any form of organized religion, and others to try to lead quiet, pious lives outside the mainstream of orthodoxy. These tendencies continued in the fifteenth century. The Great Schism in the church, when in the late fourteenth and early fifteenth centuries there were two separate popes both claiming to be the *real* pope—and for a while in the fifteenth century there were three—further eroded confidence in the organized church.

It did not help that at the end of the Middle Ages many church leaders gave the impression to their flocks that they were only in it for the money. Bishops had been elected by the local clergy since the beginnings of Christianity (though the local nobility also influenced many elections in the early Middle Ages). From the thirteenth century on, however, bishops were appointed by the popes instead. In return for a suitable payment, the papal curia would promise someone to give him a bishopric as soon as one opened up. In many areas, parish priests held the office of priest at several different churches, collecting the full revenues from each though naturally they could not do as thorough a job as if they had only held one church. (It was not all a downhill trend, however; these parish priests seem to have been better educated in the fifteenth century than their counterparts in the fourteenth century had been.) The startling splendor of the papal curia itself, though it was supposed to reflect the glory of God, looked to many critics like sheer worldliness.

In the meantime, some people began suggesting that Christians could do better reading the Bible themselves than trying to find salvation through the rituals of the church. Accordingly, for the first time the Bible began to be translated from Latin into the vernacular languages. In England, where English was just emerging as a real language with both French and Anglo-Saxon elements, the Oxford scholar John Wiclif translated the Bible into English in the late fourteenth century. The organized church attempted to ban a book that, it was feared, would give the untutored mistaken ideas of religion, but the Wiclif Bible continued to be read throughout the fifteenth century.

Private reading and study was especially important at the many new houses where groups of both priests and laymen gathered to live communally, without actually becoming monks. These first appeared in the late fourteenth century, as mentioned in Chapter 9, but they became especially common in the fifteenth century. The most influential of these groups were the Brothers and Sisters of the Common Life (or the "Modern Devotion" as they called themselves). All the members lived together, sharing their expenses and income, and prayed together, but they had no distinctive monastic habit and did not even take vows, leaving it up to the individual's conscience if he or she wanted to leave or stay. Originally they earned much of their money from copying books, but once the printing press was invented (discussed on pages 347–48), they started their own presses. Their religious emphasis was on the inner life, rather than on ceremony or liturgy, although they did retain such ceremonies as the rosary. They should not be seen as stern or harsh, because their inner life included visions, ecstacies, and outpourings of tears of repentence and joy.

In some places, the local interpretations of religion became linked with the beginnings of nationalistic feeling. This is most obvious in Bohemia (in what is now Czechoslovakia), where the preacher John Hus argued that the Bible showed that Christ, not the pope, was the head of the church, and that one must be saved through faith, not ritual. Hus himself was accused of being a heretic and burned at the stake in 1415 (accusations of heresy had become increasingly common in the late Middle Ages). But his followers, calling him a martyr, continued to oppose the organized church that had burned him, and a generation later the pope was forced to recognize a Bohemian national church, officially still part of Catholicism but with its own liturgical practices.

JOAN OF ARC

Joan of Arc was a village girl from Lorraine, on the eastern edge of France. Starting when she was about thirteen, she began to hear angel voices telling her what to do. When she was in her late teens, the voices told her to liberate France, much of which was then occupied by the English, due to their recent successes in the continuing Hundred Years' War. She first went to where the Dauphin (the French heir to the throne) was in hiding from the English, and bullied him into going to Reims in 1429 to be crowned (Reims was the traditional spot for crowning French kings, but the Dauphin had put off going there for fear of being captured). Her absolute sincerity and inspirational addresses, delivered in the plain and simple speech of one of their own level, won her the burning devotion of the common French soldier. After she won several notable military victories on the way to Reims, especially at Orléans, she took charge of all the royal armies. She made her soldiers go to mass regularly, drove the camp followers out, and managed to persuade the army that God was on the side of France. After some spectacular victories, she was captured in 1430 and turned over to the English, who naturally feared her and her inspiration of the French forces. They managed to have her accused of heresy and burned at the stake in 1431. She was still only nineteen.

In the same way, Joan of Arc combined religious fervor with military and patriotic inspiration. Even though she was burned as a heretic in 1431, she continued to be considered a martyr and a saint by the French, and with her inspiration they drove the English out of France and ended the Hundred Years' War in 1453. (Joan was not actually sainted until early in the twentieth century, but the nationalistic French church considered her a saint long before that.) This combination of religious feeling with patriotism was new in the fifteenth century but would become extremely important in the Protestant Reformation of the sixteenth century.

While there were thus religious currents tied either to personal prayer or even to nationalistic feeling, there were also other religious currents that *emphasized* ceremony and liturgy. The organized church, after all, was not trying to impose its view of religion so much as responding to one sector of the population—the one with the most resources.

It became extremely popular at the end of the Middle Ages for private individuals to collect relics of saints (King Louis XI of France had an enormous collection) and to endow private chapels and special masses. Henry VII of England arranged for no fewer than ten thousand masses to be said for his soul. Special days were treated as "good" or "bad" for ceremonial reasons; for example, if the Feast of the Innocents, the day commemorating the day Herod killed all the baby boys because he hoped to kill Jesus (December 28) fell on a Wednesday, then Wednesday would become a "bad" day for the rest of the year, on which no one would start a journey or get married. Minor saints in the church calendar were given special holy days and even their own ailments—Saint Fiacre, for example, became the special saint for curing hemorrhoids. Whether religion was expressed by full-blown participation in every new ritual (there were even special sorts of masses for each of the "joys" and "sorrows" of Mary, now long abolished), or by rejection of the forms of the organized church, it always lay just under the surface if not indeed in full view.

The Printing Press and the Universities

The fifteenth century was not as inventive a period as the fourteenth century, but in one area it made very important technical advances, and that was in the invention of the printing press. Although the spread of paper manufacture in the fourteenth century made the materials for book production less expensive, as noted in Chapter 9, books still had to be copied by hand, which meant that it took a very long time to produce each book. Such a labor-intensive process naturally meant that books were well beyond the financial means of most people.

But this changed in the mid-fifteenth century when Johann Gutenberg, a German, invented the printing press. The idea of printing was not entirely new; people had carved whole pages out of wood and then made prints by inking the raised letters and pressing the wood block onto a page. The Chinese, for example, had done printing in this manner. Gutenberg's real innovation was in the use of moveable type. One could have bins with all the different letters in them ready and waiting, and then set up a page quickly by pulling the appropriate letters out of the bins and arranging them in order. The letters, once arranged, were locked in place, forming a solid block that would be inked and pressed onto paper. (A printing press is called that because the inked page is pressed with great force onto the page, to make a clear impression.) Once one had made all the copies of a page one wanted, it could be broken up and the letters returned to the bins, to be reused.

The letters of Gutenberg's day were very clear and crisp because there had been advances in metallurgy, and he was able to pour into his molds a metal alloy that expanded as it cooled. The molds therefore were completely filled, without annoying gaps that would have left blank splotches on the page. Gutenberg used the same shapes for his letters, heavy and highly elaborate, as were then in general use in Germany, a style known to scholars who study different forms of handwriting as Gothic and to stationery engravers as Olde English. In parts of Germany, this style of printing continued to be used until the twentieth century; it was taken by the Nazis as a quintessentially "German" form of printing and thus was imposed on all printers as a patriotic measure. Actually it was not uniquely German but only the style that everyone in the late Middle Ages, including the Italians, had used until the humanists rediscovered Caroline miniscule.

Gutenberg's first book was a Bible, just as, when a new form of writing was developed at Charlemagne's court in the ninth century (see Chapter 5), it had initially been used in copying Bibles. Gutenberg's Bible was printed in large, clear letters, with the large capital letters at the beginning of each section done in bright colors by hand. (The Bible has remained the perpetual bestseller ever since, always outselling even books of erotic adventure or how-to volumes.)

The printing press immediately made books much more affordable because they could be produced so much more quickly. Although it took a little while to set up a page by hand, and the presses of the time had nothing of the speed of modern presses, once a page was set up copies could be cranked out at under a minute each. Books were now available in affordable editions for the first time (although they would still seem very expensive to us), and people could post notices and flyers or print up and distribute leaflets to argue political points. Literacy, although far from universal, spread with the lower prices for books.

The new printed books were snapped up at the universities. Although universities had first been founded in the high Middle Ages, as discussed in Chapter 8, there were originally no universities in eastern or northern Europe. But in the fifteenth century universities were founded throughout Germany and at Copenhagen in Denmark and Uppsala in Sweden. Several new universities were also founded in France, Spain, and Scotland. In part this was a response to growing nationalistic feeling; people no longer wanted to go to a foreign country to study, even though all students would be speaking Latin together. (Even the use of Latin was beginning to change; the medical school at Paris started instructing the barber-surgeons in French rather than Latin in the fifteenth century.) In part it was also due to a steadily increasing interest in learning and knowledge—more students wanted a university education—and hence more universities were needed to serve them.

Much late medieval education was like that of the high Middle Ages, but there was an increased interest in anatomy at the very end of the fifteenth century. Anatomy had not formed a major part of the medical training of the high Middle Ages, probably because most education was based on study of Greek and Arabic texts. The Arabs had had a religious prohibition against dissecting the dead, and their doctors had therefore rarely done so, meaning that little practical anatomy appeared in their texts. Christians had no such prohibitions, and surgeons regularly did post mortems (sometimes to try to determine if someone had died due to foul play) and used bodies from the gallows in order to study how a normal body was supposed to look. But only at the very end of the Middle Ages did this knowledge start to be written down and disseminated by the printing press. This happened as doctors in the West began feeling competent to compose their own textbooks, rather than just receiving others' knowledge.

Besides this new interest in anatomy at the end of the Middle Ages, as seen in the anatomical sketches of Leonardo da Vinci and many others, the other major change in medicine around 1500 was a change from using herbs to using chemicals as medicines. There had long been herbal compendiums, books listing various leaves, stems, roots, and barks with their (supposed) medicinal properties, but many of the first printed medical books also began explaining how doctors could concoct various chemical preparations from metals and liquors. Distilling was invented at the end of the Middle Ages, and brandy was prescribed as a medicine long before it became an after-dinner drink. Sprinkling precious metal, such as flakes of gold, into one's brandy was supposed to act as a preventative against the plague.

Many of the chemical medicines were quite violent, such as the widespread use of sulphur and mercury. Syphilis first appeared in Europe in the 1490s (it was thought at the time that Columbus brought it back from the New World, which may well be true), and it was often treated with mercury, in the assumption that a drastic disease needed a drastic cure. Although the new chemical cures were of doubtful medical value, their dissemination via the printing press laid the basis for the scientific study of chemistry.

The Age of Discovery

As knowledge of the printing press spread in the second half of the fifteenth century, many other books were also printed, including works of classical authors, the chivalric romances of Malory (mentioned on page 337), and scientific treatises. Some of the most avidly read scientific treatises were geographic and astronomical, works that gave information about the size of the world and about its inhabitants outside of Europe. Much of this information was based on fantasy, but it was read all the same. Men in the fifteenth century were beginning to look beyond the countries they had always known, not so much out of a pure desire for exploration as out of a desire for commercial profit. They were interested in reaching India, through or from which most luxury trade goods came, especially silks and spices.

Early in the fifteenth century, the Portuguese kings, interested in finding a sea route to India, began sponsoring explorations down the coast of Africa, going a little farther each time and setting up trading colonies on the way. Ship rigging was greatly improved in the fifteenth century by the use of a large, square-rigged sail hung from a tall mainmast. The wide, solid ships this rigging could power were much better for ocean voyages than earlier galleys had been.

At the end of the century the Portuguese at last discovered their desired sea route to the East, going all the way around Africa and through the Indian Ocean. (The present sea route is thousands of miles shorter, going from the eastern Mediterranean through the Suez Canal and the Red Sea into the Indian Ocean, but the Suez Canal was not dug for another five hundred years.) The Spanish kings were much slower than the Portuguese at getting into the explorations race, but in 1492, after having driven the last of the Muslims out of Spain (there had been Muslims in Spain since the eighth century, and the Spanish had been gradually pushing them back all during the Middle Ages), they too started

A twelfth-century depiction of a person from the "antipodes," the opposite side of the globe. He has a very large foot, designed to hold him onto the bottom of the earth.

looking for a quick sea route that would enable them to skip the middle-man and trade directly with the East.

At this time Christopher Columbus entered the picture. Columbus was an Italian who was convinced that if one sailed west one could reach India by a shortcut, without having to go all the way around Africa. He was of course wrong. His ideas were based on a miscalculation of the circumference of the earth that went back to the Greeks. Columbus thought the world was much smaller than it actually is, and he did not factor either the Pacific (which is half the globe by itself) or the width of the Americas into his calculations.

There were in fact better estimates available in the fifteenth century, which indicated that one would have to go three-quarters of the way around the world to reach India by going west, but Columbus ignored them. (It must be stressed that every person of any education knew the world was round. The idea that people thought the world was flat was invented quite recently, although it has taken a strong hold on the pop-ular imagination; this notion is even found in high school textbooks. Everything written in the fifteenth century indicates that people knew the world was a globe; the only question was how big a globe.) Colum-bus managed to persuade Ferdinand and Isabella that he was right about the size of the world—they may have been willing to try anything to get ahead of the Portuguese—and set off for what turned out to be the discovery of America. (The term "discovery" is of course something of a misnomer; Columbus discovered the New World for the Europeans, but the native Americans had known it was there all the time.)

Columbus refused to believe he had discovered a new continent. He remained convinced until the end of his life that he had found the short-cut to India, and referred to the natives he met as Indians (a name that has stuck), even though he was somewhat concerned about where the silk and spices might be. (He presumed he had reached outlying islands and attempted, in later expeditions, to go farther.) Very quickly, however, others discovered his mistake, and although the Portuguese continued to dominate the sea route to India, the Spanish kings laid claim to the New World (which is why all the Americas from Mexico south, with the exception of Brazil, are Spanish-speaking even today). With the discovery of the New World a new phase in Western history begins: the age of conquest and colonization of the rest of the world by the Europeans. But the culture they brought with them was the culture that had been formed through four thousand years of the history of antiquity and the Middle Ages.

CONCLUSIONS

THIS RAPID SURVEY of close to four thousand years of social history indicates both the enormous variety of ways that our ancestors have tried to regulate relations among members of society and the remarkable stability of some human institutions. The basic human need for food has been met primarily through raising grain for the close to five thousand years of recorded human history, and there has also been a consistency in the ways that humans have met their other basic need, the need for other people.

One of the most stable institutions has been that of marriage and the family, regardless of variations in such things as age of marriage, dowries and dower, or the like. Throughout Western history, the normal pattern has been based on the primacy of the couple, husband and wife, with their children. Husbands and wives have always been expected to stay together indefinitely; although divorce has generally been possible, in some form or other, it is the exception, with permanence the general rule. Of all the different civilizations studied, only the ancient Hebrews practiced polygamy, and then only in their pastoral, or wandering, period; settled civilization in the West has meant monogamy, one husband to one wife. Although husbands generally were allowed some license, sometimes even expected to keep concubines, it was nonetheless assumed that they should restrict themselves to liaisons that would not interfere with their primary bond.

One of the chief purposes of marriage has always been the production of children. All ancient and medieval civilizations put great store by their children, especially boys. Both boys and girls were raised primarily by women until they were at least seven years old, when, in some civilizations, boys were taken from their mothers to be raised by men. Girls generally stayed with their mothers, however, because learning to be good household managers was one of the chief duties for girls.

Age of marriage for men has varied enormously, even within the same culture, and anywhere from fifteen to forty has been considered "normal" at one time or another. Yet, throughout most of Western history, women have married very young by our standards, usually in their teens. These women were at least a few years younger than their husbands, sometimes only half their age. Without the broad experience of their older and usually better-educated husbands, wives were rarely treated as equal partners in marriage. In a few periods, marriage approached modern ideas of partnership, especially in the cities of the thirteenth and fourteenth centuries, but usually women were relegated to the home, which was considered second best to the public life of the marketplace. Here their rule was usually absolute, however, and with control over the children and the household deities women throughout history have exercised more influence over their men than the men have sometimes wanted to admit.

Although the institutions of marriage and the family are certainly central to any civilization, other factors also had a great deal of permanence throughout the ancient and medieval worlds, due in large part to the influence of each civilization on the one that followed. Education in matters beyond basic reading and arithmetic, whether those matters are astrology or theology, was always considered tremendously exciting and worthwhile. Governmental forms differed dramatically, but there was usually some sense that the governor had to rule with the consent of the governed. Except for the Egyptian pharaohs or later Roman emperors, who became gods, kings have generally been considered only slightly different from ordinary mortals; the idea of the divine right of absolute kingship was only enunciated in the sixteenth century. "The governed" and "ordinary mortals," however, were still select subgroups from the total population, for, except for medieval Europe, the civilizations surveyed in this book normally had slaves, who were considered not quite real men. Just as slavery has been a constant in history, so has warfare; pacifism has been the rare exception.

Certain aspects of government have a permanence that may make life in ancient Egypt, for example, seem very much like ours. All governments need some sort of judicial system, both to deal with criminals and to settle civil disputes between citizens. A major concern of law courts has always been trying to determine what actually happened, and calling witnesses and examining written evidence are as old as courts themselves. Governments have also always taxed, supporting the governors and magistrates by extracting something from those whom they judged and governed.

People in the West have always practiced some sort of religion, sometimes with the hope of a better life to come, sometimes out of fear of worse to come right here, sometimes because the world seems so permeated with divinity that *not* to practice religious ritual would be like not breathing. The actual content of religion has varied tremendously, but the diversity should not blind one to the similarities of the way it was practiced. Western religion, whether that of the Egyptians, the Greeks and Romans, or the Christians, involved temples served by priests. These temples were so permanent that many pagan temples became Christian churches without major upheaval. The priests were almost always men; although there was also a role for women in religion, it was generally a secondary role that left some women in the position of practicing their own version of the religion with or without official approval.

The four thousand years of history surveyed here go from the beginning of record keeping, the point at which it is first possible to have any sort of idea of human institutions, up to the beginning of the period now known as "modern," or at least "early modern." As should now be clear, the way people behave and interact is the result of more than just biology, and more than just the way that those alive at a given time decide to behave. It is also a result of history, of people being influenced from before they can remember by the institutions that their parents in turn absorbed from *their* earliest childhood.

Because of this, it does make some sort of sense for the purpose of classification to divide Western history into three great periods: antiquity, the Middle Ages, and modern times. Antiquity may be considered the time that the bases were laid down for what later became our culture, the medieval period the time that many of our "modern" institutions, from an organized church to universities to the very structure of government, were first put into place, and modern times the period in which the world we know now was given final form. But there is as much variation within each of these periods as there is between them, and none of them is expendable in understanding modern society. Western society functions the way that it does now in large part because of decisions made and institutions put into place over the last forty-five hundred years in the Near East, the Mediterranean, and western Europe, each civilization and each generation taking influences from the generation before and influencing the one that came after. During the last five hundred years, European culture has moved beyond the narrow boundaries of a small northern subcontinent to influence all the peoples of the world. This culture can only be understood, however, in relation to the lives and experiences of the people of antiquity and the Middle Ages who formed it.

SUGGESTIONS FOR FURTHER READING

THE FOLLOWING BRIEF list of suggestions for further readings is intended for those who want to find out more detail on some of the topics presented in this book. It is limited to works available in English that can readily be understood without an in-depth knowledge of the period covered, and includes both secondary and a few primary sources. (A short list of more technical works is given in the teacher's guide for each chapter.) This list is far from exhaustive, as it is limited to recent works or those that have become classics. Other books can easily be found by consulting the bibliographies of the recent titles. Books available in paperback are marked with an asterisk.

The Ancient World

An epic written during Babylonian times that provides insights into their culture and religion is *The Epic of Gilgamesh, trans. N. K. Sandars (Harmondsworth, Eng., 1960).

Overviews of life in Egypt are given in Lionel Casson, Daily Life in Ancient Egypt (New York, 1975); and in T. G. H. James, Pharaoh's People: Scenes from Life in Imperial Egypt (London, 1984).

Peter Green gives a survey of Greek history: A Concise History of Ancient Greece (London, 1973). An illustrated discussion of the Minoan society and its influence on early Greece is found in *John Chadwick, The Mycenaean World (Cambridge, 1976), a work based largely on recent archaeological discoveries. Many details on Greek life, food, and clothing are provided in Robert Flacelière, Daily Life in Greece at the Time of Pericles, trans. Peter Green (New York, 1965). For women's position in Greece and

Rome, see *Sarah B. Pomeroy, *Goddesses, Whores, Wives, and Slaves: Women in Classical Antiquity* (New York, 1975). For Greek families, see W. K. Lacey, *The Family in Ancient Greece* (Ithaca, N.Y., 1968). H. A. Harris, *Sport in Greece and Rome* (Ithaca, N.Y., 1972), covers both the Olympian games and the grander spectacles of Rome. An interesting look at how the Greeks perceived themselves and their neighbors is given in a book written in ancient Greece, *Herodotus, *The Histories*, trans. Aubrey de Sélincourt (Harmondsworth, Eng., 1972).

Socrates's and Plato's philosophy may be read firsthand in *Plato, *The Last Days of Socrates*, trans. Hugh Tredennick (Harmondsworth, Eng., 1954). One of the best writers of Greek comedies was *Aristophanes, *The Complete Plays*, ed. Moses Hades (New York, 1962).

A good introduction to ancient Rome is given by Michael Grant, *The World of Rome* (Cleveland and New York, 1960). For details on Roman life, drawn primarily from literary sources, see F. R. Cowell, *Everyday Life in Ancient Rome*, 2nd ed. (New York, 1972). Lillian M. Wilson, *The Roman Toga* (Baltimore, 1924), provides what is still the best discussion of how Roman togas were made and worn. William D. Phillips, Jr., *Slavery from Roman Times to the Early Transatlantic Trade* (Minneapolis, 1985), begins with Roman slavery and follows its persistence and influence in later centuries. For warfare in both Greece and Rome, see Yvon Garlan, *War in the Ancient World: A Social History*, trans. Janet Lloyd (London, 1975).

The great Roman epic was *The Aeneid of Virgil*, trans. Allen Mandelbaum (New York, 1961).

For northern Europe during the five centuries B.C., see *Nora Chadwick, *The Celts* (Harmondsworth, Eng., 1970).

The Early Middle Ages

For an overview of the transition from Roman to medieval society, see *Peter Brown, *The World of Late Antiquity*, A.D. 150–750 (London, 1971). A discussion of the process by which people were Christianized in the late Empire, with the emphasis on how little of the religion they actually understood, is provided by Ramsay MacMullen, *Christianizing the Roman Empire*, A.D. 100–400 (New Haven, 1984).

The early days of monasticism can best be grasped by reading works written by monks of the time; see *The Desert Fathers*, trans. and ed. Helen Waddell (Ann Arbor, Mich., 1957), and *The Rule of St. Benedict*, trans. Anthony C. Meissel and M. L. del Mastro (Garden City, N.Y., 1975). The Christian philosopher of the late Empire with the greatest impact on the Middle Ages was Augustine; see, for example, his *Confessions*, trans. John K. Ryan (New York, 1960), and his *The City of God*, trans. Marcus Dods (New York, 1950).

For Merovingian history, the best introduction is a history written at the time by a Merovingian bishop: *Gregory of Tours, *The History of the Franks*, trans. Lewis Thorpe (Harmondsworth, Eng., 1974). For the economy of the Merovingian and Carolingian periods, see *Georges Duby, *The Early Growth of the European Economy: Warriors and Peasants from the Seventh to the Twelfth Century*, trans. Howard B. Clarke (Ithaca, N.Y., 1974); and

Jean Chapelot and Robert Fossier, *The Village and House in the Middle Ages*, trans. Henry Cleere (London, 1985). These books continue to the high Middle Ages.

The best introduction to Charlemagne is the biography written by a close friend, *Einhard, *The Life of Charlemagne* (Ann Arbor, Mich., 1960). For England during this period described by a monk who lived then, see *Bede, *A History of the English Church and People*, trans. Leo Sherley-Price (Harmondsworth, Eng., 1955).

For a general introduction to the Carolingian period, see *Geoffrey Barraclough, *The Crucible of Europe: The Ninth and Tenth Centuries in European History* (Berkeley and Los Angeles, 1976), and *Jacques Boussard, *The Civilization of Charlemagne*, trans. Frances Partridge (New York, 1968). *Pierre Riché, *Daily Life in the World of Charlemagne*, trans. Jo Ann McNamara (Philadelphia, 1978), describes both the life of the court and the lives of workers.

For the Viking impact, see P. H. Sawyer, *Kings and Vikings: Scandinavia and Europe, A.D. 700–1100* (London, 1982). The Viking ethos is revealed in a work written in the early Middle Ages, *Beowulf*, trans. David Wright (Harmondsworth, Eng., 1957).

The High Middle Ages

The classic work on the rural economy of the high and late Middle Ages is *Georges Duby, *Rural Economy and Country Life in the Medieval West*, trans. Cynthia Postan (Columbia, S.C., 1968). Several agricultural treatises written during the high Middle Ages give insights into medieval farming: *Walter of Henley and Other Treatises on Estate Management and Accounting*, ed. and trans. Dorothea Oschinsky (Oxford, 1971).

For both urban and rural economic developments, see *Robert-Henri Bautier, *The Economic Development of Medieval Europe* (London, 1971). Mark Girouard, *Cities and People: A Social and Architectural History* (New Haven, 1985), discusses medieval cities extensively in a book that continues the discussion to modern times. For the "industrialization" of medieval Europe, see the lively work by *Jean Gimpel, *The Medieval Machine: The Industrial Revolution of the Middle Ages* (New York, 1976). *Joseph and Frances Gies, *Life in a Medieval City* (New York, 1969), describes medieval urban life in the city of Troyes, amid the Champagne fairs. For the role of bridges in a medieval city, illustrated with contemporary drawings, see Virginia Wylie Egbert, *On the Bridges of Medieval Paris* (Princeton, 1974). *Daniel Waley, *The Italian City-Republics* (New York, 1969), describes the government and society of Italian cities before the Renaissance.

For developments in monasticism from its foundations to the present day, see *David Knowles, *Christian Monasticism* (New York, 1969). The building of the cathedrals is described by Jean Gimpel, *The Cathedral Builders*, trans. Teresa Waugh (New York, 1983). For the investiture controversy, including translations of many contemporary documents, see *Brian Tierney, *The Crisis of Church and State, 1050–1300* (Englewood Cliffs, N.J., 1964).

*Joseph and Frances Gies, *Life in a Medieval Castle* (New York, 1974), concentrates on powerful English castles. For marriage among the medieval nobility, see Georges Duby, *Medieval Marriage: Two Models from Twelfth-Century France*, trans. Elborg Forster (Baltimore, 1978). The position of twelfth-century women as seen in art and literature is discussed by *Penny Schine Gold, *The Lady and the Virgin: Image, Attitude, and Experience in Twelfth-Century France* (Chicago, 1985). For thirteenth-century account books, showing the expenses and manpower necessary to build a castle, see H. M. Colvin, ed. and trans., *Building Accounts of Henry III* (Oxford, 1971).

Many epics and tales of fantasy were written in the high Middle Ages. These include *Gottfried von Strassburg, *Tristan*, trans. A. T. Hatto (Harmondsworth, Eng., 1960); *The Song of Roland*, trans. Robert Harrison (New York, 1970); *The Nibelungenlied*, trans. A. T. Hatto (Harmondsworth, Eng., 1965); *Wolfram von Eschenbach, *Parzival*, trans. A. T. Hatto (Harmondsworth, Eng., 1980); *Njal's Saga*, trans. Magnus Magnusson and Hermann Pálsson (Harmondsworth, Eng., 1960), which reveals the Norse ethos; *The Epic of the Cid*, trans. J. Gerald Markley (New York, 1961), which is the great Spanish epic; and *The Mabinogi*, trans. Patrick K. Ford (Berkeley and Los Angeles, 1977); this last is the Welsh national epic. The greatest work of literature of the Middle Ages is usually considered to be Dante, *The Divine Comedy*. It may be found in *The Portable Dante*, trans. Laurence Binyon (Harmondsworth, Eng., 1955).

The Late Middle Ages

The classic introduction to life and thought in the late Middle Ages is that of *J. Huizinga, *The Waning of the Middle Ages* (New York, 1949). For a highly illustrated history of the end of the Middle Ages, see *Margaret Aston, *The Fifteenth Century: The Prospect of Europe* (New York, 1968).

For late medieval peasants and townspeople, see J. F. C. Harrison, *The Common People of Great Britain: A History from the Norman Conquest to the Present* (Bloomington, Ind., 1985). For women's position in the Middle Ages, with an emphasis on the later period, see *Shulamith Shahar, *The Fourth Estate: A History of Women in the Middle Ages*, trans. Chaya Galai (London, 1983). A discussion of medieval society's most wretched members, especially in the late Middle Ages, is given by Michel Mollat, *The Poor in the Middle Ages*, trans. Arthur Goldhammer (New Haven, 1986).

For the nobility and gentry at the end of the Middle Ages, see *Mark Girouard, *Life in the English Country House* (New Haven, 1978).

The way that people lived, dressed, ate, and had families during the Renaissance is described in Charles L. Mee, Jr., *Daily Life in Renaissance Italy* (New York, 1975); and in J. Lucas-Dubreton, *Daily Life in Florence in the Time of the Medici*, trans. A. Lytton Sells (London, 1960). A history of the complex legal and emotional tangle created by the marriage of one Florentine couple is given by Gene Brucker, *Giovanni and Lusanna: Love and Marriage in Renaissance Florence* (Berkeley and Los Angeles, 1986).

For a survey of late medieval religion, see *Francis Oakley, *The Western Church in the Later Middle Ages* (Ithaca, N.Y., 1979). Jean-Claude Schmitt, *The Holy Greyhound: Guinefort, Healer of Children since the Thirteenth Century*, trans. Martin Thom (Cambridge, 1983), describes the cult of Guinefort and relates it to late medieval popular religion. For the "modern devotion," see *Thomas à Kempis, *The Imitation of Christ* (New York, 1955), a work written in the late Middle Ages.

The difficulties of life in the late Middle Ages are revealed in the very lively tales written at the time by *Boccaccio, *The Decameron*, trans. Richard Aldington (New York, 1962).

PICTURE CREDITS

2 Museo Civico Archeologico, Bologna. **4** Mesopotamian stela from Esarhaddon, ca. 680–669 B.C. Trustees of the British Museum. **11** Sumerian statues from Tell Asmar, Shrine II of Square Abu Temple. Ca. 2900–2600 B.C. Oriental Institute, The University of Chicago. **12** Pupil's copybook, ca. 2500–2000 B.C. Oriental Institute, University of Chicago. **15** Scenes of war, panel from the Standard of Ur, ca. 2700 B.C. Panel inlaid with shell, lapis lazuli, and red limestone. Trustees of the British Museum. **17** Head of a figure of Mut, bronze and light blue composition. Egyptian, Ptolemaic period, ca. 332–30 B.C. The Metropolitan Museum of Art, The Carnarvon Collection. Gift of Edward S. Harkness, 1926. **19** Wall painting: Fields of the Blest. From Tomb of Sen-Nuden, copy in tempera. Egyptian, Dynasty XIX–XX, ca. 1200 B.C. The Metropolitan Museum of Art. **24** Funerary papyrus of Princess Entiuny (detail). From Tomb of Queen Meryet-Amun at Deir el Bahri. Egyptian, Dynasty XXI, ca. 1025 B.C. The Metropolitan Museum of Art, Museum Excavations, 1928–29, and Rogers Fund, 1930. **27** Historical Pictures Service. **37** Courtesy of Constance B. Bouchard. **43** Hirmer Fotoarchiv, München. **45** Toreador scene. Fresco from Knossos, ca. 1500 B.C. Restored. The Metropolitan Museum of Art. **50** Ostraka, ca. 470 B.C. Agora Excavations, American School of Classical Studies at Athens. **53** Fallen warrior, from the east pediment of the Temple of Aphaia at Aegina. Marble. Staatliche Antikensammlungen, München. **57** Hirmer Verlag, München. **63** Black-figured Panathenaic Amphora, said to be from Etruria. Greek, end of VI century, B.C. The Metropolitan Museum of Art, Rogers Fund, 1914. **69** Staatliche Museen, Berlin. **75** Alinari/Art Resource, New York. **85** G. E. Kidder Smith, FAIA. **86** The Bettmann Archive. **89** MARBURG/Art Resource. **92** HBJ Collection. **98** Art Resource, New York. **105** SCALA/Art Resource, New York. **113** Bibliothèque Nationale, Paris. **117** Gabinetto Fotographico, Soprintendenza alle Galleria, Firenze. **120** The Metropolitan Museum of Art, Fletcher Fund, 1947. **123** © The British Museum. **128** Courtesy of Constance B. Bouchard. **130** Biblioteca Nazionale "Vittorio Emanuele, III," Naples. **144** © The British Museum. **157** Bibliothèque Nationale, Paris. **161** Foto Dr. Harald Busch. **163** From the Collection of Oland Bredsatra Parish, Antikvarisk-Topografiska Arkivet, Stockholm. **166** Bibliotèque der Reiksuniversitie, Leiden, Nederlands. **175** © Bibliothèque Royale, Bruxelles. **183** Bodleian Library, Ms. Add A, 46, fol. 4 v. **185** Aerofilms, Ltd. **187** Aerofilms, Ltd. **190** Victoria and Albert Museum, London. **198** Aerofilms, Ltd. **204** Bodleian Library, Ms. Rawl A 384, fol. 91. **212** Deutsche Fotothek, Dresden. **215** The Mansell Collection. **218** Weidenfeld and Nicolson, Ltd., Daniel Waley. **223** HBJ Photograph. **225** Courtesy of

INDEX